GED EXAM PREP

"Luck is what happens when preparation meets opportunity."
—Seneca

LUXMENTIS PRESS

TABLE OF CONTENTS

DOWNLOAD HERE YOUR FULL LENGTH SIMULATIONS!

Dear Student,

First and foremost, I want to wish you the very best of luck on your journey toward the GED exam. I know how much dedication and determination are required to reach your goal, and this book was created specifically to help you study in an effective, targeted way.

Within these pages, you'll find one complete exam, and through a convenient QR code, you can **download nine more tests at no extra cost**. I chose this format for several important reasons:

1. **Managing Costs**: Including all ten tests in the printed book would have made it bulkier and more expensive, forcing you to pay a significantly higher price.
2. **Quick Updates**: If any corrections or additions are needed, the digital format allows for immediate updates, ensuring you always have the most accurate and up-to-date materials.
3. **Flexibility**: You can print the tests at home or practice online, depending on what suits you best.

This approach lets me offer you a **comprehensive** manual while keeping it both affordable and easy to handle. I hope this guide provides all the support you need to prepare for the exam as efficiently as possible.

Remember, my goal is to help you **pass the exam** and reach your personal milestones. I'm on your side, and I wish you every success.

Good luck, and happy studying!

SCAN THE QR CODE!

You will get:

- 10 extra full length exam simulations
- Weekly extra exam bonus

INTRODUCTION

CHAPTER 1

WELCOME TO YOUR ULTIMATE GED PREPARATION GUIDE

Welcome to the **GED Exam Study Guide 2025**, the most comprehensive resource available to help you excel on the GED exam and achieve your personal and professional goals. Whether you're preparing to further your education, expand your career opportunities, or simply accomplish a long-held personal milestone, this guide is designed to make your journey as smooth and successful as possible. By using this book, you'll gain the knowledge, skills, and confidence needed to pass the GED exam with outstanding results.

The GED is not just a test—it's a life-changing opportunity. It opens doors to higher education, better job prospects, and increased self-confidence. This guide is here to walk you through every step of the process, from understanding the test structure to mastering each subject area, so you can reach your goals with ease.

What is the GED Exam?

The **General Educational Development (GED)** exam is a high school equivalency test recognized across the United States and in many other countries. It provides individuals who did not graduate from high school with the opportunity to earn a credential that is equivalent to a high school diploma. This credential is accepted by colleges, universities, employers, and the U.S. military, making it a valuable asset for advancing your future.

The GED exam consists of four subject tests:

1. **Reasoning Through Language Arts (RLA):** Focuses on reading comprehension, grammar, and essay writing.
2. **Mathematical Reasoning:** Covers arithmetic, algebra, geometry, and data analysis.
3. **Science:** Assesses understanding of life science, physical science, and earth and space science.
4. **Social Studies:** Includes U.S. history, civics and government, economics, geography, and world history.

Each test is computer-based, and the questions are designed to evaluate not only your knowledge but also your ability to apply that knowledge in real-world scenarios.

Why the GED Exam Matters

The GED exam is a stepping stone to a brighter future. It provides numerous benefits, including:

- **Access to Higher Education:** The GED credential is widely accepted by colleges, universities, and vocational schools. Scoring well can even exempt you from placement tests or remedial courses.
- **Enhanced Career Opportunities:** Many employers require a high school diploma or equivalent for entry-level positions, promotions, and career advancement.
- **Personal Achievement:** Earning your GED is a significant accomplishment that can boost your confidence and open doors to opportunities you never thought possible.
- **Military Eligibility:** The GED is recognized by the U.S. military as a valid educational credential for enlistment.

How This Guide Will Help You

This book is carefully crafted to be the **ultimate resource for GED success**. Here's what you can expect:

1. **Comprehensive Theoretical Content:** Every subject area is covered in detail, including the latest updates for the 2025 exam. You'll find explanations, examples, and clear breakdowns of concepts to help you master the material.
2. **Practical Exercises:** Test your knowledge with practice questions, exercises, and quizzes throughout the book. These activities are designed to reinforce what you've learned and build your confidence.
3. **Full-Length Practice Tests:** Simulate the real GED exam with full-length tests that mirror the official test format. Detailed answer explanations are provided for every question, helping you learn from your mistakes and improve your performance.

4. **Test Strategies and Mindset Tips:** Learn effective strategies for time management, question analysis, and stress reduction. These tips will prepare you to approach the test with confidence and poise.
5. **Tailored Study Plans:** Whether you have one month, three months, or six months to prepare, this guide includes customizable study plans to fit your schedule and help you stay on track.

A Roadmap to Success

Here's how you can use this book to maximize your preparation and ensure success on the GED exam:

1. **Start with the Basics:** Begin by reading the introductory sections to understand the structure, scoring, and purpose of the GED exam. Familiarize yourself with the format and requirements of each subject test.
2. **Master Each Subject:** Work through the theoretical sections to build a strong foundation in Reasoning Through Language Arts, Mathematical Reasoning, Science, and Social Studies. Pay attention to key concepts and take notes as you study.
3. **Practice, Practice, Practice:** Complete the practice questions and exercises provided in each chapter. Use the detailed answer explanations to identify areas where you need improvement.
4. **Take Full-Length Practice Tests:** Simulate the real exam by taking the practice tests included in this guide. Track your progress and refine your test-taking strategies based on your performance.
5. **Stay Positive and Motivated:** Use the mindset tips and motivational stories throughout the book to stay focused and confident as you prepare.

What You'll Gain from This Guide

By the time you complete this study guide, you'll have:

- A thorough understanding of the GED exam format and content.
- Confidence in your ability to tackle each subject area with skill and accuracy.
- Effective strategies for managing your time and reducing test-day stress.
- Practical experience through practice tests that replicate the real exam.
- A clear path to achieving a passing score—or even exceeding it to reach the **College Ready** or **College Ready + Credit** levels.

Final Words of Encouragement

Earning your GED is a powerful step toward achieving your dreams. It represents perseverance, dedication, and the courage to pursue a brighter future. Remember, this journey is yours, and you have the ability to succeed. With the right preparation and mindset, the GED exam is a challenge you can conquer.

Let's get started on this transformative journey together. Turn the page and take the first step toward your ultimate success on the GED exam!

CHAPTER 2

HOW TO USE THIS BOOK EFFECTIVELY

To get the most out of the **GED Exam Study Guide 2025**, it's essential to approach your preparation with a strategic and organized mindset. This book has been meticulously crafted to guide you through every step of the GED exam journey, from building foundational knowledge to applying test-day strategies. By following the guidance in this book, you can maximize your learning, improve your confidence, and ensure you're fully prepared to achieve your highest potential score.

2.1. Understand the Structure of the Book

This study guide is divided into distinct sections, each focusing on a specific aspect of GED preparation. Here's an overview of how the book is structured:

- **Introduction**: Sets the stage for your preparation, including details about the GED exam, how to use this book, and tips for effective study.
- **Subject-Specific Chapters**: Comprehensive chapters dedicated to each of the four GED subjects: Reasoning Through Language Arts (RLA), Mathematical Reasoning, Science, and Social Studies. These chapters include theoretical explanations, practical exercises, and subject-specific strategies.
- **Practice and Simulation**: Includes numerous practice questions, exercises, and full-length test simulations that replicate the real GED exam experience.
- **Mindset and Strategy**: Offers tips to develop a positive mindset, manage test-day stress, and adopt strategies for tackling different types of questions.
- **Additional Resources**: Provides study plans, online tools, and inspirational stories to keep you motivated.

By understanding the structure of the book, you'll know where to find specific information and how to navigate through the material effectively.

2.2. Customize Your Study Plan

This book includes flexible study schedules tailored to different preparation timelines:

- **One-Month Intensive Plan**: Ideal for those who need to prepare in a short amount of time.
- **Three-Month Balanced Plan**: Perfect for learners who can dedicate a few hours per week.
- **Six-Month Comprehensive Plan**: Best for individuals who prefer a more gradual and in-depth approach.

Choose the plan that best fits your schedule and follow it closely to ensure steady progress.

2.3. Study Each Subject Thoroughly

The subject-specific chapters are designed to build your understanding step by step. Here's how to use them effectively:

- **Start with the Basics**: Each chapter begins with foundational concepts, ensuring you have a solid understanding before moving to advanced topics.
- **Practice As You Go**: Complete the practice exercises embedded within each section. These exercises are designed to reinforce what you've learned and identify areas for improvement.
- **Focus on Your Weaknesses**: Use the practice questions and full-length tests to identify subjects or topics where you need additional study. Spend extra time on these areas to strengthen your understanding.

2.4. Simulate the Real Test

This book includes multiple full-length practice tests that replicate the format, timing, and difficulty of the actual GED exam. To use these tests effectively:

- **Schedule Practice Tests**: Set aside time to take a full-length test in one sitting, under conditions that mimic the real exam. This will help you build stamina and familiarize yourself with the test environment.

- **Review Your Answers**: After completing a practice test, carefully review the answer explanations provided. Understanding your mistakes is just as important as practicing.
- **Track Your Progress**: Use the results of your practice tests to measure your improvement and adjust your study plan as needed.

2.5. Master Test-Taking Strategies

Throughout the book, you'll find practical strategies for approaching each section of the GED exam. These strategies are essential for maximizing your performance on test day. Key tips include:

- **Time Management**: Learn to allocate your time effectively across different sections and questions.
- **Question Analysis**: Practice identifying keywords, eliminating incorrect answers, and understanding what the question is really asking.
- **Essay Writing**: Follow the detailed guidance provided in the Reasoning Through Language Arts section to craft a well-organized and persuasive essay.

2.6. Build a Positive Mindset

Success on the GED exam is not just about knowledge—it's also about confidence and mental preparedness. This book includes sections on:

- **Overcoming Test Anxiety**: Learn techniques to stay calm and focused during the exam.
- **Staying Motivated**: Use the motivational stories and mindset tips to keep yourself inspired throughout your preparation journey.
- **Visualizing Success**: Develop a positive outlook and envision yourself achieving your goal.

2.7. Take Advantage of Additional Resources

This guide is more than just a book—it's a comprehensive toolkit for GED success. Use the additional resources provided, including:

- **Online Tools**: Access supplementary materials and practice tests online.
- **Community Support**: Seek out local GED preparation classes or online forums to connect with other test-takers.
- **Study Aids**: Utilize the quick-reference charts, summaries, and tips included throughout the book.

2.8. Stay Consistent and Committed

Consistency is the key to success. Even if you only have 30 minutes a day to study, make it a habit. Stick to your study plan, review regularly, and celebrate your progress along the way.

Remember, this book is your ultimate companion for GED preparation. Follow the guidance provided, and you'll be well on your way to passing the GED exam and achieving your dreams.

CHAPTER 3

UNDERSTANDING THE GED EXAM: STRUCTURE, SCORING, AND PURPOSE

To prepare effectively for the GED exam, it's essential to understand its structure, how it's scored, and the purpose it serves. This chapter provides a detailed breakdown of these elements, equipping you with the knowledge to approach the test with confidence and clarity. By the end of this section, you'll have a clear understanding of what to expect and how your performance will be evaluated.

3.1. The Structure of the GED Exam

The GED exam consists of four subject tests, each designed to evaluate high school-level knowledge and skills. These tests are taken independently, meaning you can schedule them on different days or complete them all at once. Below is an overview of the four subjects:

Reasoning Through Language Arts (RLA)

- **Purpose**: Tests your ability to read, write, and analyze written texts.
- **Duration**: 150 minutes (including a 10-minute break).
- **Format**:
  - Reading comprehension questions based on informational and literary texts.
  - Language and grammar questions to test editing and revising skills.
  - An extended response (essay) requiring you to analyze and respond to a prompt.

Mathematical Reasoning

- **Purpose**: Measures your ability to solve problems using mathematical concepts.
- **Duration**: 115 minutes.
- **Format**:
  - Divided into two parts:
    - **Part 1**: No calculator allowed.
    - **Part 2**: Calculator allowed (on-screen or physical TI-30XS Multiview).
  - Covers arithmetic, algebra, geometry, and data analysis.
  - Question types include multiple-choice, fill-in-the-blank, drag-and-drop, and graphing.

Science

- **Purpose**: Assesses your understanding of life, physical, and earth/space sciences.
- **Duration**: 90 minutes.
- **Format**:
  - Questions based on scientific data, experiments, and concepts.
  - Includes multiple-choice, hotspot (selecting areas on an image), and fill-in-the-blank questions.
  - Emphasizes scientific reasoning over memorization.

Social Studies

- **Purpose**: Evaluates your knowledge of history, government, economics, and geography.
- **Duration**: 70 minutes.
- **Format**:
  - Includes questions on U.S. history, civics, economics, and geography.
  - Requires interpretation of maps, graphs, and primary/secondary documents.
  - Features multiple-choice, drag-and-drop, and hotspot questions.

3.2. Scoring System

The GED uses a scaled scoring system for each subject, ranging from **100 to 200 points**. Your performance determines whether you meet the requirements for passing, college readiness, or even college credits.

Score Ranges and What They Mean

1. **Below Passing** (100–144):
   - This indicates insufficient understanding of the subject.
   - You must retake this subject test to earn your GED credential.
2. **High School Equivalency Passing Score** (145–164):
   - Demonstrates a high school level of proficiency.
   - This score qualifies you for the GED credential.
3. **College Ready** (165–174):
   - Indicates advanced proficiency beyond high school level.
   - Colleges may waive placement tests or remedial courses if you score in this range.
4. **College Ready + Credit** (175–200):
   - Reflects exceptional performance.
   - May qualify you for up to 10 college credits, depending on the institution.

How Scoring Works

- Each subject test is scored independently. You must achieve at least **145** on each test to pass.
- The final GED credential is awarded when you pass all four subject tests.
- If you fail a subject, you can retake it without affecting your scores on other subjects.

3.3. The Purpose of the GED Exam

The GED exam serves as a gateway to new opportunities, enabling individuals to achieve their personal, educational, and professional goals. Here's why it matters:

For Education

- The GED credential is recognized as equivalent to a high school diploma by colleges and universities across the United States.
- Achieving high scores can open doors to college admissions, scholarships, and even college credits.

For Employment

- Many employers require a high school diploma or equivalent for hiring, promotions, and career advancement.
- A GED credential demonstrates your dedication, perseverance, and ability to meet educational standards.

For Personal Growth

- Completing the GED exam is a significant personal accomplishment, showcasing resilience and determination.
- It sets a positive example for family members and peers, inspiring others to pursue their goals.

For Military Service

- The GED is accepted by the U.S. military as a valid educational credential, allowing individuals to enlist and pursue specialized training programs.

3.4. What to Expect on Test Day

Understanding what happens on the day of your test can help reduce anxiety and improve your focus. Here's what you need to know:

Registration and Scheduling

- Register for the GED exam on the official website (GED.com).
- Choose a test center or opt for the online proctored exam (if eligible).

- Schedule your tests based on your availability and preparation level.

What to Bring

- A valid, government-issued photo ID.
- Approved calculator (if allowed for the specific test).
- Test center confirmation and any required documents.

Test Environment

- Tests are taken on a computer, with tools like an on-screen calculator and highlight/flag options for questions.
- Breaks are limited and only allowed during designated times.

3.5. How This Knowledge Helps You Prepare

Understanding the structure, scoring, and purpose of the GED exam allows you to:

- Set realistic goals for each subject test.
- Focus your preparation on achieving higher scores for additional benefits, such as college credits.
- Approach the test with confidence, knowing what to expect and how to excel.

The GED exam is more than a test—it's an opportunity to transform your future. With this knowledge, you're already one step closer to success. Let's move forward and dive deeper into how you can prepare effectively for each subject area.

CHAPTER 4

TIPS FOR MAXIMIZING YOUR STUDY EFFICIENCY

Preparing for the GED exam requires more than just reviewing material—it demands a strategic approach to studying that maximizes your time and effort. This chapter is designed to provide actionable tips to help you study efficiently, stay motivated, and retain the knowledge you need to succeed. By implementing these strategies, you'll optimize your preparation and build the confidence to perform your best on test day.

4.1. Create a Study Schedule

Why a Study Schedule is Essential

A structured study plan ensures that you cover all necessary material while managing your time effectively. It helps prevent last-minute cramming and reduces stress as you approach test day.

How to Build Your Study Schedule

- **Set a Target Exam Date**: Choose a realistic date based on your current level of readiness and availability. Use this as a reference point to plan your timeline.
- **Break Down the Content**: Divide the four GED subjects into manageable sections. Allocate specific days to focus on each subject, ensuring you give extra time to areas where you feel less confident.
- **Plan Study Blocks**: Dedicate consistent blocks of time each day or week to studying. For example, aim for 1–2 hours per session, depending on your schedule.
- **Incorporate Review Time**: Set aside time each week to review previously studied material and reinforce your understanding.
- **Balance Practice and Theory**: Alternate between learning theoretical content and completing practice exercises to test your knowledge.

4.2. Set SMART Goals

What are SMART Goals?

SMART goals are Specific, Measurable, Achievable, Relevant, and Time-bound. Setting these goals ensures you stay focused and motivated throughout your preparation.

Examples of SMART Goals for GED Preparation

- **Specific**: "I will complete the grammar section of the Reasoning Through Language Arts chapter by Friday."
- **Measurable**: "I will correctly answer at least 80% of the practice questions in the math chapter by the end of the week."
- **Achievable**: "I will study for 1.5 hours each evening after work."
- **Relevant**: "I will focus on improving my essay-writing skills to prepare for the extended response in RLA."
- **Time-bound**: "I will complete one full-length practice test by the end of this month."

4.3. Use Active Learning Techniques

What is Active Learning?

Active learning involves engaging with the material in a way that promotes critical thinking and retention, rather than passively reading or memorizing.

Effective Active Learning Strategies

- **Take Notes**: Summarize key points in your own words as you study. This helps you process the information and remember it more effectively.
- **Ask Questions**: Challenge yourself by asking, "Why does this work?" or "How can I apply this concept?"
- **Teach What You Learn**: Explaining a concept to someone else reinforces your understanding and highlights areas that need clarification.

- **Use Flashcards**: Create flashcards for key terms, formulas, and concepts. Test yourself regularly to reinforce your memory.
- **Practice Retrieval**: Close your book and try to recall what you just learned. Writing or saying it aloud helps solidify the information.

4.4. Minimize Distractions

Create a Productive Study Environment

- Choose a quiet, comfortable space with minimal distractions.
- Keep your phone out of reach or use apps to block notifications while studying.
- Gather all necessary materials (notes, books, calculator) before starting to avoid interruptions.

Time Management Techniques

- **Pomodoro Technique**: Study for 25 minutes, take a 5-minute break, and repeat. After four cycles, take a longer 15–30 minute break.
- **Prioritize Tasks**: Start with the most challenging subjects or topics when your energy and focus are highest.
- **Avoid Multitasking**: Focus on one subject or task at a time for maximum efficiency.

4.5. Incorporate Practice Tests Early

Why Practice Tests Are Crucial

Practice tests simulate the real exam, helping you:

- Identify strengths and weaknesses.
- Familiarize yourself with the test format and timing.
- Build endurance for the full exam.

How to Use Practice Tests Effectively

- Take a diagnostic test early in your preparation to assess your baseline knowledge.
- Use the results to focus your study efforts on weaker areas.
- Gradually increase the frequency of practice tests as you approach your exam date.

4.6. Stay Motivated

Find Your "Why"

Reflect on your reasons for taking the GED exam. Whether it's advancing your career, pursuing higher education, or achieving a personal milestone, keeping your goals in mind will help you stay motivated.

Celebrate Small Wins

Acknowledge and reward yourself for milestones, such as completing a chapter or scoring well on a practice test. Positive reinforcement boosts morale and encourages consistency.

Connect with Others

Join a GED study group or connect with fellow test-takers online. Sharing experiences, tips, and encouragement can make the process less isolating and more enjoyable.

4.7. Take Care of Your Health

Prioritize Sleep

- Aim for 7–8 hours of sleep per night to improve focus and memory.
- Avoid late-night cramming, as it can lead to burnout and reduced retention.

Eat Nutritious Meals

- Fuel your brain with healthy foods, including fruits, vegetables, whole grains, and lean protein.

- Stay hydrated by drinking plenty of water throughout the day.

Exercise Regularly

- Incorporate physical activity into your routine to reduce stress and improve concentration.
- Even short walks or stretching exercises can help refresh your mind during study breaks.

4.8. Use This Book to Its Full Potential

This book is designed to be your ultimate resource for GED preparation. Here's how to make the most of it:

- **Follow the Study Plans**: Choose a timeline that fits your schedule and stick to it.
- **Engage with the Content**: Actively read each chapter, complete practice exercises, and review the answer explanations.
- **Take Advantage of Full-Length Tests**: Simulate the real exam to build your confidence and readiness.
- **Apply Test-Taking Strategies**: Use the tips provided to approach the exam strategically and effectively.

4.9. Embrace a Growth Mindset

Approach your GED preparation with the belief that your abilities can improve through effort and persistence. Mistakes and challenges are opportunities to learn and grow. With dedication, consistency, and the strategies outlined in this book, you can achieve success.

By implementing these tips for maximizing your study efficiency, you'll not only prepare effectively for the GED exam but also develop skills and habits that will serve you well in future academic and professional endeavors. Let's move forward and begin tackling the subject-specific content in the next chapters!

PART1

PREPARING FOR SUCCESS

CHAPTER 5

BUILDING THE RIGHT MINDSET FOR THE GED

Preparing for the GED exam is not just about mastering academic subjects—it's also about cultivating the right mindset. Your attitude, motivation, and mental approach play a critical role in how well you perform. A strong mindset will help you navigate challenges, stay focused, and remain confident throughout your preparation and on test day. In this chapter, we will explore the key elements of building a mindset for success and how to maintain it.

Why Mindset Matters

Your mindset influences how you approach problems, respond to setbacks, and persevere through challenges. For the GED exam, a positive and determined mindset can:

- Increase your motivation to study consistently.
- Reduce feelings of anxiety and self-doubt.
- Help you focus on long-term goals rather than short-term obstacles.
- Boost your confidence on test day, leading to better performance.

By prioritizing your mental preparation, you'll set yourself up for success and ensure that your hard work translates into tangible results.

Key Components of a GED Success Mindset

1. Believe in Your Ability to Succeed

It's essential to believe that you are capable of passing the GED exam. Many test-takers face self-doubt, especially if they've been out of school for a while or struggled with certain subjects in the past. Remember:

- The GED exam is designed for people like you, and it's achievable with the right preparation.
- Every small step forward is progress toward your goal.
- Success stories from other GED graduates show that perseverance pays off.

2. Stay Focused on Your Goals

Your reasons for pursuing the GED are personal and meaningful. Whether it's advancing your career, continuing your education, or achieving a personal milestone, keep these goals at the forefront of your mind. Write them down and revisit them regularly to stay motivated.

3. Embrace Challenges as Opportunities

Studying for the GED will involve moments of difficulty. Instead of viewing challenges as setbacks, see them as opportunities to grow and improve. For example:

- Struggling with math? Use it as a chance to strengthen your problem-solving skills.
- Feeling nervous about essay writing? Practice consistently, and celebrate small improvements.

Practical Steps to Build a GED Mindset

1. Create a Positive Study Environment

Your surroundings can significantly impact your mindset. Choose a study space that is quiet, comfortable, and free of distractions. Personalize it with motivational quotes, photos, or reminders of your goals.

2. Visualize Success

Visualization is a powerful mental tool. Spend a few minutes each day imagining yourself:

- Confidently answering questions during the exam.
- Receiving your GED certificate.
- Using your achievement to pursue your next goal.

Visualization helps reinforce your belief in your ability to succeed and keeps you motivated.

3. Focus on Progress, Not Perfection

It's natural to make mistakes while learning. Instead of striving for perfection, aim for consistent progress. Celebrate small victories, such as mastering a challenging concept or completing a practice test, to build confidence over time.

4. Develop Resilience

Resilience is the ability to bounce back from setbacks. If you encounter difficulties, remind yourself that setbacks are temporary and can be overcome with effort and persistence. For example:

- Didn't do well on a practice test? Use the feedback to identify areas for improvement and try again.
- Feeling overwhelmed? Take a short break, refocus, and tackle your study plan one step at a time.

Staying Motivated Throughout Your Preparation

Motivation can fluctuate, especially during a long preparation period. Here are some strategies to maintain your drive:

- **Set Milestones**: Break your study goals into smaller, manageable milestones. Reward yourself when you achieve them.
- **Find Accountability**: Share your goals with a friend, family member, or study partner who can encourage you and keep you on track.
- **Reflect on Your "Why"**: Revisit your reasons for pursuing the GED whenever you feel discouraged. Remind yourself of the opportunities this achievement will unlock.

Mindset for Test Day

The right mindset is just as important on test day as it is during preparation. Keep these tips in mind:

- **Stay Calm**: Use relaxation techniques, such as deep breathing, to reduce anxiety.
- **Focus on What You Know**: Start with questions you feel confident about to build momentum.
- **Trust Your Preparation**: Remember the time and effort you've invested in studying—you're ready for this.

Building the right mindset for the GED exam is a journey, but it's one of the most rewarding aspects of your preparation. A positive, growth-oriented attitude will not only help you succeed on the exam but also empower you in other areas of life. With this foundation, you're ready to tackle the next step in preparing for success: overcoming test anxiety.

5.1 Overcoming Test Anxiety

Test anxiety is a common challenge for many GED test-takers. The pressure to perform well, coupled with fears of failure, can create stress that negatively impacts your preparation and performance. This section will guide you through understanding test anxiety, recognizing its symptoms, and adopting strategies to overcome it. By managing test anxiety effectively, you can approach the GED exam with confidence and clarity.

What is Test Anxiety?

Test anxiety is a type of performance anxiety that arises in situations where you feel evaluated or judged. It's not just about nerves—test anxiety can affect your ability to think clearly, recall information, and perform at your best. While a small amount of stress can motivate you to prepare, excessive anxiety can be counterproductive.

Symptoms of Test Anxiety

Understanding the symptoms of test anxiety can help you recognize and address it. These symptoms may be:

- **Physical**: Sweating, rapid heartbeat, shallow breathing, nausea, or headaches.
- **Emotional**: Feelings of fear, helplessness, or frustration.
- **Cognitive**: Difficulty concentrating, negative thoughts about failure, or trouble recalling information.

- **Behavioral**: Avoiding study sessions, procrastination, or difficulty starting the test.

Causes of Test Anxiety

Several factors can contribute to test anxiety, including:

1. **Fear of Failure**: High expectations, whether from yourself or others, can create pressure to perform perfectly.
2. **Lack of Preparation**: Feeling underprepared can increase stress and self-doubt.
3. **Negative Experiences**: Past failures or difficult testing experiences can lead to fear of repeating them.
4. **Perfectionism**: The belief that anything less than perfect is unacceptable can amplify anxiety.

How Test Anxiety Impacts Performance

Excessive anxiety can disrupt your ability to focus and recall information. When your mind is preoccupied with negative thoughts, it becomes harder to engage with the test material. This can create a vicious cycle: anxiety lowers performance, and poor performance increases anxiety.

Strategies to Overcome Test Anxiety

The good news is that test anxiety can be managed effectively. The following strategies will help you reduce stress and regain control over your test-taking experience.

1. Prepare Thoroughly

- **Start Early**: Give yourself ample time to study all subject areas. A rushed preparation process can increase anxiety.
- **Follow a Study Plan**: Use the study schedules in this guide to organize your preparation and cover all necessary topics.
- **Practice Regularly**: Familiarity with the test format and question types reduces uncertainty, one of the primary causes of anxiety.

2. Develop Relaxation Techniques

- **Deep Breathing**: Practice deep breathing exercises to calm your nervous system. Breathe in slowly for a count of four, hold for four, and exhale for four.
- **Progressive Muscle Relaxation**: Tense and relax different muscle groups in your body to release physical tension.
- **Visualization**: Imagine yourself successfully completing the test. Visualize calmness, focus, and confidence.

3. Replace Negative Thoughts with Positive Affirmations

- Identify negative thoughts like, "I'm going to fail," and challenge them with positive affirmations such as, "I've prepared well, and I can do this."
- Remind yourself of your progress and achievements during your preparation journey.

4. Create a Test-Day Routine

- Plan your test-day schedule in advance. Knowing what to expect reduces last-minute stress.
- Get a good night's sleep before the exam to ensure you're well-rested.
- Eat a healthy meal and stay hydrated to maintain energy levels.

5. Simulate Test Conditions

- Take full-length practice tests under timed conditions to mimic the actual exam environment. This helps you build stamina and confidence.
- Familiarize yourself with the testing tools, such as the on-screen calculator and flagging questions for review.

6. Seek Support

- **Talk to Someone**: Share your concerns with a friend, family member, or mentor. Sometimes, expressing your worries can provide relief.
- **Join a Study Group**: Connecting with other test-takers can reduce feelings of isolation and provide mutual encouragement.
- **Consider Professional Help**: If anxiety feels overwhelming, a counselor or therapist can help you develop coping strategies.

During the Test: Staying Calm and Focused

Even with preparation, anxiety can surface during the test. Use these tips to manage it effectively:

1. Start with Confidence

- Begin with questions you find easiest. This builds momentum and boosts your confidence.
- Don't dwell on difficult questions—flag them and move on. You can return to them later.

2. Use Time Wisely

- Monitor the time for each section, but don't obsess over it. Answer questions at a steady pace.
- Allocate extra time for the essay in the Reasoning Through Language Arts section, as it requires careful thought and planning.

3. Take Mini Breaks

- During the test, take a few seconds to close your eyes, breathe deeply, and refocus if you feel overwhelmed.

Building Long-Term Resilience

Overcoming test anxiety is a process, not an overnight fix. By consistently practicing the strategies outlined here, you'll build resilience and develop a healthier relationship with testing situations. Remember:

- It's okay to feel nervous—what matters is how you respond to those feelings.
- Each practice test and study session is an opportunity to grow and improve.

Success Beyond the GED

Managing test anxiety isn't just about passing the GED—it's a skill that will benefit you in other areas of life, from job interviews to further education. By taking control of your anxiety now, you're setting yourself up for future successes.

Test anxiety doesn't have to hold you back. With the right preparation, mindset, and strategies, you can overcome it and approach the GED exam with confidence. Now that you've learned how to manage anxiety, let's move on to the next step in building a success-oriented mindset: developing a growth mindset.

5.2 Developing a Growth Mindset

A growth mindset is the belief that abilities and intelligence can be developed through effort, perseverance, and learning from challenges. Unlike a fixed mindset, which assumes that talent and intelligence are static, a growth mindset encourages adaptability and resilience, two essential qualities for GED success. In this section, we'll explore what it means to have a growth mindset, why it's critical for your GED preparation, and practical ways to cultivate it.

What is a Growth Mindset?

The concept of a growth mindset, developed by psychologist Carol Dweck, emphasizes the idea that abilities are not fixed traits but can improve with time and effort. This perspective helps individuals:

- Embrace challenges rather than avoiding them.
- Persist in the face of setbacks.
- See effort as a necessary path to mastery.
- Learn from constructive criticism.
- Find inspiration in the success of others.

Adopting a growth mindset will transform how you view the GED exam. Instead of seeing obstacles as insurmountable, you'll recognize them as opportunities to grow and improve.

Why a Growth Mindset is Vital for the GED

The GED exam requires both knowledge and perseverance. A growth mindset can help you:

1. **Stay Motivated**: Even when faced with difficult subjects, you'll see progress as achievable through consistent effort.
2. **Overcome Fear of Failure**: Mistakes are viewed as part of the learning process, not as reasons to give up.

3. **Achieve Long-Term Goals**: A growth mindset encourages you to focus on the bigger picture and work steadily toward your goals.

Fixed Mindset vs. Growth Mindset

Understanding the difference between a fixed mindset and a growth mindset is the first step in making a positive change.

Fixed Mindset	Growth Mindset
"I'm not good at math, so I'll never pass the GED."	"I can improve my math skills by practicing regularly."
"If I fail, it means I'm not smart enough."	"Failure is an opportunity to learn and improve."
"I don't want to look dumb by asking questions."	"Asking questions will help me understand better."
"I'll stick to what I already know."	"I'm willing to try new strategies to succeed."

Practical Strategies to Develop a Growth Mindset

Developing a growth mindset is a gradual process, but with intentional effort, you can shift your perspective. Here's how:

1. Embrace Challenges

- **Why It Matters**: Challenges help you grow by pushing you out of your comfort zone.
- **What to Do**:
    - Tackle difficult topics first during study sessions.
    - View each problem or question as a chance to strengthen your skills.
    - Celebrate small wins when you overcome obstacles.

2. Reframe Negative Thoughts

- **Why It Matters**: Negative self-talk can limit your potential and discourage you from trying.
- **What to Do**:
    - Replace "I can't do this" with "I can't do this yet."
    - Focus on progress, not perfection.
    - Write down positive affirmations and review them daily.

3. Seek Feedback

- **Why It Matters**: Constructive feedback helps you identify areas for improvement.
- **What to Do**:
    - Review the answer explanations for practice questions you get wrong.
    - Ask a mentor, teacher, or study partner for input on your progress.
    - Use feedback as a tool for growth, not as a judgment of your abilities.

4. View Effort as a Strength

- **Why It Matters**: Consistent effort leads to mastery, regardless of initial skill level.
- **What to Do**:
    - Dedicate regular time to studying, even if it's just 30 minutes a day.
    - Focus on incremental progress, such as mastering one math concept at a time.
    - Recognize that persistence is often more important than innate ability.

5. Learn from Others

- **Why It Matters**: Observing how others succeed can inspire and guide you.
- **What to Do**:
  - Read stories of individuals who passed the GED after facing challenges.
  - Join a study group or connect with other test-takers to share tips and encouragement.
  - Observe effective study habits and strategies used by others.

Overcoming Obstacles with a Growth Mindset

As you prepare for the GED, you'll encounter obstacles. A growth mindset equips you to handle them effectively:

1. Struggling with a Subject

- **Fixed Mindset**: "I'll never understand this topic."
- **Growth Mindset**: "I need to approach this from a different angle."
- **Solution**: Break the material into smaller chunks, seek additional resources, or ask for help.

2. Low Practice Test Scores

- **Fixed Mindset**: "I'm not good enough to pass the GED."
- **Growth Mindset**: "This score shows me what I need to work on."
- **Solution**: Use the results to identify weak areas and focus your efforts there.

3. Fear of Failure

- **Fixed Mindset**: "If I fail, I'm a failure."
- **Growth Mindset**: "Failure is a stepping stone to success."
- **Solution**: Remind yourself that each attempt brings you closer to your goal.

Daily Practices to Foster a Growth Mindset

Incorporate these habits into your daily routine to strengthen your growth mindset:

1. **Reflect on Progress**: At the end of each study session, write down what you learned and how you improved.
2. **Set Achievable Goals**: Break your preparation into small, manageable steps, and celebrate milestones along the way.
3. **Surround Yourself with Positivity**: Engage with people, resources, and environments that encourage growth and optimism.
4. **Practice Gratitude**: Focus on what you've accomplished rather than what's left to do.

Long-Term Benefits of a Growth Mindset

A growth mindset doesn't just help you succeed on the GED exam—it's a valuable life skill. It fosters resilience, adaptability, and a love of learning, all of which are essential for personal and professional growth. By adopting this mindset, you'll be better equipped to handle future challenges, pursue further education, and achieve your long-term goals.

Developing a growth mindset is a powerful tool for success. By embracing challenges, persisting through difficulties, and focusing on continuous improvement, you'll not only prepare effectively for the GED but also unlock your full potential. With this mindset in place, it's time to take the next step in your journey: setting realistic goals and creating a study schedule.

5.3 Setting Realistic Goals and Creating a Study Schedule

One of the most important steps in preparing for the GED exam is establishing clear, realistic goals and creating a study schedule that fits your lifestyle. A well-structured plan ensures that you stay focused, cover all the necessary material, and have ample time to review and practice before test day. In this section, we'll discuss how to set achievable goals, craft a personalized study schedule, and maintain consistency to maximize your chances of success.

Why Setting Goals is Essential

Goals provide direction and motivation. They help you measure your progress and give you a sense of accomplishment as you reach each milestone. Without clear goals, it's easy to become overwhelmed or lose focus during the preparation process.

How to Set Realistic Goals

The key to effective goal-setting is ensuring that your objectives are achievable, measurable, and tailored to your needs. One proven method is the **SMART framework**:

1. Specific

Define your goals clearly. Instead of saying, "I want to study math," specify, "I will complete the geometry section by next Friday."

2. Measurable

Set goals that allow you to track progress. For example, aim to score at least 80% on practice questions for a specific subject.

3. Achievable

Be realistic about what you can accomplish within your timeframe. Don't aim to study for six hours a day if you have other commitments.

4. Relevant

Ensure your goals align with your ultimate objective: passing the GED. Focus on areas that need improvement rather than topics you already know well.

5. Time-Bound

Set deadlines for each goal. For instance, "I will complete one full-length practice test by the end of this month."

Breaking Down Your GED Preparation

The GED exam covers four subjects: Reasoning Through Language Arts, Mathematical Reasoning, Science, and Social Studies. Breaking your preparation into smaller, manageable tasks for each subject ensures comprehensive coverage without overwhelming you.

1. **Assess Your Starting Point**:
    - Take a diagnostic practice test to identify your strengths and weaknesses.
    - Focus your efforts on weaker areas while maintaining your skills in stronger ones.
2. **Set Milestones for Each Subject**:
    - For each subject, outline key topics to cover. For example:
        - **Math**: Arithmetic, algebra, geometry, and data analysis.
        - **RLA**: Grammar, reading comprehension, and essay writing.
        - **Science**: Life sciences, physical sciences, and interpreting data.
        - **Social Studies**: U.S. history, civics, economics, and geography.
3. **Plan for Practice and Review**:
    - Allocate time for completing practice questions and reviewing the answers.
    - Include periodic full-length practice tests to simulate the real exam environment.

Crafting Your Study Schedule

Your study schedule should be customized to fit your unique circumstances, including how much time you have before your exam and your daily responsibilities. Below are three sample plans based on different timelines:

1. One-Month Intensive Plan

- **Who It's For**: Test-takers with limited time who can dedicate several hours daily.
- **Schedule**:
    - Study for 4–6 hours per day, dividing time equally among all subjects.
    - Dedicate weekends to completing practice tests and reviewing weak areas.

2. Three-Month Balanced Plan

- **Who It's For**: Individuals with moderate time to prepare and other commitments.

- **Schedule**:
  - Study for 1–2 hours per day, focusing on one subject at a time.
  - Reserve one day per week for practice tests or reviewing previously covered material.

3. Six-Month Comprehensive Plan

- **Who It's For**: Those who prefer a gradual approach with minimal daily study time.
- **Schedule**:
  - Study for 30–60 minutes daily, covering one topic or subtopic at a time.
  - Dedicate weekends or days off to completing practice tests and addressing weak areas.

Tips for Maintaining Your Schedule

Creating a schedule is only half the battle—you must also stick to it. Here are some tips to help you stay consistent:

1. Prioritize Study Time

- Treat your study sessions like appointments that cannot be missed.
- Choose a time of day when you're most alert and focused, whether it's early morning or late evening.

2. Break it Down

- Divide study sessions into smaller, focused intervals (e.g., 25 minutes of studying followed by a 5-minute break using the Pomodoro Technique).
- This prevents burnout and keeps you engaged.

3. Use Tools to Stay Organized

- **Calendars**: Mark key milestones and test dates.
- **Planners**: Write down daily or weekly goals.
- **Apps**: Use study apps or timers to keep track of your progress and maintain focus.

4. Build in Flexibility

- Life happens, so allow room in your schedule for unexpected interruptions. If you miss a session, don't stress—just adjust your plan to make up for it.

5. Stay Accountable

- Share your schedule and goals with a friend or family member who can help keep you on track.
- Join a GED study group for mutual support and motivation.

Balancing Study with Life

For many GED test-takers, preparation must fit around work, family, and other commitments. Here's how to balance your responsibilities without compromising your study time:

1. **Combine Activities**: Listen to educational podcasts or review flashcards during your commute.
2. **Make the Most of Downtime**: Use lunch breaks or waiting periods to review notes or answer practice questions.
3. **Set Boundaries**: Communicate with family and friends about your study schedule to minimize interruptions.

Tracking Your Progress

Monitoring your progress is essential for staying motivated and ensuring that you're on track to achieve your goals. Here's how:

- **Keep a Study Journal**: Record what you study each day, what you've mastered, and what needs more attention.
- **Review Practice Test Scores**: Note improvements and pinpoint areas for additional focus.
- **Celebrate Milestones**: Reward yourself for completing chapters, mastering difficult topics, or achieving high scores on practice tests.

Adjusting Your Schedule as Needed

Your initial schedule doesn't have to be set in stone. As you progress, you may find that some subjects require more time than others or that your availability changes. Be flexible and adjust your schedule to reflect your evolving needs.

The Benefits of Setting Goals and Scheduling

By setting realistic goals and following a structured study schedule, you'll:

- Reduce stress by breaking the preparation process into manageable steps.
- Ensure that all subjects and topics are covered thoroughly.
- Build confidence as you track your progress and see your hard work paying off.

Setting realistic goals and creating a study schedule are critical components of GED success. With these tools in place, you'll have a clear roadmap for your preparation journey, ensuring that you stay organized, focused, and on track to pass with flying colors. Now that you've established the foundation for success, let's move on to the next part of this guide: test-taking strategies.

CHAPTER 6

TEST-TAKING STRATEGIES

The GED exam is not only a test of knowledge but also a test of strategy. Knowing how to approach the exam effectively can significantly impact your performance. Even the most well-prepared test-takers can struggle without a solid strategy for managing time, analyzing questions, and navigating the computer-based format. This chapter provides proven techniques to help you approach the GED exam with confidence and efficiency.

Why Test-Taking Strategies Matter

Effective test-taking strategies can:

1. Maximize your score by ensuring you answer as many questions correctly as possible within the allotted time.
2. Minimize stress by giving you a structured approach to handle the exam.
3. Help you avoid common pitfalls, such as rushing through questions or spending too much time on a single problem.

By mastering these strategies, you'll improve your chances of achieving a high score while reducing test-day anxiety.

Key Components of Successful Test-Taking

To perform well on the GED exam, you'll need to excel in four key areas:

1. **Time Management**: Ensuring you have enough time to answer all questions while avoiding the temptation to rush.
2. **Question Analysis**: Understanding what each question is asking and breaking it down into manageable steps.
3. **Eliminating Wrong Answers**: Narrowing down your choices to increase the likelihood of selecting the correct answer.
4. **Navigating the Computer-Based Format**: Familiarizing yourself with the digital tools and features of the exam platform.

Each of these components will be covered in detail throughout this chapter.

Preparing for the GED Exam Environment

Before diving into specific strategies, it's important to understand the exam environment:

- The GED is a **computer-based test**. You'll answer questions using a digital interface, which includes tools like an on-screen calculator, highlight and flagging features, and navigation options.
- Each subject test is timed, with strict limits that require you to pace yourself.
- Questions may include multiple-choice, fill-in-the-blank, drag-and-drop, and extended response formats.

Understanding this setup is the first step to building effective test-taking strategies.

Adopting a Strategic Mindset

Success on the GED exam starts with your mindset. Approach the test with the following attitudes:

1. **Stay Calm**: Anxiety can cloud your judgment. Practice relaxation techniques to stay focused.
2. **Be Flexible**: If one question is too difficult, move on and come back to it later if time permits.
3. **Trust Your Preparation**: Confidence comes from knowing you've done the work. Remind yourself of your study efforts and progress.

6.1 Managing Your Time During the Exam

Time management is one of the most critical skills for success on the GED exam. Each subject test is timed, and while the time limits are designed to be fair, many test-takers find themselves rushing to finish. By learning how to allocate your time effectively, you can ensure that you answer as many questions as possible with accuracy and confidence.

Understanding the GED Exam Time Limits

Each subject test has a specific time limit, which determines how much time you can spend on each question:

- **Reasoning Through Language Arts (RLA)**: 150 minutes, including time for an extended response (essay).

- **Mathematical Reasoning**: 115 minutes, divided into two parts (with and without a calculator).
- **Science**: 90 minutes.
- **Social Studies**: 70 minutes.

These time limits include both multiple-choice and other question formats, so efficient pacing is essential.

Common Time Management Challenges

Many test-takers struggle with time management due to the following issues:

1. Spending too much time on a single question.
2. Rushing through easier questions to "save time" for harder ones, leading to avoidable mistakes.
3. Losing track of time and running out before completing the test.

Understanding these challenges is the first step to overcoming them.

Strategies for Managing Your Time Effectively

1. Familiarize Yourself with the Test Format

Knowing what to expect will help you plan your time more effectively:

- Understand the types of questions for each subject test.
- Use the practice tests in this book to simulate the timing and format of the actual exam.

2. Allocate Time Per Question

Break down the total time allotted for each test into smaller chunks:

- **RLA**: Spend about 2 minutes per question for multiple-choice and save 45 minutes for the essay.
- **Mathematics**: Aim for 1.5 to 2 minutes per question.
- **Science**: Spend approximately 1.5 minutes per question.
- **Social Studies**: Allocate around 1 minute per question.

Remember, these are rough estimates. Some questions may take longer, while others will be quicker.

3. Prioritize Easier Questions

- Answer questions you find easy first. This builds confidence and ensures you earn points quickly.
- Use the "flag" feature to mark more challenging questions and return to them later if time permits.

4. Use the Process of Elimination

- Narrowing down answer choices can save time and increase your chances of answering correctly.
- If you're unsure about a question, eliminate obviously incorrect answers and make an educated guess.

5. Monitor the Clock

- Keep an eye on the timer displayed on the test interface.
- Check your progress periodically to ensure you're on track:
  - For example, if a section has 50 questions and 60 minutes, aim to complete 25 questions in the first 30 minutes.

6. Plan for the Extended Response (Essay)

In the RLA section, you'll need to write an essay. Here's how to manage your time:

- Spend 10 minutes planning your response.
- Use 30 minutes to write.
- Reserve 5 minutes to review and edit.

7. Avoid Perfectionism

- Don't get stuck trying to perfect an answer. If you've spent too much time on one question, make your best guess and move on.

- Remember, every question carries the same weight, so focus on answering as many as possible.

During the Test: Staying on Track

1. Start Strong

- Begin with confidence by answering questions you know well.
- Building momentum at the start will set a positive tone for the rest of the test.

2. Stay Flexible

- If you find a section particularly challenging, adjust your pace but don't let it disrupt your overall timing.

3. Use Breaks Wisely

- Some sections, like RLA, include scheduled breaks. Use this time to relax, stretch, and refocus.
- Avoid overthinking previous questions during breaks—stay focused on what's ahead.

Practice Time Management with Simulations

The best way to develop time management skills is by practicing under timed conditions:

- Use the full-length practice tests in this book to simulate the real exam.
- Track how long you spend on each question or section.
- Identify patterns: Are you spending too much time on certain question types? Adjust your approach accordingly.

Key Takeaways

- **Time is a Resource**: Treat your allotted time like a budget. Spend it wisely and prioritize where you invest it.
- **Preparation is Key**: Familiarity with the test format and timing will help you approach the exam with confidence.
- **Balance Speed and Accuracy**: While working quickly is important, don't sacrifice accuracy. Aim for a steady pace.

Effective time management ensures that you maximize your potential on the GED exam. With these strategies, you'll be able to approach each section with confidence, knowing you have a plan to finish on time.

6.2 Reading Questions Effectively

Reading and understanding questions accurately is a crucial skill for the GED exam. Misinterpreting a question can lead to incorrect answers, even if you know the material well. This section will guide you through strategies to approach and interpret questions effectively, ensuring that you fully understand what is being asked before selecting an answer.

Why Reading Questions Effectively is Important

The GED exam is designed to test not just your knowledge but also your ability to analyze, interpret, and apply information. Questions often include:

- Complex wording or scenarios requiring careful analysis.
- Distractors—incorrect answers designed to seem plausible.
- Context-dependent questions that require comprehension of accompanying text, graphs, or charts.

By mastering the skill of reading questions effectively, you'll avoid common pitfalls and increase your chances of selecting the correct answer.

Common Challenges in Reading Questions

1. **Overlooking Key Words**: Missing crucial words like "except," "not," or "best" can lead to choosing the wrong answer.
2. **Getting Distracted by Distractors**: Plausible but incorrect answer choices can confuse you if you don't fully understand the question.
3. **Overthinking**: Trying to read too much into a straightforward question can result in unnecessary mistakes.
4. **Rushing**: Skimming questions to save time can cause you to miss important details.

Strategies for Reading Questions Effectively

1. Read the Question Carefully

- **Slow Down**: Take your time to read the question thoroughly. Avoid skimming, even if it seems simple.
- **Focus on Key Words**: Look for words that indicate what the question is asking, such as:
  - **"Most likely"**: Indicates the best or most logical option.
  - **"Not" or "Except"**: Signals that you need to find the incorrect or irrelevant option.
  - **"Best describes"**: Requires interpretation and comparison of options.
- **Pay Attention to Verbs**: Words like "analyze," "explain," or "compare" provide clues about the required approach.

2. Understand the Context

Many questions include additional information, such as a passage, graph, or chart. Follow these steps:

- **Skim First, Read Later**: Quickly skim the accompanying information to understand the general context, then read the question.
- **Refer Back to the Details**: Use the information provided to find evidence or clues that support your answer.
- **Identify What is Relevant**: Not all details will be necessary. Focus on the parts that relate directly to the question.

3. Break Down Complex Questions

- For long or complicated questions, break them into smaller parts:
  - Identify the main idea or topic.
  - Note any specific instructions or conditions.
  - Eliminate unnecessary information.
- Rephrase the question in simpler terms to ensure you understand what is being asked.

4. Use the Process of Elimination

- Start by eliminating answers that are obviously incorrect.
- Compare the remaining options carefully to identify the best choice.
- If two answers seem correct, revisit the question to find subtle differences that may clarify which is better.

5. Watch for Traps

The GED exam may include questions designed to test your attention to detail. Be aware of:

- **Absolute Words**: Options with words like "always" or "never" are often incorrect, as they leave no room for exceptions.
- **Distractors**: These are incorrect answers that may include partial truths or common misconceptions. Verify each option before selecting one.

Practical Examples

Example 1: RLA (Reasoning Through Language Arts)

Question: Which sentence best summarizes the author's main argument in the passage?

- **Strategy**: Identify the passage's main idea by focusing on the introduction and conclusion. Avoid answers that include minor details or unrelated points.

Example 2: Mathematical Reasoning

Question: What is the area of a rectangle with a length of 8 inches and a width of 5 inches?

- **Strategy**: Identify the formula for area (Area=length×width\text{Area} = \text{length} \times \text{width}Area=length×width). Ignore any distractors, such as options with incorrect calculations.

Example 3: Science

Question: Based on the graph, which statement is true about the population growth of Species A over the past decade?

- **Strategy**: Focus on the graph's key details (axes labels, data points). Eliminate options that contradict the graph's trends.

Example 4: Social Studies

Question: Which of the following is NOT a principle outlined in the U.S. Constitution?

- **Strategy**: Highlight the word "NOT" to avoid overlooking it. Eliminate answers that align with the Constitution and select the exception.

Tips for Effective Question Analysis

1. **Re-Read When Needed**: If a question seems unclear, read it again slowly. Sometimes, a second reading clarifies its meaning.
2. **Highlight or Flag**: Use the test platform's tools to highlight keywords or flag questions for review.
3. **Paraphrase**: Rewriting the question in your own words can make it easier to understand.
4. **Trust Your Preparation**: Don't overthink straightforward questions. If an answer seems obvious, it likely is—provided you've read the question carefully.

Time-Saving Techniques

While reading carefully is essential, it's also important to manage your time:

- **Skip and Return**: If a question takes too long to answer, skip it and come back later.
- **Set a Pace**: Allocate a set amount of time per question and stick to it.
- **Avoid Over-Reviewing**: Don't second-guess yourself unnecessarily. Trust your first instinct unless you find clear evidence to change your answer.

Key Takeaways

- Read every question carefully, focusing on key words and context.
- Break down complex questions into manageable parts.
- Use strategies like elimination and paraphrasing to clarify your understanding.
- Stay alert for traps like distractors and absolute terms.
- Practice these techniques during preparation to make them second nature on test day.

CHAPTER 7

UNDERSTANDING THE SCORING SYSTEM

The GED scoring system is designed to provide a comprehensive evaluation of your knowledge and skills. Understanding how the scoring works and what your score represents is an essential part of your GED preparation. A clear understanding of the scoring system can help you set realistic goals, monitor your progress, and determine the level of achievement you wish to aim for, whether it's passing the exam or earning a College Ready designation.

The Basics of GED Scoring

Each of the four subject tests—Reasoning Through Language Arts, Mathematical Reasoning, Science, and Social Studies—is scored on a scale of **100 to 200 points**. To pass the GED exam, you must achieve a minimum score of **145** on each subject test. This ensures that you have demonstrated the equivalent knowledge and skills of a high school graduate.

Score Categories

Your GED score falls into one of four categories:

1. **Below Passing (100–144)**:
    - Indicates that you did not meet the minimum requirements to pass the subject test.
    - If you score in this range, you will need to retake the subject test to earn your GED credential.
2. **High School Equivalency Passing Score (145–164)**:
    - Demonstrates proficiency in the subject at a high school level.
    - Earning at least 145 on each subject test qualifies you for the GED credential.
3. **College Ready (165–174)**:
    - Indicates that you have advanced knowledge and skills beyond the high school level.
    - Many colleges and universities may waive placement tests or remedial courses for students scoring in this range.
4. **College Ready + Credit (175–200)**:
    - Reflects exceptional performance.
    - In addition to waiving placement tests, some institutions may award college credits for scores in this range.

How Scores Are Calculated

GED scores are determined using a **scaled scoring system**, which takes into account:

- **Number of Correct Answers**: The raw score is based on the number of questions answered correctly.
- **Question Weighting**: Some questions may be more challenging and therefore contribute more to the overall score.
- **Scaled Conversion**: The raw score is converted into a scaled score ranging from 100 to 200 to standardize results across different test versions.

What Passing the GED Means

Achieving the minimum passing score of 145 in all four subject tests signifies that you possess the knowledge and skills equivalent to those of a high school graduate. However, if your goals include attending college or pursuing advanced career opportunities, you may want to aim for higher scores to qualify for the College Ready or College Ready + Credit designations.

Importance of Retaking a Subject Test

If you do not pass one or more subject tests, don't be discouraged. The GED allows you to retake individual subjects without affecting your scores on the others. Use this as an opportunity to focus your study efforts on the areas where you need improvement. Retaking a subject can also help you achieve a higher overall score if you're aiming for College Ready or College Ready + Credit levels.

7.1 What Your Score Means

Your GED score is more than just a number—it reflects your academic proficiency and readiness for future opportunities. Understanding what your score means in practical terms will help you set clear goals and gauge your level of preparedness for higher education, career advancement, or personal achievement. Each score range has specific implications that can guide your next steps after completing the exam.

Breaking Down the GED Score Ranges

1. Below Passing (100–144)

- **What It Means**: This score indicates that you did not meet the minimum requirements for passing the subject test. It reflects areas where additional study and preparation are needed.
- **Next Steps**:
    - Review the specific topics where you struggled, using your test results as a guide.
    - Focus on strengthening your knowledge in weaker areas before retaking the test.
    - Take advantage of practice tests and targeted exercises to build confidence.

2. High School Equivalency Passing Score (145–164)

- **What It Means**: This range signifies that you have demonstrated the knowledge and skills equivalent to those of a high school graduate. You qualify for the GED credential, which is widely recognized as a high school diploma equivalent.
- **Opportunities**:
    - You meet the minimum requirements for most entry-level jobs.
    - You are eligible to apply for vocational training programs and some colleges.
- **Considerations**: While passing is an important milestone, consider aiming for a higher score if your goals include college admission or career advancement.

3. College Ready (165–174)

- **What It Means**: A score in this range indicates advanced proficiency. It demonstrates that you are academically prepared for college-level coursework and may exempt you from placement tests or remedial classes.
- **Opportunities**:
    - Streamlined entry into college programs.
    - Eligibility for certain scholarships or advanced placement opportunities.
- **Why It Matters**: Colleges value students who can demonstrate readiness for the academic rigors of higher education. This score can save you time and money by allowing you to skip non-credit-bearing courses.

4. College Ready + Credit (175–200)

- **What It Means**: Achieving a score in this range reflects exceptional academic performance. It not only signifies college readiness but may also qualify you for college credits, depending on the institution's policies.
- **Opportunities**:
    - You may earn up to 10 college credits, reducing the time and cost of completing a degree.
    - Increased competitiveness for scholarships and admissions to selective programs.
- **Why It Matters**: This score demonstrates mastery of the subject matter at a level comparable to high-achieving college students.

How Employers View Your GED Score

Employers often use the GED credential as a benchmark for high school equivalency. While they may not focus on the specific score, performing well can signal to employers that you are diligent, capable, and committed to self-improvement. If you're applying for jobs requiring higher skills or leadership potential, a strong score can set you apart from other candidates.

How Colleges Interpret Your Score

Colleges use GED scores to assess your readiness for academic success. Here's what they typically look for:

- **Passing (145–164)**: Indicates you meet the basic requirements for admission but may require additional assessments or remedial courses.
- **College Ready (165–174)**: Suggests you are prepared for college-level work and may bypass placement exams.
- **College Ready + Credit (175–200)**: Demonstrates exceptional readiness and can result in earned credits, reducing the overall cost and duration of your degree.

Using Your Score as a Roadmap

Your GED score provides valuable feedback on your academic strengths and weaknesses. Use it to:

- Identify areas for improvement if you plan to retake a subject test for a higher score.
- Tailor your preparation for future academic or career goals.
- Celebrate your achievements and build confidence for the next steps in your journey.

7.2 How to Aim for College Ready and College Ready + Credit Levels

Scoring in the **College Ready (165–174)** or **College Ready + Credit (175–200)** range on the GED exam is an impressive achievement that can open doors to advanced academic and professional opportunities. These scores demonstrate mastery of high school-level material, readiness for college-level work, and even the potential to earn college credits. In this section, we'll explore strategies to help you reach these higher score levels, focusing on preparation, test-taking skills, and mindset.

Why Aim for These Levels?

Achieving a score in the College Ready or College Ready + Credit range offers significant benefits:

1. **College Admission Advantages**:
   - Many colleges and universities waive placement exams or remedial courses for students scoring in this range, allowing you to start earning credits immediately.
   - High scores strengthen your college application, showcasing your readiness and commitment to academic success.
2. **Potential for College Credits**:
   - A score of **175–200** may qualify you for up to 10 college credits, depending on the institution. This can save you time and money as you pursue your degree.
3. **Scholarship Opportunities**:
   - Exceptional scores increase your eligibility for scholarships, grants, and financial aid programs targeted at high-achieving students.
4. **Personal and Professional Benefits**:
   - A high score boosts your confidence and enhances your resume, making you more competitive in the job market.

Strategies to Reach Higher Scores

Achieving a high score requires more than just passing—it demands thorough preparation, effective test-taking strategies, and a focus on accuracy and precision. Here are detailed steps to help you aim for College Ready and College Ready + Credit levels:

1. Master the Content Thoroughly

High scores are built on a strong foundation of knowledge. Focus on mastering the material in each subject:

- **Reasoning Through Language Arts (RLA)**:
  - Practice analyzing complex texts for themes, tone, and author's purpose.
  - Develop essay-writing skills by practicing extended responses with clear arguments and supporting evidence.
  - Focus on advanced grammar, syntax, and editing techniques.
- **Mathematical Reasoning**:

    - Go beyond basic arithmetic and focus on algebra, geometry, and data analysis.
    - Work on solving multi-step problems and interpreting graphs and charts.
    - Practice using the GED's on-screen calculator efficiently for the calculator-allowed section.
- **Science**:
    - Strengthen your ability to analyze data and interpret scientific experiments.
    - Focus on understanding scientific concepts like ecosystems, genetics, and physics principles.
    - Learn to evaluate hypotheses and draw conclusions from graphs and charts.
- **Social Studies**:
    - Study U.S. history, civics, economics, and geography with attention to cause-and-effect relationships.
    - Focus on analyzing historical documents and understanding how they relate to broader themes.
    - Develop skills to interpret maps, graphs, and political cartoons.

2. Aim for High Accuracy

High scores depend on answering a significant majority of questions correctly:

- Strive for an **accuracy rate of 85–90%** during practice tests.
- Prioritize answering easier questions first to secure points before tackling harder ones.
- Review incorrect answers to understand your mistakes and avoid repeating them.

3. Focus on Time Management

Efficient time management is crucial for completing the test and reviewing your answers:

- Practice completing sections within the allotted time during mock exams.
- Use the flagging feature to skip and return to difficult questions.
- Allocate time for reviewing flagged questions and double-checking answers.

4. Enhance Test-Taking Skills

Refining your approach to the exam can significantly improve your score:

- **Eliminate Distractors**: Use the process of elimination to narrow down answer choices.
- **Analyze Questions Carefully**: Pay attention to keywords like "best," "most likely," or "except."
- **Practice Multi-Step Problems**: For math and science, break down complex problems into smaller, manageable steps.

5. Practice Writing Exceptional Essays

The extended response in the RLA section contributes significantly to your score:

- Develop a clear structure: Start with a strong introduction, support your argument with evidence, and conclude effectively.
- Use specific examples from the provided texts to back up your points.
- Focus on clarity, logical flow, and proper grammar.
- Practice editing your essays to identify and correct errors.

6. Simulate Real Exam Conditions

Take full-length practice tests under timed conditions to build stamina and familiarity with the test format:

- Use practice tests in this book or online resources to simulate the GED exam environment.
- Review detailed answer explanations to understand why the correct answers are right and why others are wrong.

7. Adopt a Growth Mindset

Achieving a high score requires perseverance and a willingness to learn from mistakes:

- Treat challenges as opportunities to improve.
- Celebrate incremental progress, such as mastering a new math concept or improving your essay-writing skills.

- Stay motivated by keeping your long-term goals in mind, such as earning college credits or gaining admission to your dream school.

Advanced Study Techniques for High Scores

To push your performance into the College Ready or College Ready + Credit range, adopt advanced study techniques:

1. **Active Learning**:
    - Take detailed notes as you study.
    - Teach concepts to a friend or family member to reinforce your understanding.
2. **Targeted Review**:
    - Focus on weaker areas while maintaining strengths in other subjects.
    - Use diagnostic tests to identify specific topics that need improvement.
3. **Flashcards and Summaries**:
    - Create flashcards for key concepts, formulas, and terms.
    - Write summaries of complex topics to simplify and solidify your understanding.

What to Do After Achieving a High Score

1. **Research College Policies**:
    - Contact colleges to confirm their policies on GED scores for admissions, placement tests, and credit awards.
    - Understand the specific benefits of your score at each institution.
2. **Leverage Your Score in Applications**:
    - Highlight your high GED scores in your college applications and resumes.
    - Emphasize how your achievement demonstrates academic readiness and determination.
3. **Plan for the Next Steps**:
    - Use your GED success as a launching pad for higher education, vocational training, or career advancement.

Key Takeaways

- Aiming for College Ready (165–174) and College Ready + Credit (175–200) scores opens doors to greater academic and professional opportunities.
- Success at these levels requires mastery of content, strong test-taking strategies, and consistent practice.
- High scores can save you time and money through college credit awards and bypassing remedial courses.

By setting your sights on College Ready or College Ready + Credit levels, you're positioning yourself for exceptional opportunities and long-term success. With the strategies outlined here and your dedication to preparation, you can achieve these ambitious goals and unlock the full potential of your GED credential

PART II

REASONING THROUGH LANGUAGE ARTS (RLA)

CHAPTER 8

UNDERSTANDING THE RLA EXAM STRUCTURE

The Reasoning Through Language Arts (RLA) section of the GED exam evaluates your ability to read, comprehend, and analyze written texts, as well as write clearly and effectively. It is designed to test a broad range of skills that are essential for academic and professional success, including reading comprehension, grammar, and essay writing.

In this section, we will break down the structure of the RLA exam to help you understand what to expect and how to prepare effectively.

The Components of the RLA Exam

The RLA exam consists of three main components:

1. **Reading Comprehension**:
    - Tests your ability to understand, interpret, and analyze both informational and literary texts.
    - Requires critical thinking to determine themes, author's intent, and logical conclusions.
2. **Grammar and Language Conventions**:
    - Assesses your understanding of standard English grammar, punctuation, and sentence structure.
    - Includes questions where you edit or revise sentences for clarity and correctness.
3. **Extended Response (Essay Writing)**:
    - Requires you to write an essay responding to a specific prompt.
    - Tests your ability to construct a clear, well-organized argument supported by evidence from provided texts.

Format and Question Types

The RLA exam is computer-based and includes a variety of question formats. These include:

- **Multiple-Choice Questions**: Choose the best answer from four options.
- **Drag-and-Drop Questions**: Drag and organize text or items into the correct sequence.
- **Drop-Down Menu Questions**: Select the correct answer from a drop-down list within a sentence or paragraph.
- **Hotspot Questions**: Click on specific parts of the text to answer questions.
- **Extended Response**: Write a structured essay in response to a prompt, incorporating evidence from provided texts.

Content Breakdown

The RLA exam focuses on the following content areas:

1. **Reading Passages**:
    - **Informational Texts** (75%): Nonfiction passages from topics like science, history, or social studies.
    - **Literary Texts** (25%): Fictional excerpts, poetry, or drama.
    - Reading passages may range from 400 to 900 words in length.
2. **Language Skills**:
    - Grammar and usage, including subject-verb agreement, pronoun clarity, and sentence fragments.
    - Punctuation rules, such as correct use of commas, periods, and quotation marks.
    - Sentence structure and editing for clarity and effectiveness.

3. **Extended Response**:
    - Write an essay analyzing two opposing viewpoints presented in a pair of texts.
    - Develop a coherent argument supported by evidence from the texts.

Exam Timing

The total time for the RLA exam is **150 minutes**, divided as follows:

1. **Reading and Language Skills**: Approximately 95 minutes for multiple-choice and short-answer questions.
2. **Extended Response**: 45 minutes to plan, write, and revise your essay.
3. **Break**: A 10-minute break is included after the first section.

Skills Tested

The RLA exam evaluates a range of skills, including:

- **Reading Skills**:
    - Identifying main ideas and supporting details.
    - Determining the meaning of words in context.
    - Analyzing the structure of a text and its impact on meaning.
    - Evaluating arguments and evidence for validity and relevance.
- **Writing Skills**:
    - Constructing clear, grammatically correct sentences.
    - Organizing ideas logically and cohesively.
    - Supporting arguments with relevant evidence and examples.
    - Revising and editing for clarity and correctness.

Example Overview of the Exam Flow

Let's consider a simplified breakdown of how the exam might progress:

1. **Reading Comprehension**:
    - You are given a nonfiction passage about climate change. Questions may include:
        - Identifying the main idea.
        - Analyzing how the author supports their argument with evidence.
        - Determining the meaning of a technical term in context.
2. **Language Conventions**:
    - A paragraph contains grammatical errors, such as a misplaced modifier or incorrect punctuation. You're asked to:
        - Correct the errors.
        - Improve sentence clarity without changing the meaning.
3. **Extended Response**:
    - You're provided two articles with opposing views on renewable energy.
    - The prompt asks you to:
        - Analyze the arguments in both texts.
        - Write an essay explaining which argument is stronger, using evidence from the texts.

How the RLA Exam is Scored

- **Reading and Language Skills**:
    - These questions are scored automatically by the computer.
    - Points are awarded for each correct answer, with no penalty for incorrect responses.

- **Extended Response**:
  - The essay is graded by both an automated scoring system and trained evaluators.
  - Scoring focuses on three key areas:
    1. **Analysis of Arguments and Use of Evidence**: How well you understand and evaluate the texts.
    2. **Clarity and Organization**: The logical structure and flow of your essay.
    3. **Language Conventions and Grammar**: Proper use of grammar, punctuation, and sentence structure.

Understanding the structure of the RLA exam is the first step toward effective preparation. This overview provides the foundation you need to approach each section with confidence. Next, we'll dive deeper into the **types of questions** you'll encounter on the RLA exam and strategies for tackling them.

8.1 Types of Questions

Understanding the types of questions you will encounter on the Reasoning Through Language Arts (RLA) exam is essential for effective preparation. Each question type is designed to assess specific skills, including reading comprehension, grammar, language conventions, and written communication. By familiarizing yourself with these question formats and practicing with examples, you'll gain the confidence and ability to approach the exam with a clear strategy.

Overview of Question Types

The RLA exam includes a variety of question formats that test your ability to analyze texts, understand language conventions, and construct written responses. These question types include:

- **Multiple-Choice Questions**
- **Drag-and-Drop Questions**
- **Drop-Down Menu Questions**
- **Hotspot Questions**
- **Extended Response (Essay)**

Each question type plays a unique role in evaluating your skills, and understanding how they work will help you approach them effectively.

Multiple-Choice Questions

Description

Multiple-choice questions are the most common type on the RLA exam. These questions present a prompt or passage followed by four answer choices, from which you must select the best option.

Skills Tested

- Identifying main ideas and supporting details.
- Analyzing an author's argument, tone, or purpose.
- Understanding vocabulary in context.
- Evaluating grammatical accuracy or language usage.

Example

Passage:

"The increasing reliance on technology has brought both benefits and challenges to modern society. While technology enhances communication and access to information, it also raises concerns about privacy and dependency."

Question: What is the main idea of the passage?

A) Technology is entirely beneficial to society.
B) Technology presents both advantages and challenges.
C) Privacy concerns outweigh the benefits of technology.
D) Society is becoming too dependent on technology.

Correct Answer: B. The passage discusses both the benefits and challenges of technology, making this the best summary.

Drag-and-Drop Questions

Description

Drag-and-drop questions require you to move text or items into the correct sequence or position. These questions are often used for tasks such as organizing ideas or identifying relationships.

Skills Tested

- Recognizing logical sequences or structures in a passage.
- Organizing information for clarity and coherence.
- Understanding relationships between ideas.

Example

Prompt: Arrange the sentences below to form a clear and logical paragraph.

1. As a result, many people are now working remotely.
2. The COVID-19 pandemic significantly altered the way we work.
3. Remote work has both advantages and disadvantages.
4. For example, it allows flexibility but can lead to isolation.

Correct Order:

2 → 1 → 3 → 4.

Drop-Down Menu Questions

Description

Drop-down menu questions provide a sentence or paragraph with blanks, and you must select the correct option from a drop-down list to complete the text.

Skills Tested

- Grammar and sentence structure.
- Vocabulary and word usage.
- Logical consistency in writing.

Example

Sentence: The conference will be held on ______, and all participants are expected to arrive by noon.

Options:

- A) Monday
- B) an afternoon
- C) the building
- D) the lunchtime

Correct Answer: A. The word "Monday" fits the context of a specific day for the conference.

Hotspot Questions

Description

Hotspot questions require you to click on specific parts of a passage, graph, or image to indicate your answer. These questions often test reading comprehension and attention to detail.

Skills Tested

- Identifying evidence in a passage to support an argument or conclusion.
- Recognizing key phrases or details relevant to a question.

Example

Passage:

"Exercise is vital for maintaining physical and mental health. Regular physical activity reduces the risk of chronic diseases and improves mood and cognitive function."

Question: Click on the sentence that explains the mental health benefits of exercise.

Correct Answer: *"Regular physical activity ... improves mood and cognitive function."*

Extended Response (Essay)

Description

The extended response is the essay portion of the RLA exam. You'll be presented with two passages that present opposing viewpoints on an issue. Your task is to write an essay analyzing which argument is stronger and why, using evidence from the texts to support your analysis.

Skills Tested

- Critical thinking and analysis.
- Constructing a clear and logical argument.
- Using evidence effectively to support claims.
- Writing with proper grammar, punctuation, and sentence structure.

Steps for Success

1. **Understand the Prompt**: Carefully read the instructions and both passages.
2. **Plan Your Essay**:
    - Identify the stronger argument and why it is more convincing.
    - Note specific evidence from the texts to support your points.
3. **Write Clearly**:
    - Use a standard essay structure: introduction, body paragraphs, and conclusion.
    - Make your argument logical and well-organized.
4. **Revise**:
    - Check for clarity, grammar, and spelling before submitting.

Tips for Approaching RLA Question Types

1. **Read Carefully**:
    - For reading comprehension questions, take your time to understand the passage before answering.
    - Pay attention to details that may be critical to the question.
2. **Eliminate Wrong Answers**:
    - For multiple-choice questions, eliminate obviously incorrect options to narrow down your choices.
3. **Practice Active Reading**:
    - Highlight or underline key points in the passage to make it easier to refer back when answering questions.
4. **Time Management**:
    - Allocate time for each question type, ensuring you have enough time to complete the essay.
5. **Practice Regularly**:
    - Familiarize yourself with each question type by completing practice exercises and reviewing explanations for correct and incorrect answers.

8.2 Time Allocation

Managing your time effectively during the Reasoning Through Language Arts (RLA) section of the GED exam is critical for completing all questions, including the extended response, within the allotted 150 minutes. This section will provide a detailed breakdown of the time allocation for each part of the exam and offer strategies to help you pace yourself and maximize your performance.

Overview of RLA Exam Timing

The RLA section consists of multiple-choice questions, short-answer questions, and an extended response (essay). The total time is divided as follows:

- **Section 1**: Reading Comprehension and Language Skills – ~95 minutes.
- **Section 2**: Extended Response (Essay Writing) – 45 minutes.
- **Break**: A mandatory 10-minute break is provided between the two sections.

This division ensures you have sufficient time to demonstrate your skills in reading, analyzing, and writing.

Time Allocation for Each Component

1. Reading Comprehension and Language Skills (~95 Minutes)

This section includes multiple-choice, drag-and-drop, drop-down menu, and hotspot questions. To manage your time effectively:

- **Passage Reading**:
  - Allocate 2–3 minutes to carefully read each passage. Skim the passage for the main idea, and then re-read specific sections as needed to answer the questions.
- **Answering Questions**:
  - Spend 1–2 minutes per multiple-choice question.
  - For complex questions (e.g., drag-and-drop or hotspot), allow up to 3 minutes if needed, but flag the question if it's taking too long and return to it later.
- **Editing Tasks**:
  - For grammar and sentence structure questions, spend no more than 1–1.5 minutes per item.

Example Strategy for Timing:

If a passage has 6 questions:

1. Spend 3 minutes reading the passage.
2. Allocate an average of 1.5 minutes per question ($6 \times 1.5 = 9$ minutes).
3. Total time per passage: ~12 minutes.

2. Extended Response (Essay Writing) – 45 Minutes

The essay requires you to evaluate two passages with opposing viewpoints and write a structured response. Proper time management is essential to complete all components of the essay:

1. **Planning (10 Minutes)**:
   - Carefully read both passages (3–4 minutes).
   - Identify the stronger argument and underline key evidence (3 minutes).
   - Create a quick outline, including your thesis, main points, and supporting evidence (3 minutes).
2. **Writing (30 Minutes)**:
   - Write the essay using a standard structure:
     - **Introduction**: Clearly state your thesis and preview your main points (5 minutes).

        - **Body Paragraphs**: Develop 2–3 paragraphs analyzing the stronger argument, using evidence from the texts (20 minutes).
        - **Conclusion**: Summarize your argument and reinforce why it is stronger (5 minutes).

3. **Review and Edit (5 Minutes)**:
    - Check for grammar, punctuation, and clarity.
    - Ensure your argument is logical and supported by evidence.

Key Tip: Stick to your time allocations strictly. If you fall behind, prioritize finishing the body paragraphs over spending too much time perfecting the introduction.

Effective Pacing Strategies

1. Prioritize Easy Questions

- Answer questions you find easy first to secure points quickly.
- Flag more challenging questions and return to them later if time permits.

2. Use Time-Saving Techniques

- **Highlighting**: Use the on-screen highlighting tool to mark key sections of the passage while reading.
- **Elimination**: For multiple-choice questions, eliminate obviously wrong answers to narrow your choices quickly.

3. Monitor Your Progress

- Check the timer periodically to ensure you're staying on track. For instance:
    - By the halfway mark (approximately 47 minutes), aim to have completed about half of the questions.

4. Avoid Overthinking

- Don't spend too much time second-guessing answers. Your first instinct is often correct, especially for well-prepared test-takers.

Time Management Challenges and Solutions

Challenge 1: Spending Too Much Time on a Single Question

- **Solution**: Set a personal time limit (e.g., 2 minutes) for each question. If you exceed it, flag the question and move on.

Challenge 2: Struggling with the Essay

- **Solution**: Stick to the time allocation for planning, writing, and editing. Even if you don't perfect every sentence, completing the essay is more important than leaving it unfinished.

Challenge 3: Rushing Through the Final Questions

- **Solution**: Pace yourself early in the test by sticking to your planned time allocations. Save at least 10–15 minutes at the end to review flagged questions and finalize your answers.

Sample Time Plan for the RLA Exam

Section	Time Allocation	Task
Reading Passages	3 minutes/passage	Skim for main ideas and key details.
Answering Questions	1–2 minutes/question	Respond to multiple-choice and related tasks.
Editing and Grammar	1–1.5 minutes/task	Review sentences for clarity and correctness.
Essay Planning	10 minutes	Read passages, outline your response.
Essay Writing	30 minutes	Write introduction, body paragraphs, conclusion.
Essay Editing	5 minutes	Review for grammar, punctuation, and clarity.

Practice Makes Perfect

Time management improves with practice. Use the following techniques to refine your pacing:

1. **Simulate Exam Conditions**: Take full-length practice tests under timed conditions to get accustomed to the time constraints.
2. **Analyze Your Timing**: After each practice test, review how you allocated your time and adjust as needed.
3. **Practice Essay Writing**: Time yourself while planning, writing, and revising essays to ensure you can complete them within 45 minutes.

Final Tips for Effective Time Allocation

- **Stick to Your Plan**: Trust your preparation and follow your time allocations strictly.
- **Use Your Break**: Take advantage of the 10-minute break to rest and reset before tackling the essay.
- **Prioritize Completion**: Aim to answer all questions and complete your essay, even if some answers are not perfect.

CHAPTER 9

ESSENTIAL GRAMMAR AND LANGUAGE CONVENTIONS

A strong understanding of grammar and language conventions is essential for success on the GED Reasoning Through Language Arts (RLA) exam. This section evaluates your ability to recognize and correct errors in grammar, punctuation, and sentence structure, as well as your ability to write clear and effective sentences. Mastering these conventions is not only crucial for the exam but also a valuable skill for communication in academic and professional settings.

In this chapter, we'll explore the foundational elements of grammar and language conventions, breaking them down into manageable sections. These topics include parts of speech, sentence structure and punctuation, common grammatical errors, and subject-verb agreement with a focus on sentence clarity.

Why Grammar and Language Conventions Matter

Grammar and language conventions form the backbone of clear and effective communication. The GED exam uses these conventions to assess whether you can:

1. Construct grammatically correct sentences.
2. Edit and revise text to improve clarity and flow.
3. Use punctuation and sentence structure to convey meaning effectively.

These skills are tested in various formats, including multiple-choice questions, editing tasks, and essay writing. Mastery of these conventions will not only help you perform well on the exam but also enhance your ability to communicate in real-life situations.

Skills Tested in This Section

The Essential Grammar and Language Conventions portion of the GED RLA exam focuses on the following skills:

1. **Identifying Parts of Speech**:
    - Understanding the role of nouns, verbs, adjectives, adverbs, and other parts of speech in a sentence.
    - Recognizing how parts of speech work together to convey meaning.
2. **Understanding Sentence Structure and Punctuation**:
    - Identifying correct sentence patterns.
    - Using punctuation marks such as commas, periods, and semicolons appropriately.
3. **Correcting Common Grammatical Errors**:
    - Recognizing and fixing issues such as misplaced modifiers, incorrect pronoun usage, and run-on sentences.
4. **Applying Subject-Verb Agreement**:
    - Ensuring that subjects and verbs agree in number and tense.
    - Revising sentences for clarity and precision.

How Grammar is Tested on the GED Exam

Grammar and language conventions are assessed through various types of questions:

- **Multiple-Choice Questions**: Select the correct version of a sentence or identify errors in a passage.
- **Sentence Revision Questions**: Improve the clarity or correctness of a sentence.
- **Extended Response (Essay)**: Demonstrate mastery of grammar and conventions in your writing.

Example: **Question**: Choose the sentence that is grammatically correct.

A) She don't have any more questions to ask.
B) She doesn't have no questions to ask.
C) She doesn't have any questions to ask.
D) She don't got no questions to ask.

Correct Answer: C. This sentence uses correct subject-verb agreement and avoids double negatives.

Practical Applications of Grammar and Conventions

While these skills are critical for the GED exam, they also have real-world applications:

- **Academic Writing**: Clear grammar and conventions are essential for writing essays, reports, and other academic assignments.
- **Professional Communication**: Employers value employees who can write professional emails, reports, and proposals.
- **Everyday Communication**: Proper grammar ensures clarity in personal and social interactions.

How to Prepare for This Section

1. **Learn the Basics**:
   - Review the rules for parts of speech, sentence structure, and punctuation.
   - Practice identifying and correcting grammatical errors.
2. **Apply What You Learn**:
   - Complete exercises and quizzes to reinforce your understanding.
   - Write and revise short paragraphs, focusing on clarity and correctness.
3. **Use Practice Tests**:
   - Familiarize yourself with the types of grammar questions on the GED exam.
   - Review detailed explanations for correct and incorrect answers.

9.1 Parts of Speech

Understanding the parts of speech is fundamental to mastering grammar and language conventions. Parts of speech are the building blocks of sentences, and each plays a unique role in conveying meaning. By identifying and correctly using these elements, you can write clearly, edit effectively, and understand the grammatical relationships that form the foundation of the GED RLA exam.

In this section, we'll explore the eight main parts of speech, providing detailed explanations, examples, and practical applications to help you develop a strong grasp of these essential components.

1. Nouns

Definition

Nouns are words that name people, places, things, or ideas. They can function as the subject of a sentence, an object, or part of a prepositional phrase.

Types of Nouns

1. **Common Nouns**: General names for things (e.g., "dog," "city," "car").
2. **Proper Nouns**: Specific names, always capitalized (e.g., "Chicago," "Einstein").
3. **Abstract Nouns**: Ideas or concepts (e.g., "freedom," "happiness").
4. **Concrete Nouns**: Physical objects you can touch or see (e.g., "book," "table").
5. **Collective Nouns**: Words for groups (e.g., "team," "family").

Example in a Sentence

- Common Noun: The **cat** sat on the **mat**.
- Proper Noun: **Sarah** visited **New York** last summer.

2. Pronouns

Definition

Pronouns replace nouns to avoid repetition and make sentences clearer.

Types of Pronouns

1. **Personal Pronouns**: Refer to people or things (e.g., "I," "you," "he," "they").
2. **Possessive Pronouns**: Show ownership (e.g., "mine," "yours," "theirs").
3. **Reflexive Pronouns**: Refer back to the subject (e.g., "myself," "yourself").
4. **Demonstrative Pronouns**: Point to specific things (e.g., "this," "that," "these," "those").
5. **Relative Pronouns**: Introduce clauses (e.g., "who," "whom," "which," "that").

Example in a Sentence

- Personal Pronoun: **She** loves reading books.
- Demonstrative Pronoun: **These** are my favorite shoes.

3. Verbs

Definition

Verbs express actions, states of being, or occurrences.

Types of Verbs

1. **Action Verbs**: Show physical or mental actions (e.g., "run," "think").
2. **Linking Verbs**: Connect the subject to additional information (e.g., "is," "seem").
3. **Helping Verbs**: Assist the main verb (e.g., "has," "will," "can").

Example in a Sentence

- Action Verb: He **ran** to the store.
- Linking Verb: She **is** a great singer.

4. Adjectives

Definition

Adjectives describe or modify nouns and pronouns, providing more detail.

Functions of Adjectives

- Answer questions like "Which one?" "What kind?" and "How many?"

Example in a Sentence

- **Which one?**: That is the **red** car.
- **What kind?**: The **large** dog barked loudly.
- **How many?**: She bought **three** apples.

5. Adverbs

Definition

Adverbs modify verbs, adjectives, or other adverbs, often indicating how, when, where, or to what extent an action occurs.

Example in a Sentence

- Modifying a verb: She runs **quickly**.
- Modifying an adjective: He is **very** tall.
- Modifying another adverb: She sings **quite beautifully**.

6. Prepositions

Definition

Prepositions show relationships between nouns (or pronouns) and other words in a sentence, often indicating direction, location, or time.

Example in a Sentence

- Direction: He walked **toward** the park.

- Location: The keys are **on** the table.
- Time: We'll meet **after** lunch.

7. Conjunctions

Definition

Conjunctions connect words, phrases, or clauses.

Types of Conjunctions

1. **Coordinating Conjunctions**: Connect equal elements (e.g., "and," "but," "or").
2. **Subordinating Conjunctions**: Introduce dependent clauses (e.g., "because," "although").
3. **Correlative Conjunctions**: Work in pairs (e.g., "either/or," "neither/nor").

Example in a Sentence

- Coordinating: She wanted to go to the movies, **but** it was too late.
- Subordinating: He stayed home **because** it was raining.

8. Interjections

Definition

Interjections are words or phrases that express strong emotion. They are often followed by an exclamation point or set off by a comma.

Example in a Sentence

- **Wow!** That was amazing.
- **Oh,** I didn't see you there.

Why Knowing Parts of Speech Matters

Understanding parts of speech helps you:

1. Construct grammatically correct sentences.
2. Identify errors in sentence structure.
3. Enhance your writing clarity and variety.

Practical Application

Exercise: Identify the parts of speech in the following sentence:

The quick brown fox jumps over the lazy dog.

Answer:

- **The**: Article (a type of adjective).
- **Quick, brown**: Adjectives (describing "fox").
- **Fox**: Noun.
- **Jumps**: Verb.
- **Over**: Preposition.
- **The**: Article.
- **Lazy**: Adjective (describing "dog").
- **Dog**: Noun.

9.2 Sentence Structure and Punctuation

Sentence structure and punctuation are essential components of clear and effective communication. Understanding how sentences are built and how punctuation is used to convey meaning will enable you to write with precision and identify errors in grammar tasks on the GED RLA exam. In this section, we will explore the fundamentals of sentence structure, common sentence types, and the correct use of punctuation marks.

Sentence Structure

Sentence structure refers to how words, phrases, and clauses are organized to form sentences. Mastery of sentence structure is crucial for writing sentences that are clear, concise, and grammatically correct.

Components of a Sentence

A sentence is composed of two key parts:

1. **Subject**: The person, place, thing, or idea performing the action or being described.
2. **Predicate**: The verb or verb phrase that tells what the subject is doing or what is happening to the subject.

Example:

- Subject: The **cat**
- Predicate: **slept on the couch**
- Complete Sentence: The **cat slept on the couch**.

Types of Sentences by Structure

1. **Simple Sentence**:
   - Contains one independent clause.
   - Example: She runs every morning.
2. **Compound Sentence**:
   - Contains two or more independent clauses joined by a coordinating conjunction (e.g., *and, but, or*).
   - Example: She runs every morning, and she lifts weights in the evening.
3. **Complex Sentence**:
   - Contains one independent clause and at least one dependent clause introduced by a subordinating conjunction (e.g., *because, although, when*).
   - Example: She runs every morning because she enjoys staying active.
4. **Compound-Complex Sentence**:
   - Contains at least two independent clauses and one or more dependent clauses.
   - Example: She runs every morning, and she lifts weights in the evening because she enjoys staying active.

Common Errors in Sentence Structure

- **Fragment**: A group of words that lacks a subject, predicate, or complete thought.
  - Incorrect: Because I went to the store. (Fragment)
  - Correct: I went to the store because I needed groceries.
- **Run-On Sentence**: Two or more independent clauses joined without proper punctuation or conjunction.
  - Incorrect: I went to the store I bought milk. (Run-on)
  - Correct: I went to the store, and I bought milk.
- **Comma Splice**: Two independent clauses joined by a comma without a conjunction.
  - Incorrect: I went to the store, I bought milk.
  - Correct: I went to the store, and I bought milk.

Punctuation

Punctuation marks clarify the meaning of sentences by indicating pauses, stops, or relationships between words and ideas. Proper punctuation is essential for avoiding ambiguity and confusion.

Common Punctuation Marks

1. Period (.)

- **Use**: Marks the end of a declarative sentence or statement.
    - Example: The dog barked loudly.

2. Comma (,)

- **Use**: Indicates a pause or separates elements within a sentence.
    - **In a List**: She bought apples, oranges, and bananas.
    - **Before a Coordinating Conjunction**: I wanted to go, but it started raining.
    - **After Introductory Elements**: After the movie, we went out for dinner.

3. Semicolon (;)

- **Use**: Connects two closely related independent clauses or separates items in a complex list.
    - Example: She loves reading; however, she doesn't enjoy writing.

4. Colon (:)

- **Use**: Introduces a list, explanation, or quotation.
    - Example: She brought three things to the picnic: sandwiches, lemonade, and a blanket.

5. Quotation Marks (" ")

- **Use**: Enclose direct speech or a quotation.
    - Example: She said, "I'm excited for the trip."

6. Apostrophe (')

- **Use**: Shows possession or forms contractions.
    - **Possession**: The dog's leash was tangled.
    - **Contraction**: It's going to rain today. (*It's = It is*)

7. Dash (—)

- **Use**: Indicates a pause or emphasizes additional information.
    - Example: She decided to go—despite the bad weather.

8. Parentheses ( )

- **Use**: Enclose extra or nonessential information.
    - Example: The results (which were surprising) changed the course of the project.

Practical Applications

Identifying Sentence Errors

Exercise: Identify and correct the error in the following sentence:

The children were excited about the field trip they forgot their permission slips at home.

- **Error**: Run-on sentence.
- **Corrected Sentence**: The children were excited about the field trip, but they forgot their permission slips at home.

Using Proper Punctuation

Exercise: Add the correct punctuation to the following sentence:

After the long hike we decided to rest drink some water and enjoy the view.

- **Corrected Sentence**: After the long hike, we decided to rest, drink some water, and enjoy the view.

Tips for Mastering Sentence Structure and Punctuation

1. **Practice Identifying Errors**:
    - Use practice questions to spot fragments, run-ons, and incorrect punctuation.
2. **Understand Context**:
    - Consider the meaning and flow of the sentence when deciding on punctuation.
3. **Review Rules Regularly**:
    - Keep a quick reference guide for punctuation rules and sentence structures.
4. **Write and Revise**:
    - Practice writing sentences and editing them for clarity, grammar, and punctuation.

Why This Matters for the GED Exam

On the GED RLA exam, you'll encounter questions requiring you to identify and correct errors in sentence structure and punctuation. Additionally, your extended response (essay) will be evaluated for proper grammar and punctuation. By mastering these skills, you'll improve your ability to communicate clearly and effectively, both on the exam and in real-world situations.

9.3 Common Grammatical Errors

Mastering grammar requires recognizing and correcting common errors that can disrupt clarity and meaning in writing. On the GED RLA exam, these errors are frequently tested through questions that require you to identify mistakes and revise sentences. Here are the most common grammatical errors you need to know, along with explanations and examples.

1. Sentence Fragments

A sentence fragment is an incomplete thought that lacks either a subject, a verb, or both. Fragments cannot stand alone as complete sentences.

Example of a Fragment:

- Because I went to the store.

Revised Sentence:

- I went to the store because I needed groceries.

Tip: Ensure that every sentence has a subject and a verb and expresses a complete thought.

2. Run-On Sentences

A run-on sentence occurs when two or more independent clauses are joined without proper punctuation or conjunctions.

Example of a Run-On:

- I love pizza it's my favorite food.

Revised Sentence:

- I love pizza; it's my favorite food.
- OR: I love pizza, and it's my favorite food.

Tip: Use a period, semicolon, or a coordinating conjunction (e.g., *and, but, or*) to separate independent clauses.

3. Misplaced Modifiers

Modifiers add detail to sentences, but when placed incorrectly, they can confuse the meaning of a sentence.

Example of a Misplaced Modifier:

- She almost drove her kids to school every day.

Revised Sentence:

- She drove her kids to school almost every day.

Tip: Place modifiers as close as possible to the word or phrase they are modifying.

4. Dangling Modifiers

A dangling modifier is a phrase or clause that does not clearly modify any word in the sentence, leading to ambiguity.

Example of a Dangling Modifier:

- Driving to work, the car broke down.

Revised Sentence:

- While I was driving to work, the car broke down.

Tip: Make sure the subject being modified is explicitly stated in the sentence.

5. Subject-Verb Agreement Errors

Subjects and verbs must agree in number (singular or plural). A mismatch between the subject and verb creates grammatical errors.

Example of an Error:

- The list of items are on the table.

Revised Sentence:

- The list of items is on the table.

Tip: Ignore words or phrases that come between the subject and the verb when checking for agreement.

6. Pronoun-Antecedent Agreement Errors

Pronouns must agree with their antecedents (the nouns they replace) in number and gender.

Example of an Error:

- Each of the students must bring their textbook.

Revised Sentence:

- Each of the students must bring his or her textbook.

Tip: Use singular pronouns for singular antecedents and plural pronouns for plural antecedents.

7. Incorrect Pronoun Usage

Using the wrong pronoun can confuse the meaning of a sentence.

Example of an Error:

- Him and I went to the park.

Revised Sentence:

- He and I went to the park.

Tip: Learn the correct usage of subjective (e.g., *he, she, they*) and objective pronouns (e.g., *him, her, them*).

8. Double Negatives

Using two negatives in a sentence can cancel each other out and create confusion.

Example of an Error:

- She doesn't have no money.

Revised Sentence:

- She doesn't have any money.

Tip: Use only one negative in a sentence to express a negative idea.

9. Improper Parallel Structure

Parallel structure ensures that elements in a list or series have the same grammatical form.

Example of an Error:

- She likes reading, writing, and to paint.

Revised Sentence:

- She likes reading, writing, and painting.

Tip: Maintain consistency in lists or comparisons.

10. Incorrect Verb Tense

Inconsistent verb tenses can confuse readers about the timing of events.

Example of an Error:

- Yesterday, I walk to the store and bought groceries.

Revised Sentence:

- Yesterday, I walked to the store and bought groceries.

Tip: Ensure that verbs match the time frame being described.

11. Capitalization Errors

Capitalization errors occur when proper nouns, titles, or the first word in a sentence are not capitalized correctly.

Example of an Error:

- i visited paris last summer.

Revised Sentence:

- I visited Paris last summer.

Tip: Always capitalize proper nouns and the first word of a sentence.

12. Homophone Confusion

Homophones are words that sound the same but have different meanings and spellings. Misusing them can lead to confusion.

Example of an Error:

- Their going to the store later.

Revised Sentence:

- They're going to the store later.

Tip: Learn the meanings of common homophones (e.g., *their/there/they're, your/you're*).

Practical Exercise

Identify and Correct the Errors:

The dogs barks loudly every night, they wakes up everyone in the neighborhood.

Answer:

- Original Errors: Subject-verb disagreement (*dogs barks*), run-on sentence (*night, they*), and verb tense inconsistency (*wakes*).
- Revised Sentence: The dogs bark loudly every night, and they wake up everyone in the neighborhood.

Recognizing and correcting these common grammatical errors is key to achieving clarity in your writing and excelling on the GED RLA exam. Practice regularly to internalize these rules and apply them effectively in both grammar questions and your extended response.

9.4 Subject-Verb Agreement and Sentence Clarity

Subject-verb agreement and sentence clarity are essential for constructing grammatically correct sentences that are easy to understand. These skills are tested on the GED RLA exam through editing and revision questions, as well as in your extended response. In this section, we'll cover the rules of subject-verb agreement, strategies for ensuring sentence clarity, and common pitfalls to avoid.

Subject-Verb Agreement

Subject-verb agreement ensures that the subject and verb in a sentence match in number (singular or plural). This fundamental rule of grammar is critical for clear and correct communication.

1. Singular and Plural Subjects

- A singular subject takes a singular verb.
- A plural subject takes a plural verb.

Examples:

- Singular: The **dog** barks loudly. (*dog = singular, barks = singular verb*)
- Plural: The **dogs** bark loudly. (*dogs = plural, bark = plural verb*)

2. Compound Subjects

When two or more subjects are joined by *and*, the subject is plural and takes a plural verb.

Example:

- The **cat and dog** are playing outside.

When subjects are joined by *or* or *nor*, the verb agrees with the subject closest to it.

Example:

- Neither the **teacher** nor the **students** were late. (*students = plural, were = plural verb*)
- Either the **students** or the **teacher** is responsible. (*teacher = singular, is = singular verb*)

3. Collective Nouns

Collective nouns (e.g., *team, family, audience*) are singular when acting as a single unit but plural when referring to individual members.

Examples:

- Singular: The **team** is winning. (*acting as one unit*)
- Plural: The **team** are arguing among themselves. (*individual members*)

4. Indefinite Pronouns

Indefinite pronouns such as *everyone, each, anyone, somebody* are singular and require singular verbs.

Examples:

- **Everyone** is invited to the meeting.
- **Each** of the students has a textbook.

Some indefinite pronouns (*some, all, most*) can be singular or plural, depending on the noun they refer to.

Examples:

- Singular: **Some** of the water is cold. (*water = singular*)
- Plural: **Some** of the cookies are gone. (*cookies = plural*)

5. Interrupting Phrases

Phrases that come between the subject and the verb (e.g., *along with, as well as, including*) do not affect the verb's agreement with the subject.

Examples:

- The **teacher**, along with her students, **is** preparing for the test.
- The **books**, including the new ones, **are** on the shelf.

Common Errors in Subject-Verb Agreement

1. Mismatched Subject and Verb:

- Incorrect: The **list of names** are on the desk.
- Correct: The **list of names** is on the desk.

2. Misinterpreting Collective Nouns:

- Incorrect: The **audience** were clapping loudly. (*if viewed as a single unit*)
- Correct: The **audience** was clapping loudly.

Sentence Clarity

Clear sentences are free of ambiguity and convey meaning effectively. Achieving clarity involves choosing precise words, organizing ideas logically, and avoiding unnecessary complexity.

1. Use Active Voice

Active voice places the subject before the verb, making sentences more direct and easier to understand.

Examples:

- Active: The **manager approved** the budget.
- Passive: The budget **was approved** by the manager.

2. Avoid Wordiness

Concise sentences are more effective than overly complicated ones.

Example:

- Wordy: Due to the fact that the weather was bad, the game was canceled.
- Concise: Because the weather was bad, the game was canceled.

3. Eliminate Ambiguity

Ambiguity occurs when it's unclear what a pronoun refers to or when a sentence lacks context.

Example of Ambiguity:

- Ambiguous: The students gave their teachers a gift. They were grateful. (*Who is grateful: the students or the teachers?*)

Revised for Clarity:

- Clear: The students gave their teachers a gift, and the teachers were grateful.

4. Maintain Parallel Structure

Parallel structure ensures that items in a list or series follow the same grammatical pattern.

Example:

- Incorrect: She enjoys hiking, swimming, and to bike.
- Correct: She enjoys hiking, swimming, and biking.

5. Simplify Complex Sentences

Simplifying long or complicated sentences can improve readability.

Example:

- Complex: The report that was submitted by the student who is currently attending the university was accepted by the committee.
- Simplified: The university student's report was accepted by the committee.

6. Punctuate for Clarity

Proper punctuation clarifies sentence meaning and prevents misinterpretation.

Example Without Punctuation:

- Let's eat Grandma. **Revised with Punctuation**:
- Let's eat, Grandma.

Practical Exercise

Identify and Correct Errors:

1. Neither the employees nor the manager were satisfied with the results.
2. The team, along with their coach, are preparing for the championship.
3. Some of the water are spilling from the glass.

Answers:

1. **Correct**: Neither the employees nor the manager was satisfied with the results.
2. **Correct**: The team, along with their coach, is preparing for the championship.
3. **Correct**: Some of the water is spilling from the glass.

Strong subject-verb agreement and clear sentences are essential for effective communication and are frequently tested on the GED RLA exam. By practicing these rules and applying them to your writing and editing, you'll enhance your grammatical precision and clarity.

CHAPTER 10

READING COMPREHENSION SKILLS

Reading comprehension is a critical skill tested in the GED RLA exam. This section evaluates your ability to understand, interpret, and analyze a variety of texts, ranging from informational passages to literary works. Strong reading comprehension not only helps you answer questions accurately but also enhances your ability to write well-structured essays in the extended response section.

In this chapter, we'll delve into essential reading comprehension skills, including identifying main ideas and supporting details, understanding themes and tone, analyzing arguments, and comparing and contrasting texts. Each skill will be explored in detail, with examples and practical applications to ensure you are fully prepared for the GED RLA exam.

What to Expect in the Reading Comprehension Section

The reading comprehension portion of the RLA exam consists of passages followed by questions designed to assess various skills, such as:

- Identifying the central idea and its supporting details.
- Interpreting the author's tone, purpose, and themes.
- Evaluating arguments and evidence for validity.
- Making comparisons and drawing conclusions across texts.

Types of Passages

The exam includes two primary types of passages:

1. **Informational Texts** (75% of the test):
    - Nonfiction passages covering topics such as science, history, or current events.
    - Example: An article about the environmental impact of renewable energy.
2. **Literary Texts** (25% of the test):
    - Fictional excerpts, poetry, or dramatic works.
    - Example: A passage from a novel exploring themes of resilience.

Skills You Will Develop

To succeed in this section, you must master the following skills:

1. **Identifying Main Ideas and Supporting Details**:
    - Recognizing the central focus of a passage.
    - Understanding how details reinforce the main idea.
2. **Understanding Themes, Tone, and Author's Purpose**:
    - Interpreting the overarching message or theme of a text.
    - Analyzing the author's attitude (tone) and intent.
3. **Analyzing Arguments, Evidence, and Logical Fallacies**:
    - Evaluating the strength and validity of an author's argument.
    - Identifying flaws or logical inconsistencies in reasoning.
4. **Comparing and Contrasting Texts**:
    - Drawing connections and distinctions between multiple texts.
    - Comparing perspectives, arguments, or themes.

Question Formats

The reading comprehension section includes the following question types:

- **Multiple Choice**: Select the best answer based on the passage.
- **Hotspot Questions**: Highlight specific parts of the text to answer questions.
- **Drag-and-Drop**: Arrange details or ideas in the correct order.

Example Multiple-Choice Question

Passage:

"The industrial revolution brought about significant advancements in technology, transforming societies around the world. However, it also led to widespread environmental degradation and increased socioeconomic inequality."

Question: What is the main idea of the passage?

A) The industrial revolution was a purely positive development.
B) Technological advancements came with both benefits and drawbacks.
C) Socioeconomic inequality improved during the industrial revolution.
D) The industrial revolution had no impact on the environment.

Correct Answer: B. The passage highlights both the positive and negative effects of the industrial revolution.

Why Reading Comprehension Skills Matter

Strong reading comprehension skills will not only help you excel on the GED exam but also prepare you for real-world tasks, such as understanding workplace documents, interpreting research, or critically evaluating media. By mastering these skills, you will build the confidence to approach any text with clarity and purpose.

Next, we'll explore how to identify main ideas and supporting details, an essential foundation for effective reading comprehension.

10.1 Identifying Main Ideas and Supporting Details

The ability to identify the main idea and supporting details of a passage is a cornerstone of reading comprehension. The main idea is the central point or message the author wants to convey, while supporting details provide evidence, examples, or explanations to reinforce that main idea. On the GED RLA exam, you'll encounter questions that require you to recognize both.

This section will provide a step-by-step guide to identifying main ideas and supporting details, along with practical examples to ensure clarity.

What is the Main Idea?

The main idea is the central thought or primary focus of a passage. It answers the question: *What is the passage mostly about?*

Characteristics of the Main Idea

1. It is broad enough to encompass all parts of the passage.
2. It is not overly specific or focused on minor details.
3. It is supported by the information in the text.

How to Identify the Main Idea

1. **Read the Entire Passage**:
    - Avoid jumping to conclusions based on the first sentence. Read the passage fully to understand its overall focus.
2. **Pay Attention to the First and Last Sentences**:
    - The main idea is often introduced in the opening sentence and reiterated in the conclusion.
3. **Look for Repeated Themes**:
    - If certain words, phrases, or ideas are repeated throughout the passage, they likely relate to the main idea.
4. **Summarize the Passage in Your Own Words**:
    - After reading, ask yourself: *What is the passage mainly about?*

What are Supporting Details?

Supporting details are the facts, examples, statistics, or descriptions that explain or reinforce the main idea. These details answer questions such as:

- *Why is this important?*
- *What evidence supports this point?*

Characteristics of Supporting Details

1. They provide specific information related to the main idea.
2. They often include examples, explanations, or evidence.
3. They answer the *how* or *why* of the main idea.

How to Identify Supporting Details

1. **Locate Evidence in the Text**:
   - Supporting details often follow the main idea in the form of explanations, examples, or lists.
2. **Use Transition Words as Clues**:
   - Words like *for example, in addition, such as, because,* and *therefore* signal supporting details.
3. **Ask Questions About the Main Idea**:
   - What examples or evidence does the author use to back up their point? These are the supporting details.

Practical Examples

Example 1: Informational Text

Passage:

"Renewable energy sources, such as solar and wind power, are gaining popularity due to their environmental benefits. Solar panels, for instance, generate electricity without producing greenhouse gases. Wind turbines harness natural wind currents to produce energy efficiently. As the world faces the challenges of climate change, renewable energy is becoming a crucial solution."

- **Main Idea**: Renewable energy is becoming increasingly important due to its environmental benefits.
- **Supporting Details**:
  1. Solar panels generate electricity without greenhouse gases.
  2. Wind turbines efficiently harness natural wind currents.
  3. Renewable energy addresses the challenges of climate change.

Example 2: Literary Text

Passage:
"Sarah always found peace in her garden. It was her sanctuary, where the worries of the world seemed to fade away. Every morning, she spent hours tending to her plants, pruning the roses and watering the lilies. The rhythmic sound of the wind rustling through the leaves calmed her mind."

- **Main Idea**: Sarah finds peace and solace in her garden.
- **Supporting Details**:
  1. She considers the garden her sanctuary.
  2. She spends hours tending to her plants daily.
  3. The sounds of nature calm her mind.

Common Mistakes to Avoid

1. **Confusing Supporting Details for the Main Idea**:
   - Supporting details are specific and explain or elaborate on the main idea; they are not the central point themselves.

- Example:
    - **Main Idea**: Exercise improves mental health.
    - **Supporting Detail**: Regular exercise reduces stress and anxiety.

2. **Choosing an Overly Broad or Narrow Statement**:
    - A statement that is too broad may not capture the focus of the passage, while one that is too narrow misses the overarching point.

Practice Exercise

Passage:

"Reading regularly has numerous benefits for mental health. It can reduce stress by providing an escape from everyday worries. Additionally, reading improves cognitive function by stimulating the brain and increasing knowledge. Many people find that reading before bed helps them sleep better by relaxing the mind."

Question: What is the main idea of the passage?

A) Reading helps people sleep better at night.
B) Reading is beneficial for mental health in multiple ways.
C) Cognitive function improves with regular reading.
D) Reading reduces stress and anxiety.

Answer: B) Reading is beneficial for mental health in multiple ways.

Supporting Details:

1. Reading reduces stress.
2. It improves cognitive function.
3. It helps people relax before bed.

10.2 Understanding Themes, Tone, and Author's Purpose

To fully comprehend a passage, it's essential to understand its deeper meaning, emotional undercurrents, and the author's intentions. On the GED RLA exam, questions about themes, tone, and author's purpose assess your ability to interpret the text beyond its surface. In this section, we'll break down these elements and provide strategies to analyze them effectively.

Themes

A theme is the underlying message or central idea the author conveys in a passage. Themes are often universal concepts or insights about human nature, society, or life.

Characteristics of a Theme

1. It's broader than the main idea and often applies beyond the text itself.
2. It's implied rather than explicitly stated.
3. It reflects a lesson, moral, or universal truth.

How to Identify a Theme

1. **Summarize the Passage**:
    - Ask yourself: *What is the author trying to communicate about life, people, or the world?*
2. **Look for Repeated Ideas**:
    - Themes often emerge through recurring topics, symbols, or conflicts.
3. **Distinguish Between Theme and Topic**:
    - A topic is the subject (e.g., *friendship*), while a theme is the insight about that topic (e.g., *True friendship endures challenges*).

Examples

Informational Text:

"The relentless efforts of activists throughout history demonstrate that change often begins with small acts of courage."

- **Theme**: Significant social change requires determination and courage.

Literary Text:

"Despite their differences, the siblings realized that family was their greatest strength in overcoming adversity."

- **Theme**: The bonds of family can help overcome life's challenges.

Tone

The tone of a passage reflects the author's attitude toward the subject or audience. It's conveyed through word choice, sentence structure, and the overall style of writing.

Common Tones

- **Positive**: Optimistic, joyful, enthusiastic.
- **Negative**: Critical, somber, angry.
- **Neutral**: Objective, factual, indifferent.

How to Identify Tone

1. **Examine Word Choice**:
    - Positive tone: Words like *cheerful, vibrant, inspiring.*
    - Negative tone: Words like *harsh, bleak, ominous.*
    - Neutral tone: Words like *informative, straightforward, logical.*
2. **Look at Sentence Structure**:
    - Short, direct sentences may suggest urgency or simplicity.
    - Long, elaborate sentences may indicate a reflective or formal tone.
3. **Analyze the Subject Matter**:
    - Tone often aligns with the author's stance on the subject.

Examples

Positive Tone:

"The sunrise painted the sky with breathtaking hues of orange and pink, a reminder of the beauty in each new day."

- Tone: Optimistic, uplifting.

Critical Tone:

"The government's failure to address the crisis is a glaring example of neglect and incompetence."

- Tone: Critical, accusatory.

Author's Purpose

The author's purpose is the reason behind writing the passage. It reflects what the author intends to achieve or communicate to the reader.

Common Purposes

1. **To Inform**:
    - Provide factual information or explain a concept.
    - Example: A scientific article on climate change.
2. **To Persuade**:

- Convince the reader to adopt a viewpoint or take action.
- Example: An editorial urging readers to support renewable energy.

3. **To Entertain**:

- Engage or amuse the reader, often through storytelling.
- Example: A novel or a humorous anecdote.

How to Identify Author's Purpose

1. **Analyze Content**:

- Informative texts focus on presenting data, facts, or explanations.
- Persuasive texts include opinions, arguments, and emotional appeals.
- Entertaining texts focus on storytelling, humor, or vivid imagery.

2. **Look for Direct Clues**:

- Words like *should, must,* or *we recommend* suggest persuasion.
- Technical or detailed language suggests information.

Examples

Informational Purpose:

"The discovery of penicillin revolutionized medicine, saving millions of lives worldwide."

- Purpose: To inform about the impact of penicillin.

Persuasive Purpose:

"Recycling is not just an option; it's a necessity to preserve our planet for future generations. Join us in making a difference."

- Purpose: To persuade readers to recycle.

Entertaining Purpose:

"As the clock struck midnight, the mischievous cat leaped onto the table, sending a cascade of plates to the floor. Chaos ensued."

- Purpose: To entertain the reader with a humorous scenario.

Practical Strategies

1. **Theme**:

- Ask: *What message or lesson is the author trying to convey?*
- Look for recurring ideas or conflicts that hint at deeper meanings.

2. **Tone**:

- Identify emotionally charged words or phrases.
- Consider how the passage makes you feel—this often aligns with the tone.

3. **Author's Purpose**:

- Determine whether the passage primarily provides information, argues a point, or tells a story.

Practice Question

Passage:

"As the relentless waves pounded the shore, the lighthouse stood firm, a symbol of resilience against nature's fury."

Question: What is the tone of the passage?

A) Optimistic
B) Reflective
C) Defiant

D) Critical

Answer: C) Defiant. The description of the lighthouse standing firm against the relentless waves conveys a defiant tone.

10.3 Analyzing Arguments, Evidence, and Logical Fallacies

Analyzing arguments is a critical skill tested on the GED RLA exam. It requires evaluating how authors construct their claims, support them with evidence, and avoid or sometimes fall into logical fallacies. This skill helps you determine the strength and validity of an argument, enabling you to answer questions accurately and write better essays.

Understanding Arguments

An argument is a claim or viewpoint supported by evidence. A strong argument includes:

- **A Clear Claim**: The main point or stance the author is taking.
- **Relevant Evidence**: Facts, statistics, examples, or expert opinions that back up the claim.
- **Logical Reasoning**: A well-structured explanation of how the evidence supports the claim.

Types of Evidence

1. Facts and Data

- **Description**: Verified information, often in the form of statistics or research findings.
- **Example**: *"Studies show that students who read regularly score 20% higher on comprehension tests."*
- **Evaluation**: Strong evidence because it's objective and measurable.

2. Examples

- **Description**: Specific instances that illustrate the claim.
- **Example**: *"Jane's success in her career demonstrates the value of persistence and hard work."*
- **Evaluation**: Effective for making abstract ideas more relatable, though it may lack the objectivity of data.

3. Expert Opinions

- **Description**: Statements from professionals or authorities on the subject.
- **Example**: *"Dr. Smith, a climate scientist, asserts that renewable energy is essential for reducing carbon emissions."*
- **Evaluation**: Credible if the expert is qualified and unbiased.

4. Anecdotes

- **Description**: Personal stories or experiences.
- **Example**: *"After switching to a plant-based diet, I felt more energetic and healthier."*
- **Evaluation**: Persuasive in personal contexts but less reliable as evidence for broader claims.

Evaluating Arguments

1. Strength of Evidence

- Ask: Is the evidence relevant, credible, and sufficient to support the claim?
- Weak evidence includes vague statements, unverified data, or overgeneralizations.

2. Logical Flow

- Examine how the author connects the claim and evidence. Strong arguments are logical and free of gaps or contradictions.

3. Author Bias

- Check for signs of bias, such as emotionally charged language or selective use of evidence. While some bias is natural, excessive bias can weaken an argument.

Recognizing Logical Fallacies

Logical fallacies are errors in reasoning that undermine an argument. Understanding these helps you identify weak arguments and avoid making similar mistakes in your writing.

1. Ad Hominem

- **Definition**: Attacking the person making the argument instead of the argument itself.
- **Example**: *"You can't trust his opinion on climate change; he's not even a scientist."*
- **Why It's a Fallacy**: The argument focuses on the individual rather than addressing the claim.

2. Straw Man

- **Definition**: Misrepresenting or oversimplifying an argument to make it easier to refute.
- **Example**: *"People who oppose space exploration think science doesn't matter."*
- **Why It's a Fallacy**: The original argument is distorted.

3. Appeal to Emotion

- **Definition**: Using emotional appeals instead of logical reasoning.
- **Example**: *"Think of all the children suffering; we must act immediately."*
- **Why It's a Fallacy**: Emotions alone don't justify the argument.

4. False Dilemma

- **Definition**: Presenting only two options when more exist.
- **Example**: *"We either ban cars or accept climate disaster."*
- **Why It's a Fallacy**: Ignores alternative solutions.

5. Hasty Generalization

- **Definition**: Drawing a conclusion based on insufficient evidence.
- **Example**: *"My neighbor doesn't recycle, so no one in this city cares about the environment."*
- **Why It's a Fallacy**: The conclusion is based on a small or unrepresentative sample.

Practical Application

Example Passage:

"Renewable energy is the future of our planet. A recent study shows that countries investing in solar and wind energy have seen a 15% reduction in greenhouse gas emissions. Critics argue that renewable energy is too expensive, but this claim ignores the long-term savings and environmental benefits."

Question: Which statement evaluates the strength of the argument?

A) The author provides relevant evidence to support the claim but does not address cost concerns in depth.
B) The argument relies entirely on emotional appeals without providing any data.
C) The evidence is irrelevant because it doesn't mention traditional energy sources.
D) The author uses expert opinions, but they are biased.

Answer: A. The author uses credible data but could strengthen the argument by addressing cost concerns more thoroughly.

Strategies for Analyzing Arguments

1. **Identify the Claim**: What is the author arguing?
2. **Examine the Evidence**: Is the evidence credible, relevant, and sufficient?
3. **Check for Logical Flow**: Do the ideas connect logically, or are there gaps in reasoning?
4. **Spot Fallacies**: Look for errors in logic that weaken the argument.

By critically evaluating arguments and evidence, you can navigate the reading comprehension section of the GED RLA exam with confidence and strengthen your own writing skills.

10.4 Comparing and Contrasting Texts

The ability to compare and contrast texts is an important skill tested on the GED RLA exam. This involves identifying similarities and differences between two or more passages, analyzing how they address similar topics, and evaluating their arguments, tone, style, or purpose. Understanding this skill will help you answer questions effectively and develop a well-rounded perspective when evaluating texts.

Key Aspects of Comparing and Contrasting

1. Themes or Topics

When two texts address the same theme or topic, they may present similar or differing viewpoints. Pay attention to the central ideas and how they are explored.

Example:

- Text 1: A passage discussing the benefits of renewable energy.
- Text 2: A passage emphasizing the challenges and costs of transitioning to renewable energy.

Comparison: Both discuss renewable energy, but Text 1 highlights benefits while Text 2 focuses on challenges.

2. Tone and Style

Authors often use tone and style to convey their attitudes or engage their audience. Comparing tone and style helps you understand how the same subject can be approached differently.

Example:

- Text 1: Formal, objective tone with statistical evidence.
- Text 2: Emotional tone with personal anecdotes.

Contrast: Text 1 uses a fact-based approach, while Text 2 appeals to emotions.

3. Purpose

The purpose of a text shapes its content and presentation. Authors may aim to inform, persuade, or entertain, even when addressing the same topic.

Example:

- Text 1: An article explaining the science behind climate change (to inform).
- Text 2: An editorial urging readers to support environmental policies (to persuade).

Contrast: Text 1 provides factual information, while Text 2 advocates for action.

4. Evidence and Support

Examining the types of evidence used in each text can reveal how authors build their arguments.

Example:

- Text 1: Includes statistical data and expert opinions.
- Text 2: Relies on anecdotal evidence and hypothetical scenarios.

Contrast: Text 1 uses concrete evidence, while Text 2 relies on subjective experiences.

5. Audience

The intended audience influences the content, tone, and style of a text. Understanding the audience helps you compare how effectively each text addresses its readers.

Example:

- Text 1: A scholarly article for scientists.
- Text 2: A blog post for the general public.

Comparison: Text 1 uses technical language, while Text 2 simplifies concepts for broader accessibility.

How to Compare and Contrast Texts

1. **Identify Common Ground**:

   - Look for shared topics, themes, or questions addressed by the texts.
2. **Spot Key Differences**:
   - Compare tone, purpose, and the types of evidence used.
3. **Analyze Effectiveness**:
   - Evaluate which text provides stronger support for its claims or connects better with its audience.

Practical Example

Texts

Text 1:

"The rapid adoption of electric vehicles (EVs) offers a sustainable solution to reducing greenhouse gas emissions. EVs require less maintenance, produce zero tailpipe emissions, and help decrease dependence on fossil fuels."

Text 2:

"While electric vehicles have environmental benefits, their widespread adoption faces significant obstacles. High manufacturing costs and limited charging infrastructure remain barriers to their accessibility for many consumers."

Comparison

1. **Theme**: Both texts discuss electric vehicles.
2. **Purpose**: Text 1 aims to highlight benefits, while Text 2 focuses on challenges.
3. **Tone**: Text 1 is optimistic, while Text 2 is cautious.
4. **Evidence**: Text 1 uses benefits like reduced emissions and low maintenance. Text 2 emphasizes barriers such as costs and infrastructure.

Tips for Success

- **Use a Venn Diagram**: Create a visual representation to map similarities and differences.
- **Look for Transition Words**: Words like *however, on the other hand, similarly,* and *likewise* often signal comparisons or contrasts.
- **Answer in Context**: When asked about comparisons on the GED exam, always base your response on evidence from the text.

Practice Question

Question: How do the authors of the two texts differ in their perspectives on electric vehicles?

A) Text 1 focuses on financial benefits, while Text 2 discusses environmental issues.
B) Text 1 highlights the benefits of EVs, while Text 2 emphasizes the challenges of adopting them.
C) Text 1 argues against EVs, while Text 2 supports their adoption.
D) Text 1 discusses charging infrastructure, while Text 2 focuses on reducing emissions.

Answer: B. Text 1 highlights the benefits of EVs, while Text 2 emphasizes the challenges.

By comparing and contrasting texts effectively, you can uncover deeper insights into their themes, arguments, and styles. This skill not only enhances your performance on the GED exam but also strengthens your ability to critically evaluate information in everyday life.

CHAPTER 11

WRITING AN EFFECTIVE ESSAY

The extended response portion of the GED RLA exam is your opportunity to showcase your ability to write a clear, organized, and well-supported essay. Unlike multiple-choice questions, where you select the correct answer, the essay requires you to analyze provided texts, construct an argument, and support your points with evidence. This section is critical because it tests your writing skills, critical thinking, and ability to synthesize information.

An effective essay demonstrates your ability to:

1. Understand and respond to the prompt accurately.
2. Develop a logical structure with a clear introduction, body, and conclusion.
3. Use evidence effectively to support your argument.
4. Write with proper grammar, punctuation, and style.

This chapter provides a detailed guide to writing an impactful essay, covering everything from interpreting the prompt to avoiding common mistakes.

The Purpose of the GED Essay

The essay is designed to assess the following skills:

1. **Critical Thinking**: Can you analyze arguments and evaluate evidence?
2. **Argumentation**: Can you construct a logical and coherent argument?
3. **Writing Skills**: Can you write clearly, using proper grammar and punctuation?
4. **Synthesis**: Can you integrate information from multiple texts?

What to Expect in the Essay Section

The GED essay requires you to:

1. Read two short passages presenting opposing viewpoints on a topic.
2. Write a response analyzing which argument is stronger and why.
3. Support your analysis with evidence from the texts.

You have **45 minutes** to plan, write, and revise your essay. Effective time management is key.

Steps to Writing an Effective Essay

Step 1: Understand the Task

Carefully read the instructions and the two passages. Identify:

- The topic being debated.
- The main argument of each passage.
- The evidence each author uses to support their claims.

Step 2: Plan Your Essay

Spend the first 5–10 minutes planning your response. A strong essay has:

1. **A Clear Thesis Statement**: Identify which argument is stronger and why.
2. **Organized Structure**: Plan your introduction, body paragraphs, and conclusion.
3. **Key Evidence**: Highlight examples or data from the texts that support your thesis.

Step 3: Write Your Essay

Follow a standard structure:

1. **Introduction**:
    - Briefly introduce the topic.

- State your thesis (e.g., "Author A presents a stronger argument because…").

2. **Body Paragraphs**:
   - Analyze the strengths of the chosen argument.
   - Use specific evidence from the text to support your points.
   - Address weaknesses in the opposing argument (optional but impactful).

3. **Conclusion**:
   - Restate your thesis.
   - Summarize your key points.

Step 4: Revise and Edit

Use the last 5 minutes to:

- Check for grammar and punctuation errors.
- Ensure your essay flows logically.
- Verify that all claims are supported by evidence.

Practical Example

Sample Prompt

Passage 1:

"Recycling programs are essential for reducing waste and protecting the environment. By recycling, communities can minimize landfill use and conserve valuable resources. Additionally, recycling reduces greenhouse gas emissions, helping to combat climate change."

Passage 2:

"Recycling programs are costly and often ineffective. Many materials collected for recycling end up in landfills due to contamination or lack of demand. Instead of focusing on recycling, we should prioritize reducing waste at the source and investing in reusable products."

Essay Task:

Analyze which author presents a stronger argument and explain why, using evidence from both texts.

Example Essay

Introduction:

Recycling is a widely debated topic, with proponents emphasizing its environmental benefits and critics highlighting its limitations. While both authors provide valid points, the argument in Passage 1 is stronger due to its use of concrete benefits and broader focus on environmental impact.

Body Paragraph 1:

Passage 1 effectively demonstrates the benefits of recycling by providing clear evidence. For example, the author states that recycling reduces greenhouse gas emissions, which directly contributes to combating climate change. This argument is compelling because it connects recycling to a global issue, emphasizing its importance. Additionally, the claim about conserving resources and minimizing landfill use is supported by factual evidence, making the argument both logical and persuasive.

Body Paragraph 2:

In contrast, Passage 2 focuses primarily on the challenges of recycling programs. While the author highlights valid concerns, such as contamination and high costs, the argument lacks sufficient evidence to support these claims. For instance, the author does not provide data to quantify the costs or examples of contaminated recycling efforts. This weakens the overall argument, as it relies more on generalizations than on concrete evidence.

Conclusion:

In summary, Passage 1 presents a stronger argument by using specific evidence to highlight the environmental benefits of recycling. Although Passage 2 raises important concerns, its lack of detailed support makes it less convincing. Recycling remains a critical component of addressing environmental challenges, as demonstrated by the evidence in Passage 1.

Understanding how to construct a well-organized essay that analyzes arguments and uses evidence effectively is key to excelling on the GED RLA exam. In the next sections, we'll dive deeper into the specifics of understanding the essay prompt, structuring your response, using evidence, and avoiding common pitfalls.

11.1 Understanding the Essay Prompt

The first step in writing a successful essay for the GED RLA exam is thoroughly understanding the essay prompt. The prompt provides the instructions and framework for your response, specifying what the test expects from you. Misinterpreting or overlooking key details in the prompt can lead to an unfocused essay, no matter how well-written your response may be.

This section will guide you on how to break down the prompt, understand its components, and tailor your response to meet the expectations of the exam evaluators.

What to Look for in the Essay Prompt

The GED essay prompt typically consists of two opposing passages on the same topic, followed by instructions that guide your response. It's essential to identify the following elements:

1. The Topic

- The topic is the overarching subject or issue being debated in the passages.
- To identify it, ask: *What is the general focus of both texts?*

Example:

Passages discussing renewable energy → Topic: Renewable energy and its implications.

2. The Task

- The task specifies what you must do in your essay. For the GED, this usually involves evaluating the arguments in both passages and determining which is stronger.
- Key phrases to look for:
    - *Analyze the arguments.*
    - *Explain which argument is stronger and why.*
    - *Use evidence from the texts to support your response.*

Example:

"Explain which author presents the stronger argument about renewable energy and why."

Task: Compare the arguments, evaluate their strengths, and support your evaluation with evidence.

3. The Purpose

- The purpose defines the type of essay you're expected to write. On the GED, this is an **analytical essay**, not a persuasive or personal one.
- You are not required to provide your own opinion on the topic but rather analyze and evaluate the given texts.

Key Reminder: Focus on the evidence and reasoning within the passages, not your personal beliefs.

Breaking Down the Prompt: Practical Example

Prompt:

You will read two passages on the topic of year-round school schedules. Both authors present arguments for and against year-round schooling. Write an essay in which you analyze which author presents the stronger argument and explain why. Be sure to use evidence from both passages to support your response.

Steps to Break It Down:

1. **Identify the Topic**: Year-round school schedules.
    - Both passages will discuss this issue from opposing perspectives.
2. **Understand the Task**:
    - Analyze the arguments in the texts.
    - Determine which argument is stronger.
    - Support your analysis with evidence from the texts.
3. **Determine the Purpose**:
    - Write an analytical essay that evaluates the arguments in the texts.

Common Mistakes When Interpreting the Prompt

1. **Misidentifying the Task**:
    - Mistake: Writing a persuasive essay that argues your personal opinion.
    - Solution: Stick to analyzing the arguments in the provided texts.
2. **Focusing on Irrelevant Details**:
    - Mistake: Spending time discussing minor details that do not contribute to the strength of the argument.
    - Solution: Focus on the evidence, reasoning, and logic presented by the authors.
3. **Ignoring Key Instructions**:
    - Mistake: Failing to use evidence from both texts.
    - Solution: Highlight and annotate relevant evidence while reading.

Strategies for Understanding the Prompt

1. Annotate the Prompt

- Underline key instructions (e.g., *analyze, explain, stronger argument*).
- Circle the topic (e.g., *year-round school schedules*).

Example Annotation:

"Write an essay in which you ***analyze which author presents the stronger argument*** *and* ***explain why****. Be sure to* ***use evidence*** *from both passages to support your response."*

2. Summarize the Prompt in Your Own Words

- Paraphrasing helps ensure you fully understand what is being asked.
- Example: *"I need to evaluate which passage has a better argument about year-round schooling, explain my reasoning, and use examples from the texts."*

3. Highlight Key Words in the Texts

- Look for words or phrases that indicate the authors' positions, evidence, or tone.
- Examples: *"This data proves," "It is essential," "Critics argue," "Research shows."*

Practical Exercise

Prompt:

You will read two passages discussing the benefits and challenges of remote work. Write an essay analyzing which author presents a stronger argument and explain why. Use evidence from both passages to support your analysis.

Steps:

1. **Topic**: Remote work.
2. **Task**: Evaluate which argument is stronger.
3. **Purpose**: Analyze and explain using evidence from both texts.

Reflection Example:

- **Before Writing**: Ask yourself:
  - What are the key arguments in each passage?
  - Which author provides stronger evidence or reasoning?
  - How can I use specific evidence from the texts to support my evaluation?

By thoroughly understanding the essay prompt, you can focus your response, stay on task, and ensure that your essay meets all the requirements. In the next section, we'll discuss how to structure your response, ensuring it flows logically and effectively conveys your analysis.

11.2 Structuring Your Response: Introduction, Body, Conclusion

A well-structured essay is essential for success on the GED RLA exam. A clear and logical organization not only demonstrates your writing skills but also helps convey your argument effectively to the evaluators. The standard structure for your essay includes an introduction, body paragraphs, and a conclusion. Each section serves a specific purpose and contributes to the overall strength of your response.

Introduction: Setting the Stage

The introduction is your essay's first impression. Its primary goal is to introduce the topic, provide context, and present your thesis statement. This sets the tone for your argument and guides the reader through your analysis.

Components of a Strong Introduction

1. **Hook**: A brief sentence or two that draws the reader's attention to the topic. For example:
   - "Education systems around the world are constantly evolving, and year-round school schedules have sparked widespread debate."
2. **Context**: Provide a brief explanation of the issue at hand and summarize the perspectives in the two passages.
   - "One author advocates for year-round schooling to reduce learning loss, while the other highlights concerns about student burnout and costs."
3. **Thesis Statement**: Clearly state which argument is stronger and why.
   - "While both authors present valid points, the argument for year-round schooling is more compelling due to its focus on measurable academic benefits and long-term societal impact."

Example Introduction

Education is a cornerstone of societal progress, and the debate over year-round schooling highlights differing perspectives on how to maximize its effectiveness. One author emphasizes its potential to prevent learning loss and boost academic performance, while the other argues that the costs and emotional toll on students outweigh the benefits. After analyzing both arguments, it is clear that the first author presents a stronger case, supported by empirical evidence and long-term benefits for students and schools alike.

Body Paragraphs: Building Your Argument

The body of your essay is where you develop your analysis and support your thesis. Each paragraph should focus on one main idea, backed by specific evidence from the texts. A well-organized body creates a logical flow that reinforces your argument.

Structure of a Body Paragraph

1. **Topic Sentence**: Begin with a sentence that introduces the main point of the paragraph.
   - "The first author's argument is stronger because it relies on concrete data to support its claims."
2. **Evidence**: Use direct quotes or paraphrased examples from the texts to illustrate your point.
   - "For instance, the author states that 'students in year-round programs show a 20% improvement in test scores compared to those in traditional schedules.'"

3. **Analysis**: Explain how the evidence supports your thesis.
    - "This data highlights a measurable benefit, making the argument more persuasive and grounded in facts."
4. **Transition**: Conclude the paragraph with a sentence that connects to the next idea.
    - "While the first author's reliance on evidence strengthens their case, the second author's argument suffers from a lack of supporting data."

Number of Body Paragraphs

- Aim for **two to three body paragraphs**. Each should address a different aspect of your evaluation, such as the strength of the evidence, the logical structure, or the tone and style of the argument.

Conclusion: Summarizing and Reinforcing

The conclusion wraps up your essay by restating your thesis and summarizing your key points. This is your opportunity to leave a lasting impression on the evaluator.

Components of a Strong Conclusion

1. **Restate the Thesis**: Reiterate your main argument in different words.
    - "Ultimately, the first author's argument stands out due to its reliance on evidence and its clear focus on student success."
2. **Summarize Key Points**: Briefly recap the reasons why one argument is stronger.
    - "By providing concrete data and addressing long-term benefits, the first author presents a more compelling case compared to the second author, whose claims lack sufficient support."
3. **Closing Thought**: End with a sentence that emphasizes the importance of the issue or ties the argument to a broader context.
    - "As education evolves, evidence-based solutions like year-round schooling have the potential to transform student outcomes and address systemic challenges."

Example Conclusion

In conclusion, the first author's argument for year-round schooling is more convincing due to its use of data and focus on measurable benefits. By addressing both academic outcomes and societal impacts, the author constructs a strong case that outweighs the second author's more speculative concerns. With evidence-based approaches, educational reforms like year-round schedules can help bridge learning gaps and support future generations.

Putting It All Together: Practical Example

Full Essay Structure

Introduction:
Year-round schooling has become a contentious issue, with supporters highlighting its academic benefits and critics pointing to its financial and emotional costs. After examining both perspectives, the argument in favor of year-round schooling proves more compelling due to its reliance on evidence and long-term focus on student success.

Body Paragraph 1:

The first author strengthens their argument by presenting data to support the benefits of year-round schooling. For instance, they cite research showing that students in these programs perform 20% better on standardized tests. This reliance on evidence makes their case more credible and persuasive compared to the second author, who relies on hypothetical scenarios rather than concrete facts.

Body Paragraph 2:

In addition to evidence, the first author's argument is well-structured and logically developed. They address potential drawbacks, such as cost, but counter these with data demonstrating long-term savings for schools. This balanced approach further reinforces their position as more reasoned and reliable than the second author, whose argument lacks depth.

Conclusion:

By combining empirical evidence with a clear focus on long-term benefits, the first author presents a stronger case for year-round schooling. While concerns about cost and burnout are valid, they lack sufficient support in the second argument. As education systems continue to evolve, adopting evidence-based solutions like year-round schooling can create meaningful change.

11.3 Using Evidence to Support Your Argument

Using evidence effectively is one of the most critical aspects of crafting a strong essay for the GED RLA exam. Evidence serves as the foundation of your argument, lending credibility and substance to your claims. It shows evaluators that you can not only analyze the texts but also select and integrate relevant information to support your analysis. In this section, we'll explore how to identify strong evidence, integrate it into your essay, and analyze it to strengthen your argument.

What Counts as Evidence?

In the GED essay, evidence refers to the specific details, facts, or examples provided in the texts that you can use to support your evaluation. These might include:

1. **Statistics or Data**: Numbers that back up a claim.
    - Example: *"Research indicates that students in year-round school programs score 15% higher on standardized tests."*
2. **Direct Quotes**: Specific sentences or phrases from the text.
    - Example: *"The author argues, 'Year-round schooling reduces the impact of summer learning loss, ensuring better academic performance overall.'"*
3. **Examples or Scenarios**: Concrete illustrations that highlight a point.
    - Example: *"Programs in urban districts have already demonstrated improved test scores and attendance rates."*
4. **Logical Arguments**: Reasoning or explanations presented by the authors.
    - Example: *"By extending learning time, year-round schooling offers students more opportunities to master complex subjects."*

Not all evidence is equally strong. Focus on selecting evidence that directly supports your thesis and is clearly explained in the passage.

Selecting Strong Evidence

When choosing evidence, ask yourself:

1. **Is it relevant?**
    - Does the evidence directly support your thesis or one of your main points? Avoid including unrelated or minor details.
2. **Is it specific?**
    - General statements are less effective than concrete facts or examples.
    - Weak: *"Students benefit from more time in school."*
    - Strong: *"Studies show that students in year-round programs retain up to 20% more information."*
3. **Is it compelling?**
    - Strong evidence typically includes data, expert opinions, or well-reasoned examples.

Example Analysis

Text Excerpt:

"Year-round schooling reduces summer learning loss by allowing students to retain up to 30% more material compared to those on traditional schedules. Critics argue that the additional cost of air conditioning during summer months makes these programs impractical. However, districts that implement year-round schooling report long-term savings from fewer remedial courses."

Evidence Selection:

- Strong Evidence: *"Year-round schooling reduces summer learning loss by allowing students to retain up to 30% more material."*
  - Why? It provides a specific percentage and directly supports the idea that year-round schooling improves academic performance.
- Weak Evidence: *"Critics argue that the additional cost of air conditioning during summer months makes these programs impractical."*
  - Why? While this supports the opposing view, it lacks depth and is less relevant to evaluating the strength of the primary argument.

Integrating Evidence into Your Essay

To make your argument clear and persuasive, integrate evidence seamlessly into your essay. Avoid simply copying quotes without context—explain how the evidence supports your thesis.

Techniques for Integrating Evidence

1. **Introduce the Evidence**:
   - Provide context for the evidence by briefly explaining its source or relevance.
   - Example: *The author of Passage 1 supports their claim by citing specific statistics about learning retention.*
2. **Quote or Paraphrase the Evidence**:
   - Use direct quotes for particularly impactful or concise statements.
   - Paraphrase when the original text is too lengthy or needs to be simplified.

Direct Quote Example:

As stated in Passage 1, "Year-round schooling reduces summer learning loss by allowing students to retain up to 30% more material."

Paraphrase Example:

Passage 1 emphasizes that students in year-round programs retain significantly more material than those on traditional schedules.

1. **Analyze the Evidence**:
   - Explain why the evidence is important and how it supports your argument.
   - Example: *This statistic strengthens the argument for year-round schooling by demonstrating its measurable impact on student performance, making it more credible and persuasive than the opposing viewpoint.*
2. **Connect Back to Your Thesis**:
   - Link the evidence back to your main argument to maintain focus and cohesion.
   - Example: *By providing concrete data on improved learning retention, the author of Passage 1 builds a stronger case for year-round schooling.*

Avoiding Common Mistakes

1. **Overloading Your Essay with Quotes**:
   - Don't let quotes dominate your essay. Balance them with your own analysis.
   - Weak: *"Year-round schooling reduces summer learning loss by 30%. It also helps with attendance. Students score higher on tests."*
   - Strong: *"The statistic about learning loss strengthens the argument for year-round schooling, as it demonstrates a clear and measurable benefit."*
2. **Using Evidence Without Explanation**:
   - Always analyze evidence instead of leaving it unexplained.

- Weak: *"Passage 1 says, 'Year-round schooling reduces summer learning loss.'"*
- Strong: *"This statement highlights the long-term academic benefits of year-round schooling, making the argument more compelling than the opposing view."*

3. **Relying on Irrelevant or Weak Evidence**:
   - Choose evidence that directly relates to your thesis and is persuasive.

Practice Exercise

Text Excerpt:

"Community gardens provide numerous benefits, from improving access to fresh produce to fostering social connections among neighbors. However, critics argue that the cost of maintaining these gardens often falls on a few dedicated individuals."

Question: Select the strongest piece of evidence to support an argument in favor of community gardens: A) *"Critics argue that the cost of maintaining these gardens often falls on a few dedicated individuals."*
B) *"Community gardens improve access to fresh produce and foster social connections among neighbors."*
C) *"Some neighborhoods lack the resources to establish community gardens."*

Answer:

B. This piece of evidence directly supports the benefits of community gardens, making it the most relevant and persuasive.

11.4 Common Pitfalls to Avoid in Essays

Even the most prepared test-takers can make mistakes when writing an essay, especially under the pressure of a timed exam. Understanding the most common pitfalls and how to avoid them will help you stay focused, produce a well-crafted response, and score higher on the GED RLA essay.

Not Addressing the Prompt Fully

One of the most significant mistakes is failing to respond to the essay prompt correctly. The GED essay requires you to analyze two arguments, identify which one is stronger, and explain why. Many test-takers veer off course by summarizing the passages without evaluating them, or worse, writing about their personal opinions instead of focusing on the authors' arguments.

How to Avoid This

Always reread the prompt after reading the passages. Highlight the specific instructions, such as *"analyze," "explain,"* and *"use evidence from the texts."* Keep these instructions in mind as you plan your essay, ensuring every part of your response aligns with the task. If you find yourself straying into personal opinions, pause and refocus on the texts.

Lack of a Clear Thesis Statement

Your thesis statement is the backbone of your essay. Without a clear thesis, your essay can feel disorganized or unfocused. A weak or missing thesis leaves the evaluator guessing about your main argument.

How to Avoid This

Make sure your thesis explicitly states which argument is stronger and why. For example, instead of writing, *"Both authors make good points,"* be specific: *"Author 1 presents a stronger argument because it relies on data and addresses potential counterarguments."* A well-crafted thesis helps guide your essay and ensures your analysis stays on track.

Overloading with Evidence but Lacking Analysis

While evidence is essential, simply quoting or paraphrasing without explanation weakens your essay. The evaluator needs to see how you interpret the evidence and connect it to your thesis. Essays that are overloaded with quotes often lack original thought, making them less impactful.

How to Avoid This

For every piece of evidence you include, explain its significance. Don't assume the reader will make the connection for you. For instance, if you cite a statistic about increased test scores in year-round schooling, follow up with an analysis: *"This data demonstrates a measurable benefit, showing that year-round schooling can lead to long-term academic success."* Always tie evidence back to your thesis.

Disorganized Structure

A well-structured essay is easier to read and more persuasive. When ideas are presented haphazardly, it confuses the evaluator and makes it difficult to follow your argument. Disorganization often stems from skipping the planning stage.

How to Avoid This

Spend a few minutes outlining your essay before writing. Plan your introduction, body paragraphs, and conclusion, and decide which points you'll address in each section. Stick to one idea per paragraph, beginning with a clear topic sentence. Use transitions like *"Furthermore," "However,"* and *"In contrast"* to guide the reader through your argument seamlessly.

Failing to Address the Opposing Argument

Ignoring the opposing viewpoint can make your analysis feel one-sided and less thorough. The GED essay requires you to evaluate both arguments, even if you ultimately favor one over the other.

How to Avoid This

Dedicate at least one paragraph to discussing the weaker argument. Acknowledge its strengths but explain why it's less convincing. For example: *"While Author 2 raises a valid concern about cost, the argument lacks concrete evidence to support this claim, making it less persuasive than Author 1's evidence-based analysis."* This approach demonstrates your ability to think critically and fairly.

Grammatical Errors and Poor Word Choice

Frequent grammatical errors, spelling mistakes, or awkward phrasing can distract the evaluator and detract from your argument. Even if your analysis is strong, poor writing mechanics can lower your score.

How to Avoid This

Leave a few minutes at the end to proofread your essay. Check for common errors like subject-verb agreement, misplaced commas, or run-on sentences. Use simple, precise language instead of trying to impress with overly complex vocabulary. For example, write *"The author's evidence is compelling because it is based on research,"* instead of *"The author's substantiation is exceedingly convincing due to its empirical foundation."*

Writing Too Much or Too Little

Some test-takers feel pressured to write as much as possible, leading to lengthy essays filled with repetition or irrelevant details. Others write too little, failing to fully develop their argument or provide sufficient evidence.

How to Avoid This

Focus on quality over quantity. Aim for a concise yet comprehensive essay that thoroughly addresses the prompt. A well-structured essay with two to three strong body paragraphs is better than a rambling response. Conversely, ensure you provide enough analysis and evidence to support your thesis; a few short, undeveloped paragraphs are unlikely to score well.

Ignoring Time Management

Rushing through your essay or spending too much time on one part can leave you with an incomplete response. An essay that lacks a conclusion or is poorly edited will not showcase your full potential.

How to Avoid This

Divide your time wisely:

1. **5–10 minutes**: Read the passages, analyze the prompt, and plan your essay.
2. **25–30 minutes**: Write your essay, focusing on clarity and organization.
3. **5–10 minutes**: Review and revise your essay for grammar, structure, and adherence to the prompt.

Practical Example of Avoiding Pitfalls

Consider a prompt asking you to analyze two passages about remote work. One author argues that remote work improves productivity, citing studies and personal testimonies. The other claims it reduces collaboration, relying on anecdotal evidence. A poorly written essay might focus entirely on the first author's points, ignoring the opposing argument and failing to address weaknesses in either case. It might also include grammatical errors, such as *"The second authors argument lacks evidence its weaker."*

A stronger essay would acknowledge the second author's argument but explain why it is less convincing. For example: *"While Author 2 raises a valid concern about reduced collaboration, their reliance on anecdotal evidence undermines their argument. In contrast, Author 1 supports their claims with data, making their position more credible."* This approach balances evidence with analysis, avoids grammatical errors, and adheres to the prompt.

Avoiding these common pitfalls requires careful planning, attention to detail, and a focus on the specific demands of the GED essay prompt. By staying organized, using evidence effectively, and dedicating time to proofreading, you can craft a polished essay that demonstrates your writing and analytical abilities.

CHAPTER 12

ADVANCED LANGUAGE SKILLS

Advanced language skills are the tools that elevate writing from basic communication to polished, impactful expression. These skills encompass the ability to guide readers seamlessly through ideas, construct arguments that resonate, and refine writing for clarity and precision. On the GED RLA exam, demonstrating advanced language skills can set your essay apart, showcasing your ability to write with logic, flow, and finesse.

At the core of advanced language proficiency is the ability to create coherence and unity within your writing. This involves ensuring that every sentence contributes meaningfully to the overall message and that ideas connect logically. Strong essays don't feel like a collection of disjointed paragraphs; they read as a single, cohesive argument, leading the reader smoothly from one point to the next.

Achieving this coherence requires a mastery of several key elements. Transition words and phrases help bridge ideas, making it clear how each sentence or paragraph relates to the next. Logical flow ensures that arguments progress naturally, with each point building on the one before it. Readers should never feel lost or unsure about the direction of the essay. Instead, the argument should unfold like a well-laid path.

Equally important is the ability to tailor your writing style to suit the purpose of your essay. Whether you're crafting a persuasive argument, presenting information, or analyzing opposing viewpoints, the tone, word choice, and level of formality must align with your objectives. A persuasive argument, for instance, may employ emotionally compelling language to influence the reader, while an informative piece might rely on clear, factual statements.

Precision in writing is another hallmark of advanced language skills. This involves choosing words and phrases that convey your ideas with clarity and avoiding vagueness or redundancy. Every word should serve a purpose, contributing to the overall impact of your writing. For example, rather than writing "very important," you might choose a stronger, more precise word like "critical" or "essential." Such attention to detail enhances both the professionalism and readability of your essay.

Finally, refining your essay through editing and proofreading is an essential step in demonstrating advanced language skills. Even the most compelling arguments can be undermined by errors in grammar, punctuation, or sentence structure. Proofreading allows you to identify and correct these mistakes, ensuring that your writing is polished and professional.

In the following sections, we will delve deeper into these advanced skills, starting with the strategic use of transition words and logical flow to guide readers through your essay. From there, we'll explore how to craft persuasive and informative arguments that resonate with your audience, and finally, we'll discuss the art of editing and proofreading to refine your work. Each of these elements plays a critical role in achieving the level of writing excellence expected on the GED RLA exam.

12.1 Transition Words and Logical Flow

The use of transition words and logical flow is fundamental to writing that is clear, organized, and persuasive. Transition words act as bridges between ideas, guiding readers through your argument seamlessly. Logical flow ensures that your points build upon one another naturally, creating a cohesive and engaging piece of writing. For the GED RLA essay, mastering these skills can elevate your response, making it easier for evaluators to follow and appreciate your argument.

What Are Transition Words?

Transition words and phrases are tools that connect ideas, sentences, and paragraphs. They signal relationships between thoughts, such as cause and effect, contrast, or elaboration, helping readers understand how your ideas are related. Without transitions, your writing can feel abrupt or disjointed, leaving readers confused about how one point leads to the next.

Types of Transition Words and Their Uses

1. **Addition**: Use these to add information or continue a point.
    - Examples: *furthermore, moreover, in addition, also*
    - Example Sentence: *Year-round schooling improves retention rates. Moreover, it reduces the need for remedial classes.*

2. **Contrast**: Use these to show differences or opposing ideas.
    - Examples: *however, on the other hand, although, nevertheless*
    - Example Sentence: *Author 1 supports year-round schooling as a solution to learning loss. However, Author 2 argues that it leads to student burnout.*
3. **Cause and Effect**: Use these to explain why something happened or its result.
    - Examples: *therefore, as a result, consequently, because*
    - Example Sentence: *Year-round schooling reduces learning loss; therefore, students retain more material.*
4. **Comparison**: Use these to highlight similarities.
    - Examples: *similarly, likewise, in the same way*
    - Example Sentence: *Both authors agree that educational reforms are necessary. Similarly, they emphasize the importance of addressing learning gaps.*
5. **Conclusion or Summary**: Use these to wrap up your ideas or summarize a point.
    - Examples: *in conclusion, to summarize, ultimately, in short*
    - Example Sentence: *In conclusion, the argument for year-round schooling is stronger because it provides concrete evidence.*

Logical Flow: Building an Argument That Makes Sense

Logical flow refers to the way ideas are organized and presented in your writing. An essay with good logical flow allows readers to follow your argument effortlessly, with each point leading naturally to the next.

Steps to Achieve Logical Flow

1. **Start with a Clear Thesis**:
    - Your thesis should serve as the foundation of your essay, guiding every point you make.
    - Example: *Author 1's argument is stronger due to its reliance on evidence and clear focus on long-term benefits.*
2. **Organize Points Sequentially**:
    - Arrange your paragraphs in a logical order, starting with your strongest point.
    - Example: Begin with the evidence that supports your thesis, then address the weaknesses of the opposing argument.
3. **Use Topic Sentences**:
    - Each paragraph should start with a sentence that introduces its main idea, connecting it to your thesis.
    - Example: *The first author's reliance on statistical data strengthens their argument.*
4. **Bridge Ideas with Transitions**:
    - Smooth transitions between paragraphs and sentences maintain the flow of your essay.
    - Example: *While the first author presents concrete evidence, the second author relies heavily on anecdotal examples.*
5. **End with a Strong Conclusion**:
    - Summarize your argument and restate why your thesis is valid. The conclusion should reinforce the logical progression of your essay.

Practical Examples

Example of Poor Logical Flow

Year-round schooling helps students retain more information. The second author argues that it is expensive. Both authors discuss the importance of education. The first author uses statistics to support their point.

Why It's Weak: The points are presented without transitions or a clear connection, making it difficult to follow.

Example of Strong Logical Flow

Year-round schooling helps students retain more information, as highlighted by the first author, who provides data showing a 30% improvement in retention rates. This argument is further strengthened by addressing the long-term benefits, such as reduced need for remedial courses. In contrast, the second author argues that the costs of year-round schooling outweigh its benefits. However, this claim lacks statistical evidence, weakening the overall argument. Ultimately, the first author's reliance on concrete data makes their case more persuasive.

Why It's Strong: Each idea builds on the previous one, with transitions like *"in contrast"* and *"however"* creating a clear progression.

Tips for Using Transition Words and Ensuring Logical Flow

- **Don't Overuse Transitions**: While transitions are essential, using too many can make your writing feel forced or repetitive. Choose transitions that naturally fit the relationship between ideas.
- **Keep the Reader in Mind**: Ask yourself, *Will the reader understand how these points are connected?* If not, add a transition or clarify the relationship.
- **Read Aloud**: Reading your essay aloud can help you identify sections where the flow feels disjointed.
- **Revise for Clarity**: After writing your essay, review it to ensure that every idea is logically connected and that transitions enhance the flow.

12.2 Crafting Persuasive and Informative Arguments

Writing an essay for the GED RLA exam requires more than just summarizing ideas or stating opinions. You need to construct arguments that are persuasive and well-informed, drawing directly from the provided texts to support your analysis. This skill not only helps you succeed on the exam but also improves your ability to write effectively in real-world situations.

In this section, we will expand on the strategies to craft compelling arguments, breaking down the key elements of persuasive and informative writing, demonstrating how to integrate evidence, and providing full examples to guide you through the process.

What is a Persuasive Argument?

A persuasive argument is designed to convince the reader that your viewpoint is valid. On the GED RLA exam, this means explaining which author presents the stronger argument and why. Persuasive writing relies on three pillars:

1. **A Clear Position (Thesis Statement)**: Clearly state your stance on which argument is stronger.
2. **Logical Reasoning**: Use sound logic to explain why one argument is more compelling.
3. **Evidence-Based Support**: Incorporate specific examples, data, and quotes from the passages to substantiate your claims.

Steps to Craft a Persuasive Argument

1. **Establish a Strong Thesis**

   Your thesis is the foundation of your essay. It should answer the prompt directly, stating which author presents a stronger argument and why.

Example Thesis:

"Author 1 presents a stronger argument than Author 2 because their evidence is specific, measurable, and directly supports their claims."

Why It Works:

This thesis sets the stage for a focused essay, outlining both the evaluation (Author 1's argument is stronger) and the reason (specific, measurable evidence).

2. **Select the Most Convincing Evidence**
   Persuasive arguments rely on relevant, concrete evidence from the texts. Choose details that directly support your thesis and avoid overloading your essay with unnecessary information.

Example Evidence from the Text:

Passage 1 states, *"Remote employees completed tasks 25% faster than their in-office counterparts, according to a study conducted across 50 companies."*

Analysis:

This is a strong piece of evidence because it provides measurable results and cites a credible source, making the argument more persuasive.

3. **Address the Counterargument**
   Acknowledge the opposing author's viewpoint and explain its weaknesses. This shows evaluators that you've considered multiple perspectives, which strengthens your analysis.

Example:

"While Author 2 raises concerns about employee isolation, their argument relies on anecdotal evidence rather than concrete data, which undermines its credibility."

4. **Conclude Persuasively**
   Summarize your main points and reinforce your thesis. Leave the evaluator with a clear understanding of why your evaluation is logical and well-supported.

Example Conclusion:

"By providing specific data and addressing potential challenges with solutions, Author 1 presents a stronger argument for remote work. In contrast, Author 2's reliance on generalizations weakens their case."

What is an Informative Argument?

An informative argument focuses on presenting facts and evidence clearly and accurately. While the GED essay is primarily persuasive, it requires elements of informative writing to explain evidence and provide context.

How to Write an Informative Argument

1. **Present Evidence Objectively**
   Informative arguments emphasize clarity and accuracy. Instead of persuading the reader, focus on explaining the evidence in a neutral tone.

Example:

"Passage 1 cites a study showing that remote employees are 25% more productive. This statistic illustrates the potential benefits of remote work, particularly in industries that prioritize efficiency."

2. **Explain Evidence in Context**
   Provide background or additional details to help the reader understand the relevance of the evidence.

Example:

"The study cited in Passage 1 was conducted across 50 companies, making its findings broadly applicable to a range of industries."

3. **Avoid Bias**
   Stick to the facts and avoid language that suggests favoritism.

Example:

"Passage 2 highlights potential drawbacks of remote work, such as reduced collaboration, which may impact creative industries."

Combining Persuasive and Informative Techniques

The most effective GED essays blend elements of both persuasive and informative writing. While your primary goal is to evaluate the arguments and persuade the evaluator, providing clear explanations of the evidence ensures your essay is logical and easy to follow.

Example Paragraph:

"Author 1 presents a stronger argument for remote work by citing measurable data. For example, the study showing a 25% increase in productivity among remote employees provides concrete evidence of the benefits. In contrast, Author 2 relies on general statements, such as 'many employees feel isolated,' without providing data to support this claim. While employee connection is important, the lack of evidence weakens Author 2's argument. By focusing on measurable outcomes, Author 1 offers a more convincing perspective."

Detailed Example with Passages

Prompt:

Analyze which author presents the stronger argument about renewable energy, and explain why. Use evidence from both passages to support your response.

Passage 1:

"Renewable energy offers a sustainable solution to the growing climate crisis. Solar and wind energy are now more affordable than ever, with costs dropping by 70% over the past decade. These technologies also create jobs, with the renewable energy sector employing over 10 million people worldwide in 2023."

Passage 2:

"While renewable energy has benefits, it remains unreliable due to fluctuations in weather. Solar panels produce less energy on cloudy days, and wind turbines require consistent wind. Investing in nuclear power, a reliable and efficient alternative, may be a better solution to meet global energy demands."

Sample Analysis:

"Author 1's argument is stronger because it highlights specific, measurable benefits of renewable energy. For instance, the claim that solar and wind energy costs have decreased by 70% over the past decade is supported by clear data, making the argument credible and relevant. Additionally, the mention of 10 million jobs emphasizes the positive economic impact of renewable energy. In contrast, Author 2 focuses on the limitations of renewable energy, such as weather dependency, but does not provide data to quantify the extent of these issues. Furthermore, while nuclear power is presented as an alternative, the passage lacks evidence to support its reliability or affordability. By providing concrete data and addressing economic benefits, Author 1 builds a more compelling case for renewable energy."

Tips for Crafting Strong Arguments

1. **Always Use Evidence**: Don't make claims without backing them up with specific examples from the text.
2. **Balance Persuasion and Explanation**: Persuade the reader while clearly explaining the evidence.
3. **Stay Objective**: Even in a persuasive argument, maintain a professional tone and avoid overly emotional language.
4. **Revisit the Prompt**: Regularly refer back to the essay prompt to ensure you're addressing the task fully.

Mastering the art of crafting persuasive and informative arguments is key to writing a high-scoring essay on the GED RLA exam. By blending strong evidence, logical reasoning, and clear explanations, you can create a response that is both compelling and easy to follow.

12.3 Editing and Proofreading Techniques

Editing and proofreading are the final steps in crafting a high-quality essay. Even the most compelling argument can be undermined by errors in grammar, spelling, punctuation, or structure. These mistakes can distract readers and lower your score on the GED RLA essay. By dedicating time to review and refine your essay, you ensure that it's polished, professional, and clearly communicates your ideas.

In this section, we'll explore essential editing and proofreading techniques, provide actionable strategies, and include examples to help you identify and correct common issues in your writing.

The Importance of Editing and Proofreading

Editing focuses on improving the content, structure, and flow of your essay. This includes reviewing the clarity of your arguments, ensuring logical progression, and verifying that you've addressed the prompt fully. Proofreading, on the other hand, is the process of identifying and fixing surface-level errors, such as spelling, grammar, and punctuation mistakes.

Both steps are crucial for a strong essay. While editing ensures your ideas are well-organized and relevant, proofreading eliminates distractions caused by errors.

Steps to Edit and Proofread Effectively

Step 1: Take a Break

After finishing your essay, take a short break before editing. Even a few minutes can help you return with a fresh perspective, making it easier to spot issues you might have missed while writing.

Step 2: Check for Content and Structure

1. **Revisit the Prompt**: Ensure your essay directly addresses the task. Ask yourself:
    - Have I identified which argument is stronger and explained why?
    - Did I use evidence from both texts to support my evaluation?

Example:

Prompt: Analyze which author presents a stronger argument about environmental policies.

Your Review: Does my essay clearly state which author I chose and why their argument is stronger? Did I use evidence to back up my points?

2. **Examine the Thesis**: Verify that your thesis is clear and specific.
    - Weak Thesis: *"Both authors make good points."*
    - Strong Thesis: *"Author 1 presents a stronger argument due to their use of statistical evidence and long-term solutions."*
3. **Review Paragraph Structure**: Each paragraph should focus on one idea, starting with a topic sentence that ties back to your thesis.
    - Example of a Strong Topic Sentence: *"Author 1's reliance on concrete data strengthens their argument."*
4. **Evaluate Transitions**: Ensure smooth transitions between sentences and paragraphs for logical flow.
    - Weak Transition: *"Author 1 is good. Author 2 is not."*
    - Strong Transition: *"While Author 2 raises valid concerns, their lack of evidence makes their argument less persuasive compared to Author 1."*

Step 3: Review for Clarity and Conciseness

Effective writing is clear and concise. Eliminate unnecessary words or repetitive phrases that dilute your argument.

Before Editing:

"The author of Passage 1 provides statistics that show numbers proving that remote workers are more productive."

After Editing:

"Passage 1 provides statistics showing that remote workers are more productive."

Key Tip: Read your essay aloud to identify awkward phrasing or overly long sentences.

Step 4: Proofread for Grammar, Spelling, and Punctuation

Proofreading ensures that your writing is error-free. Focus on these common issues:

1. **Subject-Verb Agreement**:
    - Error: *"The arguments in Passage 1 is strong."*
    - Correction: *"The arguments in Passage 1 are strong."*
2. **Punctuation**:
    - Error: *"Author 1's argument is compelling it uses data to support its claims."*
    - Correction: *"Author 1's argument is compelling; it uses data to support its claims."*

3. **Spelling**:
   - Error: *"Enviromental policies are important."*
   - Correction: *"Environmental policies are important."*
4. **Consistency in Tense**:
   - Error: *"Author 2 argues that renewable energy will help and says it helped reduce emissions."*
   - Correction: *"Author 2 argues that renewable energy will help and says it reduces emissions."*

Step 5: Verify Your Evidence

Double-check that your evidence is accurate and properly integrated into your essay. Ensure quotes are correctly attributed and paraphrased ideas are faithful to the original text.

Example:

Passage 1 states, *"Students in year-round programs perform 15% better on standardized tests."*

Your Essay:

"Passage 1 highlights a 15% improvement in standardized test scores for year-round students, emphasizing the academic benefits of this system."

Step 6: Final Read-Through

Read your essay one last time from start to finish. Focus on the overall impression:

- Does the essay flow smoothly?
- Does it address the prompt fully and convincingly?
- Are there any remaining errors?

If possible, use a checklist to ensure all aspects of your essay are polished.

Practical Examples of Editing and Proofreading

Original Paragraph:

"Author 1 talks about renewable energy. They say it's good because it is cheap now. Author 2 says it's unreliable and that nuclear power is better. But Author 1's argument is better."

Edited Version:

"Author 1 argues that renewable energy is a sustainable solution, emphasizing its affordability and job creation. For example, they state that solar and wind energy costs have decreased by 70% in the past decade. In contrast, Author 2 criticizes renewable energy for its weather dependency but provides no data to support their claims. This lack of evidence weakens Author 2's argument, making Author 1's case more compelling."

Common Editing and Proofreading Mistakes to Avoid

1. **Skipping the Review Process**: Rushing to finish without reviewing your essay often results in avoidable errors.
2. **Focusing Only on Grammar**: While grammar is important, don't neglect content, structure, and clarity.
3. **Ignoring the Prompt**: Ensure your edits align with the task. For example, if the prompt asks you to evaluate arguments, avoid focusing solely on summarizing the texts.

Final Tips for Success

- **Plan for Proofreading Time**: Allocate 5–10 minutes at the end of the exam to review and refine your essay.
- **Use Tools Wisely**: If writing on a computer, use built-in spell-check tools, but don't rely on them exclusively.
- **Practice Before the Exam**: Familiarize yourself with editing and proofreading strategies by practicing with sample prompts.

Editing and proofreading are essential steps in creating a polished essay that clearly communicates your ideas and avoids costly errors. By carefully reviewing your work, you can ensure your essay meets the high standards expected on the GED RLA exam. This attention to detail can make the difference between a good essay and an outstanding one.

CHAPTER 13

PRACTICE QUESTIONS AND EXERCISES

This section provides real practice questions and exercises that mimic the structure and style of the GED RLA exam. These exercises are designed to help you improve your skills in reading comprehension, analyzing arguments, identifying evidence, and crafting a written response. Each exercise will include passages, multiple-choice questions, and extended response prompts to ensure thorough preparation.

Reading Comprehension Practice

Passage 1

"The development of electric vehicles (EVs) has transformed the automotive industry. EVs produce zero emissions during operation, making them a key solution to reducing greenhouse gases. In addition to environmental benefits, EVs are becoming more affordable, with the cost of batteries dropping significantly over the past decade. However, critics argue that the limited availability of charging infrastructure poses a challenge to widespread adoption. Despite these concerns, the potential for EVs to combat climate change and improve air quality remains undeniable."

Passage 2

"While electric vehicles are often praised for their environmental benefits, they are not without flaws. Producing EV batteries requires mining rare earth materials, a process that can cause significant environmental damage. Additionally, the energy used to charge EVs often comes from non-renewable sources, diminishing their overall impact on reducing emissions. Until renewable energy becomes the dominant source of electricity, the environmental benefits of EVs may be overstated."

Multiple-Choice Questions

1. What is the central argument of Passage 1?

A) EVs are becoming too expensive for most consumers.
B) EVs can significantly reduce greenhouse gas emissions and improve air quality.
C) The lack of charging infrastructure will prevent widespread EV adoption.
D) EVs produce harmful emissions during operation.

Correct Answer: B

2. Which statement best describes the tone of Passage 2?

A) Optimistic about the future of EVs.
B) Critical of the environmental benefits of EVs.
C) Supportive of government subsidies for EVs.
D) Neutral and factual without taking a stance.

Correct Answer: B

3. How do the authors of the two passages differ in their perspectives?

A) Passage 1 argues that EVs have limited benefits, while Passage 2 praises their environmental impact.
B) Passage 1 focuses on the positive aspects of EVs, while Passage 2 highlights their drawbacks.
C) Passage 1 discusses the affordability of EVs, while Passage 2 ignores this issue.
D) Passage 1 criticizes EVs, while Passage 2 supports their widespread use.

Correct Answer: B

Extended Response Prompt

"Analyze which author presents a stronger argument about electric vehicles and explain why. Use evidence from both passages to support your response."

Identifying Evidence Practice

Passage

"Recycling programs are essential for reducing waste and conserving natural resources. For example, one city reduced landfill waste by 40% after implementing curbside recycling. Critics argue that recycling is costly and inefficient, but studies show that the long-term environmental benefits outweigh the costs. Additionally, recycling reduces energy consumption, as manufacturing products from recycled materials requires less energy than using raw materials."

Questions

1. Which piece of evidence best supports the claim that recycling reduces waste?

A) Recycling is costly and inefficient.
B) One city reduced landfill waste by 40% after implementing curbside recycling.
C) Recycling reduces energy consumption.
D) Recycling programs conserve natural resources.

Correct Answer: B

2. What is the main purpose of the passage?

A) To argue against the cost of recycling.
B) To highlight the benefits of recycling programs.
C) To explain how recycling programs are implemented.
D) To discuss the inefficiency of recycling.

Correct Answer: B

Logical Fallacies Practice

Passage

"Opponents of year-round school schedules claim that students will feel burnt out without a long summer break. However, this argument is weak because students in year-round programs perform better on standardized tests. Furthermore, the costs of running air conditioning in the summer are a small price to pay for improved academic outcomes."

Questions

1. Which statement represents a counterargument in the passage?

A) Students will feel burnt out without a long summer break.
B) Students in year-round programs perform better on standardized tests.
C) The costs of running air conditioning in the summer are minimal.
D) Improved academic outcomes justify year-round schooling.

Correct Answer: A

2. Which logical fallacy might critics use when opposing year-round school schedules?

A) Ad hominem: attacking the proponents of year-round schooling instead of their argument.
B) Slippery slope: claiming year-round schooling will lead to the decline of family vacations.
C) Straw man: misrepresenting the argument for year-round schooling as an attack on tradition.
D) Both B and C.

Correct Answer: D

Practice Crafting a Thesis

Prompt

"Compare and contrast the arguments in two passages about remote work. Passage 1 argues that remote work improves productivity and work-life balance, while Passage 2 highlights the challenges of collaboration and employee isolation. Write a thesis statement for an essay analyzing which argument is stronger."

Example Thesis:

"Passage 1 presents a stronger argument because it uses statistical evidence to demonstrate productivity improvements, while Passage 2 relies on anecdotal claims that lack measurable support."

Practice Full Essay

Prompt:

"Analyze which author presents a stronger argument about the benefits of renewable energy, and explain why. Use evidence from both passages to support your response."

Passage 1:

"Renewable energy reduces greenhouse gas emissions, providing a sustainable alternative to fossil fuels. Wind and solar energy costs have dropped by 70% in the past decade, making them economically viable for widespread adoption."

Passage 2:

"Although renewable energy has environmental benefits, it cannot yet meet global energy demands consistently. Wind and solar energy depend on weather conditions, and storage technology is still too expensive to be practical."

EXAMPLE:

***Passage 1**:*

"Community gardens provide numerous benefits, from improving access to fresh produce to fostering social connections among neighbors. Studies show that neighborhoods with community gardens experience a 25% reduction in crime rates. Additionally, these gardens help educate residents about sustainable agriculture and healthy eating habits."

***Passage 2**:*

"While community gardens offer some advantages, they often face significant challenges. Maintaining a garden requires substantial time and resources, which can burden volunteers. Furthermore, in urban areas, limited space and zoning restrictions make it difficult to establish and sustain these gardens."

Multiple-Choice Questions

1. What is the main argument in Passage 1?

A) Community gardens reduce neighborhood crime rates by 25%.
B) Community gardens foster social connections and improve access to fresh produce.
C) Urban areas are the best locations for community gardens.
D) Maintaining a community garden requires too much effort.

***Correct Answer**: B*

2. What type of evidence does Passage 1 use to support its argument?

A) Personal anecdotes.
B) Statistical data and examples.
C) Hypothetical scenarios.
D) Generalizations.

***Correct Answer**: B*

3. Which statement best summarizes the argument in Passage 2?

A) Community gardens are beneficial but face practical challenges.
B) Urban areas are ideal for establishing community gardens.
C) Community gardens do not provide significant benefits.
D) Volunteers rarely participate in community gardens.

***Correct Answer**: A*

Extended Response Prompt

"Evaluate which author presents a stronger argument about community gardens. Use evidence from both passages to support your response."

Key Question for Critical Thinking

4. Why might the argument in Passage 1 be more persuasive than the argument in Passage 2?

A) It focuses on measurable benefits, such as crime reduction and access to fresh produce.
B) It avoids mentioning challenges or limitations.
C) It uses hypothetical examples to explain the importance of community gardens.
D) It emphasizes the burdens faced by volunteers in maintaining gardens.

***Correct Answer**: A*

EXAMPLE:

Passage 1:

"Investing in renewable energy is essential for combating climate change. Solar and wind energy are now more affordable than ever, with costs dropping by over 50% in the past decade. Transitioning to these energy sources also reduces dependence on fossil fuels, which are a major contributor to greenhouse gas emissions. Furthermore, renewable energy creates jobs in the manufacturing, installation, and maintenance of solar panels and wind turbines."

Passage 2:

"While renewable energy has its merits, overreliance on these sources could lead to energy shortages. Solar and wind energy depend on unpredictable weather conditions, making them unreliable during periods of low sunlight or wind. Additionally, large-scale solar farms and wind farms require vast amounts of land, potentially disrupting ecosystems and wildlife habitats. A balanced energy policy that includes nuclear and fossil fuels is necessary to ensure a stable energy supply."

Multiple-Choice Questions

1. What is the primary argument in Passage 1?

A) Renewable energy is unreliable and expensive.
B) Renewable energy reduces dependence on fossil fuels and creates jobs.
C) Renewable energy harms ecosystems.
D) Fossil fuels are essential for a stable energy supply.

Correct Answer: B

2. Which claim from Passage 2 highlights a limitation of renewable energy?

A) Renewable energy creates jobs in manufacturing and installation.
B) Solar and wind energy depend on unpredictable weather conditions.
C) Fossil fuels contribute to greenhouse gas emissions.
D) Costs of solar and wind energy have decreased.

Correct Answer: B

3. How does Passage 1 support its argument?

A) By providing statistics about renewable energy costs and job creation.
B) By discussing the land requirements for renewable energy.
C) By focusing on the reliability of nuclear and fossil fuels.
D) By emphasizing the ecological challenges of renewable energy.

Correct Answer: A

Extended Response Prompt

"Analyze which author presents a stronger argument about renewable energy policies. Use evidence from both passages to support your response."

Critical Thinking Question

4. Why might Passage 2's argument be considered weaker than Passage 1's argument?

A) It provides less data and relies on hypothetical scenarios.
B) It focuses exclusively on the environmental benefits of renewable energy.
C) It avoids mentioning the reliability of fossil fuels and nuclear energy.
D) It discusses renewable energy in a positive light without addressing limitations.

Correct Answer: A

Practice Writing a Thesis

Prompt: Write a thesis statement analyzing which passage provides the stronger argument and why.

Example Thesis:

"Passage 1 presents a stronger argument because it uses statistical evidence to demonstrate the affordability and benefits of renewable energy, while Passage 2 relies on hypothetical concerns without providing data to support its claims."

7. FULL-LENGTH PRACTICE TEST FOR RLA

This section includes a comprehensive set of exercises designed to mimic the actual GED RLA exam and provide readers with ample opportunities to test their knowledge and skills. It contains multiple reading passages, a variety of question types, and extended response prompts to cover all the key aspects of the RLA section. The test is divided into multiple passages, with questions ranging from multiple-choice to drag-and-drop and extended responses.

Passage 1: Renewable Energy Benefits

"Renewable energy has become a leading solution to combat climate change. Solar and wind energy are now cost-competitive with fossil fuels, and many countries are transitioning to these sustainable alternatives. For example, wind power in the United States accounted for nearly 8% of total energy production in 2022. Furthermore, renewable energy reduces air pollution, which leads to better health outcomes for communities. Despite these benefits, critics argue that renewable energy depends heavily on weather conditions, creating inconsistencies in energy supply. However, advancements in battery storage are addressing these challenges, making renewable energy more reliable than ever."

Multiple-Choice Questions

1. What is the primary argument of the passage?

A) Fossil fuels are a better energy option than renewables.
B) Renewable energy is becoming more reliable due to advancements in technology.
C) Air pollution is the main reason to avoid fossil fuels.
D) Renewable energy is too dependent on weather conditions.

Correct Answer: B

2. Which statement from the passage supports the claim that renewable energy benefits public health?

A) "Renewable energy has become a leading solution to combat climate change."
B) "Wind power accounted for nearly 8% of total energy production in 2022."
C) "Renewable energy reduces air pollution, which leads to better health outcomes for communities."
D) "Advancements in battery storage are addressing these challenges."

Correct Answer: C

3. What is the purpose of mentioning advancements in battery storage?

A) To show that renewable energy is unreliable.
B) To explain how renewable energy is overcoming its challenges.
C) To argue against transitioning to renewable energy.
D) To emphasize the costs associated with renewable energy.

Correct Answer: B

Drag-and-Drop Question

Directions:

Sort the following statements into the appropriate categories based on their relevance to renewable energy.

Statements:

1. "Solar and wind energy are cost-competitive with fossil fuels."
2. "Renewable energy reduces air pollution."
3. "Fossil fuels are a major contributor to climate change."
4. "Renewable energy depends on weather conditions."

Categories:

- **Benefits of Renewable Energy**
- **Challenges of Renewable Energy**

Correct Answer:

- **Benefits of Renewable Energy**:
  - "Solar and wind energy are cost-competitive with fossil fuels."
  - "Renewable energy reduces air pollution."
- **Challenges of Renewable Energy**:
  - "Fossil fuels are a major contributor to climate change."
  - "Renewable energy depends on weather conditions."

Passage 2: The Role of Education in Society

"Education plays a critical role in shaping a prosperous society. By fostering creativity and critical thinking, education prepares individuals to contribute meaningfully to the workforce. Moreover, higher education leads to greater financial stability, with college graduates earning an average of 50% more than those with only a high school diploma. Despite its benefits, access to quality education remains unequal, with students in low-income areas often lacking resources and opportunities. Addressing these disparities is essential for creating an equitable and thriving society."

Multiple-Choice Questions

4. What is the main idea of the passage?

A) Education is essential for societal and individual success.
B) Financial stability is the only benefit of higher education.
C) Education is unnecessary for a thriving workforce.
D) Low-income areas have better access to education.

Correct Answer: A

5. Which statement best supports the claim that higher education leads to financial stability?

A) "Education plays a critical role in shaping a prosperous society."
B) "College graduates earn an average of 50% more than those with only a high school diploma."
C) "Addressing disparities in education is essential for equity."
D) "Education fosters creativity and critical thinking."

Correct Answer: B

6. What solution does the passage suggest for educational inequality?

A) Increasing college tuition for wealthy families.
B) Addressing disparities in resources and opportunities.

C) Expanding the use of technology in education.
D) Reducing the focus on creativity in schools.

Correct Answer: B

Extended Response Question

Prompt:

Read the two passages below about the benefits and challenges of renewable energy. Write an essay analyzing which author presents a stronger argument. Use evidence from both passages to support your response.

Passage 1:

"Renewable energy reduces greenhouse gas emissions and creates jobs in the green economy. Countries that have invested heavily in renewable technologies report significant reductions in air pollution and energy costs."

Passage 2:

"While renewable energy offers benefits, it is not a complete solution. Wind and solar energy depend on weather, making them unreliable. Additionally, the production of renewable energy infrastructure, such as solar panels, has its own environmental impacts."

Additional Practice Passage: Social Media and Communication

"Social media has revolutionized communication, making it easier than ever to connect with others worldwide. Platforms like Facebook and Instagram allow users to share their lives in real-time. However, the rise of social media has also led to concerns about privacy and mental health. Studies show that excessive social media use is linked to anxiety and depression, particularly among teens. To fully benefit from these platforms, users must balance online and offline interactions."

Questions

7. What is the primary benefit of social media according to the passage?

A) It helps users connect with others worldwide.
B) It reduces anxiety and depression.
C) It eliminates privacy concerns.
D) It replaces traditional communication methods.

Correct Answer: A

8. Which statement best supports the claim that social media impacts mental health?

A) "Platforms like Facebook and Instagram allow users to share their lives in real-time."
B) "Studies show that excessive social media use is linked to anxiety and depression, particularly among teens."
C) "Social media has revolutionized communication."
D) "To fully benefit from these platforms, users must balance online and offline interactions."

Correct Answer: B

Passage 3: Urbanization and Its Impact

"Urbanization has rapidly increased in the 21st century, with more than half of the world's population now living in cities. This shift has brought economic growth and improved access to education, healthcare, and employment opportunities. However, rapid urbanization also poses significant challenges, including overcrowding, pollution, and inadequate infrastructure in some regions. To address these issues, urban planners must focus on creating sustainable cities that balance growth with environmental preservation."

Multiple-Choice Questions

9. What is the main idea of the passage?

A) Urbanization only creates problems for cities.
B) Urbanization has both benefits and challenges that need to be addressed.

C) Economic growth is the only result of urbanization.
D) Urban planners should avoid further urbanization.

Correct Answer: B

10. Which evidence from the passage supports the challenges of urbanization?

A) "More than half of the world's population now lives in cities."
B) "Urbanization has brought improved access to education, healthcare, and employment."
C) "Rapid urbanization also poses significant challenges, including overcrowding, pollution, and inadequate infrastructure."
D) "Urban planners must focus on creating sustainable cities."

Correct Answer: C

11. What solution does the passage suggest to address the challenges of urbanization?

A) Limiting the number of people allowed to live in cities.
B) Focusing on sustainable city planning.
C) Reducing economic growth to prevent urbanization.
D) Relocating people to rural areas.

Correct Answer: B

Drag-and-Drop Question

Directions:

Categorize the following statements as either a benefit or a challenge of urbanization.

Statements:

1. "Improved access to education and healthcare."
2. "Overcrowding in city centers."
3. "Economic growth and job opportunities."
4. "Inadequate infrastructure in some regions."

Categories:

- **Benefits of Urbanization**
- **Challenges of Urbanization**

Correct Answer:

- **Benefits of Urbanization**:
    - "Improved access to education and healthcare."
    - "Economic growth and job opportunities."
- **Challenges of Urbanization**:
    - "Overcrowding in city centers."
    - "Inadequate infrastructure in some regions."

Passage 4: The Value of Team Sports

"Team sports teach valuable life skills such as cooperation, leadership, and perseverance. Athletes learn to work with others to achieve a common goal, which translates to teamwork in the workplace. Additionally, participating in sports promotes physical fitness and mental well-being. However, critics argue that competitive sports can be overly stressful for some individuals, leading to burnout or a negative self-image. Despite these drawbacks, the benefits of team sports in building character and fostering social skills cannot be overlooked."

Multiple-Choice Questions

12. What is the primary argument in favor of team sports in the passage?

A) They promote physical fitness and social skills.
B) They eliminate stress in athletes.
C) They are suitable for everyone, regardless of ability.
D) They reduce the need for workplace teamwork.

Correct Answer: A

13. Which statement from the passage highlights a potential drawback of team sports?

A) "Athletes learn to work with others to achieve a common goal."
B) "Competitive sports can be overly stressful for some individuals."
C) "Team sports teach valuable life skills such as cooperation and leadership."
D) "Participating in sports promotes physical fitness and mental well-being."

Correct Answer: B

14. How does the passage address concerns about competitive sports?

A) It dismisses the concerns as irrelevant.
B) It acknowledges the concerns but emphasizes the benefits.
C) It suggests eliminating competitive sports altogether.
D) It recommends reducing the emphasis on teamwork.

Correct Answer: B

Extended Response Question

Prompt:

Analyze the benefits and challenges of urbanization based on the provided passages. Write an essay explaining which perspective—urbanization as an opportunity or urbanization as a challenge—is stronger. Use evidence from the passages to support your analysis.

Passage 5: Technology in Healthcare

"The integration of technology in healthcare has revolutionized patient care. Electronic health records allow doctors to access patient information instantly, reducing errors and improving outcomes. Telemedicine has made healthcare accessible to patients in remote areas, breaking down geographical barriers. However, critics argue that the reliance on technology can depersonalize healthcare, as patients may feel less connected to their providers during virtual consultations. Striking a balance between technological innovation and human connection is key to advancing healthcare."

Multiple-Choice Questions

15. What is the main benefit of technology in healthcare according to the passage?

A) It eliminates the need for in-person doctor visits.
B) It reduces errors and improves patient outcomes.
C) It increases the cost of healthcare services.
D) It eliminates the role of healthcare providers.

Correct Answer: B

16. Which statement from the passage highlights a challenge of technology in healthcare?

A) "Telemedicine has made healthcare accessible to patients in remote areas."
B) "Electronic health records allow doctors to access patient information instantly."
C) "Reliance on technology can depersonalize healthcare."
D) "Striking a balance between technological innovation and human connection is key."

Correct Answer: C

17. What does the passage suggest is necessary for improving healthcare?

A) Removing technology from healthcare entirely.
B) Focusing only on telemedicine solutions.
C) Balancing technological innovation with human connection.
D) Increasing the cost of healthcare technology.

Correct Answer: C

Additional Extended Response Prompt

Prompt:

Evaluate the benefits and challenges of technology in healthcare. Analyze which perspective is stronger and provide evidence from the passage to support your response.

Passage 6: Renewable Agriculture Practices

"Sustainable agriculture is crucial for ensuring long-term food security. Practices such as crop rotation, reduced chemical use, and integrated pest management help maintain soil fertility and reduce environmental damage. Research shows that farms employing these techniques produce higher yields over time compared to those relying heavily on chemical inputs. However, critics argue that sustainable practices often require more labor and can be initially expensive to implement, making them less feasible for small-scale farmers."

Multiple-Choice Questions

18. What is the main argument of the passage?

A) Sustainable agriculture is less productive than traditional methods.
B) Sustainable agriculture ensures long-term food security and reduces environmental damage.
C) Sustainable agriculture is only beneficial for large-scale farms.
D) Sustainable agriculture completely eliminates farming challenges.

Correct Answer: B

19. What evidence supports the claim that sustainable practices are effective?

A) "Sustainable practices often require more labor."
B) "Farms employing these techniques produce higher yields over time."
C) "Integrated pest management reduces the need for pesticides."
D) "Critics argue that these methods are costly for small-scale farmers."

Correct Answer: B

20. Which concern is raised about sustainable agriculture?

A) It relies heavily on chemical inputs.
B) It is initially expensive and labor-intensive for farmers.
C) It reduces soil fertility over time.
D) It produces fewer yields compared to traditional methods.

Correct Answer: B

Drag-and-Drop Question

Directions:

Categorize the following statements into benefits or challenges of sustainable agriculture.

Statements:

1. "Maintains soil fertility and reduces environmental damage."
2. "Produces higher yields over time."
3. "Requires more labor."
4. "Can be costly to implement for small-scale farmers."

Categories:

- **Benefits of Sustainable Agriculture**
- **Challenges of Sustainable Agriculture**

Correct Answer:

- **Benefits of Sustainable Agriculture**:
  - "Maintains soil fertility and reduces environmental damage."
  - "Produces higher yields over time."
- **Challenges of Sustainable Agriculture**:
  - "Requires more labor."
  - "Can be costly to implement for small-scale farmers."

Passage 7: The Effects of Music on Learning

"Listening to music while studying is a popular practice, but its effects vary depending on the type of music and the individual. Classical music has been shown to improve focus and memory retention, likely due to its calming effect. On the other hand, music with lyrics or loud, fast beats can be distracting for many students, reducing their ability to concentrate. Personal preferences also play a role—what helps one student focus might hinder another. Ultimately, understanding how music affects your learning is key to using it effectively."

Multiple-Choice Questions

21. What does the passage suggest about listening to music while studying?

A) All music improves focus and memory retention.
B) Classical music is generally more beneficial for studying.
C) Music is universally distracting during study sessions.
D) Music has no effect on learning.

Correct Answer: B

22. Which factor does the passage highlight as influencing the effects of music on studying?

A) The availability of quiet study spaces.
B) The individual's personal preference.
C) The volume of the music.
D) The length of the study session.

Correct Answer: B

23. What evidence supports the claim that classical music improves focus?

A) "Music with lyrics can be distracting."
B) "Classical music has been shown to improve focus and memory retention, likely due to its calming effect."
C) "Personal preferences play a role in the effectiveness of music."
D) "Understanding how music affects your learning is key."

Correct Answer: B

Extended Response Prompt

"Evaluate the benefits and challenges of using music while studying. Analyze which perspective—music as a tool for focus or music as a distraction—is more compelling. Use evidence from the passage to support your argument."

Passage 8: The Case for a Four-Day Workweek

"Advocates for a four-day workweek argue that it improves productivity and work-life balance. Studies show that employees working four days a week report lower stress levels and higher job satisfaction. Additionally, shorter workweeks reduce

commuting time, which decreases traffic congestion and pollution. However, critics claim that a four-day workweek may not be suitable for industries requiring continuous operations, such as healthcare or manufacturing. Implementing this change requires careful planning to ensure that productivity does not decline."

Multiple-Choice Questions

24. What is the main benefit of a four-day workweek according to the passage?

A) It decreases job satisfaction.
B) It reduces commuting time and pollution.
C) It increases stress levels among employees.
D) It benefits industries like healthcare and manufacturing.

Correct Answer: B

25. What is a key concern about the four-day workweek?

A) It may not be effective for all industries.
B) It increases traffic congestion.
C) It has no impact on work-life balance.
D) It results in lower employee satisfaction.

Correct Answer: A

26. How does the passage suggest implementing a four-day workweek successfully?

A) By limiting it to specific industries.
B) By carefully planning to maintain productivity.
C) By reducing commuting options.
D) By requiring employees to work longer shifts.

Correct Answer: B

Extended Response Prompt

"Analyze the arguments for and against a four-day workweek. Evaluate which perspective is stronger, and use evidence from the passage to support your analysis."

Passage 9: Exercise and Mental Health

"Regular exercise has been linked to numerous mental health benefits, including reduced anxiety, improved mood, and better stress management. Physical activity increases the production of endorphins, chemicals in the brain that promote feelings of well-being. However, individuals with busy schedules or physical limitations may struggle to incorporate exercise into their daily routines. Creative solutions, such as short workouts or integrating physical activity into daily tasks, can help make exercise accessible to everyone."

Multiple-Choice Questions

27. What mental health benefit is directly linked to exercise in the passage?

A) Increased stress levels.
B) Reduced production of endorphins.
C) Improved mood and stress management.
D) Physical activity is unrelated to mental health.

Correct Answer: C

28. What solution does the passage offer for people who have limited time to exercise?

A) Avoid physical activity altogether.
B) Focus solely on mental exercises.
C) Integrate short workouts into daily tasks.

D) Exercise only on weekends.

Correct Answer: C

Passage 10: The Benefits of Volunteering

"Volunteering provides individuals with opportunities to make meaningful contributions to their communities while also enhancing their personal growth. Studies show that people who volunteer regularly report higher levels of happiness and lower rates of depression. Additionally, volunteering helps individuals build new skills, expand professional networks, and gain valuable experiences that can boost career prospects. Critics argue that unpaid labor can sometimes exploit workers, particularly in organizations that rely heavily on volunteers without providing adequate support. However, when done thoughtfully, volunteering benefits both the individual and the community."

Multiple-Choice Questions

29. What is the primary argument of the passage?

A) Volunteering is a waste of time and resources.
B) Volunteering benefits both individuals and communities.
C) Volunteering is harmful due to exploitation.
D) Volunteering reduces career opportunities.

Correct Answer: B

30. Which statement from the passage supports the claim that volunteering benefits individuals?

A) "Volunteering helps individuals build new skills and expand professional networks."
B) "Unpaid labor can sometimes exploit workers."
C) "Studies show that people who volunteer regularly report higher levels of happiness."
D) Both A and C.

Correct Answer: D

31. What potential drawback of volunteering is mentioned in the passage?

A) It requires no skills or training.
B) It can sometimes exploit workers if organizations rely too heavily on unpaid labor.
C) It always benefits the individual more than the community.
D) It leads to higher rates of depression among volunteers.

Correct Answer: B

Drag-and-Drop Question

Directions:

Sort the following statements into benefits or challenges of volunteering.

Statements:

1. "Builds new skills and expands professional networks."
2. "Can lead to exploitation of unpaid workers."
3. "Boosts career prospects and provides valuable experience."
4. "Provides opportunities to make meaningful contributions to the community."

Categories:

- **Benefits of Volunteering**
- **Challenges of Volunteering**

Correct Answer:

- **Benefits of Volunteering**:

- "Builds new skills and expands professional networks."
- "Boosts career prospects and provides valuable experience."
- "Provides opportunities to make meaningful contributions to the community."

- **Challenges of Volunteering**:
  - "Can lead to exploitation of unpaid workers."

Passage 11: The Debate Over School Uniforms

"School uniforms have been a topic of debate among educators, parents, and students. Supporters argue that uniforms promote equality by reducing visible socioeconomic differences among students. They also claim that uniforms improve focus and discipline, as students are less concerned about fashion trends. Opponents, however, believe that uniforms stifle individuality and fail to address deeper issues of inequality. They argue that enforcing a uniform policy can create unnecessary tension between schools and families. While the debate continues, the effectiveness of school uniforms largely depends on how they are implemented and perceived."

Multiple-Choice Questions

32. What is the main argument in favor of school uniforms?

A) They promote equality and improve focus.
B) They are an unnecessary expense for families.
C) They stifle individuality and creativity.
D) They have no impact on student discipline.

Correct Answer: A

33. Which statement reflects an argument against school uniforms?

A) "Uniforms promote equality by reducing visible socioeconomic differences."
B) "Uniforms stifle individuality and fail to address deeper issues of inequality."
C) "Uniforms improve focus and discipline."
D) "Uniforms reduce concerns about fashion trends."

Correct Answer: B

34. How does the passage suggest the effectiveness of school uniforms is determined?

A) By analyzing the costs of implementation.
B) By considering how they are implemented and perceived.
C) By focusing solely on academic performance.
D) By eliminating socioeconomic differences entirely.

Correct Answer: B

Extended Response Prompt

"Evaluate the arguments for and against school uniforms based on the passage. Analyze which perspective is stronger, and use evidence from the text to support your response."

Passage 12: The Importance of Reading for Pleasure

"Reading for pleasure is often overlooked in today's fast-paced, technology-driven world. However, research shows that individuals who read regularly for enjoyment experience numerous cognitive and emotional benefits. Reading improves vocabulary, enhances empathy by exposing readers to different perspectives, and reduces stress levels. Despite these advantages, fewer people are reading for leisure, as distractions like social media and streaming services dominate free time. Encouraging a culture of reading is essential for fostering intellectual growth and emotional well-being."

Multiple-Choice Questions

35. What is the main argument of the passage?

A) Social media improves empathy better than reading.
B) Reading for pleasure offers significant cognitive and emotional benefits.
C) Reading for pleasure has no place in today's technology-driven world.
D) Fewer people are reading because books are outdated.

Correct Answer: B

36. What evidence supports the claim that reading improves empathy?

A) "Reading improves vocabulary and enhances empathy by exposing readers to different perspectives."
B) "Research shows that individuals who read regularly experience emotional benefits."
C) "Distractions like social media dominate free time."
D) "Encouraging a culture of reading fosters intellectual growth."

Correct Answer: A

37. What challenge to reading for pleasure is highlighted in the passage?

A) Books have become too expensive for most people.
B) Social media and streaming services dominate free time.
C) Reading does not reduce stress levels.
D) Reading fails to expose individuals to different perspectives.

Correct Answer: B

Extended Response Prompt

"Based on the passage, evaluate the importance of reading for pleasure. Analyze why it remains a valuable activity despite modern distractions, using evidence from the text to support your response."

Passage 13: Space Exploration Funding

"The debate over funding space exploration often centers on its costs versus its benefits. Supporters argue that space exploration drives technological innovation, boosts scientific understanding, and inspires future generations. They point to advancements like satellite technology and medical imaging as byproducts of space programs. Opponents, however, believe that these funds would be better spent addressing immediate issues such as poverty, healthcare, and education. While space exploration offers long-term benefits, critics question whether its value justifies the financial investment."

Multiple-Choice Questions

38. What is a key argument in favor of funding space exploration?

A) It eliminates immediate global challenges like poverty.
B) It drives technological innovation and scientific understanding.
C) It reduces costs in healthcare and education.
D) It offers short-term solutions to financial issues.

Correct Answer: B

39. Which example supports the claim that space exploration benefits society?

A) "Critics question whether its value justifies the financial investment."
B) "Space programs have led to advancements in satellite technology and medical imaging."
C) "Funds would be better spent addressing poverty and healthcare."
D) "Space exploration offers long-term benefits."

Correct Answer: B

40. What concern do opponents of space exploration funding raise?

A) It has no practical applications in daily life.
B) It fails to inspire future generations.
C) The funds could address immediate social issues.

D) It increases the financial burden on the public.

Correct Answer: C

Extended Response Prompt

"Analyze the arguments for and against funding space exploration. Evaluate which perspective is stronger and use evidence from the passage to support your response."

Passage 14: The Impact of Fast Fashion

"Fast fashion has revolutionized the clothing industry, providing consumers with trendy, affordable clothing at unprecedented speeds. However, this business model comes at a high cost to the environment and society. Fast fashion production generates significant carbon emissions and textile waste, contributing to climate change. Additionally, many workers in developing countries face poor working conditions and low wages. While some companies are beginning to adopt sustainable practices, critics argue that these efforts are insufficient to counteract the negative impacts of the fast fashion industry."

Multiple-Choice Questions

41. What is the main argument of the passage?

A) Fast fashion is a sustainable and affordable business model.
B) Fast fashion has significant environmental and societal drawbacks.
C) Companies have fully solved the issues related to fast fashion.
D) Fast fashion benefits consumers more than the environment.

Correct Answer: B

42. Which piece of evidence supports the claim that fast fashion harms the environment?

A) "Fast fashion provides consumers with trendy, affordable clothing."
B) "Fast fashion production generates significant carbon emissions and textile waste."
C) "Some companies are beginning to adopt sustainable practices."
D) "Workers in developing countries face poor working conditions."

Correct Answer: B

43. How does the passage suggest companies are addressing the challenges of fast fashion?

A) By increasing production speeds.
B) By adopting sustainable practices.
C) By lowering wages in developing countries.
D) By expanding the fast fashion business model.

Correct Answer: B

Drag-and-Drop Question

Directions:

Categorize the following statements as benefits or drawbacks of fast fashion.

Statements:

1. "Provides consumers with trendy, affordable clothing."
2. "Generates significant carbon emissions and textile waste."
3. "Workers face poor conditions and low wages."
4. "Allows quick access to the latest trends."

Categories:

- **Benefits of Fast Fashion**
- **Drawbacks of Fast Fashion**

Correct Answer:

- **Benefits of Fast Fashion**:
  - "Provides consumers with trendy, affordable clothing."
  - "Allows quick access to the latest trends."
- **Drawbacks of Fast Fashion**:
  - "Generates significant carbon emissions and textile waste."
  - "Workers face poor conditions and low wages."

Extended Response Prompt

"Analyze the benefits and drawbacks of the fast fashion industry. Evaluate which perspective—benefits or drawbacks—carries more weight and use evidence from the passage to support your analysis."

Passage 15: The Role of Artificial Intelligence

"Artificial intelligence (AI) is transforming industries by improving efficiency, reducing costs, and enhancing decision-making processes. In healthcare, AI algorithms assist doctors in diagnosing diseases with greater accuracy, while in business, AI optimizes supply chains and customer experiences. However, critics warn that increasing reliance on AI could lead to job displacement, ethical concerns, and reduced privacy. While the benefits of AI are undeniable, addressing these challenges is essential for its responsible development and implementation."

Multiple-Choice Questions

44. What is the main argument of the passage?

A) AI is universally beneficial and requires no oversight.

B) AI benefits industries but poses ethical and societal challenges.
C) AI has no real impact on industries like healthcare or business.
D) AI reduces privacy without providing meaningful benefits.

Correct Answer: B

45. Which example from the passage highlights a benefit of AI in healthcare?

A) "AI optimizes supply chains and customer experiences."
B) "AI algorithms assist doctors in diagnosing diseases with greater accuracy."
C) "Critics warn about job displacement and ethical concerns."
D) "Addressing these challenges is essential for responsible implementation."

Correct Answer: B

46. What concern is raised about the increasing use of AI?

A) It fails to improve decision-making processes.
B) It reduces job displacement in certain industries.
C) It raises ethical concerns and threatens privacy.
D) It eliminates the need for supply chain optimization.

Correct Answer: C

Drag-and-Drop Question

Directions:

Sort the following statements into benefits or challenges of AI.

Statements:

1. "Improves decision-making processes in industries."
2. "Raises ethical concerns about its use."

3. "Optimizes supply chains and customer experiences."
4. "Threatens privacy through increased data collection."

Categories:

- **Benefits of AI**
- **Challenges of AI**

Correct Answer:

- **Benefits of AI**:
    - "Improves decision-making processes in industries."
    - "Optimizes supply chains and customer experiences."
- **Challenges of AI**:
    - "Raises ethical concerns about its use."
    - "Threatens privacy through increased data collection."

Extended Response Prompt

"Evaluate the benefits and challenges of artificial intelligence as described in the passage. Analyze which perspective is more compelling and provide evidence from the text to support your response."

Passage 16: The Case for Public Transportation

"Investing in public transportation offers numerous benefits, including reducing traffic congestion, lowering greenhouse gas emissions, and providing affordable commuting options. Cities with robust public transit systems, such as New York and Tokyo, report significant reductions in air pollution. Additionally, public transportation promotes economic growth by connecting people to jobs and services. However, critics argue that expanding public transit can be costly and disruptive, particularly in densely populated urban areas. Despite these challenges, the long-term benefits of public transportation make it a worthwhile investment."

Multiple-Choice Questions

47. What is the main argument in favor of public transportation?

A) It is less efficient than private vehicles.
B) It reduces traffic congestion and air pollution.
C) It eliminates the need for urban planning.
D) It is only beneficial in rural areas.

Correct Answer: B

48. Which piece of evidence supports the claim that public transportation reduces pollution?

A) "Investing in public transportation offers numerous benefits."
B) "Cities with robust public transit systems, such as New York and Tokyo, report significant reductions in air pollution."
C) "Public transportation promotes economic growth by connecting people to jobs."
D) "Expanding public transit can be costly and disruptive."

Correct Answer: B

49. What concern about public transportation is raised in the passage?

A) It eliminates traffic congestion entirely.
B) It is costly and disruptive in urban areas.
C) It increases greenhouse gas emissions.
D) It prevents people from accessing jobs and services.

Correct Answer: B

Extended Response Prompt

"Based on the passage, evaluate whether the benefits of public transportation outweigh its challenges. Use evidence from the text to support your argument."

Passage 17: The Pros and Cons of Remote Work

"Remote work has become increasingly common, offering employees the flexibility to work from anywhere. Proponents argue that remote work improves productivity and reduces commuting time, which can lead to lower stress levels. Additionally, businesses benefit from reduced office expenses. However, critics claim that remote work can isolate employees, leading to weaker collaboration and diminished team morale. Balancing the advantages and disadvantages of remote work requires thoughtful policies to ensure both employee well-being and organizational success."

Multiple-Choice Questions

50. What is the primary argument in favor of remote work?

A) It weakens collaboration among employees.
B) It offers flexibility and reduces commuting stress.
C) It leads to higher office expenses.
D) It reduces the need for employee well-being policies.

Correct Answer: B

51. Which statement from the passage highlights a drawback of remote work?

A) "Remote work improves productivity and reduces commuting time."
B) "Businesses benefit from reduced office expenses."
C) "Remote work can isolate employees, leading to weaker collaboration."
D) "Balancing advantages and disadvantages requires thoughtful policies."

Correct Answer: C

52. How does the passage suggest remote work challenges can be addressed?

A) By eliminating remote work entirely.
B) By implementing thoughtful policies to balance its pros and cons.
C) By encouraging employees to work more hours remotely.
D) By increasing commuting time for remote employees.

Correct Answer: B

Drag-and-Drop Question

Directions:

Categorize the following statements as benefits or challenges of remote work.

Statements:

1. "Reduces commuting time and stress."
2. "Improves productivity and flexibility."
3. "Leads to weaker collaboration."
4. "Can isolate employees."

Categories:

- **Benefits of Remote Work**
- **Challenges of Remote Work**

Correct Answer:

- **Benefits of Remote Work**:
  - "Reduces commuting time and stress."
  - "Improves productivity and flexibility."

- **Challenges of Remote Work**:
    - "Leads to weaker collaboration."
    - "Can isolate employees."

Extended Response Prompt

"Analyze the advantages and disadvantages of remote work as presented in the passage. Evaluate which perspective is stronger and provide evidence from the text to support your argument."

Passage 18: The Decline of Pollinators

"Pollinators such as bees and butterflies play a critical role in maintaining ecosystems by facilitating plant reproduction. However, their populations are in decline due to habitat loss, pesticide use, and climate change. This decline poses serious risks to global food security, as many crops depend on pollinators for production. Efforts to protect pollinators include creating pollinator-friendly habitats, reducing pesticide use, and promoting public awareness. While these measures show promise, reversing the trend will require global cooperation and long-term commitment."

Multiple-Choice Questions

53. What is the main argument of the passage?

A) Pollinators are no longer necessary for food production.
B) Protecting pollinators is essential for ecosystems and food security.
C) Pollinator populations are increasing due to climate change.
D) Pesticide use has no impact on pollinator populations.

Correct Answer: B

54. Which solution does the passage suggest for protecting pollinators?

A) Increasing pesticide use to control pests.
B) Encouraging habitat destruction to create farmland.
C) Promoting public awareness and reducing pesticide use.
D) Ignoring pollinator populations and focusing on technology.

Correct Answer: C

55. How does the decline of pollinators affect food security?

A) It has no measurable impact on food production.
B) Many crops depend on pollinators for production.
C) It reduces the availability of fertilizers.
D) It increases the need for pesticide use.

Correct Answer: B

Drag-and-Drop Question

Directions:

Categorize the following factors as causes of the decline of pollinators or solutions to protect pollinators.

Statements:

1. "Habitat loss and climate change."
2. "Reducing pesticide use."
3. "Creating pollinator-friendly habitats."
4. "Pesticide use and habitat destruction."

Categories:

- **Causes of Pollinator Decline**

- **Solutions to Protect Pollinators**

Correct Answer:

- **Causes of Pollinator Decline**:
    - "Habitat loss and climate change."
    - "Pesticide use and habitat destruction."
- **Solutions to Protect Pollinators**:
    - "Reducing pesticide use."
    - "Creating pollinator-friendly habitats."

Extended Response Prompt

"Evaluate the significance of protecting pollinators as described in the passage. Analyze the proposed solutions and their potential effectiveness, using evidence from the text to support your response."

Passage 19: Universal Basic Income (UBI)

"Universal Basic Income (UBI) is a policy where all citizens receive a regular, unconditional payment from the government. Advocates argue that UBI reduces poverty, provides financial stability, and allows individuals to pursue education or entrepreneurship without fear of economic failure. Opponents, however, claim that UBI is too expensive to implement and may discourage people from seeking employment. While pilot programs have shown mixed results, the debate over UBI continues to grow as automation transforms the global job market."

Multiple-Choice Questions

56. What is the primary benefit of UBI according to its proponents?

A) It reduces the costs of government programs.
B) It discourages people from seeking employment.
C) It provides financial stability and reduces poverty.
D) It prevents automation from affecting the job market.

Correct Answer: C

57. Which argument is raised by opponents of UBI?

A) It promotes entrepreneurship and education.
B) It is too expensive and may reduce employment motivation.
C) It allows individuals to explore creative pursuits.
D) It solves all issues caused by automation.

Correct Answer: B

58. How has UBI been evaluated so far?

A) It has been universally successful.
B) It has shown mixed results in pilot programs.
C) It has consistently reduced unemployment rates.
D) It has led to the elimination of automation.

Correct Answer: B

Drag-and-Drop Question

Directions:

Categorize the following statements as arguments for or against UBI.

Statements:

1. "Provides financial stability and reduces poverty."
2. "Too expensive to implement."
3. "Allows individuals to pursue education or entrepreneurship."
4. "May discourage people from seeking employment."

Categories:

- **Arguments For UBI**
- **Arguments Against UBI**

Correct Answer:

- **Arguments For UBI**:
    - "Provides financial stability and reduces poverty."
    - "Allows individuals to pursue education or entrepreneurship."
- **Arguments Against UBI**:
    - "Too expensive to implement."
    - "May discourage people from seeking employment."

Extended Response Prompt

"Evaluate the arguments for and against Universal Basic Income as described in the passage. Analyze which perspective is stronger, and use evidence from the text to support your argument."

PART III

MATHEMATICAL REASONING

CHAPTER 14

OVERVIEW OF THE MATH EXAM

The Mathematical Reasoning section of the GED exam is designed to test your ability to solve problems and apply mathematical concepts in practical, real-world scenarios. This section assesses a wide range of skills, from basic arithmetic to more advanced algebra and geometry. Understanding the structure and expectations of this part of the test is essential to your preparation and success.

The GED Math test is divided into two main parts: a **Calculator-Allowed Section** and a **Non-Calculator Section**. Both sections include multiple-choice questions, drag-and-drop problems, fill-in-the-blank items, and questions that require selecting multiple answers. These variations ensure that test-takers demonstrate not only their mathematical knowledge but also their problem-solving and reasoning skills.

The Structure of the Math Exam

The Math section consists of approximately **46 questions** and has a total time limit of **115 minutes**. The questions are not grouped by topic; instead, they are presented in a mixed format, covering a variety of mathematical concepts. This format reflects the real-world application of math, where different skills may be required simultaneously.

1. **Non-Calculator Section**
   - This is the first part of the exam, comprising about 5–7 questions.
   - As the name suggests, calculators are not allowed during this section.
   - The questions here are typically designed to assess your mental math skills, logical reasoning, and ability to work with basic operations without technological assistance.
2. **Calculator-Allowed Section**
   - After completing the non-calculator section, you will move on to the larger portion of the test, where calculators are permitted.
   - You will use an **on-screen scientific calculator** provided by the GED testing software (or a physical TI-30XS Multiview calculator, depending on the testing center's rules).
   - This section includes a broader range of questions, requiring more complex calculations and applications.

Key Areas of Focus

The GED Math test assesses four primary areas of mathematical reasoning. These areas align with high school curriculum standards and ensure you are equipped with the skills needed for both academic and everyday problem-solving.

1. **Quantitative Problem Solving**
   - This area covers basic arithmetic, fractions, percentages, ratios, and proportions.
   - You may encounter questions that involve interpreting graphs, tables, or charts.
2. **Algebraic Problem Solving**
   - Topics include solving equations and inequalities, understanding functions, and working with algebraic expressions.
   - Algebra questions often test your ability to identify relationships between variables and solve for unknowns.
3. **Geometry**
   - Geometry questions assess your understanding of shapes, angles, and measurements.
   - You will be asked to calculate perimeters, areas, and volumes or apply the Pythagorean theorem.

4. **Data Analysis and Probability**
    - This section includes interpreting data from graphs and charts, calculating statistical measures (mean, median, mode), and understanding probabilities.
    - These questions often simulate real-life scenarios, such as analyzing survey results or making predictions based on data.

The Role of Mathematical Reasoning

Mathematical reasoning on the GED goes beyond rote memorization or simple calculations. The test requires you to analyze problems, determine the correct methods for solving them, and apply your skills efficiently. For instance, you might need to decide whether to use a proportional relationship or an algebraic equation to solve a word problem. This practical focus ensures that the skills tested on the GED Math exam align with those needed in the workplace or in postsecondary education.

Why This Section Matters

The Math section is critical for demonstrating your quantitative and analytical abilities. Whether you are planning to pursue higher education, advance in your career, or achieve personal goals, strong math skills are essential. The GED Math test serves as a benchmark to prove your competency in these areas.

By mastering the structure of the test and understanding the types of questions you will encounter, you can approach this section with confidence and clarity. The following chapters will delve deeper into each aspect of the exam, providing you with the tools and strategies you need to excel.

14.1 Calculator vs. Non-Calculator Sections

The GED Math test is divided into two distinct sections: the **Non-Calculator Section** and the **Calculator-Allowed Section**. Each section is designed to test different aspects of your mathematical reasoning skills, ensuring you are proficient in both fundamental calculations and more complex problem-solving.

Understanding how these sections are structured and what is expected in each will help you manage your time effectively and approach the exam with confidence. Let's examine each section in detail.

The Non-Calculator Section

This section is the first part of the GED Math test and typically includes **5–7 questions**. The primary goal of the non-calculator section is to evaluate your ability to perform basic mathematical operations without technological assistance. It emphasizes mental math, number sense, and logical reasoning.

What to Expect in the Non-Calculator Section

1. **Basic Arithmetic**
    - Operations with whole numbers, fractions, and decimals.
    - Examples include addition, subtraction, multiplication, and division.
2. **Ratios and Proportions**
    - Questions that involve comparing quantities or solving for missing values.
3. **Estimation**
    - Determining approximate answers to ensure accuracy in calculations.
4. **Number Properties**
    - Understanding concepts such as prime numbers, greatest common factors, and least common multiples.
5. **Simplifying Expressions**
    - Basic algebraic tasks like combining like terms or solving for a variable in simple equations.

Sample Non-Calculator Question

A store sells apples for $0.85 each. If you buy 12 apples, how much will they cost in total?

Solution:

You must calculate 12×0.8512 \times 0.8512×0.85 without a calculator. Start by breaking the calculation into steps:

- Multiply 12×0.80=9.6012 \times 0.80 = 9.6012×0.80=9.60.
- Multiply 12×0.05=0.6012 \times 0.05 = 0.6012×0.05=0.60.
- Add 9.60+0.60=10.209.60 + 0.60 = 10.209.60+0.60=10.20.

The total cost is **$10.20**.

Key Strategies for Success

- **Practice Mental Math**: Familiarize yourself with quick calculation methods, such as rounding or breaking numbers into manageable parts.
- **Write Out Your Work**: Use the scratch paper provided during the test to organize your calculations and avoid errors.
- **Double-Check Answers**: If time allows, review your calculations to ensure they are accurate.

The Calculator-Allowed Section

The second and much larger portion of the Math test is the calculator-allowed section, which typically contains **39–41 questions**. Here, you can use a **TI-30XS Multiview scientific calculator**, either on-screen or as a physical device, depending on the test environment. This section focuses on more complex mathematical concepts where a calculator is a valuable tool.

What to Expect in the Calculator-Allowed Section

1. **Algebra and Functions**
    - Solving linear equations and inequalities.
    - Graphing linear functions.
    - Working with quadratic equations.
2. **Geometry and Measurement**
    - Calculating perimeters, areas, and volumes.
    - Applying the Pythagorean theorem.
    - Understanding coordinate geometry.
3. **Data Analysis and Statistics**
    - Interpreting graphs, charts, and tables.
    - Calculating statistical measures like mean, median, and mode.
    - Working with probabilities.
4. **Word Problems**
    - Multi-step problems requiring analysis and logical application of mathematical concepts.

Sample Calculator-Allowed Question

The area of a rectangle is 72 square feet, and its width is 8 feet. What is its length?

Solution:

The formula for the area of a rectangle is $\text{Area} = \text{Length} \times \text{Width}$.

Given $\text{Area} = 72$ and $\text{Width} = 8$, solve for Length:

$$\text{Length} = \frac{\text{Area}}{\text{Width}} = \frac{72}{8} = 9 \text{ feet.}$$

The length is **9 feet**.

Using the Calculator Effectively

- Familiarize yourself with the **TI-30XS Multiview calculator** before the test. Understand its functions, including fractions, exponents, and parentheses.

- Always verify that you've entered calculations correctly. Miskeys can lead to incorrect answers.
- For multi-step problems, write down intermediate steps on your scratch paper.

Comparing the Two Sections

Feature	Non-Calculator Section	Calculator-Allowed Section
Purpose	Test basic arithmetic and logical reasoning	Test advanced math concepts and applications
Number of Questions	~5–7	~39–41
Focus Areas	Mental math, ratios, and estimation	Algebra, geometry, data analysis
Calculator Allowed?	No	Yes

Balancing Your Approach

The non-calculator section may seem intimidating, but it tests fundamental skills that are essential for everyday problem-solving. Practicing these skills will improve your confidence and efficiency. The calculator-allowed section, while offering technological assistance, requires a deep understanding of more complex concepts. Use the calculator as a tool, not a crutch—understand the problem-solving process to ensure accuracy.

14.2 Types of Questions and Time Allocation

The GED Math test is designed to evaluate a wide range of mathematical skills through a variety of question types. These questions assess your ability to apply mathematical concepts, solve problems, and interpret data in real-world contexts. Understanding the types of questions you'll encounter and how to manage your time effectively is crucial for success.

Types of Questions

The GED Math test includes several question formats, each requiring different approaches. Here's a detailed breakdown of the types of questions and how to tackle them:

1. Multiple-Choice Questions

These questions provide four answer choices, and your task is to select the correct one. Multiple-choice questions may test basic arithmetic, algebra, geometry, or data analysis.

Example:

What is the sum of $5/6 + 3/4$*?*

A) $1\,1/2$
B) $19/12$
C) $2\,1/3$
D) $11/12$

Solution:

Convert the fractions to have a common denominator:

$$\frac{5}{6} = \frac{10}{12}, \frac{3}{4} = \frac{9}{12}.$$

Add the fractions:

$$\frac{10}{12} + \frac{9}{12} = \frac{19}{12}.$$

The correct answer is **B**.

2. Drag-and-Drop Questions

These interactive questions require you to move answer options into specific categories or positions. Drag-and-drop questions often involve sorting data, completing equations, or labeling graphs.

Example:

Sort the following fractions into "Greater than 1" and "Less than 1."

- $\frac{3}{2}, \frac{4}{5}, \frac{7}{3}, \frac{2}{7}$

Solution:

- **Greater than 1**: $\frac{3}{2}, \frac{7}{3}$
- **Less than 1**: $\frac{4}{5}, \frac{2}{7}$

3. Fill-in-the-Blank Questions

In this type, you'll enter a numeric answer instead of choosing from options. These questions often test basic calculations or solving equations.

Example:

Solve for x: $3x + 5 = 14$.

Solution:

$$3x = 14 - 5 \Rightarrow 3x = 9 \Rightarrow x = \frac{9}{3}. = 3$$

The correct answer is **3**.

4. Drop-Down Menu Questions

These questions allow you to select answers from drop-down menus embedded in equations or sentences. They often test your ability to complete a formula or identify the correct term.

Example:

Select the correct operation to complete the equation: 12 [add/subtract/multiply] 3 = 36.

Solution:

The correct operation is **multiply**.

5. Graphing Questions

Graphing questions require you to plot points, interpret data from graphs, or analyze relationships between variables.

Example:

The equation $y = 2x + 3$ *is graphed. What is the y-intercept?*

Solution:

The y-intercept is where $x = 0$:

$$y = 2(0) + 3 = 3.$$

The y-intercept is **3**.

Time Allocation

The GED Math test has a total time limit of **115 minutes**, split across two sections: the **Non-Calculator Section** and the **Calculator-Allowed Section**. Managing your time effectively is essential to completing the test confidently.

Recommended Time Allocation

1. **Non-Calculator Section** (~5–7 questions): **10–15 minutes**

   - Focus on quick mental math and basic calculations.
   - Do not dwell too long on any one question; prioritize accuracy and efficiency.

2. **Calculator-Allowed Section** (~39–41 questions): **95–100 minutes**
   - Allocate time evenly, spending about **2–2.5 minutes per question**.
   - Use the calculator for complex calculations but double-check your work.

3. **Extended or Complex Problems**
   - Some questions, such as multi-step word problems or graphing tasks, may require extra time.
   - Balance these by quickly solving simpler problems first.

Strategies for Effective Time Management

- **Skip and Return**: If you encounter a difficult question, skip it and come back later. Don't let one problem consume too much time.
- **Use Your Scratch Paper**: Write down calculations and steps to keep your work organized and reduce errors.
- **Monitor Your Progress**: Periodically check the time and ensure you are on track to complete all questions.
- **Double-Check Key Calculations**: If time allows, review your answers to confirm accuracy, especially for complex problems.

Why Understanding Question Types and Timing Matters

Knowing the types of questions and how much time to spend on each section helps you feel more prepared and confident on test day. Familiarity with the format ensures that you can focus on solving problems rather than deciphering instructions. By practicing with real examples and timing yourself, you can build the skills and speed necessary to excel on the GED Math test.

In the next chapter, we'll dive deeper into arithmetic fundamentals, starting with operations on whole numbers, fractions, and decimals. These foundational skills are crucial for success in both the calculator and non-calculator sections of the test.

CHAPTER 15

ARITHMETIC FUNDAMENTALS

15.1 Operations with Whole Numbers, Fractions, and Decimals

Arithmetic is the foundation of all mathematics, and mastering operations with whole numbers, fractions, and decimals is essential for success on the GED Math test. These concepts appear in both the non-calculator and calculator-allowed sections, and they are often presented within real-world contexts, such as solving word problems or interpreting data.

This chapter will review the key operations—addition, subtraction, multiplication, and division—across whole numbers, fractions, and decimals. Practical examples are provided to illustrate each concept.

Operations with Whole Numbers

Whole numbers include all non-negative integers (e.g., 0, 1, 2, 3...). Basic operations with whole numbers form the foundation of arithmetic.

Addition and Subtraction

- **Addition** combines two or more numbers into a total.
- **Subtraction** determines the difference between two numbers.

Example 1:

Find the total number of apples if one basket has 45 apples and another has 32.

$$45 + 32 = 77 \text{ apples.}$$

Example 2:

A store has 120 shirts. If 35 are sold, how many remain?

$$120 - 35 = 85 \text{ shirts.}$$

Multiplication and Division

- **Multiplication** represents repeated addition.
- **Division** splits a quantity into equal parts.

Example 3:

Each box contains 8 pencils. How many pencils are in 12 boxes?

$$12 \times 8 = 96 \text{ pencils.}$$

Example 4:

A baker divides 240 cookies equally among 12 trays. How many cookies are on each tray?

$$240 \div 12 = 20 \text{ cookies per tray.}$$

Operations with Fractions

Fractions represent parts of a whole. Operations with fractions require understanding numerators (the top number) and denominators (the bottom number).

Addition and Subtraction of Fractions

- **Step 1**: Ensure the denominators are the same (common denominators).
- **Step 2**: Add or subtract the numerators, keeping the denominator unchanged.
- **Step 3**: Simplify the fraction if necessary.

Example 5:

Add $\frac{2}{5} + \frac{3}{10}$.

Find a common denominator: $\frac{2}{5} = \frac{4}{10}$.

$$\frac{4}{10} + \frac{3}{10} = \frac{7}{10}.$$

Example 6:

Subtract $\frac{7}{8} - \frac{5}{12}$.

Find a common denominator: $\frac{7}{8} = \frac{21}{24}, \frac{5}{12} = \frac{10}{24}$.

$$\frac{21}{24} - \frac{10}{24} = \frac{11}{24}.$$

Multiplication and Division of Fractions

- **Multiplication**: Multiply the numerators and denominators.
- **Division**: Multiply by the reciprocal of the second fraction.

Example 7:

Multiply $\frac{3}{4} \times \frac{5}{6}$.

$$\frac{3}{4} \times \frac{5}{6} = \frac{15}{24} = \frac{5}{8} \text{ (simplified)}.$$

Example 8:

Divide $\frac{7}{9} \div \frac{2}{3}$.

Find the reciprocal of $\frac{2}{3}$: $\frac{3}{2}$.

$$\frac{7}{9} \times \frac{3}{2} = \frac{21}{18} = \frac{7}{6} \text{ (improper fraction)}.$$

Operations with Decimals

Decimals represent parts of a whole using a base-10 system. Operations with decimals are similar to those with whole numbers but require careful alignment of the decimal point.

Addition and Subtraction of Decimals

Align the decimal points and perform the operation as with whole numbers.

Example 9:

Add $12.34 + 5.678$.

Align decimals:

$$12.340 + 5.678 = 18.018.$$

Example 10:

Subtract $45.6 - 12.345$.

Align decimals:

$$45.600 - 12.345 = 33.255.$$

Multiplication of Decimals

- Ignore the decimal points and multiply the numbers as whole numbers.
- Count the total number of decimal places in both numbers and adjust the decimal point in the result.

Example 11:

Multiply 3.2×1.5.

$$32 \times 15 = 480.$$

Adjust for two decimal places: 4.80.

Division of Decimals

- Move the decimal point in the divisor (and dividend if necessary) to make the divisor a whole number.
- Perform division as usual.

Example 12:

Divide $4.5 \div 1.5$.

Adjust the decimal point: $45 \div 15 = 3$.

The result is **3**.

Real-World Applications

Understanding operations with whole numbers, fractions, and decimals is crucial in real-world scenarios, such as:

1. **Budgeting**: Adding expenses, dividing bills, or calculating discounts.
2. **Cooking**: Scaling recipes that require fractional measurements.
3. **Measurements**: Converting between units using decimals and fractions.

Example 13:

A recipe requires $\frac{3}{4}$ *cup of sugar. If you want to make half the recipe, how much sugar will you need?*

$$\frac{3}{4} \times \frac{1}{2} = \frac{3}{8}.$$

You will need $\frac{3}{8}$ **cup of sugar**.

Tips for Mastering Arithmetic

1. **Practice Mental Math**: This builds confidence in handling non-calculator questions.
2. **Use Scratch Paper**: Write out each step to reduce errors.
3. **Understand Concepts**: Don't just memorize formulas; understand why they work.
4. **Check Your Work**: Review your answers to ensure accuracy.

Mastering these operations provides a solid foundation for tackling more advanced topics like algebra, geometry, and data analysis, which are covered in later chapters. These skills will serve you well on both the GED exam and in everyday life.

15.2 Ratios, Proportions, and Percentages

Understanding ratios, proportions, and percentages is essential for solving real-world problems, ranging from comparing quantities to calculating discounts or interest rates. These concepts are frequently tested on the GED Math exam, often within practical contexts like word problems, graphs, and data interpretation. Mastering them will enable you to analyze relationships and make informed decisions efficiently.

Ratios

A **ratio** is a comparison of two quantities that shows the relative size of one value to another. Ratios can be written in three forms:

1. **Fraction Form**: $\frac{3}{5}$
2. **Colon Form**: $3:5$
3. **Word Form**: "3 to 5"

How to Interpret Ratios

Ratios express how many times one quantity fits into another. For example, a ratio of 2: 3 means for every 2 parts of one quantity, there are 3 parts of another.

Example 1:

The ratio of cats to dogs in a shelter is 5: 3. If there are 15 cats, how many dogs are there?

Solution:

Set up a proportion:

$$\frac{5}{3} = \frac{15}{x}.$$

Cross-multiply:

$$5\text{x} = 45 \Rightarrow x = 9$$

There are **9 dogs**.

Proportions

A **proportion** is an equation that shows two ratios are equal. Proportions are commonly used to solve problems involving scaling or finding missing values in equivalent relationships.

How to Solve Proportions

5. Write the proportion.
6. Cross-multiply.
7. Solve for the unknown variable.

Example 2:

A map uses a scale of 1: 100, meaning 1 inch on the map represents 100 miles. If two cities are 2.5 inches apart on the map, what is the actual distance between them?

Solution:

Set up the proportion:

$$\frac{1}{100} = \frac{2.5}{x}.$$

Cross-multiply:

$$1\text{x} = 2.5\ X\ 100 \Rightarrow x = 250$$

The actual distance is **250 miles**.

Percentages

A **percentage** is a way to express a number as a fraction of 100. The symbol "%" means "per hundred." Percentages are widely used in contexts like discounts, interest rates, and population statistics.

Basic Percentage Formula

$$\text{Percentage} = \frac{\text{Part}}{\text{Whole}} \times 100$$

Finding Percentages

Example 3:

What percentage of 50 is 20?

Solution:

$$\text{Percentage} = \frac{\text{Part}}{\text{Whole}} \times 100 = \frac{20}{50} \times 100 = 40\%.$$

Answer: 20 is **40%** of 50.

Finding the Part Given the Percentage

Example 4:

What is 25% of 200?

Solution:

$$\text{Part} = \frac{\text{Percentage}}{100} \times \text{Whole} = \frac{25}{100} \times 200 = 50.$$

Answer: 25% of 200 is **50**.

Finding the Whole Given the Percentage

Example 5:

30 is 15% of what number?

Solution:

$$\text{Whole} = \frac{\text{Part}}{\text{Percentage}} \times 100 = \frac{30}{15} \times 100 = 200.$$

Answer: The whole is **200**.

Real-World Applications of Percentages

1. **Discounts and Sales**
   - A $200 item is on sale for 25% off. What is the sale price?

     Solution:

$$\text{Discount} = \frac{25}{100} \times 200 = 50.$$

$$\text{Sale Price} = 200 - 50 = 150.$$

   Answer: $150.

2. **Interest Rates**
   - A savings account earns 4% annual interest. If the balance is $1,000, how much interest is earned in a year?

     Solution:

$$\text{Interest} = \frac{4}{100} \times 1000 = 40.$$

   Answer: $40.

Using Ratios, Proportions, and Percentages Together

Complex problems may involve combining these concepts.

Example 6:

A school has 300 students. The ratio of boys to girls is 3: 2. What percentage of the students are girls?

Solution:

1. Find the number of girls:

$$\frac{3}{2} = \frac{Boys}{Girls} \Rightarrow Girl = \frac{2}{5} X\ 300 = 120$$

2. Calculate the percentage:

$$\frac{\text{Girls}}{\text{Total Students}} \times 100 = \frac{120}{300} \times 100 = 40\%.$$

Answer: 40% of the students are girls.

Tips for Mastering These Concepts

1. **Practice Word Problems**: Many GED Math questions embed ratios, proportions, and percentages in real-life scenarios.
2. **Write Equations Clearly**: Organize your work to avoid errors.
3. **Use a Calculator When Allowed**: For percentages and proportions, the calculator can save time, especially in multi-step problems.
4. **Understand Units**: Always verify that your answer makes sense in the context of the problem.

Mastering ratios, proportions, and percentages equips you to handle a significant portion of the GED Math exam confidently. These skills are also invaluable in daily life, from budgeting to interpreting data. In the next section, we will explore **conversions between units of measurement**, an essential tool for solving practical problems.

15.3 Conversions Between Units of Measurement

Conversions between units of measurement are a critical skill for solving real-world problems, especially in areas like cooking, construction, and scientific experiments. On the GED Math test, you'll encounter questions that require you to convert between different units of length, weight, volume, and time. These questions often include both customary (imperial) units and metric units.

This chapter will review the most common unit conversions, provide practical examples, and explain how to approach conversion problems step by step.

Understanding Units of Measurement

Units of measurement are grouped into two main systems:

1. **Customary (Imperial) System**
   a. Used primarily in the United States.
   b. Common units: inches, feet, pounds, ounces, gallons, cups, and Fahrenheit.
2. **Metric System**
   a. Used internationally and in scientific contexts.
   b. Based on powers of 10.
   c. Common units: meters, liters, grams, and Celsius.

Key Conversion Factors

Length

- **Customary System**:
    - 1 foot = 12 inches
    - 1 yard = 3 feet
    - 1 mile = 1,760 yards
- **Metric System**:
    - 1 kilometer (km) = 1,000 meters (m)
    - 1 meter = 100 centimeters (cm)
    - 1 centimeter = 10 millimeters (mm)
- **Customary to Metric**:
    - 1 inch ≈ 2.54 cm
    - 1 foot ≈ 0.3048 m

Weight

- **Customary System**:

- 1 pound (lb) = 16 ounces (oz)
    - 1 ton = 2,000 pounds
- **Metric System**:
    - 1 kilogram (kg) = 1,000 grams (g)
    - 1 gram = 1,000 milligrams (mg)
- **Customary to Metric**:
    - 1 pound ≈ 0.4536 kg

Volume

- **Customary System**:
    - 1 gallon = 4 quarts
    - 1 quart = 2 pints
    - 1 pint = 2 cups
    - 1 cup = 8 fluid ounces
- **Metric System**:
    - 1 liter (L) = 1,000 milliliters (mL)
- **Customary to Metric**:
    - 1 gallon ≈ 3.785 liters

Time

Time conversions are straightforward:

- 1 hour = 60 minutes
- 1 minute = 60 seconds
- 1 day = 24 hours

Steps for Solving Conversion Problems

1. **Identify the Given Value**: Determine the quantity you need to convert.
2. **Determine the Conversion Factor**: Use the appropriate conversion rate between units.
3. **Set Up the Equation**: Multiply (or divide) the given value by the conversion factor.
4. **Simplify and Solve**: Perform the calculation and check your work.

Examples of Conversions

Example 1: Converting Inches to Feet

How many feet are in 36 inches?

Solution:

Use the conversion factor: $1\text{ foot} = 12\text{ inches}$.

$$\text{Feet} = \frac{36}{12} = 3.$$

Answer: 36 inches = **3 feet**.

Example 2: Converting Pounds to Kilograms

Convert 50 pounds to kilograms.

Solution:

Use the conversion factor: $1\text{ pound} \approx 0.4536\,\text{kg}$.

$$\text{Kilograms} = 50 \times 0.4536 = 22.68.$$

Answer: 50 pounds ≈ **22.68 kilograms**.

Example 3: Converting Gallons to Liters

A car's fuel tank holds 15 gallons. How many liters does it hold?

Solution:

Use the conversion factor: 1 gallon ≈ 3.785 liters.

$$\text{Liters} = 15 \times 3.785 = 56.775.$$

Answer: 15 gallons ≈ **56.78 liters**.

Example 4: Converting Minutes to Hours

How many hours are in 150 minutes?

Solution:

Use the conversion factor: 1 hour = 60 minutes.

$$\text{Hours} = \frac{150}{60} = 2.5.$$

Answer: 150 minutes = **2.5 hours**.

Example 5: Multi-Step Conversion

A truck drives 200 miles. Convert this distance to kilometers.

Solution:

Use the conversion factor: 1 mile ≈ 1.609 km.

$$\text{Kilometers} = 200 \times 1.609 = 321.8.$$

Answer: 200 miles ≈ **321.8 kilometers**.

Real-World Applications of Unit Conversions

1. **Travel**: Converting distances between miles and kilometers.
2. **Cooking**: Adjusting recipes with different volume or weight units.
3. **Health**: Understanding weight and height measurements in different systems.
4. **Science**: Converting units in experiments or data analysis.

Example 6:

You are baking a cake, and the recipe calls for 250 grams of flour. How many ounces is this?

Solution:

Use the conversion factor: 1 ounce ≈ 28.35 grams.

$$\text{Ounces} = \frac{250}{28.35} \approx 8.82.$$

Answer: 250 grams ≈ **8.82 ounces**.

Tips for Mastering Conversions

5. **Memorize Common Conversion Factors**: Focus on frequently used conversions like inches to feet, pounds to kilograms, and gallons to liters.
6. **Write Out Each Step**: Setting up the equation properly reduces errors.
7. **Use Estimation for Sanity Checks**: Ensure your answer makes sense. For example, converting 50 pounds to kilograms should give a value significantly less than 50.
8. **Practice Real-World Problems**: Incorporate conversions into everyday activities to reinforce your skills.

CHAPTER 16

ALGEBRA BASICS

16.1 Understanding Variables and Expressions

Algebra is a cornerstone of mathematics, and it plays a significant role on the GED Math test. Understanding variables and expressions is the foundation of algebraic reasoning. These concepts are crucial for solving equations, analyzing relationships, and interpreting real-world scenarios mathematically.

In this chapter, we'll explore the meaning of variables and expressions, how they're used, and how to manipulate them effectively. Practical examples will ensure clarity and prepare you for related questions on the exam.

What Are Variables?

A **variable** is a symbol, often a letter, that represents an unknown or changing value. Variables allow us to create general mathematical models for real-world situations.

Example 1:

The equation $x + 5 = 10$ uses the variable x to represent a value that makes the equation true. Here, $x = 5$.

What Are Expressions?

An **expression** is a mathematical phrase that combines numbers, variables, and operations (addition, subtraction, multiplication, and division). Unlike an equation, an expression does not include an equals sign.

Components of an Expression

- **Constants**: Numbers without variables (e.g., 3, -7).
- **Coefficients**: Numbers that multiply variables (e.g., in $5x$, the coefficient is 5).
- **Variables**: Letters representing unknown values (e.g., x, y).
- **Operators**: Mathematical symbols for operations (e.g., $+, -, \times, \div$).

Example 2:

The expression $3x + 7$ contains:

- The coefficient 3,
- The variable x,
- The constant 7,
- The addition operator.

Simplifying Expressions

Simplifying an expression means combining like terms or performing operations to write it in its simplest form.

Like Terms

Terms are "like" if they have the same variable raised to the same power. Constants are also considered like terms.

Example 3:

Simplify $2x + 3x - 7 + 4$.

1. Combine like terms involving x: $2x + 3x = 5x$.
2. Combine constants: $-7 + 4 = -3$.
3. **Simplified Expression**: $5x - 3$.

Evaluating Expressions

To evaluate an expression, substitute a specific value for the variable and perform the operations.

Example 4:

Evaluate $4x + 6$ when $x = 3$.

1. Substitute $x = 3$: $4(3) + 6$.
2. Perform operations: $12 + 6 = 18$.
3. **Answer**: 18.

Combining Variables and Constants

Expressions often involve multiple variables and constants. Simplify and evaluate these expressions step by step.

Example 5:

Simplify $2a + 4b - 3a + 7$.

1. Combine like terms: $2a - 3a = -a$.
2. Keep $4b$ unchanged since there are no like terms.
   Simplified Expression: $-a + 4b + 7$.

Distributive Property

The distributive property is a key concept in algebra that allows you to multiply a term outside parentheses by each term inside the parentheses.

Formula:

$$a(b + c) = ab + ac$$

Example 6:

Simplify $3(x + 5)$.

1. Distribute 3: $3(x) + 3(5) = 3x + 15$.
   Simplified Expression: $3x + 15$.

Example 7:

Simplify $4(2y - 3)$.

1. Distribute 4: $4(2y) - 4(3) = 8y - 12$.
   Simplified Expression: $8y - 12$.

Combining the Distributive Property and Like Terms

Sometimes, you'll need to simplify an expression by applying the distributive property first and then combining like terms.

Example 8:

Simplify $2(3x + 4) + 5x - 7$.

1. Apply the distributive property: $6x + 8 + 5x - 7$.
2. Combine like terms: $6x + 5x = 11x$ and $8 - 7 = 1$.
   Simplified Expression: $11x + 1$.

Writing Expressions for Real-World Problems

Many GED Math problems involve translating real-world scenarios into algebraic expressions.

Example 9:

A taxi company charges a base fee of $3plus2$ *per mile driven. Write an expression for the cost of a trip of* m *miles.*

Solution:

The cost consists of the base fee $(3)and2$ per mile ($2m$).

Expression: $3 + 2m$.

Practical Application: Writing and Evaluating Expressions

1. **Budgeting**:

   If you spend $15 on lunch daily, the monthly cost is $ 15d , where d $ is the number of days. For 30 days:

   $$15(30) = 450.$$

   Answer: $450.

2. **Distance Problems**:

   A car travels at 60 miles per hour. The distance covered in t hours is $60t$. For 3 hours:

   $$60(3) = 180.$$

   Answer: 180 miles.

16.2 Solving Linear Equations and Inequalities

Solving linear equations and inequalities is a fundamental skill in algebra and a key component of the GED Math test. These concepts involve finding the value(s) of a variable that make an equation or inequality true. Linear equations represent straight lines when graphed, while inequalities define ranges of solutions.

In this chapter, we'll cover how to solve linear equations, interpret inequalities, and apply these skills to real-world problems.

Linear Equations

A **linear equation** is an equation where the variable is raised to the power of 1. The general form of a linear equation is:

$$ax + b = c,$$

where a, b, and c are constants, and x is the variable.

Steps to Solve a Linear Equation

1. Simplify both sides of the equation by combining like terms.
2. Isolate the variable using inverse operations (addition/subtraction, multiplication/division).
3. Solve for the variable.
4. Check your solution by substituting it back into the original equation.

Examples of Linear Equations

Example 1: Solve $3x + 5 = 20$.

Solution:

1. Subtract 5 from both sides:

$$3x = 15.$$

2. Divide both sides by 3:

$$x = 5.$$

Answer: $x = 5$.

Example 2: Solve $4x - 7 = 2x + 9$.

Solution:

1. Subtract $2x$ from both sides:

$$2x - 7 = 9.$$

2. Add 7 to both sides:

$$2x = 16.$$

3. Divide by 2:

$$x = 8.$$

Answer: $x = 8$.

Equations with Fractions

Example 3: Solve $\frac{2x}{3} + 4 = 10$.

Solution:

1. Subtract 4 from both sides:

$$\frac{2x}{3} = 6.$$

2. Multiply both sides by 3:

$$2x = 18.$$

3. Divide by 2:

$$x = 9.$$

Answer: $x = 9$.

Linear Inequalities

A **linear inequality** is similar to a linear equation but uses inequality symbols ($<, \leq, >, \geq$) instead of an equals sign. The solution to an inequality is a range of values rather than a single value.

Key Rules for Solving Inequalities

1. Use the same steps as solving equations: isolate the variable and simplify.
2. When multiplying or dividing both sides by a **negative number**, reverse the inequality symbol.

Examples of Linear Inequalities

Example 4: Solve $3x + 5 > 20$.

Solution:

1. Subtract 5 from both sides:

$$3x > 15.$$

2. Divide by 3:

$$x > 5.$$

Answer: $x > 5$. The solution is all values of x greater than 5.

Example 5: Solve $-4x + 3 \leq 11$.

Solution:

1. Subtract 3 from both sides:

$$-4x \leq 8.$$

2. Divide by -4 and reverse the inequality:

$$x \geq -2.$$

Answer: $x \geq -2$. The solution is all values of x greater than or equal to -2.

Graphing Inequalities

Graphing inequalities helps visualize the range of solutions.

1. **One Variable**:

    - Plot the boundary point on a number line.
    - Use an open circle for < or > and a closed circle for ≤ or ≥.
    - Shade to the left or right to show the solution set.

Example: Graph $x > 3$.

- Place an open circle at 3.
- Shade all values to the right of 3.

2. **Two Variables**:

    - Graph the related equation as a boundary line.
    - Use a dashed line for < or > and a solid line for ≤ or ≥.
    - Shade above or below the line based on the inequality.

Real-World Applications of Linear Equations and Inequalities

Budgeting

Example 6:

You want to spend no more than $50 on groceries. Write and solve an inequality to determine how many $8 items you can buy.

Solution:

Let x represent the number of items.

$$8x \leq 50.$$

Divide by 8:

$$x \leq 6.25.$$

Since x must be a whole number, $x \leq 6$.

Answer: You can buy at most 6 items.

Travel

Example 7:

A car rental company charges $40 per day plus $0.15 per mile driven. If you have $100 to spend, how many miles can you drive in one day?

Solution:

Let x represent the number of miles.

$$40 + 0.15x \leq 100.$$

1. Subtract 40 from both sides:

$$0.15x \leq 60.$$

2. Divide by 0.15:

$$x \leq 400.$$

Answer: You can drive up to 400 miles.

16.3 Working with Quadratic Equations

Quadratic equations are an essential part of algebra and are characterized by a variable raised to the power of 2. They are widely used to model real-world situations, such as projectile motion, optimization problems, and more. On the GED Math test, you'll encounter questions that require solving quadratic equations, interpreting their solutions, and understanding their graphical representation.

This chapter will cover the basics of quadratic equations, methods for solving them, and practical examples to solidify your understanding.

What Is a Quadratic Equation?

A **quadratic equation** is any equation that can be written in the standard form:

$$ax^2 + bx + c = 0,$$

where:

- $a, b,$ and c are constants (with $a \neq 0$), and
- x is the variable.

Examples of Quadratic Equations

1. $x^2 + 5x + 6 = 0$
2. $2x^2 - 8x = 0$
3. $x^2 - 9 = 0$

Methods for Solving Quadratic Equations

1. Factoring

Factoring is the process of rewriting the quadratic equation as a product of two binomials.

Steps:

1. Write the equation in standard form: $ax^2 + bx + c = 0$.
2. Factor the quadratic expression into two binomials.
3. Set each factor equal to zero and solve for x.

Example 1: Solve $x^2 + 5x + 6 = 0$.

1. Factor: $(x + 2)(x + 3) = 0$.
2. Solve each factor:

$X + 2=0 \Rightarrow x = -2$, $x + 3 = 0 \Rightarrow x = -3$.

Answer: $x = -2$ and $x = -3$.

2. The Quadratic Formula

The quadratic formula is a universal method for solving any quadratic equation:

$$x = \frac{-b \pm \sqrt{b^2 - 4ac}}{2a}.$$

Steps:

1. Identify $a, b,$ and c from the equation $ax^2 + bx + c = 0$.
2. Substitute these values into the formula.
3. Simplify to find the solutions.

Example 2: Solve $2x^2 - 4x - 6 = 0$.

1. Identify coefficients: $a = 2, b = -4, c = -6$.
2. Substitute into the formula:

$$x = \frac{-(-4) \pm \sqrt{(-4)^2 - 4(2)(-6)}}{2(2)}.$$

3. Simplify:

$$x = \frac{4 \pm \sqrt{16+48}}{4} = \frac{4 \pm \sqrt{64}}{4}.$$

4. Solve:

$$x = \frac{4+8}{4} = 3, \quad x = \frac{4-8}{4} = -1.$$

Answer: $x = 3$ and $x = -1$.

3. Completing the Square

Completing the square involves rewriting the quadratic equation so that one side is a perfect square trinomial.

Steps:

1. Rewrite the equation in the form $ax^2 + bx = -c$.
2. Divide through by a (if $a \neq 1$).
3. Add $\left(\frac{b}{2}\right)^2$ to both sides to complete the square.
4. Solve for x.

Example 3: Solve $x^2 + 6x - 7 = 0$.

1. Move the constant: $x^2 + 6x = 7$.
2. Add $\left(\frac{6}{2}\right)^2 = 9$ to both sides:

$$x^2 + 6x + 9 = 16.$$

3. Factor: $(x+3)^2 = 16$.
4. Solve:

X + 3 = ± 4 ⟹ x = 1 or x = −7.

Answer: $x = 1$ and $x = -7$.

4. Graphical Method

The solutions of a quadratic equation correspond to the x-intercepts (roots) of its graph. These intercepts are the points where the parabola crosses the x-axis.

Steps:

1. Write the equation in standard form.
2. Graph the parabola using a table of values or graphing software.
3. Identify the x-intercepts.

Example 4: Graph $y = x^2 - 4$.

The parabola opens upwards with intercepts at $x = -2$ and $x = 2$.

Key Features of Quadratic Graphs

Quadratic equations produce **parabolas** when graphed. Important features include:

1. **Vertex**: The highest or lowest point of the parabola.
2. **Axis of Symmetry**: A vertical line passing through the vertex.
   - Formula: $x = \frac{-b}{2a}$.
3. **Direction**: The parabola opens upward if $a > 0$ and downward if $a < 0$.

Real-World Applications of Quadratic Equations

Example 5: Projectile Motion

A ball is thrown upward, and its height h in feet after t seconds is given by:

$$h = -16t^2 + 32t + 48.$$

Find the time it takes for the ball to hit the ground.

Solution:

1. Set $h = 0$:

$$-16t^2 + 32t + 48 = 0.$$

2. Divide by -16:

$$t^2 - 2t - 3 = 0.$$

3. Factor:

$$(t - 3)(t + 1) = 0.$$

4. Solve:

$$t = 3 \text{ or } t = -1.$$

Since time cannot be negative, $t = 3$.

Answer: The ball hits the ground after **3 seconds**.

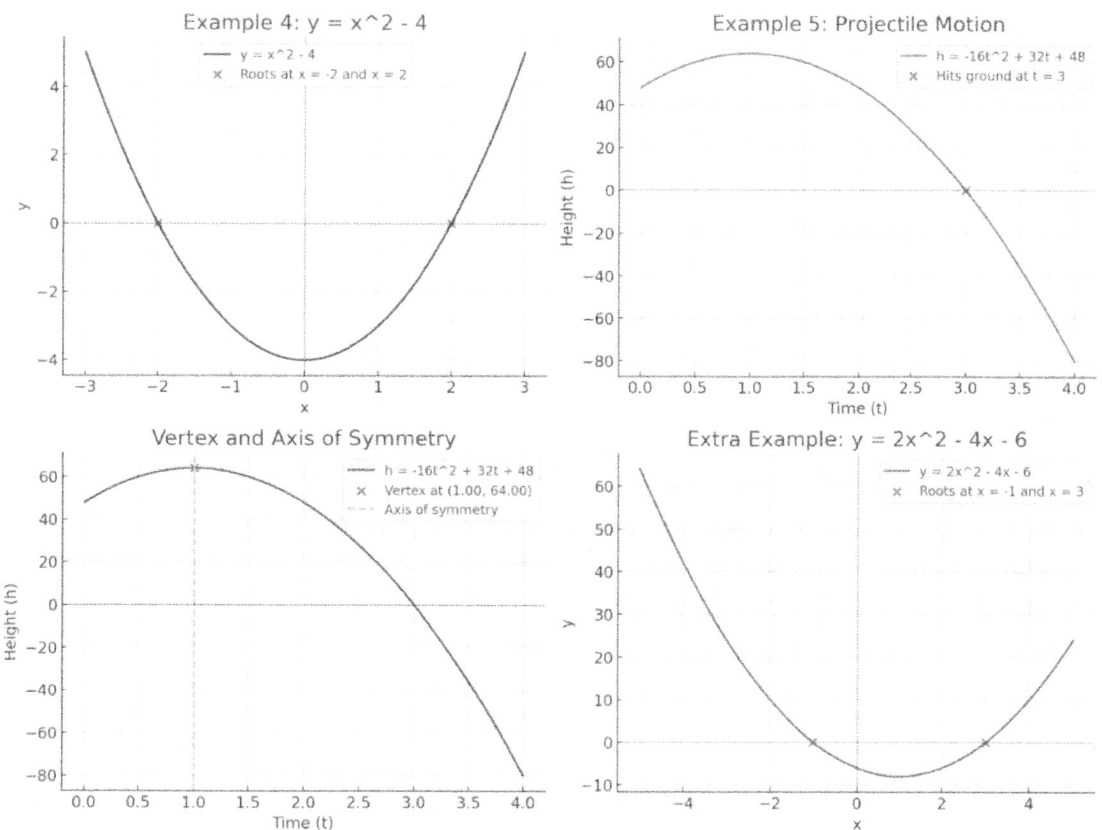

16.4 Graphing Linear Equations and Functions

Graphing linear equations and functions is a crucial skill in algebra and an essential part of the GED Math test. Linear equations represent straight lines on a coordinate plane and are commonly used to model real-world relationships. In this chapter, we'll explore the basics of graphing, step-by-step techniques, and practical examples to ensure a thorough understanding.

What Is a Linear Equation?

A **linear equation** is any equation that can be written in the form:

$$y = mx + b,$$

where:

- m is the **slope**, which represents the steepness of the line,
- b is the **y-intercept**, which is the point where the line crosses the y-axis,
- x and y are variables.

Examples of Linear Equations

1. $y = 2x + 3$
2. $y = -x + 5$
3. $y = \frac{1}{2}x - 4$

Key Features of Linear Equations

1. **Slope** (m):
    - Measures the rate of change.
    - Calculated as:

$$m = \frac{\text{Change in } y}{\text{Change in } x} = \frac{y_2 - y_1}{x_2 - x_1}.$$

    - Positive slope: Line rises from left to right.
    - Negative slope: Line falls from left to right.
    - Zero slope: Horizontal line.
2. **Y-Intercept** (b):
    - The point where the line crosses the y-axis ($x = 0$).
3. **X-Intercept**:
    - The point where the line crosses the x-axis ($y = 0$).

Steps for Graphing Linear Equations

- **Identify the Slope and Y-Intercept**: Start with the equation in slope-intercept form ($y = mx + b$).
- **Plot the Y-Intercept**: Mark the point $(0, b)$ on the graph.
- **Use the Slope**: From the y-intercept, apply the slope ($rise/run$) to find another point.
- **Draw the Line**: Connect the points with a straight line.

Graphing Examples

Example 1: Graph $y = 2x + 1$

1. Identify the slope ($m = 2$) and y-intercept ($b = 1$).
2. Plot the y-intercept $(0,1)$.
3. Use the slope $m = \frac{2}{1}$ (rise 2, run 1) to find another point $(1,3)$.
4. Draw the line through these points.

Example 2: Graph $y = -\frac{1}{2}x + 4$

1. Identify the slope ($m = -\frac{1}{2}$) and y-intercept ($b = 4$).
2. Plot the y-intercept (0,4).
3. Use the slope $m = -\frac{1}{2}$ (fall 1, run 2) to find another point (2,3).
4. Draw the line through these points.

Using Tables to Graph

Another way to graph is by creating a table of values. Choose several x-values, substitute them into the equation, and calculate the corresponding y-values.

Example 3: Graph $y = x - 2$ Using a Table

x	y
-2	-4
0	-2
2	0

Plot the points $(-2, -4)$, $(0, -2)$, and (2,0) on the graph, and connect them to form the line.

Parallel and Perpendicular Lines

1. **Parallel Lines**:
   - Have the same slope (m).
   - Example: $y = 2x + 3$ and $y = 2x - 4$.
2. **Perpendicular Lines**:
   - Slopes are negative reciprocals ($m_1 \times m_2 = -1$).
   - Example: $y = 2x + 1$ and $y = -\frac{1}{2}x + 3$.

Graphs

Graph 1: $y = 2x + 1$ and $y = -\frac{1}{2}x + 4$

These lines demonstrate how to plot using slope and y-intercept.

Graph 2: $y = x - 2$ Using a Table

This graph shows the points calculated in the table, connected by a straight line.

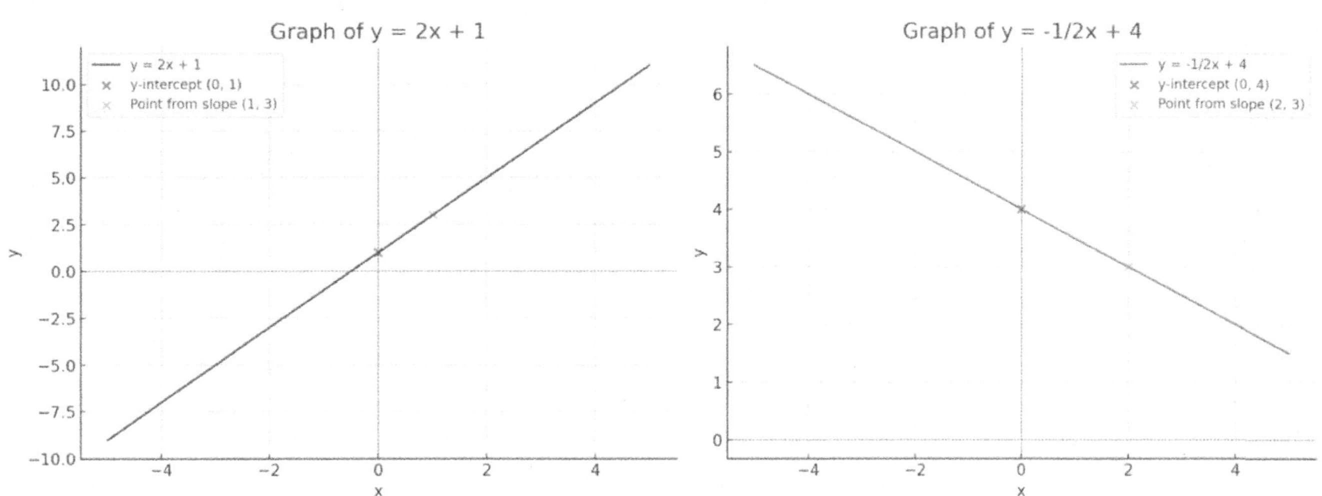

Graph of $y = 2x + 1$:

- The blue line represents the equation $y = 2x + 1$.
- The y-intercept is $(0,1)$, marked in red.
- Another point $(1,3)$, calculated using the slope, is marked in orange.

Graph of $y = -\frac{1}{2}x + 4$:

- The green line represents the equation $y = -\frac{1}{2}x + 4$.
- The y-intercept is $(0,4)$, marked in red.
- Another point $(2,3)$, calculated using the slope, is marked in orange.

CHAPTER 17

GEOMETRY AND MEASUREMENT

17.1 Properties of Shapes and Angles

Geometry is a key area of the GED Math test, focusing on understanding the properties of shapes and the relationships between angles. This section lays the groundwork for solving problems related to polygons, circles, and three-dimensional shapes. Mastering these concepts will help you analyze and interpret geometric scenarios, both in real-world applications and on the test.

Understanding Basic Geometric Shapes

Shapes are classified based on the number of sides, angles, and overall structure. The most common categories include polygons, circles, and three-dimensional figures.

Polygons

Polygons are closed, two-dimensional shapes with straight sides. Key polygons include triangles, quadrilaterals, pentagons, hexagons, and octagons.

- **Triangle**: A three-sided polygon with three angles. The sum of the angles is always 180°.
    - Types: Equilateral, isosceles, scalene.
    - Special cases: Right triangle (one 90° angle).
- **Quadrilateral**: A four-sided polygon with angles summing to 360°.
    - Types: Rectangle, square, parallelogram, trapezoid, rhombus.
- **Pentagon, Hexagon, Octagon**: These polygons have 5, 6, and 8 sides, respectively. The formula for the sum of interior angles is:

  $$\text{Sum of Interior Angles} = (n-2)\times 180,$$

  where n is the number of sides.

Circles

A circle is a two-dimensional shape defined by all points equidistant from a central point (the center).

- Key terms: Radius (distance from center to edge), diameter (distance across the circle, passing through the center), and circumference (distance around the circle).
- Important relationships:

  $$\text{Circumference} = 2\pi r, \quad \text{Area} = \pi r^2,$$

  where r is the radius.

Angles and Their Properties

Angles are formed when two rays share a common endpoint (vertex). They are measured in degrees and are categorized based on their size.

Types of Angles

- **Acute Angle**: Less than 90°.
- **Right Angle**: Exactly 90°.
- **Obtuse Angle**: Greater than 90° but less than 180°.
- **Straight Angle**: Exactly 180°.

Angle Relationships

- **Complementary Angles**: Two angles whose sum is $90°$.
- *Example*: If one angle is $40°$, the other is $50°$.
- **Supplementary Angles**: Two angles whose sum is $180°$.
- *Example*: If one angle is $110°$, the other is $70°$.
- **Vertical Angles**: Opposite angles formed by two intersecting lines. Vertical angles are always equal.
- **Adjacent Angles**: Angles that share a common side and vertex.

Special Angle Properties in Polygons

Each polygon has specific angle properties that help solve problems involving missing angles or verifying shapes.

- **Interior Angles**: The sum of the interior angles of a polygon is given by the formula:

  $$\text{Sum of Interior Angles} = (n - 2) \times 180,$$

  where n is the number of sides.

  Example: For a hexagon ($n = 6$), the sum is $(6 - 2) \times 180 = 720°$.

- **Exterior Angles**: The sum of the exterior angles of any polygon is always $360°$, regardless of the number of sides.

Real-World Applications

1. **Architecture**: Calculating the angles in roof designs, window frames, or floor layouts.
   Example: Determining the angles for a triangular gable roof where one angle is $90°$ and another is $45°$. The third angle can be calculated as $180° - (90° + 45°) = 45°$.
2. **Construction**: Using angle properties to measure and cut materials for precise fits.
   Example: Ensuring a corner is a perfect $90°$ angle when laying tile.
3. **Engineering**: Solving for angles in gears or bridges, ensuring stability and function.

Sample Problem 1: Finding a Missing Angle

Question: A quadrilateral has angles measuring $90°, 110°$, and $80°$. Find the missing angle.

Solution:

The sum of the angles in a quadrilateral is $360°$. Subtract the known angles:

$$360° - (90° + 110° + 80°) = 80°.$$

Answer: The missing angle is $80°$.

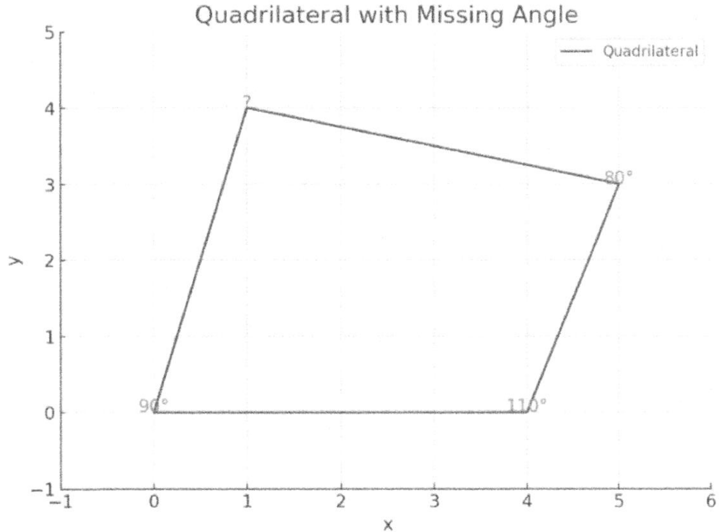

Sample Problem 2: Verifying a Polygon

Question: A pentagon has four angles measuring $100°, 120°, 90°$, and $85°$. What is the fifth angle?

Solution:

The sum of interior angles of a pentagon is $(5-2) \times 180 = 540°$. Subtract the known angles:

$$540° - (100° + 120° + 90° + 85°) = 145°.$$

Answer: The fifth angle is $145°$.

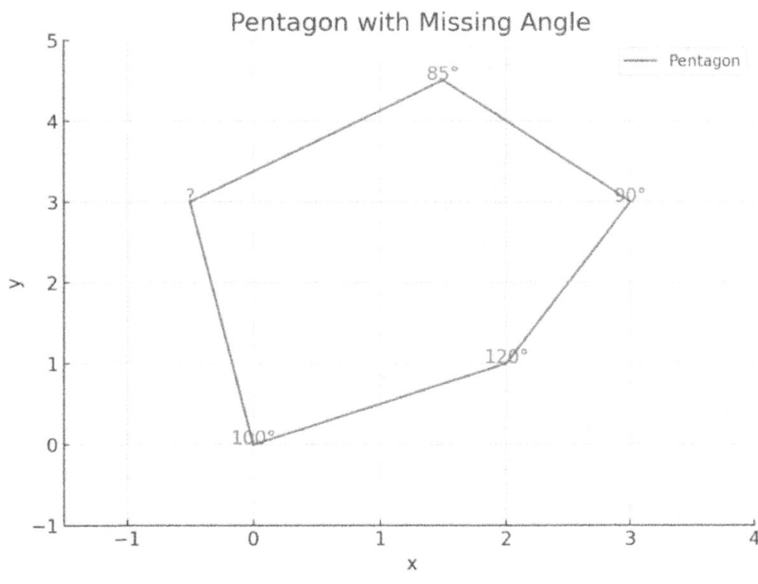

17.2 Perimeter, Area, and Volume Calculations

Understanding perimeter, area, and volume is fundamental for solving geometry problems on the GED Math test. These measurements are used to describe the boundaries, surface coverage, and space occupied by two-dimensional and three-dimensional shapes, respectively. This chapter provides formulas, practical examples, and visual representations to ensure clarity.

Perimeter

The **perimeter** of a shape is the total distance around its boundary. It applies to all two-dimensional shapes and is calculated by summing the lengths of all sides.

Formulas for Common Shapes

- **Rectangle**:

$$P = 2l + 2w,$$

 where l is the length and w is the width.

- **Square**:

$$P = 4s,$$

 where s is the side length.

- **Triangle**:

$$P = a + b + c,$$

 where $a, b,$ and c are the side lengths.

- **Circle (Circumference)**:

$$C = 2\pi r,$$

 where r is the radius.

Example 1: Find the Perimeter of a Rectangle

A rectangular garden measures 8 feet by 6 feet. What is its perimeter?

Solution:

$$P = 2(8) + 2(6) = 16 + 12 = 28 \text{ feet.}$$

Answer: 28 feet.

Area

The **area** measures the surface covered by a two-dimensional shape.

Formulas for Common Shapes

- **Rectangle**:

$$A = l \times w.$$

- **Square**:

$$A = s^2.$$

- **Triangle**:

$$A = \frac{1}{2} \times b \times h,$$

 where b is the base and h is the height.

- **Circle**:

$$A = \pi r^2.$$

Example 2: Find the Area of a Triangle

A triangle has a base of 10 cm and a height of 5 cm. What is its area?

Solution:

$$A = \frac{1}{2} \times 10 \times 5 = 25\,\text{cm}^2.$$

Answer: $25\,\text{cm}^2$.

Volume

The **volume** measures the space occupied by a three-dimensional object.

Formulas for Common Shapes

- **Rectangular Prism (Box)**:

$$V = l \times w \times h,$$

where $l, w,$ and h are the length, width, and height.

- **Cube**:

$$V = s^3,$$

where s is the side length.

- **Cylinder**:

$$V = \pi r^2 h,$$

where r is the radius of the base, and h is the height.

- **Sphere**:

$$V = \frac{4}{3}\pi r^3.$$

Example 3: Find the Volume of a Cylinder

A cylinder has a radius of 4 cm and a height of 10 cm. What is its volume?

Solution:

$$V = \pi r^2 h = \pi(4^2)(10) = \pi(16)(10) = 160\pi\,\text{cm}^3.$$

Using $\pi \approx 3.14$:

$$V \approx 160 \times 3.14 = 502.4\,\text{cm}^3.$$

Answer: $502.4\,\text{cm}^3$.

Real-World Applications

1. **Perimeter**: Fencing a yard or framing a picture.
   Example: To surround a rectangular field measuring 20m by 15m, calculate:

$$P = 2(20) + 2(15) = 70\,\text{meters}.$$

2. **Area**: Determining paint coverage or floor space.
   Example: To carpet a room that is 12 feet long and 10 feet wide, calculate:

$$A = 12 \times 10 = 120\,\text{square feet}.$$

3. **Volume**: Filling a tank or designing a container.
   Example: A box measuring 4 feet by 3 feet by 2 feet has a volume:

$$V = 4 \times 3 \times 2 = 24\,\text{cubic feet}.$$

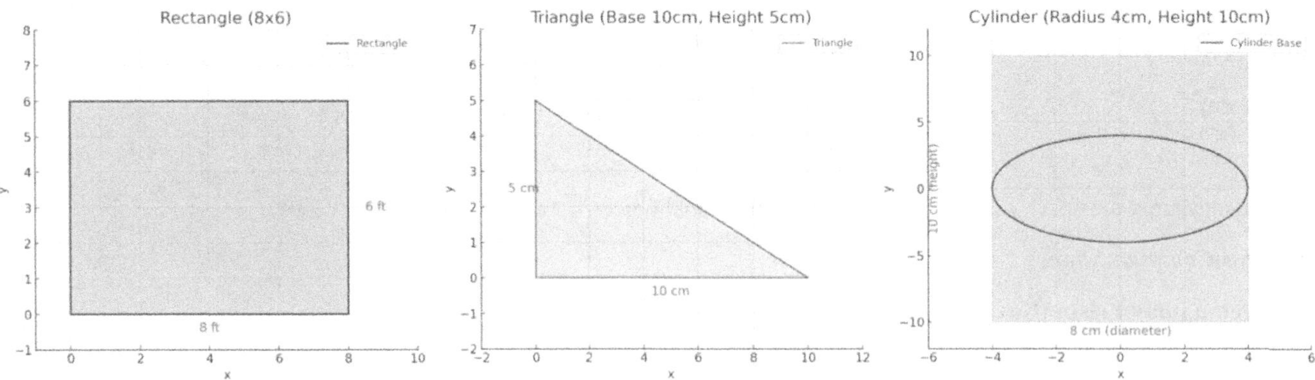

17.3 Applying the Pythagorean Theorem

The **Pythagorean Theorem** is one of the most important concepts in geometry, providing a way to solve problems involving right triangles. This theorem states that in any right triangle, the square of the length of the hypotenuse (the side opposite the right angle) is equal to the sum of the squares of the lengths of the other two sides.

The theorem is expressed mathematically as:

$$a^2 + b^2 = c^2,$$

where:

- a and b are the lengths of the two legs of the triangle,
- c is the length of the hypotenuse.

In this chapter, we'll explore the applications of the Pythagorean Theorem, solve practical problems, and explain its real-world uses.

Understanding the Pythagorean Theorem

The Pythagorean Theorem only applies to **right triangles**. A right triangle has one angle equal to 90°, and the hypotenuse is always the longest side. The two shorter sides are called the legs.

Key Points

- If you know the lengths of two sides, you can calculate the third.
- The theorem can be used to determine whether a triangle is a right triangle by checking if $a^2 + b^2 = c^2$.

How to Use the Pythagorean Theorem

1. **Identify the Sides**: Determine which side is the hypotenuse (c) and which are the legs (a and b).
2. **Apply the Formula**: Plug the known values into $a^2 + b^2 = c^2$.
3. **Solve for the Unknown**: Use algebraic techniques to find the missing side.
4. **Check Your Work**: Verify the solution by substituting it back into the formula.

Examples

Example 1: Finding the Hypotenuse

A right triangle has legs measuring 3 units and 4 units. Find the hypotenuse.

Solution:

1. Identify the sides: $a = 3, b = 4, c = ?$.
2. Apply the formula:

$$3^2 + 4^2 = c^2.$$

Simplify:

$9 + 16 = c^2 \Rightarrow c^2 = 25.$

1. Take the square root:

$$c = \sqrt{25} = 5.$$

Answer: The hypotenuse is 5 units.

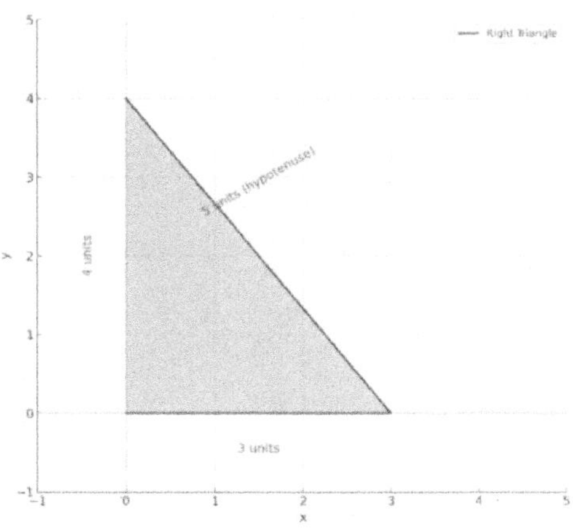

Example 2: Finding a Leg

A right triangle has a hypotenuse of 13 units and one leg of 5 units. Find the other leg.

Solution:

1. Identify the sides: $a = 5, b = ?, c = 13.$
2. Apply the formula:

$$5^2 + b^2 = 13^2.$$

Simplify:

$25 + b^2 = 169 \Rightarrow b^2 = 169 - 25 = 144$

1. Take the square root:

$$b = \sqrt{144} = 12.$$

Answer: The other leg is 12 units.

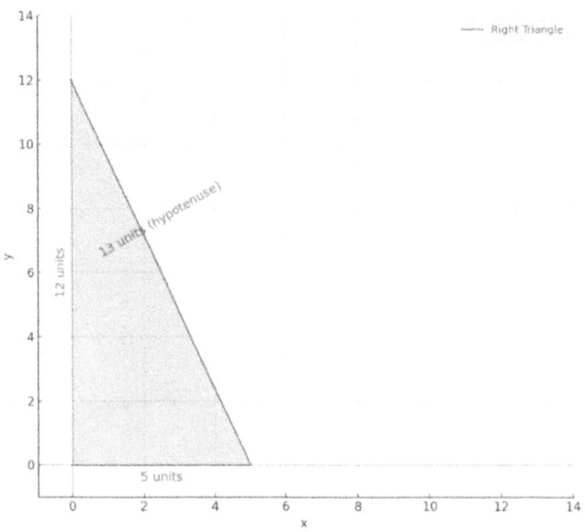

Example 3: Verifying a Right Triangle

Determine whether a triangle with sides 6, 8, and 10 is a right triangle.

Solution:

1. Identify the sides: $a = 6, b = 8, c = 10$.
2. Check if $a^2 + b^2 = c^2$:

$$6^2 + 8^2 = 10^2.$$

   Simplify:

36 + 64 = 100 ⟹ 100 = 100.

Answer: Yes, the triangle is a right triangle.

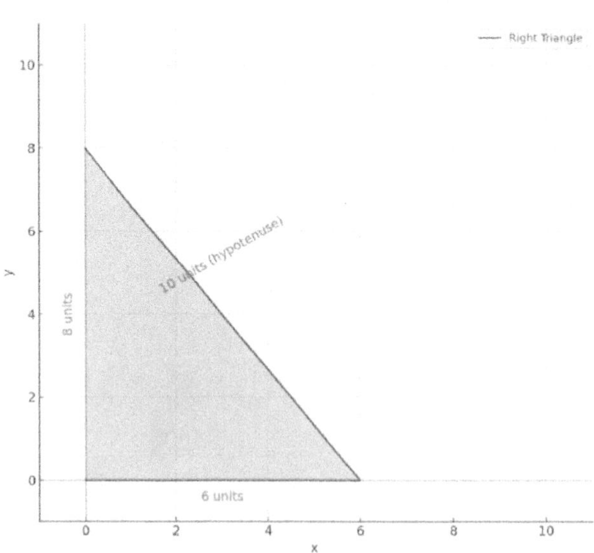

Real-World Applications

1. **Construction**: Builders use the Pythagorean Theorem to create perfectly square corners for walls and foundations.

Example: To ensure a corner is square, measure 3 feet on one side, 4 feet on the other, and check if the diagonal measures 5 feet.

2. **Navigation**: Calculate the shortest distance between two points.
Example: If a boat travels 8 km north and then 15 km east, the straight-line distance back to the starting point is:

$$\sqrt{8^2 + 15^2} = \sqrt{64 + 225} = \sqrt{289} = 17\,\text{km}.$$

3. **Design and Art**: Determine the dimensions of diagonal elements in frames, designs, or architectural features.

17.4 Understanding Coordinate Geometry

Coordinate geometry, also known as analytic geometry, combines algebra and geometry to study shapes and their properties using a coordinate system. This is an essential concept in the GED Math test, as it forms the basis for solving problems involving points, lines, distances, and slopes on the Cartesian plane.

In this chapter, we will explore the fundamentals of coordinate geometry, including the coordinate plane, formulas for distance and midpoint, slopes of lines, and equations of lines. We'll also include examples and visual aids to clarify these concepts.

The Coordinate Plane

The coordinate plane is a two-dimensional grid formed by two perpendicular number lines: the horizontal x-axis and the vertical y-axis. These axes intersect at the **origin** $(0,0)$.

- **Quadrants**: The plane is divided into four quadrants:
    a. Quadrant I $(x > 0, y > 0)$
    b. Quadrant II $(x < 0, y > 0)$
    c. Quadrant III $(x < 0, y < 0)$
    d. Quadrant IV $(x > 0, y < 0)$
- **Points**: Each point on the plane is represented as an ordered pair (x, y), where x is the horizontal position and y is the vertical position.

Distance Formula

The **distance formula** calculates the straight-line distance between two points (x_1, y_1) and (x_2, y_2):

$$d = \sqrt{(x_2 - x_1)^2 + (y_2 - y_1)^2}.$$

Example 1: Finding the Distance Between Two Points

Find the distance between the points $(1,2)$ and $(4,6)$.

Solution:

$$d = \sqrt{(4-1)^2 + (6-2)^2} = \sqrt{3^2 + 4^2} = \sqrt{9 + 16} = \sqrt{25} = 5.$$

Answer: The distance is 5 units.

Example 1: Distance Between Two Points

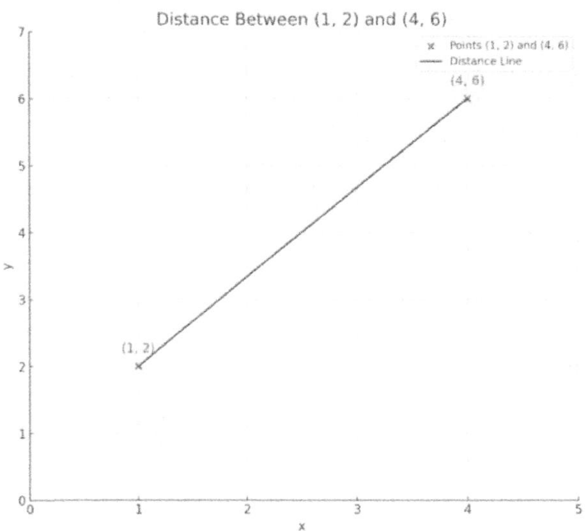

Midpoint Formula

The **midpoint formula** calculates the point exactly halfway between two points (x_1, y_1) and (x_2, y_2):

$$M = \left(\frac{x_1 + x_2}{2}, \frac{y_1 + y_2}{2}\right).$$

Example 2: Finding the Midpoint Between Two Points

Find the midpoint between (2,4) and (6,8).

Solution:

$$M = \left(\frac{2+6}{2}, \frac{4+8}{2}\right) = (4,6).$$

Answer: The midpoint is (4,6).

Example 2: Midpoint Between Two Points

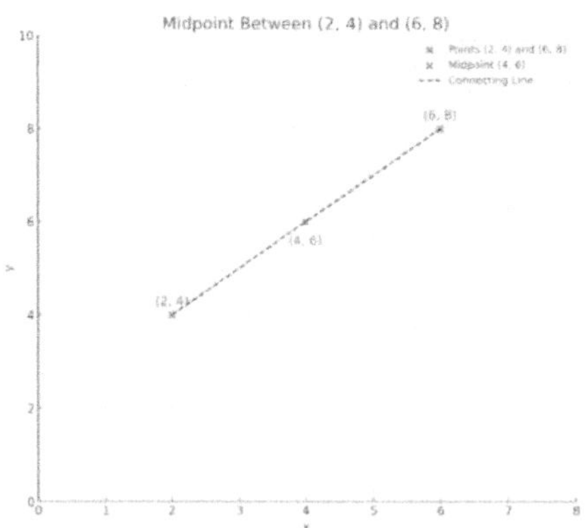

Slope of a Line

The **slope** of a line measures its steepness and is defined as the ratio of the change in y (rise) to the change in x (run) between two points on the line:

$$m = \frac{y_2 - y_1}{x_2 - x_1}.$$

Example 3: Finding the Slope of a Line

Find the slope of the line passing through $(-1,2)$ and $(3,6)$.

Solution:

$$m = \frac{6-2}{3-(-1)} = \frac{4}{4} = 1.$$

Answer: The slope is 1.

Example 3: Slope of the Line

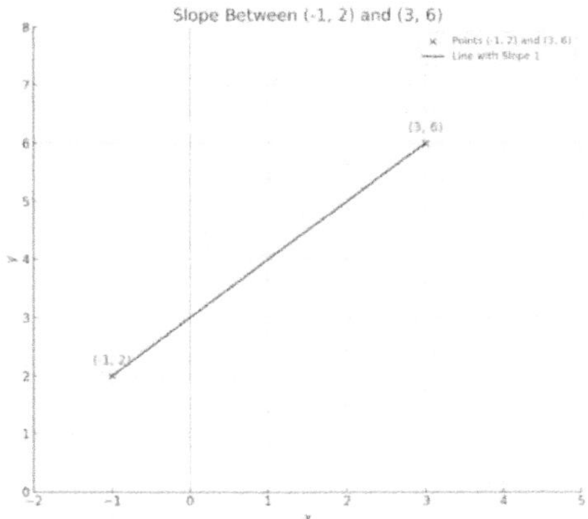

Equations of Lines

There are several forms of equations to represent lines:

1. **Slope-Intercept Form**:

$$y = mx + b,$$

   where m is the slope and b is the y-intercept.

2. **Point-Slope Form**:

$$y - y_1 = m(x - x_1),$$

   where m is the slope and (x_1, y_1) is a point on the line.

3. **Standard Form**:

$$Ax + By = C,$$

   where $A, B,$ and C are integers.

Example 4: Writing the Equation of a Line

Write the equation of the line passing through $(1,3)$ with a slope of 2.

Solution:

Using slope-intercept form:

$$y = mx + b.$$

Substitute $m = 2$ and $(1,3)$:

$3 = 2\,(1) + b \Rightarrow b = 1$

The equation is:

$$y = 2x + 1.$$

Answer: $y = 2x + 1$.

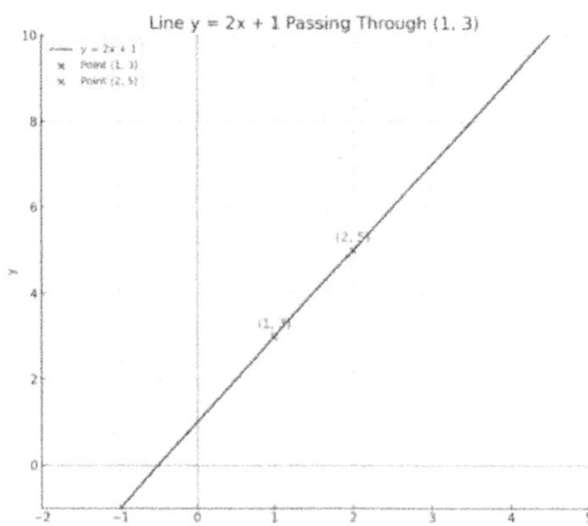
Example 4: Line Equation and Slope Representation
Line y = 2x + 1 Passing Through (1, 3)
y = 2x + 1
Point (1, 3)
Point (2, 5)
(2, 5)
(1, 3)
10
8
6
4
2
0
-2
-1
0
1
2
3
4
5
x
y

CHAPTER 18

DATA ANALYSIS AND STATISTICS

18.1 Interpreting Graphs, Charts, and Tables

Interpreting data presented in graphs, charts, and tables is an essential skill tested on the GED Math section. These visual tools provide a way to summarize, analyze, and communicate information effectively. To succeed, students must be able to read and extract relevant data, identify patterns, and make logical conclusions.

In this chapter, we will cover the main types of graphs, charts, and tables commonly encountered on the exam, explain how to interpret them, and include examples with visual aids to enhance understanding.

Common Types of Graphs and Charts

1. Bar Graphs

Bar graphs display data using rectangular bars of varying lengths. They are used to compare quantities across different categories.

- **Key Features**:
  - The x-axis represents categories.
  - The y-axis represents numerical values.
  - Bars can be vertical or horizontal.

Example: A bar graph comparing the number of books read by students in four months.

Month	Books Read
January	8
February	12
March	10
April	15

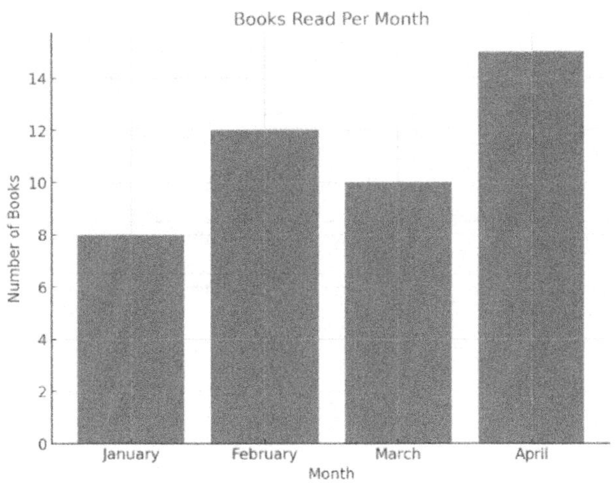

2. Line Graphs

Line graphs show trends or changes over time. Points are plotted and connected by lines to illustrate the movement of data.

- **Key Features**:

- The x-axis represents time or a sequence.
- The y-axis represents values.

Example: A line graph showing a student's monthly test scores.

Month	Test Score
January	80
February	85
March	90
April	88

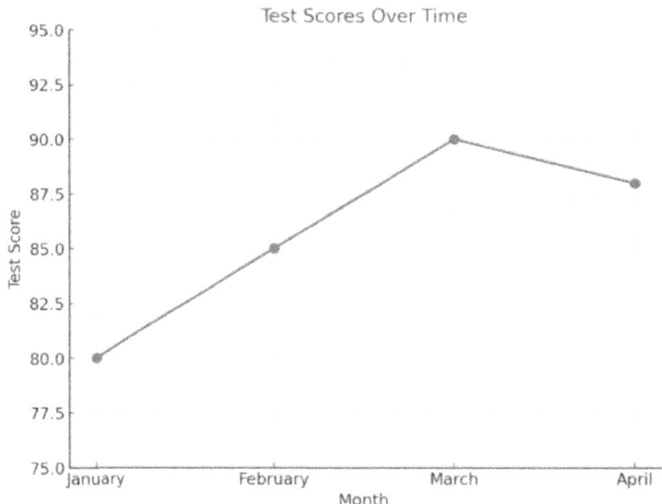

3. Pie Charts

Pie charts represent proportions as slices of a circular "pie." Each slice corresponds to a percentage of the whole.

Example: A pie chart showing the percentage of time a student spends on activities in a day.

Activity	Percentage
Studying	40%
Sleeping	35%
Recreation	15%
Meals	10%

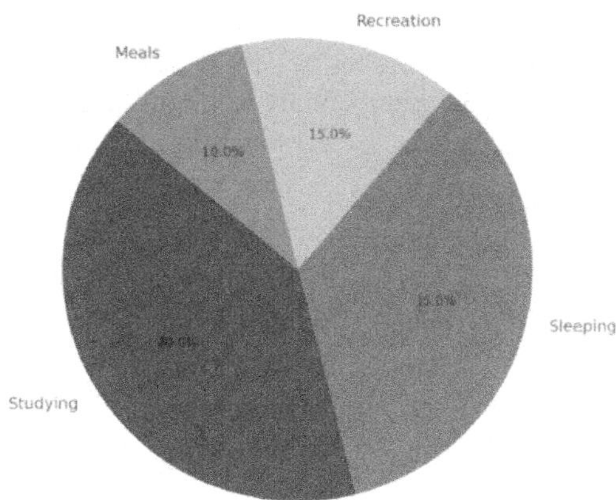

4. Tables

Tables organize data into rows and columns, making it easier to read and interpret numerical information. Tables are often used to display large datasets.

Example: A table showing sales for a product over a year.

Month	**Sales ($)**
January	2,000
February	1,800
March	2,500

18.2 Calculating Mean, Median, Mode, and Range

Understanding how to calculate and interpret **mean**, **median**, **mode**, and **range** is essential for the GED Math test. These are fundamental statistical concepts used to summarize and analyze data. This chapter explains each concept, provides formulas, and includes practical examples to ensure mastery.

Mean (Average)

The **mean** is the sum of all values in a dataset divided by the number of values. It provides a central value that represents the dataset.

Formula:

$$\text{Mean} = \frac{\text{Sum of all values}}{\text{Number of values}}.$$

Example 1: Calculating the Mean

Find the mean of the dataset: $5, 8, 12, 10, 15$.

Solution:

1. Add all the values:

$$5 + 8 + 12 + 10 + 15 = 50.$$

2. Divide by the number of values:

$$\text{Mean} = \frac{50}{5} = 10.$$

Answer: The mean is 10.

Median

The **median** is the middle value in a dataset when the numbers are arranged in order. If there is an even number of values, the median is the average of the two middle numbers.

Steps to Find the Median:

1. Arrange the data in ascending order.
2. Identify the middle value (or average the two middle values if the dataset size is even).

Example 2: Finding the Median

Find the median of the dataset: 7,3,9,1,5.

Solution:

1. Arrange the values in order: 1,3,5,7,9.
2. Identify the middle value: 5.
   Answer: The median is 5.

Mode

The **mode** is the value that appears most frequently in a dataset. A dataset may have one mode, multiple modes, or no mode at all.

Example 3: Finding the Mode

Find the mode of the dataset: 4,6,6,8,9,6,4.

Solution:

1. Count the frequency of each value:
   - 4: appears 2 times.
   - 6: appears 3 times.
   - 8,9: each appear 1 time.
2. Identify the value with the highest frequency: 6.
   Answer: The mode is 6.

Range

The **range** is the difference between the highest and lowest values in a dataset. It measures the spread of the data.

Formula:

$$\text{Range} = \text{Maximum value} - \text{Minimum value}.$$

Example 4: Calculating the Range

Find the range of the dataset: 12,18,5,7,25.

Solution:

1. Identify the maximum value: 25.
2. Identify the minimum value: 5.
3. Subtract the minimum from the maximum:

$$25 - 5 = 20.$$

Answer: The range is 20.

Practical Application

1. **Mean**: Used to find the average of daily expenses or test scores.

2. **Median**: Helpful in understanding the middle value in salary distributions to avoid the impact of extreme outliers.
3. **Mode**: Useful in identifying popular choices, such as the most common shoe size in a store.
4. **Range**: Important in analyzing variability, such as temperature changes over a week.

Graphical Representations

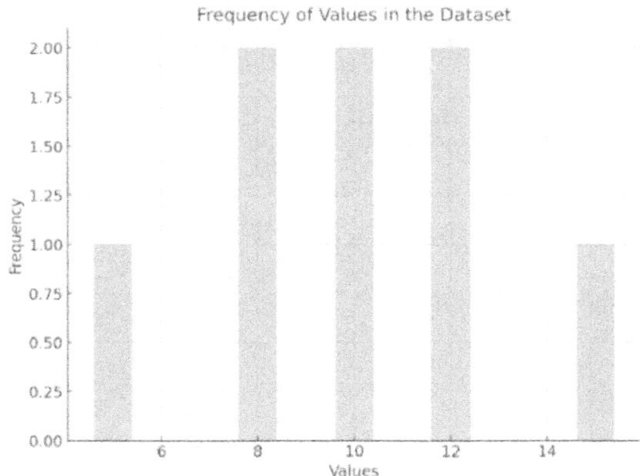

Dataset Representation: Mean, Median, and Range

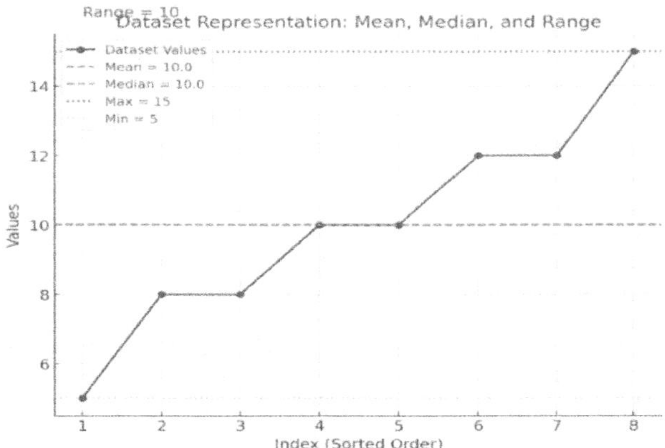

18.3 Understanding Probability and Its Applications

Probability is the measure of how likely an event is to occur. It is a fundamental concept in statistics, often used to predict outcomes, assess risks, and make informed decisions in various real-world scenarios. In the GED Math test, understanding probability involves calculating simple probabilities, working with compound events, and interpreting related problems.

This chapter will explain the basics of probability, explore its formulas, provide practical examples, and highlight real-world applications.

What is Probability?

Probability is expressed as a ratio, fraction, or percentage that represents the likelihood of an event happening. It is calculated using the formula:

$$P(\text{Event}) = \frac{\text{Number of Favorable Outcomes}}{\text{Total Number of Outcomes}}.$$

Key Properties of Probability:

- **Range**: Probability values range from 0 to 1.
  - $P = 0$: The event is impossible.
  - $P = 1$: The event is certain.
- **Complementary Probability**: The probability of an event not occurring is:

$$P(\text{Not Event}) = 1 - P(\text{Event}).$$

Types of Events

1. **Simple Events**: Involve a single outcome or scenario.
    a. Example: Rolling a die and getting a 4.
2. **Compound Events**: Involve two or more outcomes combined.
    a. Example: Drawing a red card and a face card from a deck of cards.
3. **Independent Events**: The outcome of one event does not affect the other.
    a. Example: Tossing a coin and rolling a die.
4. **Dependent Events**: The outcome of one event affects the other.
    a. Example: Drawing two cards without replacement.

How to Calculate Probability

Simple Probability

Example 1: What is the probability of rolling a 3 on a six-sided die?

Solution:

1. Total number of outcomes: 6 (faces of the die).
2. Favorable outcome: 1 (rolling a 3).

$$P(\text{Rolling a 3}) = \frac{1}{6}.$$

Answer: $\frac{1}{6}$ or approximately 0.167.

Compound Probability

Example 2: What is the probability of flipping a coin and getting heads, and then rolling a die and getting a 5?

Solution:

1. Probability of heads: $P(\text{Heads}) = \frac{1}{2}$.
2. Probability of rolling a 5: $P(5) = \frac{1}{6}$.
3. Multiply probabilities (independent events):

$$P(\text{Both}) = P(\text{Heads}) \times P(5) = \frac{1}{2} \times \frac{1}{6} = \frac{1}{12}.$$

Answer: $\frac{1}{12}$ or approximately 0.083.

Probability with Percentages

Example 3*: A survey shows that 30% of people prefer chocolate ice cream. If you randomly select one person, what is the probability they prefer chocolate ice cream?*

Solution:
Probability is given directly as 30%, or 0.3.

Answer: 0.3.

Real-World Applications

1. **Weather Forecasting**:
    a. Probability is used to predict the likelihood of rain, snow, or other weather conditions. *Example*: A 70% chance of rain means rain is likely.
2. **Risk Assessment**:
    a. Businesses assess probabilities to make decisions, such as determining the risk of investing in a new product.

3. **Games and Gambling**:
    a. Probability is key in calculating odds for games of chance, like rolling dice, drawing cards, or spinning a wheel.
4. **Medical Studies**:
    a. Probability helps researchers determine the effectiveness of treatments or the likelihood of side effects.

18.4 Working with Statistical Data in Real-Life Scenarios

Statistics play a vital role in understanding and interpreting the world around us. From analyzing trends in business and healthcare to evaluating personal finances or understanding sports performance, working with statistical data is a practical skill with broad applications. In this chapter, we will explore how to analyze and interpret statistical data in real-world scenarios, focusing on key techniques like identifying patterns, understanding variability, and drawing conclusions from data.

Understanding Real-Life Statistical Data

Statistical data is often presented in tables, charts, or graphs to summarize and simplify complex information. In real-world scenarios, the following types of data analysis are commonly used:

1. **Descriptive Statistics**: Summarizes data using measures like mean, median, mode, range, and standard deviation.
    a. Example: Determining the average monthly sales for a business.
2. **Inferential Statistics**: Makes predictions or inferences about a population based on a sample.
    a. Example: Using survey results from 1,000 people to estimate the opinions of an entire city.

Steps to Analyze Statistical Data

1. **Identify the Purpose**: Understand what the data represents and the question it aims to answer.
    a. Example: A sales report may aim to identify which products perform best.
2. **Organize the Data**: Arrange data in tables, charts, or graphs for easy interpretation.
    a. Example: A bar graph showing sales by month.
3. **Analyze Central Tendency**: Use measures like mean, median, and mode to summarize the data.
    a. Example: The mean daily temperature for a week.
4. **Examine Variability**: Consider how data values differ using measures like range or standard deviation.
    a. Example: Analyzing fluctuations in stock prices.
5. **Draw Conclusions**: Use patterns or trends in the data to make informed decisions.
    a. Example: Noticing that sales peak during holidays might lead to increased inventory planning.

Real-Life Scenarios

Scenario 1: Business Performance Analysis

A business wants to determine which product category generates the most revenue. The sales data is as follows:

Product Category	Revenue ($)
Electronics	50,000
Furniture	30,000
Clothing	20,000

Analysis:

- Use descriptive statistics to identify the top-performing category (Electronics).
- Calculate the percentage contribution of each category to total revenue:

$$\text{Percentage} = \frac{\text{Revenue of Category}}{\text{Total Revenue}} \times 100.$$

Example: For Electronics:

$$\frac{50{,}000}{100{,}000} \times 100 = 50\%.$$

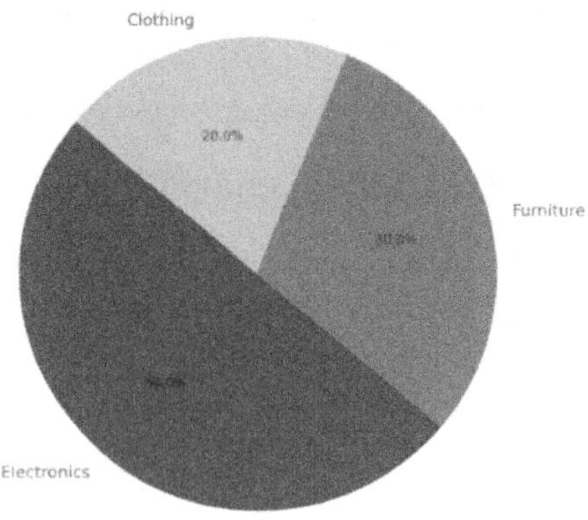

Scenario 2: Healthcare Monitoring

A clinic tracks patient recovery times (in days) for a treatment. The data is as follows:

Patient	Recovery Time (days)
A	5
B	7
C	4
D	6
E	8

Analysis:

- Calculate the mean recovery time:

$$\text{Mean} = \frac{5+7+4+6+8}{5} = 6 \text{ days.}$$

- Identify variability using the range:

$$\text{Range} = \text{Maximum} - \text{Minimum} = 8 - 4 = 4 \text{ days.}$$

- Use this data to assess the effectiveness of the treatment.

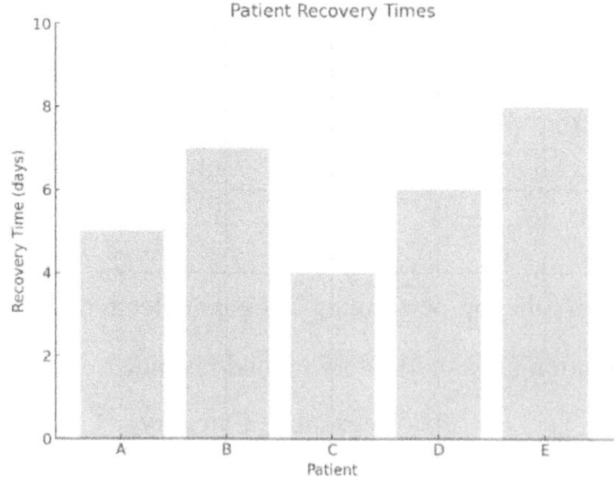

Scenario 3: Sports Performance

A basketball team tracks the points scored by players in a game:

Player	Points Scored
Player 1	15
Player 2	22
Player 3	18
Player 4	30
Player 5	25

Analysis:

- Find the player with the highest score (Player 4 with 30 points).
- Calculate the mean score:

$$\text{Mean} = \frac{15 + 22 + 18 + 30 + 25}{5} = 22.$$

- Consider the range to assess consistency:

$$\text{Range} = 30 - 15 = 15\,\text{points}.$$

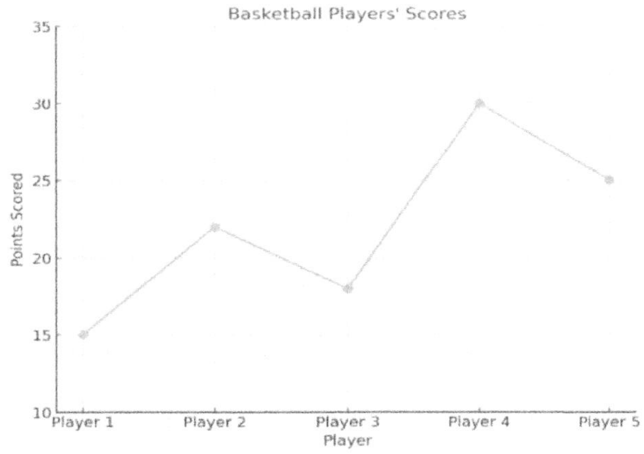

CHAPTER 19

MATH PRACTICE QUESTIONS AND SOLUTIONS

Arithmetic

Fundamentals

Question 1: Bakery Discount

A bakery sells cookies for $2.50 each. If a customer buys 8 cookies, and there is a 10% discount on the total purchase, how much does the customer pay?

Solution:

1. Calculate the total cost without a discount:

$$8 \times 2.50 = 20.00 \text{ USD}.$$

2. Calculate the discount:

$$10\% \text{ of } 20.00 = 0.10 \times 20.00 = 2.00 \text{ USD}.$$

3. Subtract the discount:

$$20.00 - 2.00 = 18.00 \text{ USD}.$$

Answer: The customer pays $18.00.

Question 2: Coffee Shop Bill

A coffee shop charges $3.75 for a cup of coffee. A customer buys 3 cups of coffee and leaves a tip of 20% of the total bill. How much does the customer pay in total?

Solution:

1. Calculate the total cost of the coffee:

$$3 \times 3.75 = 11.25 \text{ USD}.$$

2. Calculate the tip:

$$20\% \text{ of } 11.25 = 0.20 \times 11.25 = 2.25 \text{ USD}.$$

3. Add the tip to the total cost:

$$11.25 + 2.25 = 13.50 \text{ USD}.$$

Answer: The customer pays $13.50.

Question 3: Car Rental

A car rental company charges $45 per day to rent a car. If a customer rents a car for 6 days and gets a $50 discount on the total, what is the final amount they pay?

Solution:

1. Calculate the cost for 6 days:

$$6 \times 45 = 270 \text{ USD}.$$

2. Subtract the discount:

$$270 - 50 = 220 \text{ USD}.$$

Answer: The final amount is $220.

Question 4: Hardware Store

A hardware store sells screws for $0.25 each. If a contractor buys 120 screws and there is a 5% discount on the total purchase, what is the discounted total?

Solution:

1. Calculate the total cost without the discount:

$$120 \times 0.25 = 30.00 \text{ USD}.$$

2. Calculate the discount:

$$5\% \text{ of } 30.00 = 0.05 \times 30.00 = 1.50 \text{ USD.}$$

3. Subtract the discount:

$$30.00 - 1.50 = 28.50 \text{ USD.}$$

Answer: The discounted total is $28.50.

Question 5: Grocery Store

A grocery store sells apples for $1.20 per pound. If a shopper buys 3.5 pounds of apples, how much do they pay?

Solution:

1. Multiply the price per pound by the weight:

$$1.20 \times 3.5 = 4.20 \text{ USD.}$$

Answer: The shopper pays $4.20.

Question 6: Concert Tickets

A concert ticket costs $85. If a person buys 4 tickets and there is a 10% service fee added to the total, how much does the person pay?

Solution:

1. Calculate the cost of 4 tickets:

$$4 \times 85 = 340 \text{ USD.}$$

2. Calculate the service fee:

$$10\% \text{ of } 340 = 0.10 \times 340 = 34.00 \text{ USD.}$$

3. Add the service fee to the total cost:

$$340 + 34 = 374 \text{ USD.}$$

Answer: The person pays $374.

Question 7: Teacher's Notebooks

A teacher buys 25 notebooks for her class. Each notebook costs $1.50. If the store offers a "buy 10, get 1 free" deal, how much does the teacher pay in total?

Solution:

1. Calculate the number of free notebooks:

$$\lfloor 25 \div 10 \rfloor = 2 \text{ free notebooks.}$$

2. Calculate the number of notebooks to pay for:

$$25 - 2 = 23.$$

3. Calculate the total cost:

$$23 \times 1.50 = 34.50 \text{ USD.}$$

Answer: The teacher pays $34.50.

Question 8: Pizza Delivery

A pizza place charges $14.99 per pizza. If a family orders 3 pizzas and adds a delivery fee of $5.50, what is the total cost?

Solution:

1. Calculate the cost of the pizzas:

$$3 \times 14.99 = 44.97 \text{ USD.}$$

2. Add the delivery fee:

$$44.97 + 5.50 = 50.47 \text{ USD.}$$

Answer: The total cost is $50.47.

Question 9: Bag of Rice

A bag of rice weighing 10 pounds costs $22. If there is a 15% discount on the price, how much does the bag of rice cost?

Solution:

1. Calculate the discount:

$$15\% \text{ of } 22 = 0.15 \times 22 = 3.30 \text{ USD.}$$

2. Subtract the discount:

$$22 - 3.30 = 18.70 \text{ USD.}$$

Answer: The bag of rice costs $18.70.

Question 10: Phone Bill

A phone company charges a base rate of $50 per month and $0.10 for every text message sent. If a customer sends 150 texts in one month, what is their total bill?

Solution:

1. Calculate the cost of the texts:

$$150 \times 0.10 = 15.00 \text{ USD.}$$

2. Add the base rate:

$$50 + 15.00 = 65.00 \text{ USD.}$$

Answer: The total bill is $65.00.

Question 11: Gas Station Cost

A gas station charges $3.85 per gallon of gasoline. If a driver fills their car with 12.5 gallons, how much do they pay?

Solution:

1. Multiply the price per gallon by the amount of gas:

$$3.85 \times 12.5 = 48.125 \text{ USD.}$$

2. Round to the nearest cent:

$$48.13 \text{ USD.}$$

Answer: The driver pays $48.13.

Question 12: Daily Wages

A worker earns $18.75 per hour. If they work 7.5 hours in a day, what is their daily wage?

Solution:

1. Multiply the hourly wage by the hours worked:

$$18.75 \times 7.5 = 140.625 \text{ USD.}$$

2. Round to the nearest cent:

$$140.63 \text{ USD.}$$

Answer: The daily wage is $140.63.

Question 13: Bulk Purchase

A wholesaler sells boxes of pencils at $12.50 per box. If a school buys 45 boxes, how much do they pay?

Solution:

1. Multiply the price per box by the number of boxes:

$$12.50 \times 45 = 562.50 \text{ USD.}$$

Answer: The school pays $562.50.

Question 14: Water Bottle Discount

A store sells water bottles for $1.20 each. If a customer buys 15 bottles and receives a 10% discount, what is the total cost?

Solution:

1. Calculate the total cost without the discount:

$$15 \times 1.20 = 18.00 \text{ USD.}$$

2. Calculate the discount:

$$10\% \text{ of } 18.00 = 0.10 \times 18.00 = 1.80 \text{ USD.}$$

3. Subtract the discount:

$$18.00 - 1.80 = 16.20 \text{ USD}.$$

Answer: The total cost is $16.20.

Question 15: Hourly Pay Raise

An employee's hourly pay increases from $15.50 to 17.25$. If the employee works 40 hours per week, how much more do they earn in a week after the raise?

Solution:

1. Calculate the old weekly earnings:

$$15.50 \times 40 = 620.00 \text{ USD}.$$

2. Calculate the new weekly earnings:

$$17.25 \times 40 = 690.00 \text{ USD}.$$

3. Find the difference:

$$690.00 - 620.00 = 70.00 \text{ USD}.$$

Answer: They earn $70.00 more per week.

Question 16: Phone Plan Comparison

Plan A charges $0.08 per minute for calls. Plan B charges a flat fee of $10 per month plus $0.05 per minute. If you make 200 minutes of calls in a month, which plan is cheaper and by how much?

Solution:

1. Cost of Plan A:

$$0.08 \times 200 = 16.00 \text{ USD}.$$

2. Cost of Plan B:

$$10 + (0.05 \times 200) = 10 + 10 = 20.00 \text{ USD}.$$

3. Difference:

$$20.00 - 16.00 = 4.00 \text{ USD}.$$

Answer: Plan A is cheaper by $4.00.

Question 17: Grocery Bill

A shopper buys the following items:

- Milk: $3.49
- Bread: $2.25
- Eggs: $4.79
- Cereal: $5.99

If the sales tax is 8%, what is the total bill?

Solution:

1. Calculate the subtotal:

$$3.49 + 2.25 + 4.79 + 5.99 = 16.52 \text{ USD}.$$

2. Calculate the tax:

$$0.08 \times 16.52 = 1.32 \text{ USD}.$$

3. Add the tax to the subtotal:

$$16.52 + 1.32 = 17.84 \text{ USD}.$$

Answer: The total bill is $17.84.

Question 18: Group Trip Cost

A group of 12 friends rents a cabin for a weekend. The cabin costs $960 for two nights. If the cost is split equally among the friends, how much does each person pay?

Solution:

1. Divide the total cost by the number of friends:

$$960 \div 12 = 80\,\text{USD}.$$

Answer: Each person pays $80.00.

Question 19: Parking Fee

A parking lot charges $1.25 for the first hour and $0.75 for each additional hour. How much does it cost to park for 5 hours?

Solution:

1. Calculate the cost for the first hour:

$$1.25\,\text{USD}.$$

2. Calculate the cost for the remaining 4 hours:

$$4 \times 0.75 = 3.00\,\text{USD}.$$

3. Add the costs:

$$1.25 + 3.00 = 4.25\,\text{USD}.$$

Answer: The total cost is $4.25.

Question 20: Investment Growth

An investment of $2,000 earns 6% annual interest. How much is the total value of the investment after one year?

Solution:

1. Calculate the interest earned:

$$0.06 \times 2000 = 120\,\text{USD}.$$

2. Add the interest to the principal:

$$2000 + 120 = 2120\,\text{USD}.$$

Answer: The total value is $2,120.

Algebra Basics: 30 Practice Questions with Solution

Solving for x: Single Variable Equations

Question 1:

Solve for x:

$$6x + 8 = 20.$$

Solution:

1. Subtract 8 from both sides:

$$6x = 12.$$

2. Divide by 6:

$$x = 2.$$

Answer: $x = 2$.

Question 2:

Solve for x:

$$4x - 5 = 3x + 9.$$

Solution:

1. Subtract $3x$ from both sides:

$$x - 5 = 9.$$

2. Add 5 to both sides:

$$x = 14.$$

Answer: $x = 14$.

Question 3:

Solve for x:

$$9x - 3 = 6x + 18.$$

Solution:

1. Subtract $6x$ from both sides:

$$3x - 3 = 18.$$

2. Add 3 to both sides:

$$3x = 21.$$

3. Divide by 3:

$$x = 7.$$

Answer: $x = 7$.

Question 4:

Solve for x:

$$7x + 15 = 2x - 5.$$

Solution:

1. Subtract $2x$ from both sides:

$$5x + 15 = -5.$$

2. Subtract 15 from both sides:

$$5x = -20.$$

3. Divide by 5:

$$x = -4.$$

Answer: $x = -4$.

Question 5:

Solve for x:

$$10x + 50 = 100.$$

Solution:

1. Subtract 50 from both sides:

$$10x = 50.$$

2. Divide by 10:

$$x = 5.$$

Answer: $x = 5$.

Simplifying and Expanding Expressions

Question 6:

Simplify:

$$3(2x + 4) - 5x.$$

Solution:

1. Distribute 3:

$$6x + 12 - 5x.$$

2. Combine like terms:

$$x + 12.$$

Answer: $x + 12$.

Question 7:

Simplify:

$$(2x+3)(x-4).$$

Solution:

1. Apply the distributive property:

$$2x^2 - 8x + 3x - 12.$$

2. Combine like terms:

$$2x^2 - 5x - 12.$$

Answer: $2x^2 - 5x - 12.$

Question 8:

Simplify:

$$4x^2 - 8x + 12x - 16.$$

Solution:

Combine like terms:

$$4x^2 + 4x - 16.$$

Answer: $4x^2 + 4x - 16.$

Factoring

Question 9:

Factor:

$$x^2 + 6x + 8.$$

Solution:

Find two numbers that multiply to 8 and add to 6: 4 and 2.

Write as:

$$(x+4)(x+2).$$

Answer: $(x+4)(x+2).$

Question 10:

Factor:

$$x^2 - 9x + 18.$$

Solution:

Find two numbers that multiply to 18 and add to -9: -6 and -3.

Write as:

$$(x-6)(x-3).$$

Answer: $(x-6)(x-3).$

Word Problems

Question 11:

A rectangle has a width of 5 units and a length of $2x+3$ units. If the perimeter is 26 units, what is x?

Solution:

1. Write the perimeter formula:

$$P = 2(\text{Length} + \text{Width}).$$

2. Substitute values:

$$26 = 2(2x + 3 + 5).$$

3. Simplify inside parentheses:

$$26 = 2(2x + 8).$$

4. Expand:

$$26 = 4x + 16.$$

5. Subtract 16 from both sides:

$$10 = 4x.$$

6. Divide by 4:

$$x = 2.5.$$

Answer: $x = 2.5$.

Question 12:

A number is increased by 7 and equals three times the number. What is the number?

Solution:

1. Write the equation:

$$x + 7 = 3x.$$

2. Subtract x from both sides:

$$7 = 2x.$$

3. Divide by 2:

$$x = 3.5.$$

Answer: $x = 3.5$.

Question 13:

The sum of three consecutive integers is 27. Find the integers.

Solution:

1. Represent the integers as x, $x + 1$, and $x + 2$.
2. Write the equation:

$$x + (x + 1) + (x + 2) = 27.$$

3. Simplify:

$$3x + 3 = 27.$$

4. Subtract 3 from both sides:

$$3x = 24.$$

5. Divide by 3:

$$x = 8.$$

The integers are 8,9, and 10.

Answer: 8,9,10.

Question 14:

The product of a number and 4 is 28. What is the number?

Solution:

1. Write the equation:

$$4x = 28.$$

2. Divide by 4:

$$x = 7.$$

Answer: $x = 7$.

Question 15:

Twice a number is decreased by 9 and equals 15. What is the number?

Solution:

1. Write the equation:

$$2x - 9 = 15.$$

2. Add 9 to both sides:

$$2x = 24.$$

3. Divide by 2:

$$x = 12.$$

Answer: $x = 12$.

Question 16:

The perimeter of a triangle is 30 units. The sides are x, $x + 2$, and $x + 3$. What is the value of x?

Solution:

1. Write the perimeter equation:

$$x + (x + 2) + (x + 3) = 30.$$

2. Simplify:

$$3x + 5 = 30.$$

3. Subtract 5 from both sides:

$$3x = 25.$$

4. Divide by 3:

$$x = \frac{25}{3} \approx 8.33.$$

Answer: $x \approx 8.33$.

Question 17:

Simplify:

$$(x + 3)^2.$$

Solution:

1. Expand using the formula $(a + b)^2 = a^2 + 2ab + b^2$:

$$x^2 + 6x + 9.$$

Answer: $x^2 + 6x + 9$.

Question 18:

Solve for x:

$$2(x - 3) = 4x + 6.$$

Solution:

1. Expand $2(x - 3)$:

$$2x - 6 = 4x + 6.$$

2. Subtract $2x$ from both sides:

$$-6 = 2x + 6.$$

3. Subtract 6 from both sides:

$$-12 = 2x.$$

4. Divide by 2:

$$x = -6.$$

Answer: $x = -6$.

Question 19:

Solve for x:

$$3x + 4 > 16.$$

Solution:

1. Subtract 4 from both sides:

$$3x > 12.$$

2. Divide by 3:

$$x > 4.$$

Answer: $x > 4$.

Question 20:

Solve for x:

$$2x + 5 \leq 15.$$

Solution:

1. Subtract 5 from both sides:

$$2x \leq 10.$$

2. Divide by 2:

$$x \leq 5.$$

Answer: $x \leq 5$.

Question 21:

Factor:

$$x^2 - 16.$$

Solution:

1. Use the difference of squares formula $a^2 - b^2 = (a + b)(a - b)$:

$$x^2 - 16 = (x + 4)(x - 4).$$

Answer: $(x + 4)(x - 4)$.

Question 22:

Factor:

$$x^2 - 5x + 6.$$

Solution:

1. Find two numbers that multiply to 6 and add to -5: -3 and -2.

$$x^2 - 5x + 6 = (x - 3)(x - 2).$$

Answer: $(x - 3)(x - 2)$.

Question 23:

Simplify:

$$3(x - 4) + 2(x + 5).$$

Solution:

1. Distribute:

$$3x - 12 + 2x + 10.$$

2. Combine like terms:

$$5x - 2.$$

Answer: $5x - 2$.

Question 24:

The area of a rectangle is 36 square units. The length is $2x + 4$, and the width is $x - 2$. Find x.

Solution:

1. Use the area formula $A = \text{length} \times \text{width}$:
$$(2x + 4)(x - 2) = 36.$$
2. Expand:
$$2x^2 - 4x + 4x - 8 = 36.$$
3. Simplify:
$$2x^2 - 8 = 36.$$
4. Add 8 to both sides:
$$2x^2 = 44.$$
5. Divide by 2:
$$x^2 = 22.$$
6. Take the square root:
$$x = \sqrt{22} \approx 4.69.$$

Answer: $x \approx 4.69$.

Question 25:

Solve for x:

$$\frac{x + 4}{3} = 5.$$

Solution:

1. Multiply both sides by 3:
$$x + 4 = 15.$$
2. Subtract 4 from both sides:
$$x = 11.$$

Answer: $x = 11$.

Question 26:

Solve for x:

$$5x - 3x + 8 = 12.$$

Solution:

1. Combine like terms:
$$2x + 8 = 12.$$
2. Subtract 8 from both sides:
$$2x = 4.$$
3. Divide by 2:
$$x = 2.$$

Answer: $x = 2$.

Question 27:

Solve for x:

$$3(x + 2) = 18.$$

Solution:

1. Divide both sides by 3:
$$x + 2 = 6.$$
2. Subtract 2 from both sides:

$$x = 4.$$

Answer: $x = 4$.

Question 28:

Solve for x:

$$4x + 12 = 2x + 24.$$

Solution:

1. Subtract $2x$ from both sides:

$$2x + 12 = 24.$$

2. Subtract 12 from both sides:

$$2x = 12.$$

3. Divide by 2:

$$x = 6.$$

Answer: $x = 6$.

Question 29:

Simplify:

$$(3x + 4)^2.$$

Solution:

1. Expand using the square formula $(a + b)^2 = a^2 + 2ab + b^2$:

$$9x^2 + 24x + 16.$$

Answer: $9x^2 + 24x + 16$.

Question 30:

Solve for x:

$$\frac{2x - 3}{4} = 5.$$

Solution:

1. Multiply both sides by 4:

$$2x - 3 = 20.$$

2. Add 3 to both sides:

$$2x = 23.$$

3. Divide by 2:

$$x = 11.5.$$

Answer: $x = 11.5$

Geometry and Measurement Practice Questions with Solutions

Below are 10 practice questions for the **Geometry and Measurement** part of the GED Math exam. Each question includes detailed solutions and graphs or charts where necessary.

Question 1: Calculating the Perimeter of a Rectangle

A rectangle has a length of 12 cm and a width of 8 cm. What is its perimeter?

Solution:

1. Use the perimeter formula for a rectangle:

$$P = 2 \times (\text{length} + \text{width}).$$

2. Substitute the values:

$$P = 2 \times (12 + 8) = 2 \times 20 = 40 \text{ cm}.$$

Answer: The perimeter is **40 cm**.

Question 2: Finding the Area of a Triangle

A triangle has a base of 10 m and a height of 6 m. What is its area?

Solution:

1. Use the area formula for a triangle:

$$A = \frac{1}{2} \times \text{base} \times \text{height}.$$

2. Substitute the values:

$$A = \frac{1}{2} \times 10 \times 6 = 30\,\text{m}^2.$$

Answer: The area is **30 m²**.

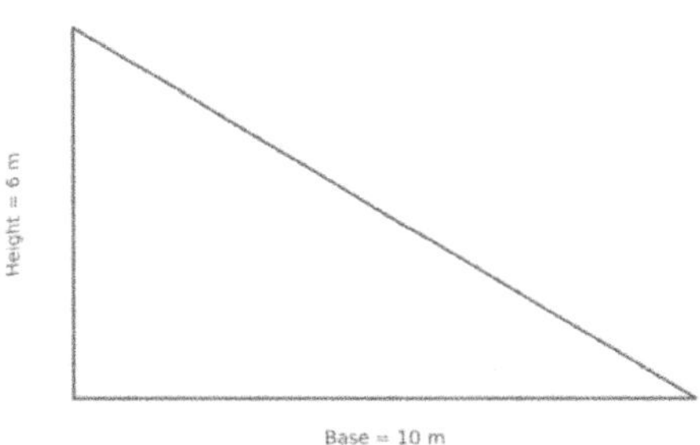

Question 3: Volume of a Rectangular Prism

A rectangular prism has a length of 5 inches, a width of 3 inches, and a height of 4 inches. What is its volume?

Solution:

1. Use the volume formula for a rectangular prism:

$$V = \text{length} \times \text{width} \times \text{height}.$$

2. Substitute the values:

$$V = 5 \times 3 \times 4 = 60\,\text{in}^3.$$

Answer: The volume is **60 in³**.

Question 4: Circumference of a Circle

A circle has a radius of 7 cm. What is its circumference? Use $\pi \approx 3.14$.

Solution:

1. Use the circumference formula:

$$C = 2\pi r.$$

2. Substitute the radius:

$$C = 2 \times 3.14 \times 7 = 43.96\,\text{cm}.$$

Answer: The circumference is **43.96 cm**.

Circle Diagram: Circumference

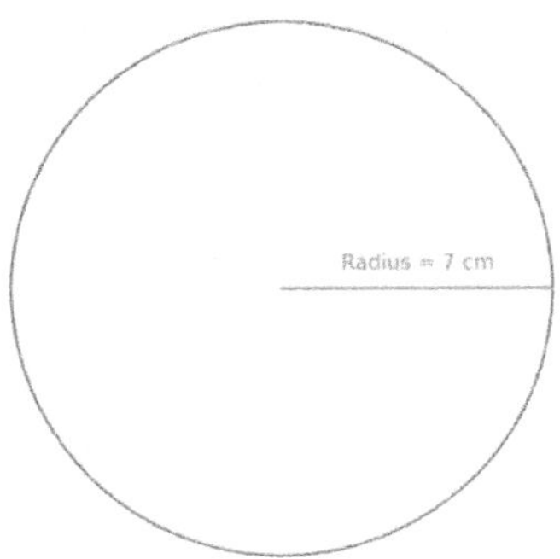

Question 5: Pythagorean Theorem

A right triangle has legs of 9 ft and 12 ft. What is the length of the hypotenuse?

Solution:

1. Use the Pythagorean theorem:

$$c^2 = a^2 + b^2.$$

2. Substitute the values:

$$c^2 = 9^2 + 12^2 = 81 + 144 = 225.$$

3. Take the square root:

$$c = \sqrt{225} = 15 \text{ ft}.$$

Answer: The hypotenuse is **15 ft**.

Pythagorean Theorem: Right Triangle

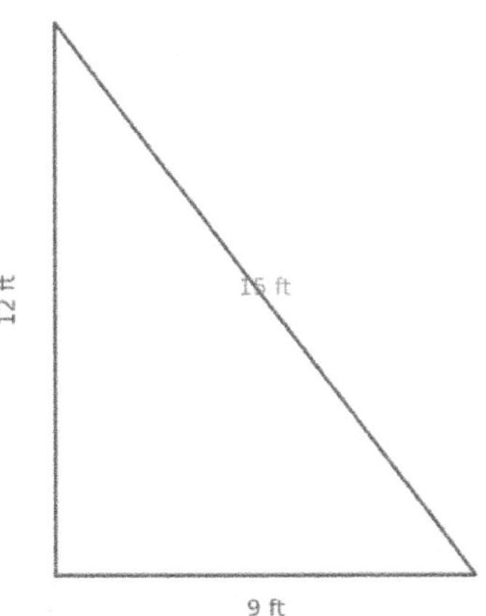

Question 6: Area of a Circle

A circular garden has a radius of 5 meters. What is its area? Use $\pi \approx 3.14$.

Solution:

1. Use the area formula for a circle:

$$A = \pi r^2.$$

2. Substitute the radius:

$$A = 3.14 \times 5^2 = 3.14 \times 25 = 78.5 \, \text{m}^2.$$

Answer: The area is **78.5 m²**.

Circle Diagram: Area

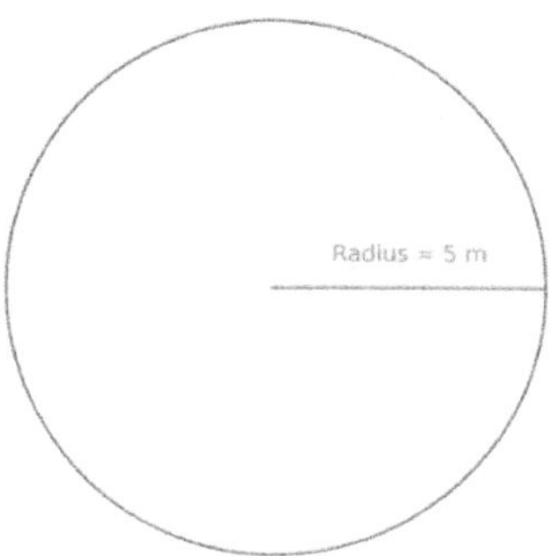

Question 7: Surface Area of a Cube

A cube has an edge length of 4 inches. What is its surface area?

Solution:

1. Use the surface area formula for a cube:

$$SA = 6 \times \text{side}^2.$$

2. Substitute the edge length:

$$SA = 6 \times 4^2 = 6 \times 16 = 96 \text{ in}^2.$$

Answer: The surface area is **96 in²**.

Question 8: Identifying Angles

Two angles are complementary. If one angle measures 35°, what is the measure of the other angle?

Solution:

1. Complementary angles sum to 90°:

$$90° - 35° = 55°.$$

Answer: The other angle is **55°**.

Question 9: Volume of a Cylinder

A cylindrical water tank has a radius of 3 feet and a height of 10 feet. What is its volume? Use $\pi \approx 3.14$.

Solution:

1. Use the volume formula for a cylinder:

$$V = \pi r^2 h.$$

2. Substitute the values:

$$V = 3.14 \times 3^2 \times 10 = 3.14 \times 9 \times 10 = 282.6 \text{ ft}^3.$$

Answer: The volume is **282.6 ft³**.

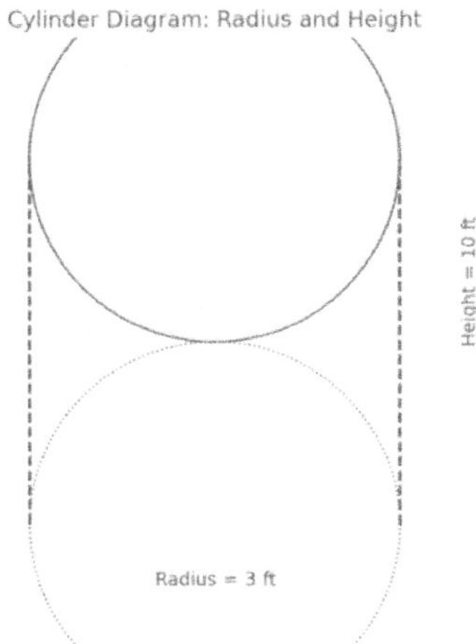

Question 10: Perimeter of a Trapezoid

A trapezoid has sides measuring 8 cm, 12 cm, 10 cm, and 6 cm. What is its perimeter?

Solution:

1. Add the lengths of all sides:

$$P = 8 + 12 + 10 + 6 = 36\,\text{cm}.$$

Answer: The perimeter is **36 cm**.

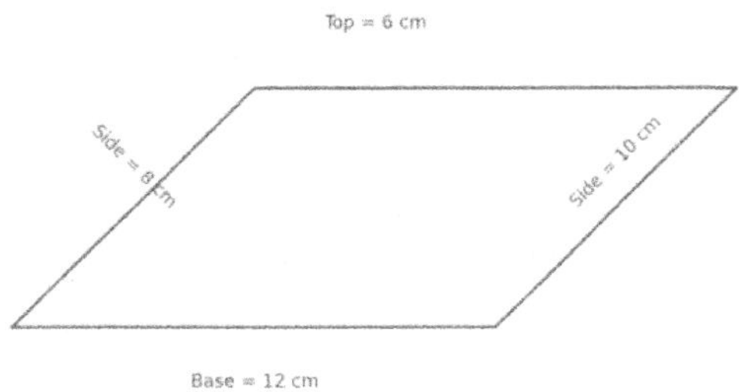

Question 11: Finding the Missing Angle in a Triangle

A triangle has two angles measuring 45° and 65°. What is the measure of the third angle?

Solution:

1. The sum of angles in a triangle is always 180°.
2. Add the known angles:

$$45^\circ + 65^\circ = 110^\circ.$$

3. Subtract the sum of the known angles from 180°:

$$180^\circ - 110^\circ = 70^\circ.$$

Answer: The third angle is **70°**.

Question 12: Calculating the Area of a Trapezoid

A trapezoid has bases measuring 10 cm and 14 cm, and a height of 6 cm. What is its area?

Solution:

1. Use the formula for the area of a trapezoid:

$$A = \frac{1}{2} \times (\text{base}_1 + \text{base}_2) \times \text{height}.$$

2. Substitute the values:

$$A = \frac{1}{2} \times (10 + 14) \times 6 = \frac{1}{2} \times 24 \times 6 = 72\,\text{cm}^2.$$

Answer: The area is **72 cm²**.

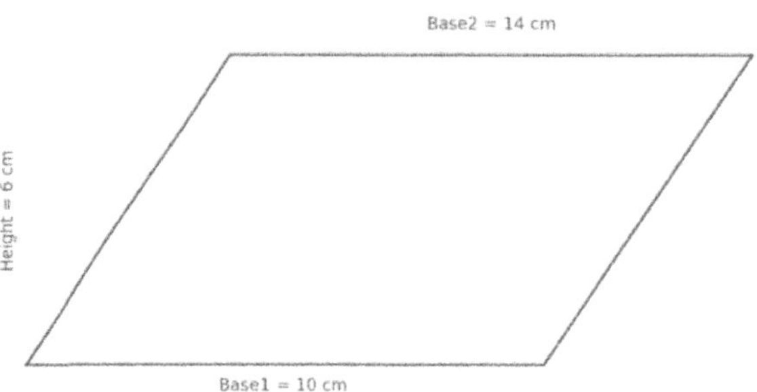

Question 13: Surface Area of a Rectangular Prism

A rectangular prism has a length of 8 cm, a width of 5 cm, and a height of 4 cm. What is its surface area?

Solution:

1. Use the formula for surface area:

$$SA = 2(\text{lw} + \text{lh} + \text{wh}),$$

where l is length, w is width, and h is height.

2. Substitute the values:

$$SA = 2(8 \times 5 + 8 \times 4 + 5 \times 4) = 2(40 + 32 + 20) = 2(92) = 184\,\text{cm}^2.$$

Answer: The surface area is **184 cm²**.

Question 14: Volume of a Cone

A cone has a radius of 3 cm and a height of 8 cm. What is its volume? Use $\pi \approx 3.14$.

Solution:

1. Use the formula for the volume of a cone:

$$V = \frac{1}{3}\pi r^2 h.$$

2. Substitute the values:

$$V = \frac{1}{3} \times 3.14 \times 3^2 \times 8 = \frac{1}{3} \times 3.14 \times 9 \times 8 = \frac{1}{3} \times 226.08 = 75.36\,\text{cm}^3.$$

Answer: The volume is **75.36 cm³**.

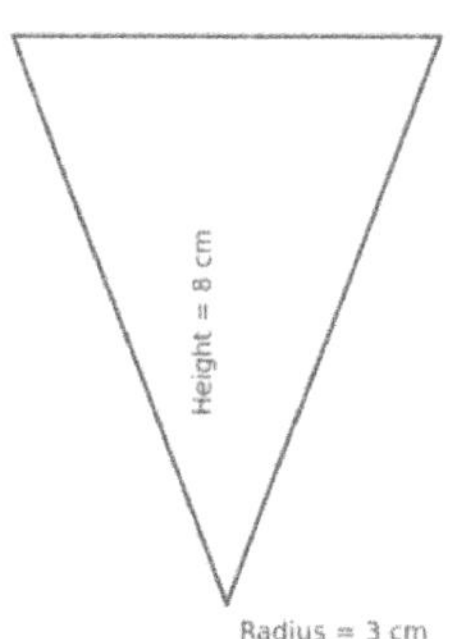

Question 15: Identifying Parallel Lines

Two lines in a coordinate plane have equations $y = 2x + 3$ and $y = 2x - 4$. Are these lines parallel?

Solution:

1. Parallel lines have the same slope but different y-intercepts.
2. The slope of both lines is 2.
3. **Answer:** Yes, the lines are **parallel** because their slopes are equal.

Question 16: Diagonal of a Rectangle

A rectangle has a length of 12 cm and a width of 5 cm. What is the length of its diagonal?

Solution:

1. Use the Pythagorean theorem:

$$d^2 = l^2 + w^2.$$

2. Substitute the values:

$$d^2 = 12^2 + 5^2 = 144 + 25 = 169.$$

3. Take the square root:

$$d = \sqrt{169} = 13 \text{ cm}.$$

Answer: The diagonal is **13 cm**.

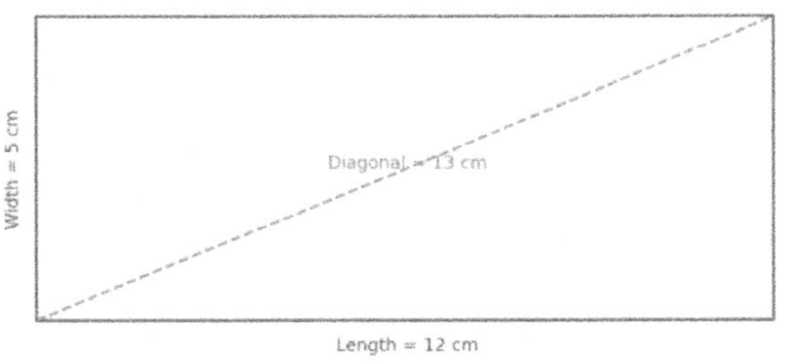

Question 17: Angle of a Regular Polygon

What is the measure of each interior angle of a regular pentagon?

Solution:

1. Use the formula for the interior angle of a regular polygon:

$$\text{Interior Angle} = \frac{(n-2) \times 180}{n},$$

where n is the number of sides.

2. Substitute $n = 5$:

$$\text{Interior Angle} = \frac{(5-2) \times 180}{5} = \frac{3 \times 180}{5} = \frac{540}{5} = 108°.$$

Answer: Each interior angle is **108°**.

Question 18: Area of a Parallelogram

A parallelogram has a base of 15 m and a height of 7 m. What is its area?

Solution:

1. Use the formula for the area of a parallelogram:

$$A = \text{base} \times \text{height}.$$

2. Substitute the values:

$$A = 15 \times 7 = 105 \text{ m}^2.$$

Answer: The area is **105 m²**.

Question 19: Volume of a Sphere

A sphere has a radius of 6 inches. What is its volume? Use $\pi \approx 3.14$.

Solution:

1. Use the formula for the volume of a sphere:

$$V = \frac{4}{3}\pi r^3.$$

2. Substitute the radius:

$$V = \frac{4}{3} \times 3.14 \times 6^3 = \frac{4}{3} \times 3.14 \times 216 = \frac{4}{3} \times 678.24 = 904.32 \text{ in}^3.$$

Answer: The volume is **904.32 in³**.

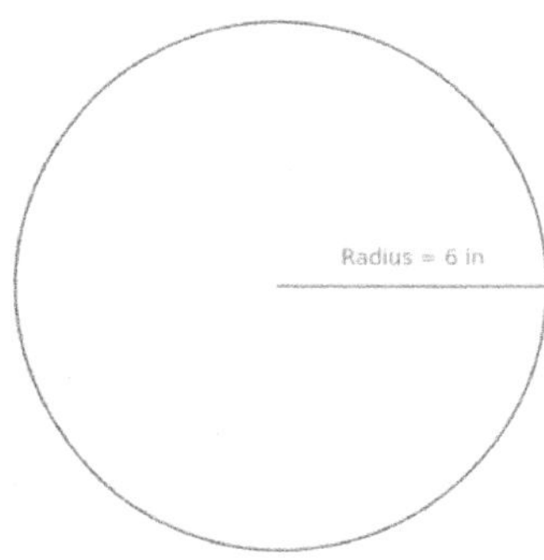

Question 20: Finding the Missing Side of a Trapezoid

A trapezoid has one base of 10 cm, another base of 6 cm, and two equal legs. If the perimeter is 36 cm, what is the length of each leg?

Solution:

1. Write the perimeter equation:

$$\text{Perimeter} = \text{base}_1 + \text{base}_2 + 2 \times \text{leg}.$$

2. Substitute known values:

$$36 = 10 + 6 + 2 \times \text{leg}.$$

3. Simplify:

$$36 = 16 + 2 \times \text{leg}.$$

4. Subtract 16 from both sides:

$$20 = 2 \times \text{leg}.$$

5. Divide by 2:

$$\text{leg} = 10 \text{ cm}.$$

Answer: Each leg is **10 cm**.

Data Analysis and Statistics Practice Questions

Question 1: Weekly Sales

The following table shows the weekly sales (in dollars) of five stores:

Store	Sales ($)
A	700
B	850
C	780
D	720
E	700

Tasks:

1. Find the mean sales.
2. Determine the mode.
3. Calculate the range.

Solution:

Mean:

$$\text{Mean} = \frac{\text{Sum of Sales}}{\text{Number of Stores}} = \frac{700 + 850 + 780 + 720 + 700}{5} = \frac{3750}{5} = 750\ \text{USD}.$$

Mode:

The mode is **700 USD**, as it appears twice.

Range:

$$\text{Range} = \text{Maximum} - \text{Minimum} = 850 - 700 = 150\ \text{USD}.$$

Answer: Mean = 750 USD, Mode = 700 USD, Range = 150 USD.

Question 2: Monthly Temperatures

The following table shows the monthly high temperatures (in °F) for a city:

Month	Temperature (°F)
Jan	45
Feb	48
Mar	52
Apr	50
May	48

Tasks:

1. Calculate the mean temperature.
2. Identify the mode.
3. Find the range.

Solution:

Mean:

$$\text{Mean} = \frac{45 + 48 + 52 + 50 + 48}{5} = \frac{243}{5} = 48.6^\circ\ \text{F}.$$

Mode:

The mode is **48°F**, as it appears twice.

Range:

$$\text{Range} = \text{Maximum} - \text{Minimum} = 52 - 45 = 7^\circ\ \text{F}.$$

Answer: Mean = 48.6°F, Mode = 48°F, Range = 7°F.

Question 3: Student Test Scores

The following table shows the test scores of six students:

Student	Score
A	85
B	90
C	78
D	85
E	92
F	85

Tasks:

1. Compute the mean score.
2. Determine the mode.
3. Find the range.

Solution:

Mean:

$$\text{Mean} = \frac{85 + 90 + 78 + 85 + 92 + 85}{6} = \frac{515}{6} \approx 85.83.$$

Mode:

The mode is **85**, as it appears three times.

Range:

$$\text{Range} = 92 - 78 = 14.$$

Answer: Mean ≈ 85.83, Mode = 85, Range = 14.

Question 4: Daily Expenses

The following table shows the daily expenses (in dollars) of a family over five days:

Day	Expense ($)
Mon	45
Tue	50
Wed	45
Thu	40
Fri	55

Tasks:

1. Find the mean expense.
2. Determine the mode.
3. Calculate the range.

Solution:

Mean:

$$\text{Mean} = \frac{45 + 50 + 45 + 40 + 55}{5} = \frac{235}{5} = 47\,\text{USD}.$$

Mode:

The mode is **45 USD**, as it appears twice.

Range:

$$\text{Range} = 55 - 40 = 15\,\text{USD}.$$

Answer: Mean = 47 USD, Mode = 45 USD, Range = 15 USD.

Question 5: Weekly Rainfall

The following table shows the weekly rainfall (in inches) for five weeks:

Week	Rainfall (in)
1	2.5
2	3.0
3	2.5
4	3.5
5	3.0

Tasks:

1. Calculate the mean rainfall.
2. Identify the mode.
3. Find the range.

Solution:

Mean:

$$\text{Mean} = \frac{2.5 + 3.0 + 2.5 + 3.5 + 3.0}{5} = \frac{14.5}{5} = 2.9 \text{ in.}$$

Mode:

The mode is **2.5 in** and **3.0 in**, as both appear twice.

Range:

$$\text{Range} = 3.5 - 2.5 = 1 \text{ in.}$$

Answer: Mean = 2.9 in, Mode = 2.5 in and 3.0 in, Range = 1 in.

Question 6: Employee Working Hours

The following table shows the weekly working hours for six employees:

Employee	Hours
A	35
B	40
C	38
D	35
E	42
F	35

Tasks:

1. Compute the mean hours worked.
2. Determine the mode.
3. Calculate the range.

Solution:

Mean:

$$\text{Mean} = \frac{35 + 40 + 38 + 35 + 42 + 35}{6} = \frac{225}{6} = 37.5 \text{ hours.}$$

Mode:

The mode is **35 hours**, as it appears three times.

Range:

$$\text{Range} = 42 - 35 = 7 \text{ hours.}$$

Answer: Mean = 37.5 hours, Mode = 35 hours, Range = 7 hours.

Question 7: Car Prices

The following table shows the prices of six cars (in $1,000s):

Car	Price ($)
A	22
B	25
C	24
D	20
E	25
F	22

Tasks:

1. Find the mean price.
2. Identify the mode.
3. Calculate the range.

Solution:

Mean:

$$\text{Mean} = \frac{22 + 25 + 24 + 20 + 25 + 22}{6} = \frac{138}{6} = 23 \text{ (in thousands).}$$

Mode:

The mode is **22** and **25 (in thousands)**, as both appear twice.

Range:

$$\text{Range} = 25 - 20 = 5 \text{ (in thousands).}$$

Answer: Mean = 23, Mode = 22 and 25, Range = 5.

Question 8: Monthly Utility Bills

The following table shows the monthly utility bills (in dollars) for five households:

Household	Utility Bill ($)
A	120
B	150
C	140
D	130
E	150

Tasks:

1. Find the mean utility bill.
2. Identify the mode.
3. Calculate the range.

Solution:

Mean:

$$\text{Mean} = \frac{120 + 150 + 140 + 130 + 150}{5} = \frac{690}{5} = 138 \text{ USD.}$$

Mode:

The mode is **150 USD**, as it appears twice.

Range:

$$\text{Range} = 150 - 120 = 30\ \text{USD.}$$

Answer: Mean = 138 USD, Mode = 150 USD, Range = 30 USD.

Question 9: Weekly Study Hours

The following table shows the weekly study hours for six students:

Student	Study Hours
A	12
B	14
C	10
D	12
E	16
F	14

Tasks:

1. Compute the mean study hours.
2. Identify the mode.
3. Find the range.

Solution:

Mean:

$$\text{Mean} = \frac{12 + 14 + 10 + 12 + 16 + 14}{6} = \frac{78}{6} = 13\ \text{hours.}$$

Mode:
The mode is **12 hours** and **14 hours**, as both appear twice.

Range:

$$\text{Range} = 16 - 10 = 6\ \text{hours.}$$

Answer: Mean = 13 hours, Mode = 12 and 14 hours, Range = 6 hours.

Question 10: Product Prices

The following table shows the prices of five products (in dollars):

Product	Price ($)
A	25
B	30
C	35
D	30
E	40

Tasks:

1. Calculate the mean price.
2. Identify the mode.
3. Find the range.

Solution:
Mean:

$$\text{Mean} = \frac{25 + 30 + 35 + 30 + 40}{5} = \frac{160}{5} = 32\ \text{USD.}$$

Mode:

The mode is **30 USD**, as it appears twice.

Range:

$$\text{Range} = 40 - 25 = 15\,\text{USD}.$$

Answer: Mean = 32 USD, Mode = 30 USD, Range = 15 USD.

Question 11: Employee Bonuses

The following table shows the bonuses (in dollars) received by five employees:

Employee	Bonus ($)
A	500
B	700
C	600
D	500
E	800

Tasks:

1. Compute the mean bonus.
2. Determine the mode.
3. Calculate the range.

Solution:

Mean:

$$\text{Mean} = \frac{500 + 700 + 600 + 500 + 800}{5} = \frac{3100}{5} = 620\,\text{USD}.$$

Mode:

The mode is **500 USD**, as it appears twice.

Range:

$$\text{Range} = 800 - 500 = 300\,\text{USD}.$$

Answer: Mean = 620 USD, Mode = 500 USD, Range = 300 USD.

Question 12: Monthly Rents

The following table shows the monthly rents (in dollars) of six apartments:

Apartment	Rent ($)
A	1200
B	1400
C	1300
D	1200
E	1500
F	1400

Tasks:

1. Find the mean rent.
2. Determine the mode.
3. Calculate the range.

Solution:

Mean:

$$\text{Mean} = \frac{1200 + 1400 + 1300 + 1200 + 1500 + 1400}{6} = \frac{8000}{6} \approx 1333.33\,\text{USD}.$$

Mode:

The mode is **1200 USD** and **1400 USD**, as both appear twice.

Range:

$$\text{Range} = 1500 - 1200 = 300\text{ USD.}$$

Answer: Mean ≈ 1333.33 USD, Mode = 1200 and 1400 USD, Range = 300 USD.

Question 13: Test Scores

The following table shows the test scores of seven students:

Student	Score
A	78
B	85
C	80
D	85
E	90
F	85
G	88

Tasks:

1. Calculate the mean score.
2. Identify the mode.
3. Find the range.

Solution:

Mean:

$$\text{Mean} = \frac{78 + 85 + 80 + 85 + 90 + 85 + 88}{7} = \frac{591}{7} \approx 84.43.$$

Mode:

The mode is **85**, as it appears three times.

Range:

$$\text{Range} = 90 - 78 = 12.$$

Answer: Mean ≈ 84.43, Mode = 85, Range = 12.

Question 14: Weekly Savings

The following table shows the weekly savings (in dollars) of five individuals:

Person	Savings ($)
A	20
B	25
C	30
D	20
E	25

Tasks:

1. Compute the mean savings.
2. Determine the mode.
3. Find the range.

Solution:

Mean:

$$\text{Mean} = \frac{20 + 25 + 30 + 20 + 25}{5} = \frac{120}{5} = 24\text{ USD.}$$

Mode:
The mode is **20 USD** and **25 USD**, as both appear twice.

Range:

$$\text{Range} = 30 - 20 = 10 \text{ USD}.$$

Answer: Mean = 24 USD, Mode = 20 and 25 USD, Range = 10 USD.

Question 15: Probability of Selecting a Red Marble

A bag contains 5 red marbles, 7 blue marbles, and 8 green marbles.

Task:

What is the probability of randomly selecting a red marble?

Solution:

1. Total number of marbles:

$$5 + 7 + 8 = 20.$$

2. Probability of selecting a red marble:

$$\frac{\text{Number of Red Marbles}}{\text{Total Marbles}} = \frac{5}{20} = 0.25 \text{ or } 25\%.$$

Answer: The probability is **0.25 (25%)**.

Question 16: Comparing Averages

The table below shows the test scores for two classes:

Class A	78, 82, 85, 88, 90
Class B	70, 75, 80, 85, 90

Task:

Which class has the higher average score?

Solution:

Class A Mean:

$$\text{Mean} = \frac{78 + 82 + 85 + 88 + 90}{5} = \frac{423}{5} = 84.6.$$

Class B Mean:

$$\text{Mean} = \frac{70 + 75 + 80 + 85 + 90}{5} = \frac{400}{5} = 80.$$

Answer: Class A has a higher average score of **84.6** compared to Class B's **80**.

Question 17: Interpreting a Bar Chart

A bar chart shows the number of books read by four students in a month:

- Student A: 5 books
- Student B: 7 books
- Student C: 6 books
- Student D: 8 books

Tasks:

1. Find the mean number of books read.
2. Determine the range.

Solution:

Mean:

$$\text{Mean} = \frac{5+7+6+8}{4} = \frac{26}{4} = 6.5\,\text{books.}$$

Range:

$$\text{Range} = 8 - 5 = 3\,\text{books.}$$

Answer: Mean = **6.5 books**, Range = **3 books**.

Question 18: Percentage of a Total

A company has 120 employees. Of these, 36 are in the sales department.

Task:

What percentage of employees work in the sales department?

Solution:

1. Use the percentage formula:

$$\text{Percentage} = \frac{\text{Part}}{\text{Whole}} \times 100 = \frac{36}{120} \times 100 = 30\%.$$

Answer: 30% of employees work in the sales department.

Question 19: Median Household Income

The table below shows the annual household incomes (in $1,000s) for seven households:

Household	Income ($1,000s)
A	42
B	38
C	50
D	45
E	40
F	55
G	48

Task:

Find the median income.

Solution:

1. Arrange the incomes in ascending order: $38, 40, 42, 45, 48, 50, 55$.
2. The median is the middle value:

$$\text{Median} = 45.$$

Answer: Median = **45 (in $1,000s)**.

Question 20: Probability from a Deck of Cards

A standard deck of 52 playing cards contains 13 cards in each suit.

Task:

What is the probability of randomly selecting a heart?

Solution:

1. Number of hearts in the deck: 13.
2. Total number of cards: 52.
3. Probability:

$$\frac{13}{52} = \frac{1}{4} = 0.25 \text{ or } 25\%.$$

Answer: The probability is **0.25 (25%)**.

Question 21: Comparing Data Sets

Two stores sell a product at these daily prices over five days:

Day	Store A ($)	Store B ($)
Monday	50	52
Tuesday	48	50
Wednesday	52	54
Thursday	51	53
Friday	50	51

Task:

Which store had the lower average price?

Solution:

Store A Mean:

$$\text{Mean} = \frac{50 + 48 + 52 + 51 + 50}{5} = \frac{251}{5} = 50.2\,\text{USD}.$$

Store B Mean:

$$\text{Mean} = \frac{52 + 50 + 54 + 53 + 51}{5} = \frac{260}{5} = 52\,\text{USD}.$$

Answer: Store A had the lower average price of **50.2 USD**.

Question 22: Percent Increase

The price of a product increased from $40 to 50$.

Task:

What is the percentage increase?

Solution:

1. Find the increase:

$$\text{Increase} = 50 - 40 = 10.$$

2. Calculate the percentage increase:

$$\frac{\text{Increase}}{\text{Original Price}} \times 100 = \frac{10}{40} \times 100 = 25\%.$$

Answer: The percentage increase is **25%**.

Question 23: Interpreting a Table

The table below shows the number of hours worked by employees in a week:

Employee	Hours Worked
A	35
B	40
C	42
D	38
E	45

Task:

1. Find the mean hours worked.
2. Identify the range.

Solution:

Mean:

$$\text{Mean} = \frac{35 + 40 + 42 + 38 + 45}{5} = \frac{200}{5} = 40 \text{ hours.}$$

Range:

$$\text{Range} = 45 - 35 = 10 \text{ hours.}$$

Answer: Mean = **40 hours**, Range = **10 hours**.

PART IV

SCIENCE

CHAPTER 20

OVERVIEW OF THE SCIENCE EXAM

The Science portion of the GED exam is designed to assess your understanding of key scientific concepts, your ability to apply scientific practices, and your skill in interpreting and analyzing scientific data. This section focuses on three core areas: Life Science, Physical Science, and Earth and Space Science. Beyond simply testing your knowledge of facts, the exam challenges your ability to think critically about scientific problems, draw logical conclusions, and apply scientific reasoning to real-world scenarios.

The Science exam includes a mix of multiple-choice, drag-and-drop, fill-in-the-blank, and hotspot questions. Additionally, you may encounter short-answer questions where you will need to provide a written response based on a given scenario or dataset. Each question is designed to test not only your recall of scientific information but also your ability to analyze and interpret data, understand experimental designs, and evaluate evidence.

This section is timed, with approximately 90 minutes allocated to complete the questions. The exam comprises around 34 to 40 questions, divided into the following content areas:

- **Life Science (40% of the test):** This area includes topics related to cells, genetics, ecosystems, and the interactions between human body systems.
- **Physical Science (40% of the test):** This section focuses on physics and chemistry concepts, such as force, motion, energy, chemical reactions, and the properties of matter.
- **Earth and Space Science (20% of the test):** This area explores topics like Earth's structure, weather patterns, natural disasters, the solar system, and the impact of human activity on the environment.

In addition to content knowledge, the exam evaluates your ability to engage in scientific practices. This includes analyzing experimental designs, interpreting data from tables and graphs, identifying trends, and evaluating the validity of conclusions based on evidence. The questions often involve real-world contexts, such as climate change, medical advancements, or energy conservation, to help connect scientific principles to everyday life.

The Science exam does not require advanced mathematical calculations, but a basic understanding of mathematical concepts, such as interpreting graphs or calculating percentages, is essential. A calculator is provided for specific questions, and you will also have access to a formula sheet containing commonly used equations, such as those for speed, force, and density.

Preparation for this section requires a balanced focus on theoretical knowledge and practical skills. Understanding key scientific concepts is essential, but so is the ability to critically analyze data, evaluate hypotheses, and draw evidence-based conclusions. The questions are designed to assess your ability to think like a scientist, focusing on logical reasoning and problem-solving.

In the following sections, we will delve into the specific areas covered on the exam, including detailed explanations of Life Science, Physical Science, and Earth and Space Science topics. We will also provide tips for mastering scientific practices and strategies for interpreting scientific data effectively. With thorough preparation, you will be equipped to tackle this section of the exam confidently.

20.1 Exam Structure and Question Types

The Science section of the GED exam is structured to assess both your understanding of scientific concepts and your ability to apply scientific reasoning to analyze and interpret information. This part of the test consists of a variety of question formats designed to evaluate not only your factual knowledge but also your critical thinking and problem-solving skills. The questions are organized into three primary scientific domains—Life Science, Physical Science, and Earth and Space Science—each representing a different percentage of the test. Below, we will explore the structure and types of questions you can expect on the Science exam.

Structure of the Exam

The Science exam consists of approximately 34 to 40 questions, which you are given 90 minutes to complete. The questions are evenly distributed among the three scientific domains:

- **Life Science (40% of the test):** This includes questions on cellular biology, genetics, ecosystems, and the human body.
- **Physical Science (40% of the test):** Topics include physics and chemistry, such as force, energy, chemical reactions, and properties of matter.
- **Earth and Space Science (20% of the test):** Questions focus on Earth's systems, weather, climate, natural disasters, and space exploration.

The exam is presented in a computer-based format, with a range of interactive question types that simulate real-world scenarios. You will also have access to a basic scientific calculator for specific questions and a formula sheet that includes key equations, such as those for speed, force, and energy.

Question Types

The Science exam incorporates several types of questions to evaluate your ability to apply scientific principles and reasoning effectively. These question formats include:

1. **Multiple-Choice Questions** Multiple-choice questions require you to select the correct answer from four options. These questions assess your understanding of scientific concepts, interpretation of data, and ability to apply knowledge to solve problems. For example:
   - **Example:**
     Which organelle is responsible for energy production in a cell?
   - a) Nucleus
   - b) Mitochondria
   - c) Ribosome
   - d) Chloroplast
     Answer: b) Mitochondria
2. **Drag-and-Drop Questions**
   These questions ask you to drag labels or data points into the correct positions on a diagram or chart. For instance, you might label the parts of a plant cell or arrange the steps of a scientific process in the correct order.
   - **Example:** Label the following parts of a plant cell: nucleus, chloroplast, cell wall, and mitochondria.
3. **Hotspot Questions**
   In hotspot questions, you will click directly on specific areas of an image, graph, or diagram to identify the correct answer. For example:
   - **Example:** Click on the area of the graph where the population reaches its carrying capacity.
4. **Fill-in-the-Blank Questions**
   These questions require you to type your answer into a blank field. The answer might be a numerical value, a short phrase, or a single word. For example:
   - **Example:**
     The chemical formula for water is ______
     Answer: H_2O
5. **Short-Answer Questions**
   Short-answer questions involve writing a brief response, usually one or two sentences. These questions often ask you to explain a scientific concept, describe an experimental outcome, or make a prediction based on given data.
   - **Example:**
     Explain why plants are considered producers in an ecosystem.
     Answer: Plants are considered producers because they use sunlight to create energy through photosynthesis, forming the base of the food chain.
6. **Data Interpretation Questions**
   These questions require you to analyze information presented in tables, graphs, or charts. You may be asked to identify trends, make predictions, or evaluate conclusions based on the data provided.
   - **Example:**
     A graph shows the growth of a bacterial population over time. At what point does the population reach its maximum?
     Answer: At 48 hours, when the graph levels off at 1,000 bacteria.
7. **Scenario-Based Questions**

These questions present a real-world problem or scientific scenario and require you to analyze the situation and apply scientific principles to answer the questions. For example, you might evaluate the results of a clinical trial or analyze data on climate change.

Skills Assessed

In addition to content knowledge, the Science exam evaluates several critical scientific skills:

- **Understanding Scientific Texts:** The ability to read and comprehend passages about scientific topics, such as descriptions of experiments or explanations of natural phenomena.
- **Analyzing Data:** The ability to interpret tables, graphs, and charts, identify patterns, and draw conclusions.
- **Applying Scientific Practices:** The ability to evaluate hypotheses, predict outcomes, and assess the validity of conclusions.
- **Problem-Solving:** The ability to use scientific reasoning to address complex questions, often involving multiple steps.

Time Management Tips

Managing your time effectively during the Science exam is essential. Here are some strategies:

- **Prioritize Questions:** Answer easier questions first and return to more challenging ones later.
- **Interpret Graphics Efficiently:** Spend extra time understanding charts and graphs before answering related questions.
- **Pace Yourself:** With approximately 90 minutes for 34–40 questions, aim to spend about 2 minutes per question. Save a few minutes at the end to review your answers.

Understanding the structure and question types of the Science exam is the first step in effective preparation. As you move through this study guide, you'll gain the tools and knowledge needed to master these question formats and excel in this section of the GED exam.

20.2 Key Scientific Practices

The Science section of the GED exam is not only about memorizing facts but also about understanding and applying scientific practices. These practices involve analyzing data, interpreting evidence, designing experiments, and making logical conclusions based on observations. The exam evaluates your ability to think like a scientist and apply critical reasoning to solve real-world problems. Below, we will explore the key scientific practices you need to master for the exam.

1. Understanding Experimental Design

One of the foundational skills in science is the ability to understand and evaluate experimental designs. This includes identifying the components of an experiment, such as:

- **Hypothesis:** A testable statement or prediction that the experiment seeks to confirm or refute.
  - *Example:* If plants receive more sunlight, then they will grow faster.
- **Independent Variable:** The factor that is changed or manipulated in the experiment.
  - *Example:* The amount of sunlight the plants receive.
- **Dependent Variable:** The factor that is measured or observed in response to the independent variable.
  - *Example:* The growth rate of the plants.
- **Control Variables:** Factors that are kept constant to ensure a fair test.
  - *Example:* The type of soil, amount of water, and temperature.
- **Control Group vs. Experimental Group:**
  - *Control Group:* Does not receive the experimental treatment, used for comparison.
  - *Experimental Group:* Receives the treatment being tested.

2. Interpreting Data

Another critical practice is the ability to interpret data presented in various forms, such as tables, graphs, and charts. You may be asked to identify trends, compare data points, or make predictions based on the information provided.

- **Line Graphs:** Often used to show changes over time or continuous data.
  - *Example:* A graph showing the increase in a population over several years.
- **Bar Graphs:** Useful for comparing discrete categories.
  - *Example:* Comparing the rainfall in different cities.
- **Pie Charts:** Represent proportions or percentages of a whole.
  - *Example:* The percentage of energy produced by different sources (solar, wind, coal, etc.).
- **Tables:** Organize data into rows and columns, often requiring you to identify relationships or calculate averages.

    - *Example:* A table showing the temperature at different times of the day.

3. Making Predictions and Inferences

You will often encounter questions that ask you to make predictions or inferences based on the given data or scenarios. This requires logical reasoning and the application of scientific principles.

- *Example Question:* A graph shows the population of deer in a forest declining over ten years. What might happen if predators are removed from the ecosystem?
    - *Answer:* The deer population may increase due to reduced predation.

4. Evaluating Evidence

Another essential skill is evaluating the reliability and validity of evidence. You may need to assess whether conclusions drawn from an experiment are justified based on the data.

- **Key Considerations:**
    - Are the sample sizes large enough to ensure accurate results?
    - Were control variables properly maintained?
    - Is there bias in the interpretation of results?
- *Example Question:* A study claims that a new drug is effective in treating a disease, but the sample size is only 10 patients. What is a potential issue with this conclusion?
    - *Answer:* The small sample size may not provide reliable results.

5. Scientific Argumentation

The ability to construct and evaluate scientific arguments is crucial. This involves analyzing claims, supporting them with evidence, and considering alternative explanations.

- **Example of Constructing a Scientific Argument:**
    - **Claim:** Increased carbon dioxide levels contribute to global warming.
    - **Evidence:** Data shows a correlation between rising CO_2 levels and global temperatures over the past century.
    - **Reasoning:** CO_2 is a greenhouse gas that traps heat, leading to temperature increases.

6. Applying Scientific Models

Scientific models are simplified representations of complex systems or processes. You may be asked to use these models to predict outcomes or explain phenomena.

- **Examples of Models:**
    - The water cycle: Shows how water moves through evaporation, condensation, and precipitation.
    - DNA replication: A model illustrating how genetic material is copied in cells.

7. Problem-Solving Using Scientific Methods

Scientific problem-solving involves applying the scientific method to address questions or challenges. This method includes the following steps:

1. **Observation:** Identify a problem or phenomenon.
2. **Question:** Ask a specific, testable question.
3. **Hypothesis:** Propose a possible explanation or prediction.
4. **Experimentation:** Design and conduct an experiment to test the hypothesis.
5. **Analysis:** Evaluate the results and determine whether they support the hypothesis.
6. **Conclusion:** Summarize findings and suggest future research.

- *Example Question:* A scientist observes that a specific plant species grows faster in acidic soil. What step should they take next to confirm this observation?
    - *Answer:* Design an experiment to test the effect of soil pH on plant growth.

8. Understanding Cause-and-Effect Relationships

You will often need to identify cause-and-effect relationships in scientific contexts. This involves determining how one variable influences another.

- *Example Question:* A study shows that an increase in fertilizer use leads to higher crop yields. What is the cause, and what is the effect?
    - *Answer:* The cause is the increase in fertilizer use, and the effect is the higher crop yields.

CHAPTER 21

LIFE SCIENCE

21.1 Cells and Their Functions

Cells are the fundamental building blocks of all living organisms, often referred to as the "basic units of life." Every organism, from the simplest single-celled bacteria to the most complex multicellular organisms like humans, is made up of cells. The study of cells, their structure, and their functions is essential to understanding life processes.

At their core, cells are responsible for carrying out all the processes necessary for life, including energy production, reproduction, and responding to environmental stimuli. Despite their diversity, all cells share some common features and structures, each playing a vital role in maintaining life.

Structure of Cells

Cells are categorized into two main types: **prokaryotic cells** and **eukaryotic cells**. Prokaryotic cells, such as bacteria, are simpler and lack a nucleus or membrane-bound organelles. Eukaryotic cells, found in plants, animals, fungi, and protists, are more complex and contain a variety of specialized structures known as organelles.

Eukaryotic cells are enclosed by a plasma membrane, a selectively permeable barrier that regulates what enters and exits the cell. Inside the cell, the cytoplasm is filled with organelles, each performing specific functions.

Key Organelles and Their Functions

1. **Nucleus**: Often referred to as the "control center" of the cell, the nucleus houses the cell's DNA, which contains instructions for protein synthesis and cell reproduction. The nuclear envelope surrounds the nucleus, and pores within it allow the exchange of materials between the nucleus and the cytoplasm.
2. **Mitochondria**: Known as the "powerhouse" of the cell, mitochondria are responsible for producing energy in the form of ATP (adenosine triphosphate) through cellular respiration. They are crucial for energy-intensive processes like muscle contraction and cell division.
3. **Ribosomes**: These small structures are the site of protein synthesis. Ribosomes can be found floating freely in the cytoplasm or attached to the rough endoplasmic reticulum.
4. **Endoplasmic Reticulum (ER)**: The ER is a network of membranes involved in the production and transport of materials. The rough ER is studded with ribosomes and specializes in protein synthesis, while the smooth ER is involved in lipid synthesis and detoxification.
5. **Golgi Apparatus**: This organelle modifies, sorts, and packages proteins and lipids for transport within the cell or secretion outside the cell.
6. **Lysosomes**: These are the cell's "recycling centers." They contain enzymes that break down waste materials and cellular debris.
7. **Chloroplasts**: Found only in plant cells and some protists, chloroplasts are the site of photosynthesis. They contain the pigment chlorophyll, which captures light energy to produce glucose.
8. **Vacuoles**: These storage organelles are larger in plant cells, where they help maintain cell structure and store nutrients, waste products, and water.
9. **Cytoskeleton**: The cytoskeleton provides structural support to the cell, maintains its shape, and facilitates the movement of organelles and other materials within the cell.
10. **Cell Wall**: Found in plant cells, fungi, and some prokaryotes, the cell wall provides additional support and protection. It is composed of cellulose in plants.

Cellular Processes

Cells perform a variety of functions that are critical to the survival of organisms. These processes include:

- **Energy Production**: In eukaryotic cells, mitochondria convert glucose and oxygen into ATP through cellular respiration. In plants, chloroplasts perform photosynthesis, converting sunlight into chemical energy stored in glucose.
- **Protein Synthesis**: Proteins are essential for virtually every function within the cell. This process begins in the nucleus, where DNA is transcribed into messenger RNA (mRNA). The mRNA is then translated by ribosomes into a specific sequence of amino acids, forming proteins.

- **Transport of Materials**: The plasma membrane controls the movement of substances into and out of the cell. Processes like diffusion, osmosis, and active transport regulate the exchange of materials, ensuring that nutrients enter the cell and waste products are removed.
- **Cell Division**: Cells reproduce by dividing. In eukaryotic cells, this occurs through mitosis (for growth and repair) or meiosis (for sexual reproduction). During division, the cell duplicates its DNA to ensure that each daughter cell receives a complete set of genetic information.
- **Communication**: Cells communicate with each other through chemical signals, such as hormones and neurotransmitters. These signals bind to receptors on the cell surface, triggering specific responses.

The Importance of Cells in Multicellular Organisms

In multicellular organisms, cells do not function in isolation. Instead, they work together to form tissues, organs, and organ systems. For example, muscle cells contract to enable movement, while nerve cells transmit signals that coordinate bodily functions. The specialization of cells allows organisms to perform complex activities, from digesting food to responding to environmental changes.

Application to the GED Exam

Understanding the structure and functions of cells is a key component of the Life Science section of the GED Science exam. You may encounter questions that ask you to:

- Identify the function of specific organelles, such as the mitochondria or chloroplasts.
- Analyze diagrams of cells and label their parts.
- Apply knowledge of cellular processes to real-world scenarios, such as explaining how photosynthesis contributes to energy production in plants.
- Compare and contrast prokaryotic and eukaryotic cells.

21.2 Human Body Systems and Their Interactions

The human body is a complex, interconnected network of systems, each playing a vital role in maintaining life. These systems work together seamlessly, enabling us to move, breathe, think, and respond to our environment. Understanding how these systems function and interact is key to grasping the fundamentals of human biology.

The Circulatory System: Transporting Life's Essentials

The circulatory system serves as the body's transportation network. The heart pumps blood through a network of arteries, veins, and capillaries, delivering oxygen and nutrients to cells while removing waste products like carbon dioxide. This system also plays a role in distributing hormones and regulating body temperature.

For example, during physical activity, the heart beats faster, increasing blood flow to muscles. At the same time, oxygen from the respiratory system and nutrients from the digestive system are delivered to meet the body's energy demands.

The Respiratory System: Breathing in Vital Oxygen

The respiratory system is responsible for gas exchange. When you inhale, oxygen enters your lungs and diffuses into the bloodstream. When you exhale, carbon dioxide—a waste product of cellular metabolism—is expelled. This exchange occurs in tiny air sacs called alveoli.

The respiratory and circulatory systems are closely linked. Oxygen picked up in the lungs is carried by the blood to tissues, while carbon dioxide from the tissues is transported back to the lungs for removal.

The Digestive System: Breaking Down and Building Up

The digestive system converts food into energy and nutrients that the body can use. It begins in the mouth, where food is chewed and mixed with saliva, and continues in the stomach and intestines, where enzymes break down carbohydrates, proteins, and fats.

Nutrients absorbed in the small intestine enter the bloodstream and are delivered to cells for energy and repair. Meanwhile, waste products move to the large intestine for elimination. This system works closely with the circulatory system to distribute nutrients and with the excretory system to remove waste.

The Nervous System: Commanding and Coordinating

The nervous system acts as the body's control center, regulating voluntary actions like walking and involuntary processes like heartbeat. It consists of the brain, spinal cord, and nerves, which transmit signals throughout the body.

Sensory organs gather information about the environment, such as light or sound, and send it to the brain for processing. In turn, the brain sends signals to muscles, enabling movement, or to glands, influencing processes like digestion or stress responses.

The Muscular and Skeletal Systems: Support and Movement

The skeletal system provides structure and protection, while the muscular system enables movement. Bones support the body and protect vital organs, such as the brain and heart. Muscles attach to bones and contract to create motion.

These systems work together to perform everyday actions, from simple tasks like picking up a cup to complex movements like running. Joints, ligaments, and cartilage ensure flexibility and smooth motion.

The Immune System: Defending Against Threats

The immune system protects the body from harmful invaders like bacteria and viruses. It includes white blood cells, antibodies, and lymph nodes, which work together to identify and neutralize pathogens. The skin also serves as a physical barrier against infections.

When an injury occurs, the immune system triggers inflammation to prevent infection and promote healing. This system often interacts with the circulatory system, as blood carries immune cells to affected areas.

The Endocrine System: Regulating Through Hormones

The endocrine system uses hormones to control bodily functions. Glands such as the thyroid, pancreas, and adrenal glands release hormones into the bloodstream, influencing processes like metabolism, growth, and reproduction.

For instance, the pancreas produces insulin, which regulates blood sugar levels. If insulin production is disrupted, as in diabetes, multiple systems—including the circulatory and excretory systems—are affected.

The Excretory System: Removing Waste

The excretory system eliminates waste products from the body. The kidneys filter blood to produce urine, removing toxins and excess water. The skin helps excrete waste through sweat, while the lungs expel carbon dioxide.

This system plays a critical role in maintaining chemical balance and preventing the buildup of harmful substances.

The Reproductive System: Sustaining Life

The reproductive system ensures the continuation of species. In males, the testes produce sperm, while in females, the ovaries produce eggs. This system is regulated by hormones that also influence secondary sexual characteristics, such as voice changes and body hair growth during puberty.

Interactions Between Systems

The human body is a web of interconnected systems. During exercise, the respiratory system increases oxygen intake, the circulatory system delivers that oxygen to muscles, and the muscular and skeletal systems work together to produce motion. Meanwhile, the nervous system monitors the body's needs, adjusting heart rate and respiration as necessary.

When the body experiences a threat, such as an infection, the immune system activates. White blood cells target pathogens, while the endocrine system releases stress hormones like cortisol to manage the body's response. At the same time, the circulatory system transports immune cells to the affected area, and the excretory system eliminates waste generated during the immune response.

21.3 Genetics, DNA, and Heredity

Genetics, DNA, and heredity are central to understanding how traits are passed from one generation to the next and how living organisms develop, function, and evolve. These concepts provide insight into why individuals have unique physical characteristics and how certain conditions or traits can run in families. In this chapter, we will explore the structure of DNA, the principles of heredity, and the mechanisms that govern genetic inheritance.

DNA: The Blueprint of Life

DNA, or deoxyribonucleic acid, is a molecule that carries the genetic instructions necessary for the growth, development, functioning, and reproduction of all living organisms. It is often referred to as the "blueprint of life" because it contains the information needed to build and maintain an organism.

DNA is found in the nucleus of cells, packaged into structures called chromosomes. In humans, there are 23 pairs of chromosomes (46 in total). Half of these chromosomes come from the mother, and the other half come from the father, ensuring a mix of genetic information.

The structure of DNA is a double helix, resembling a twisted ladder. The "sides" of the ladder are made of sugar and phosphate molecules, while the "rungs" are pairs of nitrogenous bases. There are four types of bases:

- **Adenine (A)** pairs with **Thymine (T).**
- **Cytosine (C)** pairs with **Guanine (G).**

The sequence of these bases encodes genetic information, much like letters form words and sentences. Specific sequences of bases make up genes, which determine traits such as eye color, hair color, and height.

Genes and Their Function

Genes are segments of DNA that provide instructions for making proteins, which perform most of the functions in a cell. Each gene has a specific location on a chromosome and can vary in length. For example, one gene may code for a protein that determines skin pigmentation, while another may influence blood type.

The combination of all an individual's genes is called their **genotype**, while the observable characteristics resulting from these genes are referred to as their **phenotype**. Environmental factors can also influence phenotypes, meaning that genetics and the environment often work together to shape an organism.

Heredity: Passing Traits to Offspring

Heredity is the process by which genetic information is passed from parents to offspring. This occurs through the transmission of chromosomes during reproduction. Humans inherit one set of 23 chromosomes from each parent, resulting in a unique combination of genetic material.

Traits are inherited according to principles first described by **Gregor Mendel**, the "father of genetics." Mendel's experiments with pea plants revealed how traits are passed down in predictable patterns. He identified two key principles:

1. **The Principle of Dominance:** Some traits are controlled by dominant alleles, which mask the expression of recessive alleles. For example, in pea plants, tall height (T) is dominant over short height (t). A plant with the genotype "Tt" will be tall because the dominant "T" allele is expressed.
2. **The Principle of Segregation:** During the formation of gametes (sperm and egg cells), alleles separate so that each gamete carries only one allele for each gene. Offspring inherit one allele from each parent.

Punnett Squares: Predicting Genetic Outcomes

A **Punnett square** is a tool used to predict the likelihood of specific genetic outcomes. By organizing the alleles from each parent, the Punnett square shows the possible genotypes and phenotypes of offspring.

For example, if both parents have the genotype "Tt" (heterozygous for tall height), the Punnett square looks like this:

	T (Parent 1)	**t (Parent 1)**
T (Parent 2)	TT	Tt
t (Parent 2)	Tt	tt

- **Genotypes:** 1 TT, 2 Tt, 1 tt
- **Phenotypes:** 3 Tall (TT or Tt), 1 Short (tt)

This illustrates that there is a 75% chance of offspring being tall and a 25% chance of being short.

Mutations and Genetic Variation

Mutations are changes in the DNA sequence. These can occur naturally during DNA replication or be caused by environmental factors like radiation or chemicals. Some mutations have no effect, while others can lead to genetic disorders or provide beneficial traits that enhance survival.

For example:

- **Beneficial Mutation:** A mutation that increases resistance to a disease.
- **Harmful Mutation:** A mutation in a gene that leads to conditions like cystic fibrosis or sickle cell anemia.

Mutations contribute to genetic variation within populations, which is essential for evolution and adaptation.

Applications of Genetics

Genetics has numerous applications in fields such as medicine, agriculture, and forensic science. Here are a few examples:

- **Medicine:** Genetic testing can identify inherited conditions or predispositions to diseases, enabling early intervention.
- **Agriculture:** Genetic engineering allows scientists to create crops with desirable traits, such as resistance to pests or drought.
- **Forensics:** DNA fingerprinting is used to identify individuals in criminal investigations.

21.4 Ecosystems, Biodiversity, and Environmental Science

Ecosystems, biodiversity, and environmental science are critical topics for understanding the complex interactions between living organisms and their environment. These concepts form the foundation for comprehending how ecosystems function, the role of biodiversity in maintaining balance, and the ways human activities impact the natural world. For the GED exam, it is essential to grasp these principles in detail, as they not only appear in scientific questions but also relate to real-world environmental issues.

What Are Ecosystems?

An **ecosystem** is a community of living organisms (biotic factors) interacting with their nonliving environment (abiotic factors) in a specific area. These interactions create a network of energy flow and nutrient cycling that sustains life. Ecosystems can be as small as a puddle or as vast as a rainforest.

- **Biotic factors** include plants, animals, fungi, and microorganisms that depend on one another for survival.
- **Abiotic factors** include sunlight, water, air, soil, temperature, and nutrients, all of which influence the living components.

Types of Ecosystems:

- **Terrestrial Ecosystems:** These are land-based ecosystems such as forests, grasslands, deserts, and tundra. Each has unique characteristics shaped by climate, geography, and the organisms that inhabit it.
- **Aquatic Ecosystems:** These include freshwater ecosystems (lakes, rivers, streams) and marine ecosystems (oceans, coral reefs). Aquatic ecosystems cover about 71% of Earth's surface and are vital for global oxygen production and climate regulation.

Example of Ecosystem Interactions:

In a forest ecosystem, trees produce oxygen and provide shelter and food for animals. Decomposers like fungi and bacteria break down dead organic material, recycling nutrients into the soil, which supports plant growth. These interdependent relationships ensure the ecosystem functions effectively.

Energy Flow in Ecosystems

Energy flows through ecosystems in a unidirectional manner, beginning with the sun. Plants, also called **producers** or autotrophs, capture solar energy through photosynthesis and convert it into chemical energy stored in glucose. This energy is then passed through various **trophic levels**:

1. **Producers:** Plants, algae, and some bacteria form the base of the food chain.
2. **Primary Consumers:** Herbivores, such as deer or rabbits, that feed on plants.
3. **Secondary Consumers:** Carnivores, such as snakes, that feed on herbivores.
4. **Tertiary Consumers:** Top predators, such as eagles or lions, that feed on other carnivores.
5. **Decomposers:** Fungi and bacteria break down dead organisms, returning nutrients to the soil.

Food Chain and Food Webs:

- A **food chain** is a linear sequence showing who eats whom, while a **food web** is a more complex representation of interconnected food chains in an ecosystem.
- **Example:** In a grassland, grass (producer) is eaten by a grasshopper (primary consumer), which is eaten by a frog (secondary consumer), and the frog is eaten by a snake (tertiary consumer).

The 10% Rule:

Only about 10% of the energy from one trophic level is transferred to the next. The rest is lost as heat. This explains why energy decreases as you move up the food chain and why ecosystems can only support a limited number of top predators.

Biodiversity: The Variety of Life

Biodiversity refers to the variety of life on Earth, encompassing the diversity of genes, species, and ecosystems. It is essential for ecosystem stability, resilience, and productivity.

Levels of Biodiversity:

1. **Genetic Diversity:** Variations within a species' DNA. Greater genetic diversity allows populations to adapt to environmental changes.
2. **Species Diversity:** The variety of species within a specific area. Ecosystems with high species diversity, like tropical rainforests, are more resilient to disturbances.
3. **Ecosystem Diversity:** The variety of ecosystems across the planet, from deserts to wetlands, each contributing uniquely to global processes.

Importance of Biodiversity:

Biodiversity supports essential ecosystem services, such as:

- Pollination of crops by insects.
- Natural pest control by predators.
- Nutrient cycling and soil formation.
- Water purification and climate regulation.

Environmental Science and Human Impact

Environmental science explores the relationship between humans and the natural world, focusing on how human activities affect ecosystems. Many modern environmental challenges stem from human interference.

Major Human Impacts:

1. **Deforestation:** Cutting down forests for agriculture, logging, or urbanization destroys habitats and contributes to climate change by reducing carbon storage.
2. **Pollution:** Air, water, and soil pollution harm ecosystems. For example, plastic waste in oceans entangles marine life, while pesticides can poison non-target species.
3. **Climate Change:** Rising temperatures, caused by greenhouse gas emissions, disrupt ecosystems, alter weather patterns, and threaten species unable to adapt quickly.
4. **Overfishing:** Depletes fish populations, disrupting marine ecosystems and food chains.
5. **Invasive Species:** Non-native species introduced to new areas often outcompete native species, reducing biodiversity.

Example of Human Impact:

The Great Barrier Reef, one of the most biodiverse marine ecosystems, is under threat from coral bleaching caused by rising sea temperatures. This illustrates how climate change directly affects ecosystems.

Ecosystem Services: Nature's Contributions

Ecosystem services are the benefits that humans derive from nature. These include:

- **Provisioning Services:** Food, water, timber, and medicine.
- **Regulating Services:** Climate control, flood prevention, and water purification.
- **Cultural Services:** Recreational, spiritual, and educational opportunities.
- **Supporting Services:** Processes like soil formation and nutrient cycling that support other services.

Conservation and Restoration

Protecting ecosystems and biodiversity is crucial for maintaining ecological balance and securing resources for future generations. Conservation efforts include:

- Establishing protected areas, like national parks and wildlife reserves.
- Enforcing anti-poaching laws and sustainable fishing regulations.
- Promoting reforestation and habitat restoration.
- Using renewable energy to reduce reliance on fossil fuels.

Ecosystems in the GED Exam

For the GED Science exam, understanding ecosystems, biodiversity, and environmental science involves analyzing graphs, interpreting data, and applying knowledge to real-world scenarios. You may encounter questions that ask you to:

- Explain how energy flows through a food chain.
- Interpret a chart showing the effects of deforestation on biodiversity.
- Evaluate human impacts on an ecosystem and propose solutions for restoration.

CHAPTER 22

PHYSICAL SCIENCE

22.1 Principles of Force, Motion, and Energy

Understanding the principles of force, motion, and energy is essential for analyzing how objects interact and move within their environment. These concepts are foundational in the field of physics and are often applied in everyday situations, from the motion of vehicles to the operation of machines. In this chapter, we will explore the fundamental laws governing these principles and their real-world applications.

Force: The Push and Pull of the Universe

A **force** is a push or pull acting on an object, capable of changing its motion, direction, or shape. Forces are measured in **newtons (N)** and are vector quantities, meaning they have both magnitude and direction.

Types of Forces

1. **Contact Forces:** These require physical contact between objects. Examples include:
   - **Frictional Force:** Opposes the motion of an object sliding across a surface.
   - **Tension Force:** Experienced by a rope or cable when it is pulled taut.
   - **Normal Force:** The support force exerted by a surface perpendicular to an object resting on it.
2. **Non-Contact Forces:** These act over a distance without physical contact. Examples include:
   - **Gravitational Force:** The attraction between two objects due to their mass.
   - **Electromagnetic Force:** Associated with electric and magnetic fields.
   - **Nuclear Force:** Acts within the nucleus of an atom, holding protons and neutrons together.

Net Force and Equilibrium

- **Net Force:** The total force acting on an object is the sum of all individual forces. If forces are balanced (net force = 0), the object remains at rest or moves at a constant velocity. If forces are unbalanced, the object accelerates.

Motion: Describing How Objects Move

Motion occurs when an object changes its position relative to a reference point. The study of motion, known as **kinematics**, involves analyzing speed, velocity, and acceleration.

Key Concepts of Motion

1. **Speed:** The distance an object travels per unit of time. It is a scalar quantity (magnitude only).
   - Formula:

$$\text{Speed} = \frac{\text{Distance}}{\text{Time}}$$

2. **Velocity:** Similar to speed but includes direction. It is a vector quantity.
   - Example: A car moving at 60 mph eastward has a velocity of 60 mph east.
3. **Acceleration:** The rate at which velocity changes over time. Acceleration occurs when an object speeds up, slows down, or changes direction.
   - Formula:

$$\text{Acceleration} = \frac{\text{Change in Velocity}}{\text{Time}}$$

Newton's Laws of Motion

1. **First Law (Law of Inertia):** An object remains at rest or in uniform motion unless acted upon by an external force.
   - Example: A book on a table will not move unless pushed.
2. **Second Law:** The acceleration of an object is directly proportional to the net force acting on it and inversely proportional to its mass.
   - Formula:

$$F = ma$$

   $(Force = Mass \times Acceleration)$
   - Example: A heavier object requires more force to accelerate than a lighter object.

3. **Third Law:** For every action, there is an equal and opposite reaction.
   - Example: When you jump off a boat, the boat moves backward as you push forward.

Energy: The Ability to Do Work

Energy is the capacity to perform work or cause change. It exists in various forms and can be transferred or transformed but never created or destroyed (**Law of Conservation of Energy**).

Types of Energy

1. **Kinetic Energy:** Energy of motion.
   - Formula:

$$KE = \frac{1}{2}mv^2$$

     (*Kinetic Energy = ½ × Mass × Velocity²*)
   - Example: A rolling ball has kinetic energy.
2. **Potential Energy:** Stored energy based on an object's position or configuration.
   - Formula:

$$PE = mgh$$

     (*Potential Energy = Mass × Gravity × Height*)
   - Example: A rock at the top of a hill has potential energy.
3. **Thermal Energy:** Energy associated with the motion of particles in a substance. It increases as temperature rises.
4. **Chemical Energy:** Stored in chemical bonds and released during chemical reactions.
5. **Mechanical Energy:** The sum of kinetic and potential energy in a system.

Work and Power

Work is done when a force is applied to an object, and the object moves in the direction of the force.

- Formula:

$$W = Fd\cos\theta$$

  (*Work = Force × Distance × Cosine of the Angle*)
- Example: Lifting a box involves work because a force is applied, and the box moves upward.

Power is the rate at which work is done.

- Formula:

$$P = \frac{W}{t}$$

  (*Power = Work ÷ Time*)
- Example: A motor lifting a weight quickly is more powerful than one lifting it slowly.

Real-World Applications

- **Transportation:** Understanding motion and force helps engineers design safer and more efficient vehicles.
- **Sports:** Athletes use principles of energy and motion to optimize performance.
- **Energy Production:** Kinetic and potential energy principles are applied in hydroelectric plants, wind turbines, and other renewable energy sources.

Practice Problem Example

Problem 1:

A car with a mass of 1,500 kg accelerates at a rate of 2 m/s². What is the force exerted by the engine?

Solution:

Using Newton's Second Law:

$$F = ma$$

$$F = 1500\ \text{kg} \times 2\ \text{m/s}^2 = 3000\ \text{N}$$

Answer: The force exerted by the engine is **3,000 N**.

Problem 2:

A 2-kg object is held at a height of 5 m. Calculate its potential energy.

Solution:

$$PE = mgh$$

$$PE = 2\,\text{kg} \times 9.8\,\text{m/s}^2 \times 5\,\text{m} = 98\,\text{J}$$

Answer: The potential energy is **98 J**.

22.2 Chemical Reactions and Properties of Matter

Chemical reactions and the properties of matter are at the heart of understanding how substances interact, transform, and form the building blocks of everything around us. From the air we breathe to the food we eat, chemical reactions and the physical and chemical properties of matter are fundamental concepts in physical science. In this chapter, we will explore the nature of matter, its properties, and the principles behind chemical reactions.

What is Matter?

Matter is anything that has mass and occupies space. It can exist in different forms, such as solids, liquids, gases, and plasma. All matter is composed of atoms, which are the smallest units of an element that retain its chemical properties. Atoms combine to form molecules, the smallest units of compounds.

States of Matter

1. **Solids:** Have a definite shape and volume. The particles are tightly packed and only vibrate in place.
   - Example: Ice, metal, wood.
2. **Liquids:** Have a definite volume but take the shape of their container. Particles are less tightly packed than in solids and can flow past one another.
   - Example: Water, oil, milk.
3. **Gases:** Have neither a definite shape nor volume. Particles are far apart and move freely.
   - Example: Oxygen, carbon dioxide.
4. **Plasma:** A high-energy state where electrons are separated from atoms. Common in stars and lightning.

Matter can change from one state to another through physical processes such as melting, freezing, evaporation, and condensation.

Physical and Chemical Properties of Matter

Physical Properties

Physical properties can be observed or measured without changing the identity of a substance. Examples include:

- **Color**
- **Density** (mass per unit volume)
- **Boiling and Melting Points**
- **Solubility** (ability to dissolve in a solvent)

Chemical Properties

Chemical properties describe how a substance interacts with other substances. Examples include:

- **Flammability** (ability to burn)
- **Reactivity** (how it reacts with acids, bases, or oxygen)
- **Toxicity**

Understanding Chemical Reactions

A **chemical reaction** occurs when one or more substances, called reactants, transform into new substances, called products. This involves breaking chemical bonds in the reactants and forming new bonds in the products.

Signs of a Chemical Reaction

- Color change
- Formation of a gas (bubbles)
- Formation of a solid (precipitate) in a solution

- Release or absorption of energy (light, heat, sound)

Key Components of a Chemical Reaction

1. **Reactants:** The starting substances.
2. **Products:** The substances formed after the reaction.
3. **Chemical Equation:** A representation of the reaction.
   - Example:

$$2H_2 + O_2 \rightarrow 2H_2O$$

(Two molecules of hydrogen react with one molecule of oxygen to form water.)

Balancing Chemical Equations

Chemical equations must be balanced to obey the **Law of Conservation of Mass**, which states that matter cannot be created or destroyed in a chemical reaction. The number of atoms of each element must be the same on both sides of the equation.

- **Unbalanced Equation:**

$$H_2 + O_2 \rightarrow H_2O$$

(This equation is unbalanced because there are two oxygen atoms on the left but only one on the right.)

- **Balanced Equation:**

$$2H_2 + O_2 \rightarrow 2H_2O$$

(Now, there are two oxygen atoms and four hydrogen atoms on both sides.)

Types of Chemical Reactions

Chemical reactions can be categorized into several types:

1. **Synthesis (Combination) Reactions:** Two or more reactants combine to form a single product.
   - Example:

$$2Na + Cl_2 \rightarrow 2NaCl$$

(Sodium reacts with chlorine to form sodium chloride, or table salt.)

2. **Decomposition Reactions:** A single compound breaks down into two or more products.
   - Example:

$$2H_2O \rightarrow 2H_2 + O_2$$

(Water decomposes into hydrogen and oxygen gas when electricity is applied.)

3. **Single Replacement Reactions:** One element replaces another in a compound.
   - Example:

$$Zn + 2HCl \rightarrow ZnCl_2 + H_2$$

(Zinc replaces hydrogen in hydrochloric acid.)

4. **Double Replacement Reactions:** Two compounds exchange elements to form new compounds.
   - Example:

$$NaCl + AgNO_3 \rightarrow NaNO_3 + AgCl$$

(Sodium chloride reacts with silver nitrate to form sodium nitrate and silver chloride.)

5. **Combustion Reactions:** A substance reacts with oxygen, releasing energy in the form of heat and light.
   - Example:

$$CH_4 + 2O_2 \rightarrow CO_2 + 2H_2O$$

(Methane burns in oxygen to produce carbon dioxide and water.)

Energy in Chemical Reactions

Chemical reactions either absorb or release energy:

- **Exothermic Reactions:** Release energy, usually as heat.
  - Example: Combustion of fuels.
- **Endothermic Reactions:** Absorb energy, often causing a drop in temperature.
  - Example: Photosynthesis.

Real-Life Applications of Chemical Reactions

1. **Cooking:** Heat causes chemical reactions in food, such as caramelization or the Maillard reaction, which gives browned foods their flavor.
2. **Medicine:** Chemical reactions are used to create pharmaceuticals and deliver treatments.
3. **Environment:** Reactions like the breakdown of pollutants help clean air and water.
4. **Energy Production:** Combustion reactions power engines and generate electricity.

Practice Problem Example

Problem 1: Balance the equation:

$$C_3H_8 + O_2 \rightarrow CO_2 + H_2O$$

Solution:

1. Balance carbon (C):

$$C_3H_8 + O_2 \rightarrow 3CO_2 + H_2O$$

2. Balance hydrogen (H):

$$C_3H_8 + O_2 \rightarrow 3CO_2 + 4H_2O$$

3. Balance oxygen (O):

$$C_3H_8 + 5O_2 \rightarrow 3CO_2 + 4H_2O$$

Answer: The balanced equation is:

$$C_3H_8 + 5O_2 \rightarrow 3CO_2 + 4H_2O$$

Problem 2: Classify the reaction:

$$2H_2O_2 \rightarrow 2H_2O + O_2$$

Answer: This is a **decomposition reaction** because hydrogen peroxide breaks down into water and oxygen.

22.3 Basics of Electricity and Magnetism

Electricity and magnetism are fundamental forces of nature that play a crucial role in powering modern life. These forces are interconnected and form the basis of electromagnetism, a branch of physics that explains how electric charges and currents interact with magnetic fields. Understanding the basics of electricity and magnetism is essential for interpreting how devices work, from simple circuits to advanced technologies.

Electricity: Understanding Electric Charge and Current

Electricity is the flow of electric charge, which is carried by particles like electrons and protons. The study of electricity involves understanding charges, currents, and their effects.

Electric Charge

- **Definition:** Electric charge is a property of particles that causes them to experience a force when placed in an electric field. Charges can be positive (protons) or negative (electrons).
- **Law of Charges:** Like charges repel, and opposite charges attract.
- **Unit of Charge:** The unit of electric charge is the **coulomb (C).**

Electric Current

- **Definition:** Electric current is the flow of electric charge through a conductor, such as a wire.
- **Measurement:** It is measured in **amperes (A)** using an ammeter.
- **Formula:**

$$I = \frac{Q}{t}$$

  Where I is the current, Q is the charge in coulombs, and t is the time in seconds.

Voltage

- **Definition:** Voltage, or electric potential difference, is the energy per unit charge that drives the flow of electrons.
- **Unit:** It is measured in **volts (V)** using a voltmeter.
- **Source:** Batteries and generators provide voltage to circuits.

Resistance

- **Definition:** Resistance is the opposition to the flow of electric current in a material.
- **Unit:** Resistance is measured in **ohms (Ω).**
- **Factors Affecting Resistance:** Material, length, thickness, and temperature of the conductor.

Ohm's Law

Ohm's Law describes the relationship between voltage, current, and resistance:

$$V = IR$$

Where V is voltage, I is current, and R is resistance. This law is fundamental for understanding how circuits function.

Circuits: Pathways for Electricity

An electric circuit is a closed loop that allows current to flow. Circuits can be classified into two main types:

1. **Series Circuit:**
   - Components are connected end-to-end.
   - Current is the same through all components, but voltage is divided.
   - Example: Old Christmas lights, where one bulb failing breaks the circuit.
2. **Parallel Circuit:**
   - Components are connected across the same two points.
   - Voltage is the same across all branches, but current divides.
   - Example: Modern home wiring, where multiple devices can operate independently.

Magnetism: The Force of Attraction and Repulsion

Magnetism arises from the motion of electric charges, typically electrons in atoms. Magnets and magnetic fields are central to many technologies, from compasses to motors.

Magnetic Fields

- **Definition:** A magnetic field is the region around a magnet where magnetic forces can be detected.
- **Field Lines:** Magnetic field lines show the direction of the magnetic force, emerging from the north pole and looping back to the south pole.
- **Earth's Magnetic Field:** Earth acts as a giant magnet, with a magnetic field that protects the planet from solar radiation.

Properties of Magnets

- Magnets have two poles: north and south.
- Like poles repel, and opposite poles attract.
- Breaking a magnet results in two smaller magnets, each with its own north and south poles.

Electromagnetism: The Link Between Electricity and Magnetism

Electricity and magnetism are interconnected. When an electric current flows through a wire, it creates a magnetic field around the wire. This principle is the basis for electromagnets and many modern devices.

Electromagnets

- **Definition:** An electromagnet is a temporary magnet created by passing electric current through a coil of wire wrapped around a core, usually made of iron.
- **Uses:** Electromagnets are used in electric motors, generators, and MRI machines.

Faraday's Law of Electromagnetic Induction

Faraday's Law explains how a changing magnetic field can induce an electric current in a conductor. This principle is used in:

- Generators: Convert mechanical energy into electrical energy.
- Transformers: Transfer electrical energy between circuits by varying voltage.

Real-Life Applications of Electricity and Magnetism

Electricity and magnetism are essential for powering modern life. Some everyday applications include:

1. **Power Generation:** Power plants use generators to produce electricity for homes and industries.
2. **Transportation:** Electric vehicles and trains use principles of electromagnetism for propulsion.

3. **Communication:** Devices like radios, televisions, and smartphones rely on electromagnetic waves to transmit information.
4. **Healthcare:** MRI machines use strong magnetic fields to produce detailed images of the human body.
5. **Household Appliances:** Devices like refrigerators, fans, and microwaves operate using electric circuits and motors.

Practice Problem Examples

Problem 1: A circuit has a voltage of 12 V and a resistance of 4 Ω. What is the current flowing through the circuit?

Solution:

Using Ohm's Law:

$$I = \frac{V}{R}$$

$$I = \frac{12\ \text{V}}{4\,\Omega} = 3\ \text{A}$$

Answer: The current is **3 A**.

Problem 2: A wire carrying an electric current generates a magnetic field. If the current increases, what happens to the strength of the magnetic field?

Answer: The strength of the magnetic field increases because the magnetic field is directly proportional to the current.

Problem 3: In a parallel circuit with two branches, one branch has a resistance of 2 Ω and the other has a resistance of 4 Ω. Which branch will carry more current?

Answer: The branch with 2 Ω resistance will carry more current, as current is inversely proportional to resistance.

22.4 Understanding Waves: Light and Sound

Waves are essential to understanding how energy travels through different mediums, including light and sound. These concepts are crucial not only for their applications in science and technology but also for interpreting phenomena we encounter daily, such as seeing colors or hearing music. This chapter explores the properties, behaviors, and differences between light and sound waves and how they impact the world around us.

What Are Waves?

A wave is a repeating disturbance or vibration that transfers energy from one place to another. Waves can move through a medium (like air, water, or solid materials) or, in the case of electromagnetic waves, through a vacuum.

Two Main Types of Waves

1. **Mechanical Waves:** Require a medium to travel through, such as air, water, or solid objects.
   - **Examples:** Sound waves, water waves, and seismic waves.
2. **Electromagnetic Waves:** Do not require a medium and can travel through a vacuum.
   - **Examples:** Light, radio waves, and X-rays.

Properties of Waves

All waves share certain characteristics that define their behavior:

- **Wavelength (λ):** The distance between two consecutive crests or troughs of a wave.
- **Frequency (f):** The number of wave cycles passing a point per second, measured in hertz (Hz).
- **Amplitude:** The height of the wave, related to the wave's energy. Higher amplitude means greater energy.
- **Speed (v):** The rate at which a wave travels through a medium.
  - Formula:

$$v = f\lambda$$

Where v is wave speed, f is frequency, and λ is wavelength.

Light Waves

Light is an electromagnetic wave that travels through space at a speed of approximately 3.0×10^8 m/s (the speed of light). Light waves have both electric and magnetic components, which oscillate perpendicular to each other and to the direction of travel.

Key Properties of Light

1. **Reflection:** Light bounces off a surface.
   - Example: A mirror reflects light, forming an image.
2. **Refraction:** Light bends as it passes from one medium to another due to a change in speed.
   - Example: A straw appears bent in a glass of water.
3. **Diffraction:** Light spreads out when it passes through a narrow opening or around an obstacle.
4. **Absorption:** Certain materials absorb light, converting it into heat.
   - Example: Dark clothing absorbs more sunlight than light-colored clothing.

The Visible Spectrum

Light waves are part of the electromagnetic spectrum, which ranges from gamma rays (short wavelength, high energy) to radio waves (long wavelength, low energy). The visible spectrum includes wavelengths that human eyes can detect, ranging from violet (short wavelength) to red (long wavelength).

Sound Waves

Sound is a mechanical wave that requires a medium, such as air, water, or solids, to travel. It is produced by vibrations and propagates as a longitudinal wave, where particles of the medium oscillate parallel to the wave's direction of travel.

Key Properties of Sound

1. **Pitch:** Determined by the frequency of the sound wave. Higher frequencies produce higher-pitched sounds.
2. **Loudness:** Related to the amplitude of the sound wave. Greater amplitude means louder sound.
3. **Speed of Sound:** Varies depending on the medium:
   - Travels fastest in solids, slower in liquids, and slowest in gases.
   - In air at room temperature, the speed of sound is approximately 343 m/s.

Comparing Light and Sound Waves

Property	Light Waves	Sound Waves
Type of Wave	Electromagnetic (transverse)	Mechanical (longitudinal)
Medium Required	No (can travel in a vacuum)	Yes (requires air, water, or solids)
Speed	3.0×10^8 m/s	343 m/s in air
Behavior	Can reflect, refract, and diffract	Can reflect, refract, and diffract
Examples	Sunlight, X-rays, microwaves	Music, speech, sonar

Wave Behavior in Real Life

- **Reflection of Sound (Echo):** Sound waves bounce off surfaces like canyon walls, creating echoes.
- **Sonar Technology:** Uses sound waves to detect objects underwater by measuring the time it takes for a reflected wave to return.
- **Prisms and Rainbows:** Refraction of light waves through water droplets separates light into its spectrum of colors.
- **Noise-Canceling Headphones:** Use destructive interference to reduce unwanted sound waves.

Practice Problem Examples

Problem 1: A light wave has a frequency of 5×10^{14} Hz. If the speed of light is 3.0×10^8 m/s, what is its wavelength?

Solution:

Using the formula $v = f\lambda$:

$$\lambda = \frac{v}{f} = \frac{3.0 \times 10^8 \text{ m/s}}{5 \times 10^{14} \text{ Hz}} = 6 \times 10^{-7} \text{ m}$$

Answer: The wavelength is 6×10^{-7} m or 600 nm.

Problem 2: A sound wave travels through air at 343 m/s and has a frequency of 256 Hz. What is its wavelength?

Solution:

Using the formula $v = f\lambda$:

$$\lambda = \frac{v}{f} = \frac{343 \text{ m/s}}{256 \text{ Hz}} = 1.34 \text{ m}$$

Answer: The wavelength is 1.34 m.

CHAPTER 23

EARTH AND SPACE SCIENCE

23.1 The Earth's Structure and Systems

The Earth is a dynamic planet, constantly shaped and reshaped by its internal and external forces. Understanding the Earth's structure and the systems that interact to sustain life is essential for interpreting natural processes and their impact on ecosystems and human activities. In this chapter, we delve into the Earth's layers, its geologic cycles, and the systems that regulate life and climate.

The Earth's Layers

The Earth is composed of several distinct layers, each with unique characteristics that contribute to its overall structure and function. These layers are categorized by their composition and physical properties.

1. **The Crust**
   The crust is the outermost layer of the Earth, where we live. It is relatively thin, ranging from about 5 km beneath the oceans (oceanic crust) to about 70 km beneath continents (continental crust). Made primarily of silicate minerals, the crust is divided into tectonic plates that float on the semi-fluid mantle beneath. These plates interact at their boundaries, causing earthquakes, volcanic activity, and mountain formation.
2. **The Mantle**
   Beneath the crust lies the mantle, which extends to a depth of about 2,900 km. The mantle is primarily composed of silicate rocks rich in iron and magnesium. Its upper portion, called the asthenosphere, is partially molten, allowing tectonic plates to move. Convection currents in the mantle, driven by heat from the Earth's core, play a critical role in plate tectonics.
3. **The Outer Core**
   The outer core is a layer of molten iron and nickel, extending from a depth of 2,900 km to 5,150 km. The movement of these liquid metals generates the Earth's magnetic field, which protects the planet from harmful solar radiation.
4. **The Inner Core**
   At the Earth's center is the inner core, a solid sphere of iron and nickel with temperatures reaching up to 5,700°C. Despite its extreme heat, the immense pressure at this depth keeps it solid.

The Rock Cycle

The Earth's crust is continuously recycled through the rock cycle, a natural process that transforms rocks from one type to another over time. This cycle includes the formation, breakdown, and reformation of rocks through various geological processes.

1. **Igneous Rocks** form when molten magma cools and solidifies, either beneath the Earth's surface (intrusive igneous rocks) or after erupting from a volcano (extrusive igneous rocks).
   - Example: Granite and basalt.
2. **Sedimentary Rocks** develop from the accumulation and compression of sediments, such as sand, silt, and organic material, often in layers.
   - Example: Limestone and sandstone.
3. **Metamorphic Rocks** arise when existing rocks are subjected to intense heat and pressure, altering their structure and mineral composition.
   - Example: Marble and schist.

These transformations occur over millions of years, driven by processes like erosion, deposition, and tectonic activity.

Earth's Systems: The Interconnected Spheres

The Earth operates as a system composed of four interdependent "spheres," each playing a vital role in maintaining balance and supporting life.

1. **Geosphere**
   The geosphere includes all the solid parts of the Earth, such as rocks, minerals, and landforms. It provides the foundation for ecosystems and influences natural events like earthquakes and volcanic eruptions.

2. **Hydrosphere**
   The hydrosphere encompasses all water on Earth, including oceans, rivers, lakes, glaciers, and groundwater. Water cycles through evaporation, condensation, and precipitation, connecting the atmosphere, biosphere, and geosphere.
3. **Atmosphere**
   The atmosphere is the layer of gases surrounding Earth, composed mainly of nitrogen (78%) and oxygen (21%), with traces of other gases. It regulates temperature, protects the planet from harmful solar radiation, and provides the air we breathe.
4. **Biosphere**
   The biosphere includes all living organisms on Earth. It interacts with other spheres to support life, with plants exchanging gases with the atmosphere, animals relying on water from the hydrosphere, and organisms using minerals from the geosphere.

Plate Tectonics and Continental Drift

The theory of **plate tectonics** explains the movement of the Earth's lithospheric plates and their role in shaping the planet's surface. This movement is driven by convection currents in the mantle and has led to the formation of continents, mountains, and ocean basins.

- **Divergent Boundaries:** Plates move apart, creating new crust.
  - Example: The Mid-Atlantic Ridge.
- **Convergent Boundaries:** Plates collide, forming mountains or subduction zones where one plate is forced beneath another.
  - Example: The Himalayas.
- **Transform Boundaries:** Plates slide past each other, causing earthquakes.
  - Example: The San Andreas Fault.

Natural Cycles Supporting Life

The Earth's systems are interconnected through natural cycles that sustain life:

1. **The Water Cycle:** Water moves through evaporation, condensation, precipitation, and runoff, distributing fresh water across the planet.
2. **The Carbon Cycle:** Carbon flows between the atmosphere, oceans, plants, animals, and soil, playing a critical role in regulating Earth's climate.
3. **The Nitrogen Cycle:** Nitrogen moves through the atmosphere, soil, and living organisms, supporting plant growth and ecosystem productivity.

Practice Problem Example

Problem 1:
Explain how the movement of tectonic plates can lead to the formation of volcanoes.
Answer:
Volcanoes often form at convergent plate boundaries where one plate is forced beneath another in a process called subduction. As the subducted plate sinks into the mantle, it melts, forming magma. This magma rises through the crust, leading to volcanic eruptions. Volcanoes can also form at divergent boundaries, where plates move apart and magma rises to fill the gap.
Problem 2:
If the Earth's core generates the magnetic field, why is the outer core liquid while the inner core is solid?
Answer:
The outer core is liquid because the temperature there exceeds the melting point of its iron and nickel components at the pressures present. The inner core, despite being hotter, remains solid due to the immense pressure at the Earth's center, which prevents the atoms from moving freely to form a liquid.

23.2 Weather, Climate, and Natural Disasters

Weather and climate are integral aspects of Earth science, shaping ecosystems, influencing human activities, and interacting with other planetary systems. Understanding their differences, causes, and impacts, as well as the phenomena of natural disasters, is essential for interpreting the environment and addressing global challenges.

Weather vs. Climate: What's the Difference?

Weather and climate are often used interchangeably, but they refer to different phenomena:

- **Weather:** The short-term atmospheric conditions in a specific place at a specific time. It includes factors like temperature, humidity, precipitation, wind, and pressure.
    - Example: A thunderstorm in the afternoon or a sunny morning.
- **Climate:** The average weather conditions of a region over a long period, typically 30 years or more. It reflects patterns such as seasonal temperatures and rainfall.
    - Example: The hot, dry summers and mild winters of a Mediterranean climate.

Factors Affecting Weather and Climate

Several factors influence weather and climate, ranging from global phenomena to localized conditions:

1. **Solar Energy:** The sun is the primary driver of weather and climate. Uneven heating of the Earth's surface creates temperature differences that drive wind and ocean currents.
2. **Atmospheric Circulation:** Wind patterns, such as trade winds and jet streams, distribute heat and moisture around the globe.
3. **Ocean Currents:** Currents like the Gulf Stream transfer heat between the equator and poles, moderating temperatures.
4. **Topography:** Mountains can block or direct wind and precipitation, creating rain shadows or enhanced rainfall.
    - Example: The Pacific Northwest receives high rainfall due to moist air rising over coastal mountains.
5. **Latitude:** Regions near the equator receive more direct sunlight, leading to warmer climates, while polar regions are colder due to indirect sunlight.
6. **Human Activity:** Greenhouse gas emissions, deforestation, and urbanization affect climate by altering the atmosphere's composition and the Earth's surface.

Weather Phenomena

Weather is shaped by interactions between the atmosphere, hydrosphere, and solar energy. Key weather phenomena include:

1. **Precipitation:** Rain, snow, sleet, or hail that forms when water vapor condenses in the atmosphere.
2. **Cloud Formation:** Clouds form when moist air rises, cools, and condenses around particles like dust or pollen.
3. **Storms:** Weather systems like thunderstorms, hurricanes, and tornadoes result from unstable atmospheric conditions.
4. **Wind:** Air movement caused by pressure differences in the atmosphere. Winds are classified by their speed and direction.

Example of Weather Interaction:

During a warm summer day, the sun heats the ground, causing warm air to rise. This creates a low-pressure area, pulling in cooler air, which can lead to thunderstorms if moisture is present.

Climate Zones

The Earth is divided into climate zones based on temperature, precipitation, and vegetation:

1. **Tropical:** Hot and humid, with significant rainfall. Found near the equator.
2. **Arid:** Dry climates with low rainfall, such as deserts.
3. **Temperate:** Moderate climates with distinct seasons, common in mid-latitudes.
4. **Polar:** Cold and dry, found near the poles.
5. **Mediterranean:** Hot, dry summers and mild, wet winters, common in regions like California and southern Europe.

Natural Disasters

Natural disasters are extreme weather or geological events that cause significant damage to life, property, and ecosystems. These events often result from natural processes intensified by human activities.

Types of Natural Disasters

1. **Tornadoes:** Violently rotating columns of air that form under specific conditions in thunderstorms. Tornadoes are most common in regions like the central United States, known as Tornado Alley.
2. **Hurricanes:** Intense tropical storms with sustained winds of at least 74 mph. Hurricanes form over warm ocean waters and can cause flooding, storm surges, and wind damage.
3. **Floods:** Occur when water overflows onto normally dry land. They can result from heavy rainfall, hurricanes, or melting snow.
4. **Droughts:** Prolonged periods of below-average precipitation that lead to water shortages and crop failures.

5. **Earthquakes and Tsunamis:** While primarily geological, these disasters can be exacerbated by atmospheric conditions, such as undersea earthquakes triggering tsunamis.
6. **Wildfires:** Fires that spread rapidly in forests or grasslands, often sparked by lightning or human activity and intensified by dry, windy conditions.

Global Climate Change and Extreme Weather

Global climate change has intensified many natural disasters, increasing their frequency and severity. Key impacts include:

- **Rising Sea Levels:** Contributing to more frequent coastal flooding.
- **Warmer Oceans:** Fueling stronger hurricanes and cyclones.
- **Drier Conditions:** Leading to more frequent and severe droughts and wildfires.
- **Shifting Weather Patterns:** Altering precipitation and temperature trends, impacting agriculture and biodiversity.

Practice Problem Examples

Problem 1:
What is the primary difference between weather and climate?
Answer:
Weather refers to short-term atmospheric conditions, such as daily temperature and precipitation. Climate describes the long-term average weather patterns in a region over decades.
Problem 2:
How do ocean currents influence climate?
Answer:
Ocean currents transfer heat across the planet. Warm currents, like the Gulf Stream, raise temperatures in coastal regions, while cold currents, like the California Current, cool nearby areas.
Problem 3:
Why are hurricanes more common in warm ocean regions?
Answer:
Hurricanes form over warm ocean waters where heat and moisture provide the energy needed to develop and sustain these powerful storms.

By understanding weather, climate, and natural disasters, you gain insight into the forces that shape our environment and impact human activities. These principles not only form a critical part of the GED Science exam but also provide the knowledge needed to address global environmental challenges.

23.3 The Solar System, Stars, and Galaxies

The universe is vast and complex, containing billions of stars, planets, and galaxies. At its core, our Solar System is just one of countless systems in the universe, yet it plays a vital role in shaping life on Earth. This chapter explores the components of the Solar System, the life cycle of stars, and the structure of galaxies to provide a comprehensive understanding of celestial phenomena.

The Solar System

Our Solar System consists of the Sun, planets, moons, dwarf planets, comets, asteroids, and other celestial bodies, all bound by the Sun's gravitational pull. Formed approximately 4.6 billion years ago, it is located in the Milky Way galaxy.

Key Components of the Solar System

1. **The Sun:**
    - A medium-sized star at the center of the Solar System.
    - Composed primarily of hydrogen and helium, the Sun generates energy through nuclear fusion, converting hydrogen into helium in its core.
    - Its energy supports life on Earth and drives processes like photosynthesis and the water cycle.
2. **Planets:**
    - There are eight planets, categorized into **terrestrial planets** (rocky surfaces) and **gas giants** (composed mostly of gases).

- **Terrestrial Planets:** Mercury, Venus, Earth, Mars.
- **Gas Giants:** Jupiter, Saturn (with significant hydrogen and helium).
- **Ice Giants:** Uranus, Neptune (rich in water, ammonia, and methane ices).

3. **Moons:**
   - Natural satellites that orbit planets.
   - Earth's Moon influences tides and stabilizes the planet's axial tilt.
   - Jupiter and Saturn have dozens of moons, including Europa (potentially harboring subsurface oceans) and Titan (with a thick atmosphere).
4. **Asteroids and Comets:**
   - **Asteroids:** Small, rocky objects primarily found in the asteroid belt between Mars and Jupiter.
   - **Comets:** Composed of ice, dust, and rock, comets develop glowing tails as they approach the Sun.
5. **Dwarf Planets:**
   - Objects like Pluto, Ceres, and Eris that orbit the Sun but do not clear their orbital paths of other debris.

The Life Cycle of Stars

Stars are massive spheres of plasma that emit light and heat through nuclear fusion. Their life cycle depends on their mass and involves several stages:

1. **Nebula:**
   - Stars form in a nebula, a vast cloud of gas and dust. Gravity causes the material to collapse and heat up, forming a protostar.
2. **Main Sequence:**
   - The star reaches equilibrium, with gravity pulling inward and nuclear fusion pushing outward.
   - Example: The Sun is a main-sequence star.
3. **Red Giant or Supergiant:**
   - When a star exhausts its hydrogen fuel, it expands into a red giant (low-mass stars) or supergiant (high-mass stars).
   - The core begins fusing helium or heavier elements.
4. **End Stages:**
   - **Low-Mass Stars:** Shed outer layers to form a planetary nebula, leaving behind a white dwarf.
   - **High-Mass Stars:** Explode in a supernova, leading to a neutron star or black hole.

Galaxies: The Universe's Star Systems

A galaxy is a massive collection of stars, planets, gas, dust, and dark matter held together by gravity. There are billions of galaxies in the universe, each with unique characteristics.

Types of Galaxies

1. **Spiral Galaxies:**
   - Have a central bulge surrounded by spiral arms.
   - Example: The Milky Way, our galaxy, is a barred spiral galaxy.
2. **Elliptical Galaxies:**
   - Range from spherical to elongated shapes, containing older stars.
   - Example: M87, a giant elliptical galaxy.
3. **Irregular Galaxies:**
   - Lack a defined shape and often form from galaxy collisions.
   - Example: The Magellanic Clouds, satellite galaxies of the Milky Way.

Gravity: The Force Holding It All Together

Gravity is the fundamental force that governs celestial motion:

- It keeps planets in orbit around the Sun.
- It holds galaxies together.
- It influences tides on Earth and the trajectories of comets and asteroids.

Exploration of the Solar System and Beyond

Humans have made significant strides in exploring the Solar System:

- **Space Missions:** NASA's Voyager probes, Mars rovers like Perseverance, and the James Webb Space Telescope have expanded our understanding of the cosmos.
- **Future Plans:** Upcoming missions aim to explore Europa's icy surface, collect samples from Mars, and search for exoplanets capable of supporting life.

Practice Problem Examples

Problem 1: Which planet in the Solar System has the most moons?
Answer: Jupiter, with over 90 confirmed moons, has the most moons in the Solar System.

Problem 2: Describe the process that powers the Sun.
Answer: The Sun generates energy through nuclear fusion, where hydrogen nuclei combine to form helium, releasing energy in the form of light and heat.

Problem 3: What is the main difference between a terrestrial planet and a gas giant?
Answer: Terrestrial planets, like Earth, have solid rocky surfaces, while gas giants, like Jupiter, are composed mostly of gases and lack a defined surface.

Problem 4: How do spiral galaxies differ from elliptical galaxies?
Answer: Spiral galaxies have a distinct structure with a central bulge and spiral arms, while elliptical galaxies are more rounded or elongated without defined arms.

23.4 Human Impact on Earth Systems

Humans have become one of the most influential forces shaping the Earth's systems. While natural processes such as volcanic eruptions and tectonic movements play a role in shaping the planet, human activities over the past few centuries have increasingly disrupted the balance of Earth's interconnected systems. Understanding these impacts is crucial for addressing global challenges and creating a sustainable future.

How Humans Interact with Earth Systems

The Earth is composed of four main systems: the geosphere, hydrosphere, atmosphere, and biosphere. Human activities affect each of these systems, often in interconnected ways:

1. **Geosphere (Land):**
    - **Deforestation:** Clearing forests for agriculture, urban development, or logging leads to soil erosion, loss of biodiversity, and changes in the local climate.
    - **Mining and Extraction:** Removing minerals and fossil fuels from the Earth disrupts landscapes and can result in sinkholes, deforestation, and contamination of soil and water.
    - **Urbanization:** Building cities changes land use, reduces green spaces, and increases impervious surfaces, which affects water drainage and local temperatures.
2. **Hydrosphere (Water):**
    - **Pollution:** Industrial waste, agricultural runoff, and plastics contaminate rivers, lakes, and oceans, harming aquatic ecosystems.
    - **Overuse of Water Resources:** Excessive water withdrawal for irrigation, industry, and domestic use depletes groundwater and affects ecosystems reliant on these water sources.
    - **Climate Change Effects:** Rising temperatures lead to the melting of glaciers, rising sea levels, and disruptions in ocean currents, such as the weakening of the Gulf Stream.
3. **Atmosphere (Air):**
    - **Greenhouse Gas Emissions:** Burning fossil fuels for energy releases carbon dioxide (CO_2), methane (CH_4), and other gases that trap heat, contributing to global warming.

- **Air Pollution:** Emissions from vehicles, factories, and agricultural activities release pollutants like nitrogen oxides (NO_x) and sulfur dioxide (SO_2), causing smog, acid rain, and respiratory issues.
- **Ozone Layer Depletion:** Certain industrial chemicals, such as chlorofluorocarbons (CFCs), have damaged the ozone layer, increasing the risk of harmful ultraviolet (UV) radiation.

4. **Biosphere (Living Organisms):**
    - **Habitat Destruction:** Land clearing, deforestation, and urban sprawl lead to the loss of habitats for countless species.
    - **Biodiversity Loss:** Overhunting, poaching, pollution, and climate change have driven many species to extinction or placed them at risk.
    - **Introduction of Invasive Species:** Humans transport non-native species that outcompete local flora and fauna, disrupting ecosystems.

Human Activities and Global Climate Change

Climate change, driven largely by human activity, is one of the most significant threats to Earth's systems. Key contributors include:

1. **Fossil Fuels:** Burning coal, oil, and natural gas for electricity, transportation, and industry is the largest source of greenhouse gas emissions.
2. **Deforestation:** Trees absorb CO_2, so removing forests reduces the planet's capacity to regulate carbon levels.
3. **Agriculture:** Livestock, particularly cattle, produce methane, a potent greenhouse gas. Fertilizers release nitrous oxide, another significant contributor.
4. **Industrial Processes:** Factories release greenhouse gases and pollutants, including CO_2, methane, and fluorinated gases.

Impacts of Climate Change

- **Rising Temperatures:** Global temperatures have increased by about 1°C since the late 19th century, affecting weather patterns, ecosystems, and species distribution.
- **Melting Ice and Rising Sea Levels:** Glaciers and polar ice caps are melting, causing sea levels to rise and threatening coastal areas with flooding.
- **Extreme Weather:** Climate change has led to more frequent and intense hurricanes, heatwaves, droughts, and floods.
- **Ocean Acidification:** Increased CO_2 absorption by oceans lowers pH levels, harming marine life like coral reefs and shellfish.

Human Actions and Resource Depletion

Humans rely on Earth's natural resources for survival, but overuse and unsustainable practices have led to significant depletion of these resources:

- **Forests:** Rapid deforestation reduces biodiversity, disrupts the water cycle, and accelerates climate change.
- **Water:** Unsustainable irrigation, industrial use, and urban consumption have strained freshwater supplies, with some regions facing chronic shortages.
- **Soil:** Intensive farming and deforestation lead to soil degradation, reducing fertility and increasing desertification.
- **Fossil Fuels:** These non-renewable energy sources are being consumed faster than they can form, pushing the need for renewable alternatives.

Efforts to Mitigate Human Impact

Many global initiatives aim to reduce the negative effects of human activities on Earth's systems. These include:

1. **Renewable Energy:** Transitioning to solar, wind, hydroelectric, and geothermal energy reduces reliance on fossil fuels and lowers greenhouse gas emissions.
2. **Conservation and Reforestation:** Protecting forests and replanting trees help absorb CO_2, restore habitats, and improve soil health.
3. **Water Conservation:** Efficient irrigation techniques, wastewater recycling, and public awareness campaigns help preserve freshwater resources.
4. **Pollution Control:** Regulations on industrial emissions, wastewater treatment, and single-use plastics reduce pollution in air, water, and soil.
5. **Sustainable Agriculture:** Practices like crop rotation, organic farming, and agroforestry enhance soil health, reduce chemical use, and maintain biodiversity.

Practice Problem Examples

Problem 1: How does deforestation contribute to climate change?
Answer: Deforestation reduces the number of trees available to absorb CO_2 from the atmosphere. Additionally, clearing forests often involves burning trees, which releases stored carbon into the atmosphere, further increasing greenhouse gas levels.

Problem 2: Which human activity is the largest contributor to greenhouse gas emissions?
Answer: Burning fossil fuels for energy (electricity, transportation, and industry) is the largest contributor to greenhouse gas emissions.

Problem 3: What is one way humans can reduce their impact on the hydrosphere?
Answer: Humans can reduce their impact by conserving water, using efficient irrigation techniques, and treating wastewater to prevent pollution of freshwater sources.

CHAPTER 24

INTERPRETING SCIENTIFIC DATA

24.1 Analyzing Graphs, Charts, and Experimental Results

The ability to analyze graphs, charts, and experimental results is a critical skill for interpreting scientific data. In this chapter, we will explore how to read, understand, and extract valuable insights from visual data representations, a skill heavily tested on the GED Science exam.

Understanding Graphs and Charts

Graphs and charts are visual tools used to represent data. They make it easier to identify patterns, trends, and relationships in scientific experiments or studies. Below are the most common types of graphs and charts and how to interpret them:

1. Line Graphs

Line graphs show changes over time or continuous data, with data points connected by a line.

Example: Temperature Over a Day

Time (Hours)	Temperature (°C)
6 AM	15
9 AM	18
12 PM	22
3 PM	25
6 PM	20

Graph:

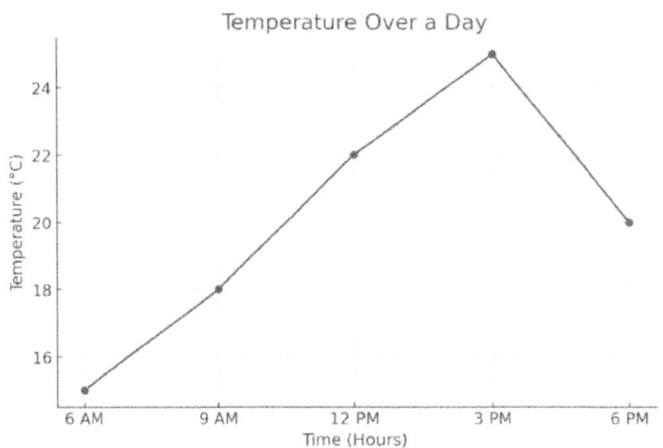

How to Interpret:

- Look for trends (e.g., rising, falling, or steady).
- Identify peaks (maximum temperature) or troughs (minimum temperature).

2. Bar Graphs

Bar graphs compare data between categories, with bars representing quantities.

Example: Average Monthly Rainfall

Month	Rainfall (mm)
January	80
February	60
March	100
April	120

Graph:

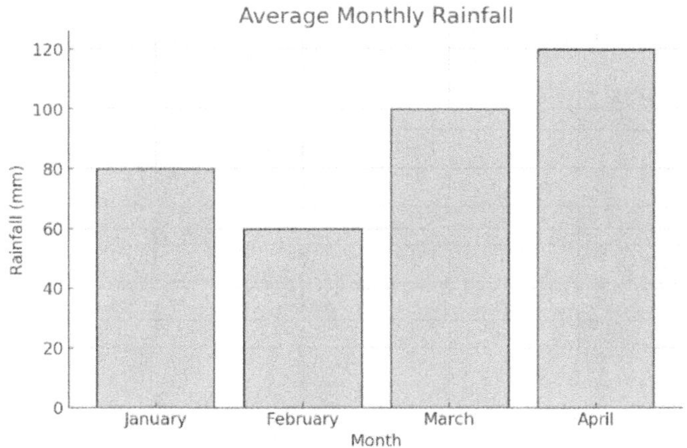

How to Interpret:

- Compare bar heights to identify the highest or lowest values.
- Examine differences between categories.

3. Pie Charts

Pie charts show proportions or percentages of a whole.

Example: Energy Sources Used in a City

Energy Source	Percentage (%)
Solar	30
Wind	25
Coal	20
Hydro	15
Nuclear	10

Chart:

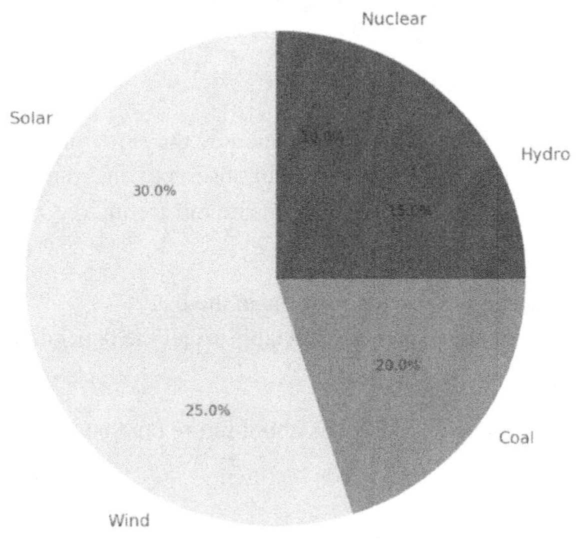

How to Interpret:

- Determine the largest and smallest segments.

- Calculate proportions based on percentages.

4. Scatter Plots

Scatter plots display relationships between two variables, with points plotted on an x-y axis.

Example: Study Hours vs. Test Scores

Study Hours	Test Score (%)
2	50
4	60
6	75
8	90

Graph:

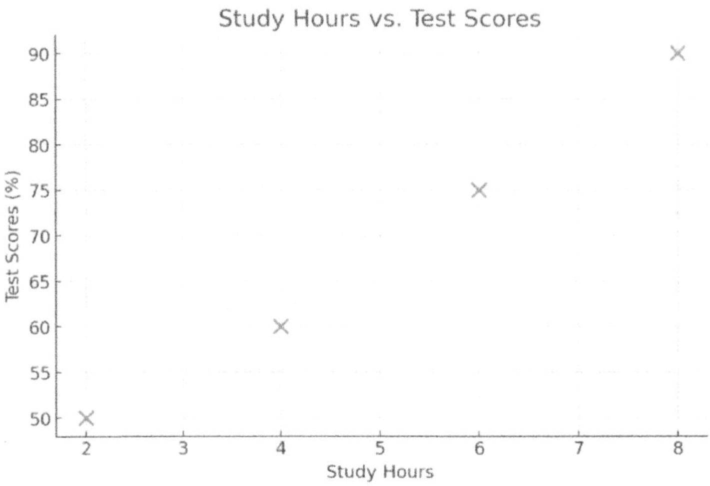

How to Interpret:

- Look for patterns or correlations (positive, negative, or no correlation).
- Identify outliers (points far from the trend line).

Experimental Results: Interpreting Data

Interpreting experimental results often requires analyzing data presented in tables, graphs, or written summaries. Key steps include:

1. **Identifying Variables:**
   - **Independent Variable:** The variable manipulated by the experimenter (e.g., amount of sunlight).
   - **Dependent Variable:** The variable measured or observed (e.g., plant growth).
   - **Control Variables:** Factors kept constant to ensure fair testing (e.g., type of soil, water amount).
2. **Analyzing Trends and Patterns:**
   - Identify increases, decreases, or steady patterns in the data.
   - Consider how changes in the independent variable affect the dependent variable.
3. **Making Predictions:**
   - Use data trends to make logical predictions about future outcomes.

Practical Example

Scenario: Measuring Plant Growth

A scientist conducted an experiment to determine how different amounts of water affect plant growth. The data is presented in a table and graph:

Water per Day (mL)	Average Plant Growth (cm)
50	5

Water per Day (mL)	Average Plant Growth (cm)
100	10
150	15
200	14

Graph:

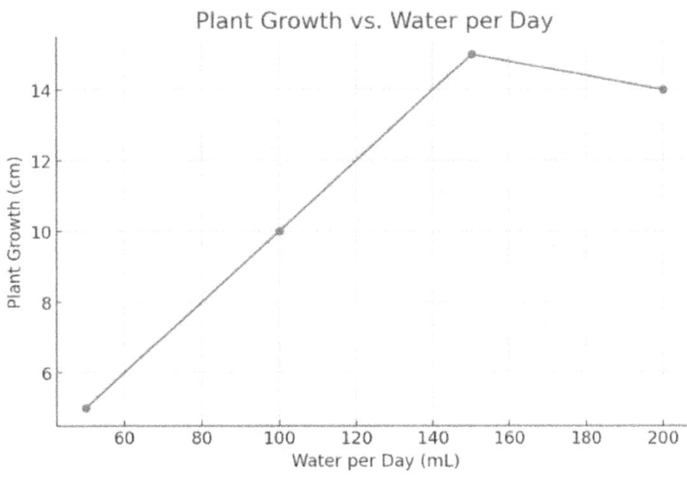

Analysis:

- Plant growth increases as water increases up to 150 mL/day.
- Excessive water (200 mL/day) slightly reduces growth, possibly due to overwatering.

Tips for the GED Exam

- **Read Titles and Labels Carefully:** Always check the title, axes, and legend to understand what the graph or chart represents.
- **Pay Attention to Units:** Units (e.g., cm, mL, °C) provide critical information about the data.
- **Look for Key Points:** Identify trends, peaks, and outliers.
- **Consider the Context:** Relate the graph or chart to the scientific question or hypothesis being tested.

Practice Problem Example

Problem 1: Analyzing a Line Graph

A line graph shows the population of rabbits in a field over six months:

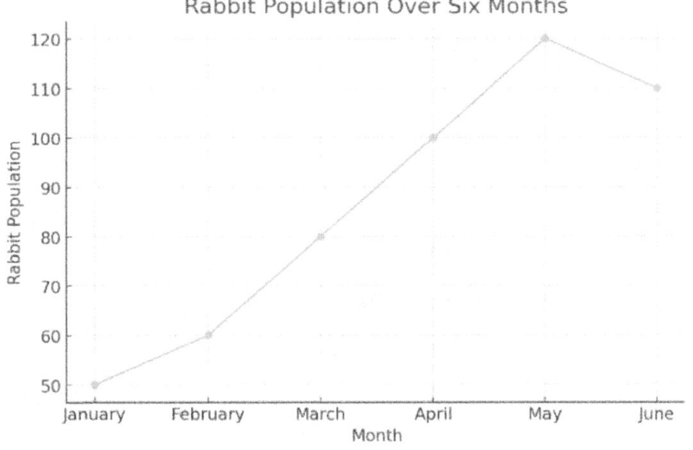

Month	Rabbit Population
January	50
February	60
March	80
April	100
May	120
June	110

Question:

What can you conclude about the rabbit population in this field?

Answer:

The rabbit population increased steadily from January to May, peaking at 120 in May. However, the population slightly decreased in June, suggesting possible environmental factors like food scarcity or predation.

Problem 2: Interpreting a Pie Chart

A pie chart shows energy consumption in a city:

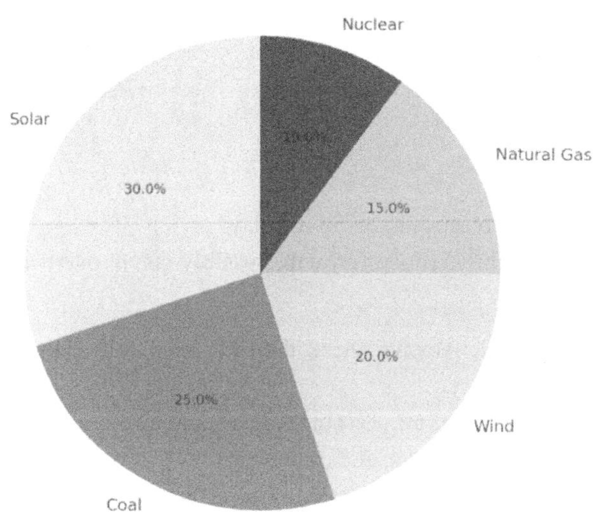

- Solar: 30%
- Coal: 25%
- Wind: 20%
- Natural Gas: 15%
- Nuclear: 10%

Question:

What is the largest source of energy consumption in the city?

Answer:

The largest source of energy consumption is **solar energy (30%)**.

24.2 Designing and Understanding Scientific Experiments

Scientific experiments are the foundation of research, allowing scientists to investigate questions, test hypotheses, and uncover patterns in the natural world. Understanding how to design and interpret experiments is a key skill for success on the GED Science exam and for making informed decisions in everyday life.

The Scientific Method: The Basis of Experiments

The **scientific method** is a systematic process used to investigate phenomena, answer questions, and solve problems. It involves the following steps:

1. **Ask a Question:** Identify a specific problem or question to explore.
    - Example: Does the amount of sunlight affect plant growth?
2. **Conduct Background Research:** Gather information about the topic to better understand the context and refine the question.
3. **Formulate a Hypothesis:** Develop a testable prediction about the outcome.
    - Example: Plants exposed to more sunlight will grow taller.
4. **Design and Conduct an Experiment:** Create a procedure to test the hypothesis, ensuring it is controlled and repeatable.
5. **Analyze Data:** Examine the results to determine whether they support or refute the hypothesis.
6. **Draw Conclusions:** Interpret the findings and consider their implications.
7. **Communicate Results:** Share the findings through reports, graphs, or charts.

Key Components of a Well-Designed Experiment

1. **Independent Variable:** The factor you change in the experiment.
    - Example: The amount of sunlight plants receive.
2. **Dependent Variable:** The factor you measure or observe.
    - Example: The height of the plants.
3. **Control Variables:** Factors kept constant to ensure a fair test.
    - Example: Type of plant, soil quality, water amount.
4. **Control Group:** A group that does not receive the experimental treatment, used for comparison.
    - Example: Plants kept in the dark.
5. **Experimental Group:** The group that receives the treatment or variable being tested.
    - Example: Plants exposed to varying amounts of sunlight.
6. **Sample Size:** The number of subjects or items tested. Larger sample sizes improve reliability.
7. **Repetition:** Repeating the experiment multiple times ensures consistent results and reduces error.

Types of Experiments

1. **Controlled Experiments:** Only one variable is changed while others are held constant.
    - Example: Testing how fertilizer affects plant growth by varying fertilizer amounts but keeping sunlight, water, and soil the same.
2. **Observational Studies:** Researchers observe and collect data without manipulating variables.
    - Example: Studying the migration patterns of birds.
3. **Field Experiments:** Conducted in natural settings rather than controlled environments.
    - Example: Measuring water quality in different rivers.

Interpreting Experimental Results

Once data is collected, it must be analyzed to determine patterns or trends. Use the following steps:

1. **Organize Data:** Present data in tables, graphs, or charts for clarity.
    - Example: A line graph showing plant growth over time.
2. **Look for Trends:** Identify increases, decreases, or relationships between variables.
    - Example: Plants receiving 8 hours of sunlight grew taller than those receiving 4 hours.
3. **Check for Anomalies:** Look for outliers or unexpected results.
    - Example: One plant in the 8-hour group did not grow, possibly due to disease.
4. **Compare Results to Hypothesis:** Determine whether the data supports or refutes the hypothesis.
    - Example: If all plants in the sunlight group grew taller, the hypothesis is supported.

Practice Experiment Example

Question: Does water temperature affect the time it takes for sugar to dissolve?

Hypothesis: Sugar dissolves faster in warmer water.

Experiment Design:

- **Independent Variable:** Temperature of the water (hot, room temperature, cold).
- **Dependent Variable:** Time taken for the sugar to dissolve.
- **Control Variables:** Amount of water, type of sugar, amount of stirring.
- **Procedure:**
    a. Fill three identical glasses with 200 mL of water at different temperatures (10°C, 25°C, 60°C).

b. Add one teaspoon of sugar to each glass.
c. Stir each glass at the same speed and record the time taken for the sugar to completely dissolve.

Results:

Temperature (°C)	Dissolving Time (seconds)
10	60
25	45
60	20

Conclusion: Sugar dissolves faster in warmer water, supporting the hypothesis.

Common Errors in Experiments

1. **Bias:** Favoring a specific outcome. Avoid bias by randomizing samples and using blind or double-blind methods.
2. **Confounding Variables:** Variables other than the independent variable that affect the results. Control all other variables to minimize their impact.
3. **Small Sample Size:** A small sample may not represent the population accurately. Use larger groups when possible.
4. **Misinterpreting Data:** Drawing conclusions not supported by the data. Ensure conclusions align with the evidence.

Practice Problem Examples

Problem 1:

A student wants to test whether fertilizer affects plant growth. They grow one plant without fertilizer and another with fertilizer for two weeks. Both plants receive the same amount of sunlight and water. The plant with fertilizer grows 10 cm, while the plant without fertilizer grows 5 cm.

Question: What is the independent variable in this experiment?
Answer: The independent variable is the use of fertilizer.

Problem 2:

A scientist tests the effect of temperature on bacterial growth. They incubate bacteria at 20°C, 30°C, and 40°C and measure the growth after 24 hours.

Temperature (°C)	Bacterial Growth (units)
20	50
30	100
40	75

Question: At which temperature did the bacteria grow the most?

Answer: The bacteria grew the most at 30°C.

24.3 Applying Scientific Reasoning to Real-World Problems

Scientific reasoning is the application of critical thinking, logic, and evidence-based methods to analyze real-world problems and devise practical solutions. On the GED Science exam, understanding how to apply these skills is essential for interpreting data, making informed decisions, and solving complex issues. In this chapter, we will explore the principles of scientific reasoning and how they relate to everyday challenges and larger global problems.

What is Scientific Reasoning?

Scientific reasoning involves:

1. **Analyzing Evidence:** Using reliable data to evaluate claims.
2. **Forming Logical Connections:** Drawing conclusions based on patterns, trends, or causal relationships in the data.
3. **Testing Hypotheses:** Designing experiments or observations to validate ideas.
4. **Evaluating Outcomes:** Considering the implications and accuracy of results.

This approach enables individuals to tackle issues like public health challenges, environmental concerns, and technological advancements.

Steps in Applying Scientific Reasoning

1. **Identify the Problem:** Define the issue clearly and ask specific questions.
   - Example: Why are honeybee populations declining?
2. **Gather Relevant Data:** Collect evidence from observations, experiments, or credible sources.
   - Example: Monitor pesticide levels in environments where honeybee populations are decreasing.
3. **Analyze the Evidence:** Look for patterns, correlations, or causal relationships.
   - Example: Determine if increased pesticide use corresponds to declining bee populations.
4. **Formulate Conclusions:** Use the evidence to support or refute hypotheses.
   - Example: Conclude that certain pesticides negatively impact honeybee health.
5. **Develop Solutions:** Propose actionable strategies based on findings.
   - Example: Recommend limiting pesticide use during pollination seasons.

Real-World Applications of Scientific Reasoning

1. Public Health

Scientific reasoning is critical in addressing health crises and improving public health outcomes:

- **Problem:** Rising obesity rates in a population.
- **Reasoning Process:**
  - Collect data on dietary habits and physical activity.
  - Analyze the relationship between lifestyle choices and weight gain.
  - Implement public health campaigns promoting balanced diets and exercise.

2. Environmental Conservation

Scientific reasoning helps address ecological issues:

- **Problem:** Deforestation causing habitat loss and climate change.
- **Reasoning Process:**
  - Analyze satellite imagery to measure forest cover loss.
  - Study the impact of deforestation on local climates and biodiversity.
  - Develop reforestation projects and sustainable logging practices.

3. Technology and Innovation

Scientific reasoning drives technological advancements:

- **Problem:** Need for renewable energy sources to reduce carbon emissions.
- **Reasoning Process:**
  - Evaluate the efficiency and costs of solar, wind, and geothermal energy.
  - Test new materials for improved energy storage.
  - Develop cost-effective, scalable renewable energy systems.

Common Errors in Scientific Reasoning

Even with a structured approach, errors can occur:

1. **Correlation vs. Causation:** Just because two events occur together doesn't mean one causes the other.
   - Example: Ice cream sales and drowning rates both increase in summer, but one does not cause the other.
2. **Bias:** Allowing personal opinions or incomplete data to influence conclusions.
   - Avoid by using blind or double-blind study methods and ensuring data is comprehensive.
3. **Overgeneralization:** Applying findings from a small sample to a larger population without sufficient evidence.
4. **Ignoring Confounding Variables:** Overlooking factors that may influence results.
   - Example: In studying student performance, failing to account for socioeconomic factors beyond school resources.

Practice Problem Examples

Problem 1: Public Health Scenario

Scenario: A city observes an increase in respiratory illnesses during the winter. The city council hypothesizes that increased use of wood-burning stoves contributes to the problem.
Question: What type of data should the city collect to test this hypothesis?
Answer: The city should collect data on:

- Air quality levels (e.g., particulate matter concentrations) during winter.
- The number of households using wood-burning stoves.
- The incidence of respiratory illnesses reported during the same period.

Problem 2: Environmental Conservation Scenario

Scenario: A coastal town is experiencing increased flooding. Scientists hypothesize that rising sea levels due to climate change are responsible.

Question: What evidence would support this hypothesis?

Answer:

- Historical data showing rising sea levels in the area over time.
- Records of flooding frequency and intensity increasing in correlation with sea-level rise.
- Satellite images showing coastal erosion or loss of land.

Problem 3: Technological Innovation Scenario

Scenario: An electric car manufacturer claims that their new battery design increases driving range by 20%.

Question: How could this claim be tested?

Answer:

- Conduct controlled tests comparing the driving range of cars with the new battery to those with the previous design.
- Analyze the battery's energy efficiency and charge capacity under identical conditions.
- Review third-party verification or peer-reviewed studies supporting the manufacturer's claim.

Critical Thinking in Everyday Life

Scientific reasoning isn't just for laboratories or classrooms; it applies to daily decision-making:

- **Example 1:** Comparing nutritional labels to choose healthier food options.
- **Example 2:** Evaluating the reliability of news sources before believing or sharing information.
- **Example 3:** Assessing the effectiveness of a product based on user reviews, manufacturer claims, and independent studies.

Right

Wrong

Steps in Applying Scientific Reasoning

1. **Identify the Problem:** Define the issue clearly and ask specific questions.
   - Example: Why are honeybee populations declining?
2. **Gather Relevant Data:** Collect evidence from observations, experiments, or credible sources.
   - Example: Monitor pesticide levels in environments where honeybee populations are decreasing.
3. **Analyze the Evidence:** Look for patterns, correlations, or causal relationships.
   - Example: Determine if increased pesticide use corresponds to declining bee populations.
4. **Formulate Conclusions:** Use the evidence to support or refute hypotheses.
   - Example: Conclude that certain pesticides negatively impact honeybee health.
5. **Develop Solutions:** Propose actionable strategies based on findings.
   - Example: Recommend limiting pesticide use during pollination seasons.

Real-World Applications of Scientific Reasoning

1. Public Health

Scientific reasoning is critical in addressing health crises and improving public health outcomes:

- **Problem:** Rising obesity rates in a population.
- **Reasoning Process:**
  - Collect data on dietary habits and physical activity.
  - Analyze the relationship between lifestyle choices and weight gain.
  - Implement public health campaigns promoting balanced diets and exercise.

2. Environmental Conservation

Scientific reasoning helps address ecological issues:

- **Problem:** Deforestation causing habitat loss and climate change.
- **Reasoning Process:**
  - Analyze satellite imagery to measure forest cover loss.
  - Study the impact of deforestation on local climates and biodiversity.
  - Develop reforestation projects and sustainable logging practices.

3. Technology and Innovation

Scientific reasoning drives technological advancements:

- **Problem:** Need for renewable energy sources to reduce carbon emissions.
- **Reasoning Process:**
  - Evaluate the efficiency and costs of solar, wind, and geothermal energy.
  - Test new materials for improved energy storage.
  - Develop cost-effective, scalable renewable energy systems.

Common Errors in Scientific Reasoning

Even with a structured approach, errors can occur:

1. **Correlation vs. Causation:** Just because two events occur together doesn't mean one causes the other.
   - Example: Ice cream sales and drowning rates both increase in summer, but one does not cause the other.
2. **Bias:** Allowing personal opinions or incomplete data to influence conclusions.
   - Avoid by using blind or double-blind study methods and ensuring data is comprehensive.
3. **Overgeneralization:** Applying findings from a small sample to a larger population without sufficient evidence.
4. **Ignoring Confounding Variables:** Overlooking factors that may influence results.
   - Example: In studying student performance, failing to account for socioeconomic factors beyond school resources.

Practice Problem Examples

Problem 1: Public Health Scenario

Scenario: A city observes an increase in respiratory illnesses during the winter. The city council hypothesizes that increased use of wood-burning stoves contributes to the problem.

Question: What type of data should the city collect to test this hypothesis?

Answer: The city should collect data on:

CHAPTER 25

SCIENCE PRACTICE QUESTIONS AND SOLUTIONS

Multiple-Choice Questions

Question 1

What is the primary source of energy for life on Earth?

a) Wind
b) The Sun
c) Fossil fuels
d) Water
Answer: b) The Sun

Question 2

Which organ system is responsible for transporting oxygen and nutrients to the body's cells?

a) Nervous system
b) Circulatory system
c) Digestive system
d) Endocrine system
Answer: b) Circulatory system

Question 3

Which molecule in plant cells captures sunlight for photosynthesis?

a) Chlorophyll
b) Glucose
c) Oxygen
d) ATP
Answer: a) Chlorophyll

Question 4

What is the role of DNA in a cell?

a) Providing energy for cellular activities
b) Transporting oxygen to tissues
c) Storing genetic information
d) Breaking down nutrients
Answer: c) Storing genetic information

Question 5

What type of rock is formed by cooling and solidifying molten magma or lava?

a) Sedimentary
b) Metamorphic
c) Igneous
d) Fossilized
Answer: c) Igneous

Question 6

Which layer of the atmosphere contains the ozone layer?

a) Troposphere
b) Stratosphere
c) Mesosphere
d) Thermosphere

Answer: b) Stratosphere

Question 7

Which gas contributes most to the greenhouse effect?

a) Nitrogen
b) Oxygen
c) Carbon dioxide
d) Helium
Answer: c) Carbon dioxide

Question 8

What process is responsible for water moving from the ocean to the atmosphere?

a) Precipitation
b) Evaporation
c) Condensation
d) Runoff
Answer: b) Evaporation

Question 9

What is the primary function of red blood cells?

a) Fighting infections
b) Carrying oxygen
c) Producing hormones
d) Regulating body temperature
Answer: b) Carrying oxygen

Question 10

Which planet in the Solar System is known as the "Red Planet"?

a) Venus
b) Jupiter
c) Mars
d) Saturn
Answer: c) Mars

Question 11

Which of the following is an example of a renewable energy source?

a) Coal
b) Natural gas
c) Wind
d) Nuclear
Answer: c) Wind

Question 12

What is the smallest unit of life?

a) Organ
b) Tissue
c) Molecule
d) Cell
Answer: d) Cell

Question 13

What type of energy transformation occurs in photosynthesis?

a) Chemical to thermal
b) Solar to chemical
c) Mechanical to electrical
d) Nuclear to chemical
Answer: b) Solar to chemical

Question 14

What causes seasons on Earth?

a) The distance of Earth from the Sun
b) The tilt of Earth's axis
c) The speed of Earth's rotation
d) The shape of Earth's orbit
Answer: b) The tilt of Earth's axis

Question 15

Which part of the water cycle involves water vapor cooling and forming clouds?

a) Evaporation
b) Transpiration
c) Precipitation
d) Condensation
Answer: d) Condensation

Question 16

What is a possible effect of deforestation?

a) Increased biodiversity
b) Enhanced carbon dioxide absorption
c) Loss of habitat for wildlife
d) Decreased soil erosion
Answer: c) Loss of habitat for wildlife

Question 17

What is the function of the mitochondria in a cell?

a) Producing energy
b) Storing genetic material
c) Controlling cell division
d) Synthesizing proteins
Answer: a) Producing energy

Question 18

What type of bond holds water molecules together?

a) Ionic
b) Covalent
c) Hydrogen
d) Metallic
Answer: c) Hydrogen

Question 19

Which of the following best describes a hypothesis?

a) A proven fact
b) A testable prediction
c) A conclusion drawn from data
d) An experimental result
Answer: b) A testable prediction

Question 20

Which of the following is an abiotic factor in an ecosystem?

a) Plants
b) Animals
c) Soil
d) Microorganisms
Answer: c) Soil

Question 21

What is the primary reason that Earth's magnetic field exists?

a) Movement of tectonic plates
b) The spinning of the Earth's solid inner core
c) The flow of liquid iron in the outer core
d) Gravitational pull from the Moon
Answer: c) The flow of liquid iron in the outer core

Question 22

Which of the following is an example of chemical weathering?

a) Wind eroding a rock
b) Freezing water cracking a rock
c) Acid rain dissolving limestone
d) Roots growing into cracks in a rock
Answer: c) Acid rain dissolving limestone

Question 23

What causes ocean tides?

a) Coal
b) Natural gas
c) Wind
d) Nuclear
Answer: c) Wind

Question 12

What is the smallest unit of life?

a) Organ
b) Tissue
c) Molecule
d) Cell
Answer: d) Cell

Question 13

What type of energy transformation occurs in photosynthesis?

a) Chemical to thermal
b) Solar to chemical
c) Mechanical to electrical
d) Nuclear to chemical
Answer: b) Solar to chemical

Question 14

What causes seasons on Earth?

a) The distance of Earth from the Sun
b) The tilt of Earth's axis
c) The speed of Earth's rotation
d) The shape of Earth's orbit
Answer: b) The tilt of Earth's axis

Question 15

Which part of the water cycle involves water vapor cooling and forming clouds?

a) Evaporation
b) Transpiration
c) Precipitation
d) Condensation
Answer: d) Condensation

Question 16

What is a possible effect of deforestation?

a) Increased biodiversity
b) Enhanced carbon dioxide absorption
c) Loss of habitat for wildlife
d) Decreased soil erosion
Answer: c) Loss of habitat for wildlife

Question 17

What is the function of the mitochondria in a cell?

a) Producing energy
b) Storing genetic material
c) Controlling cell division
d) Synthesizing proteins
Answer: a) Producing energy

Question 18

What type of bond holds water molecules together?

a) Ionic
b) Covalent
c) Hydrogen
d) Metallic
Answer: c) Hydrogen

Question 19

Which of the following best describes a hypothesis?

a) A proven fact
b) A testable prediction
c) A conclusion drawn from data
d) An experimental result
Answer: b) A testable prediction

Question 20

Which of the following is an abiotic factor in an ecosystem?

a) Plants
b) Animals
c) Soil
d) Microorganisms
Answer: c) Soil

Question 21

What is the primary reason that Earth's magnetic field exists?

a) Movement of tectonic plates
b) The spinning of the Earth's solid inner core
c) The flow of liquid iron in the outer core
d) Gravitational pull from the Moon
Answer: c) The flow of liquid iron in the outer core

Question 22

Which of the following is an example of chemical weathering?

a) Wind eroding a rock
b) Freezing water cracking a rock
c) Acid rain dissolving limestone
d) Roots growing into cracks in a rock
Answer: c) Acid rain dissolving limestone

Question 23

What causes ocean tides?

a) The Earth's rotation
b) Wind patterns
c) Gravitational pull from the Moon and Sun
d) Earth's axial tilt
Answer: c) Gravitational pull from the Moon and Sun

Question 24

What is the function of chloroplasts in plant cells?

a) To store water
b) To produce energy from sunlight
c) To control cell division
d) To transport nutrients
Answer: b) To produce energy from sunlight

Question 25

Which layer of the Earth is the thickest?

a) Crust
b) Mantle
c) Outer core
d) Inner core
Answer: b) Mantle

Question 26

What is the primary benefit of using renewable energy sources like wind and solar power?

a) They are less expensive than fossil fuels.
b) They produce less pollution and are sustainable.
c) They are easier to install than fossil fuel plants.
d) They require no maintenance.
Answer: b) They produce less pollution and are sustainable.

Question 27

Which element is most abundant in Earth's atmosphere?

a) Oxygen
b) Carbon dioxide
c) Nitrogen
d) Hydrogen
Answer: c) Nitrogen

Question 28

Which phase of the water cycle is directly responsible for replenishing groundwater supplies?

a) Evaporation
b) Transpiration
c) Infiltration
d) Condensation
Answer: c) Infiltration

Question 29

Which of the following structures is found in both plant and animal cells?

a) Cell wall
b) Chloroplast
c) Mitochondria
d) Central vacuole
Answer: c) Mitochondria

Question 30

What is a major cause of acid rain?

a) Deforestation
b) Emission of sulfur dioxide and nitrogen oxides from factories
c) Increased levels of methane in the atmosphere
d) Excessive use of fertilizers in agriculture
Answer: b) Emission of sulfur dioxide and nitrogen oxides from factories

Question 31

Which process releases energy from glucose in cells?

a) Photosynthesis
b) Respiration
c) Fermentation
d) Transpiration
Answer: b) Respiration

Question 32

What is the function of ribosomes in a cell?

a) Producing proteins
b) Generating energy
c) Storing genetic material
d) Regulating cell division
Answer: a) Producing proteins

Question 33

What do scientists call the process by which new species evolve from existing ones?

a) Mutation
b) Natural selection
c) Speciation
d) Genetic drift
Answer: c) Speciation

Question 34

Which property of water allows it to dissolve many substances?

a) Its high surface tension
b) Its polar nature
c) Its ability to absorb heat
d) Its neutral pH
Answer: b) Its polar nature

Question 35

Why do we see different phases of the Moon?

a) The Moon rotates on its axis.
b) The Earth casts a shadow on the Moon.
c) The Moon reflects light from the Sun, and its position changes relative to Earth.
d) The Moon emits its own light.
Answer: c) The Moon reflects light from the Sun, and its position changes relative to Earth.

Question 36

What happens during a solar eclipse?

a) The Moon casts a shadow on the Earth.
b) The Earth casts a shadow on the Moon.
c) The Sun is blocked by a cloud of dust.
d) The Sun moves behind the Earth.
Answer: a) The Moon casts a shadow on the Earth.

Question 37

Which of the following is an example of kinetic energy?

a) A compressed spring
b) A rolling ball
c) A chemical bond in a glucose molecule
d) A battery in a remote control
Answer: b) A rolling ball

Question 38

Which is an example of an adaptation?

a) A bird migrating to a warmer climate during winter
b) An animal eating more food before hibernating
c) A plant growing toward sunlight
d) A polar bear's thick fur for insulation
Answer: d) A polar bear's thick fur for insulation

Question 39

Which type of macromolecule is primarily used for energy storage in the human body?

a) Proteins
b) Lipids
c) Nucleic acids
d) Carbohydrates
Answer: b) Lipids

Question 40

Which is a primary driver of ocean currents?

a) Salinity differences
b) Gravitational pull of the Moon
c) Earth's magnetic field
d) Precipitation patterns
Answer: a) Salinity differences

Drag-and-Drop Questions

In drag-and-drop questions, you organize items into the correct categories, sequence steps, or match concepts.

Question 1: Steps of the Water Cycle

Drag the following steps into the correct order:

- Precipitation
- Condensation
- Evaporation
- Collection

Answer:

1. Evaporation
2. Condensation
3. Precipitation
4. Collection

Question 2: Scientific Method

Drag these steps into the correct sequence of the scientific method:

- Analyze data
- Form a hypothesis
- Conduct an experiment
- Ask a question

Answer:

1. Ask a question
2. Form a hypothesis
3. Conduct an experiment
4. Analyze data

Question 3: Layers of the Atmosphere

Match each description with the appropriate atmospheric layer:

- **Troposphere**: Weather occurs here.
- **Stratosphere**: Contains the ozone layer.
- **Mesosphere**: Meteors burn up in this layer.
- **Thermosphere**: Northern lights occur here.

Answer:

- Troposphere → Weather occurs here.
- Stratosphere → Contains the ozone layer.
- Mesosphere → Meteors burn up in this layer.
- Thermosphere → Northern lights occur here.

Question 4: Types of Rocks

Drag the following rock types into their correct processes of formation:

- Igneous
- Sedimentary
- Metamorphic

Processes:

- **Cooling and solidification of magma or lava**
- **Compaction and cementation of sediments**
- **Heat and pressure applied to existing rock**

Answer:

- Igneous → Cooling and solidification of magma or lava
- Sedimentary → Compaction and cementation of sediments
- Metamorphic → Heat and pressure applied to existing rock

Question 5: Plant Cell Parts

Match each part of a plant cell to its function:

- **Chloroplast**: Captures sunlight for photosynthesis.
- **Cell Wall**: Provides structural support.
- **Vacuole**: Stores water and nutrients.
- **Mitochondria**: Generates energy for the cell.

Answer:

- Chloroplast → Captures sunlight for photosynthesis.
- Cell Wall → Provides structural support.
- Vacuole → Stores water and nutrients.
- Mitochondria → Generates energy for the cell.

Question 6: Human Body Systems

Drag each organ to the correct body system:

- **Heart**: Circulatory system
- **Lungs**: Respiratory system
- **Stomach**: Digestive system
- **Kidneys**: Excretory system

Answer:

- Heart → Circulatory system
- Lungs → Respiratory system
- Stomach → Digestive system
- Kidneys → Excretory system

Question 7: Phases of Mitosis

Drag the phases of mitosis into the correct order:

- Anaphase
- Metaphase
- Prophase
- Telophase

Answer:

1. Prophase
2. Metaphase
3. Anaphase
4. Telophase

Question 8: Greenhouse Gases

Match the following greenhouse gases with their sources:

- **Carbon dioxide (CO_2)**: Burning fossil fuels
- **Methane (CH_4)**: Livestock and landfills
- **Nitrous oxide (N_2O)**: Fertilizers
- **Water vapor**: Evaporation

Answer:

- Carbon dioxide → Burning fossil fuels
- Methane → Livestock and landfills
- Nitrous oxide → Fertilizers
- Water vapor → Evaporation

Question 9: Renewable vs. Non-Renewable Energy

Sort the following energy sources into renewable or non-renewable:

- Coal
- Solar
- Wind
- Natural Gas

Answer:

- Renewable → Solar, Wind
- Non-renewable → Coal, Natural Gas

Question 10: States of Matter

Drag the following states of matter to their correct descriptions:

- Solid
- Liquid
- Gas

Descriptions:

- **Has a definite shape and volume.**
- **Takes the shape of its container but has a definite volume.**
- **Fills the container completely and has no definite shape.**

Answer:

- Solid → Has a definite shape and volume.
- Liquid → Takes the shape of its container but has a definite volume.
- Gas → Fills the container completely and has no definite shape.

Question 11: Functions of DNA

Drag the following descriptions to their correct role of DNA:

- **Storing genetic information**
- **Transmitting genetic information to offspring**
- **Providing instructions for protein synthesis**

Answer:

- Storing genetic information → DNA contains genetic blueprints.
- Transmitting genetic information to offspring → DNA is inherited during reproduction.
- Providing instructions for protein synthesis → DNA codes for proteins.

Question 12: Types of Forces

Match the following forces with their examples:

- **Gravity**: An apple falling from a tree
- **Friction**: A book sliding across a table
- **Magnetic force**: A compass needle pointing north
- **Tension**: A rope pulling a sled

Answer:

- Gravity → An apple falling from a tree
- Friction → A book sliding across a table
- Magnetic force → A compass needle pointing north
- Tension → A rope pulling a sled

Question 13: Properties of Water

Match each property of water to its description:

- **Cohesion**: Water molecules sticking together
- **Adhesion**: Water molecules sticking to other surfaces
- **High specific heat**: Water absorbs heat without a large temperature change

Answer:

- Cohesion → Water molecules sticking together
- Adhesion → Water molecules sticking to other surfaces
- High specific heat → Water absorbs heat without a large temperature change

Question 14: Stages of Photosynthesis

Sort these stages into their correct order:

- Light absorption
- ATP and NADPH production
- Carbon fixation in the Calvin cycle

Answer:

1. Light absorption
2. ATP and NADPH production
3. Carbon fixation in the Calvin cycle

Question 15: Renewable Energy Benefits

Drag each benefit to the correct renewable energy source:

- **Solar**: Reduces reliance on fossil fuels, generates power from sunlight
- **Wind**: Uses natural wind currents, generates clean energy

Answer:

- Solar → Reduces reliance on fossil fuels, generates power from sunlight
- Wind → Uses natural wind currents, generates clean energy

Question 16: Earth's Layers

Match each description to the correct layer of Earth:

- **Crust**: Thinnest layer, where life exists
- **Mantle**: Thickest layer, contains convection currents
- **Core**: Generates Earth's magnetic field

Answer:

- Crust → Thinnest layer, where life exists
- Mantle → Thickest layer, contains convection currents
- Core → Generates Earth's magnetic field

Question 17: Moon Phases

Arrange the phases of the Moon in order:

- Waxing crescent
- First quarter
- Full Moon
- Waning gibbous

Answer:

1. Waxing crescent
2. First quarter
3. Full Moon
4. Waning gibbous

Question 18: Heat Transfer

Match each type of heat transfer to its example:

- **Conduction**: A metal spoon heating in hot soup
- **Convection**: Warm air rising in a heated room
- **Radiation**: Feeling heat from sunlight

Answer:

- Conduction → A metal spoon heating in hot soup
- Convection → Warm air rising in a heated room
- Radiation → Feeling heat from sunlight

Question 19: Ecosystem Components

Sort the following into biotic or abiotic components:

- Rocks
- Plants
- Animals
- Water

Answer:

- Biotic → Plants, Animals
- Abiotic → Rocks, Water

Question 20: Levels of Organization in Biology

Arrange these levels in order from smallest to largest:

- Tissue
- Organ
- Cell
- Organism

Answer:

1. Cell
2. Tissue
3. Organ
4. Organism

Fill-in-the-Blank Questions for GED Science Exam

Question 1

The process by which plants convert sunlight into chemical energy is called __________.

Answer: Photosynthesis

Question 2

The smallest unit of life that can carry out all life processes is the __________.

Answer: Cell

Question 3
In the water cycle, water vapor cools and changes back into liquid form during the process of __________.
Answer: Condensation
Question 4
The primary gas that animals exhale as a waste product of respiration is __________.
Answer: Carbon dioxide
Question 5
The two main types of cells are __________ and __________.
Answer: Prokaryotic, Eukaryotic
Question 6
The __________ system is responsible for transporting oxygen and nutrients throughout the body.
Answer: Circulatory
Question 7
The Moon's gravitational pull on Earth is the primary cause of __________.
Answer: Tides
Question 8
DNA stands for __________.
Answer: Deoxyribonucleic acid
Question 9
The __________ is the part of the Earth where life exists.
Answer: Biosphere
Question 10
In an atom, protons have a __________ charge, electrons have a __________ charge, and neutrons have __________ charge.
Answer: Positive, negative, no
Question 11
A scientist makes a __________ when they use their senses to gather information about the natural world.
Answer: Observation
Question 12
The process by which organisms maintain a stable internal environment is called __________.
Answer: Homeostasis
Question 13
The total amount of living matter in a given area is called __________.
Answer: Biomass
Question 14
The point in the Earth's orbit when it is closest to the Sun is called __________.
Answer: Perihelion
Question 15
The __________ scale is used to measure the strength of an earthquake.
Answer: Richter
Question 16
The movement of tectonic plates is caused by convection currents in the __________.
Answer: Mantle
Question 17
The outermost layer of a plant cell is called the __________.
Answer: Cell wall
Question 18
An organism that makes its own food is called a(n) __________.
Answer: Autotroph
Question 19
The process of water moving through a semi-permeable membrane is called __________.
Answer: Osmosis

Question 20
The Sun is primarily composed of two elements: __________ and __________.
Answer: Hydrogen, Helium

20 Short Answer Questions

Question 1
What is the primary role of chloroplasts in plant cells?
Answer: The primary role of chloroplasts is to capture sunlight and convert it into chemical energy through the process of photosynthesis.
Question 2
Explain why water is considered a universal solvent.
Answer: Water is considered a universal solvent because its polar molecules can dissolve a wide variety of substances, including salts, sugars, and gases.
Question 3
What is one way humans can reduce their carbon footprint?
Answer: Humans can reduce their carbon footprint by using renewable energy sources, such as solar or wind power, instead of fossil fuels.
Question 4
Why do hurricanes lose strength when they move over land?
Answer: Hurricanes lose strength over land because they are cut off from their primary energy source: warm ocean waters.
Question 5
Describe the difference between weather and climate.
Answer: Weather refers to short-term atmospheric conditions, such as temperature and precipitation, while climate describes long-term patterns and averages of weather in a specific region.
Question 6
What happens to the energy in a food chain as it moves from one trophic level to the next?
Answer: Energy decreases as it moves up the food chain because only a small portion of energy (around 10%) is transferred to the next trophic level; the rest is lost as heat.
Question 7
How does deforestation contribute to climate change?
Answer: Deforestation contributes to climate change by reducing the number of trees that absorb carbon dioxide during photosynthesis, leading to increased levels of CO_2 in the atmosphere.
Question 8
What is the function of red blood cells in the human body?
Answer: The function of red blood cells is to transport oxygen from the lungs to the body's tissues and carry carbon dioxide back to the lungs for exhalation.
Question 9
Explain why the ozone layer is important for life on Earth.
Answer: The ozone layer is important because it absorbs and blocks most of the Sun's harmful ultraviolet (UV) radiation, protecting living organisms from its damaging effects.
Question 10
What causes the seasons on Earth?
Answer: The tilt of Earth's axis as it orbits the Sun causes the seasons. Different parts of Earth receive varying amounts of sunlight throughout the year.
Question 11
How do fossil fuels form?
Answer: Fossil fuels form over millions of years from the remains of dead plants and animals that are buried under sediment and subjected to heat and pressure.
Question 12
What is biodiversity, and why is it important?
Answer: Biodiversity is the variety of life in an ecosystem, and it is important because it supports ecosystem stability, resilience, and the provision of resources like food and medicine.

Question 13

What is the difference between renewable and non-renewable resources?

Answer: Renewable resources can be replenished naturally over time (e.g., solar energy), while non-renewable resources, like fossil fuels, are finite and take millions of years to form.

Question 14

Why does ice float on water?

Answer: Ice floats on water because it is less dense than liquid water due to the unique arrangement of hydrogen bonds in its solid form.

Question 15

What is one reason why invasive species can harm ecosystems?

Answer: Invasive species can harm ecosystems by outcompeting native species for resources, leading to population declines or extinctions of native organisms.

Question 16

What is the primary function of the mitochondria in cells?

Answer: The mitochondria produce energy for the cell in the form of ATP through the process of cellular respiration.

Question 17

What role do decomposers play in an ecosystem?

Answer: Decomposers break down dead organisms and recycle nutrients back into the soil, supporting plant growth and maintaining the nutrient cycle.

Question 18

Why is the greenhouse effect important for life on Earth?

Answer: The greenhouse effect is important because it traps heat in Earth's atmosphere, keeping the planet warm enough to sustain life.

Question 19

How does vaccination prevent the spread of diseases?

Answer: Vaccination prevents diseases by stimulating the immune system to recognize and fight specific pathogens, reducing the likelihood of infection and transmission.

Question 20

What happens to light when it passes through a prism?

Answer: When light passes through a prism, it is refracted (bent) and separated into its component colors, creating a spectrum.

10 GRAPH AND DATA INTERPRETATION QUESTIONS

Question 1

The following line graph shows the deer population in a forest over five years:

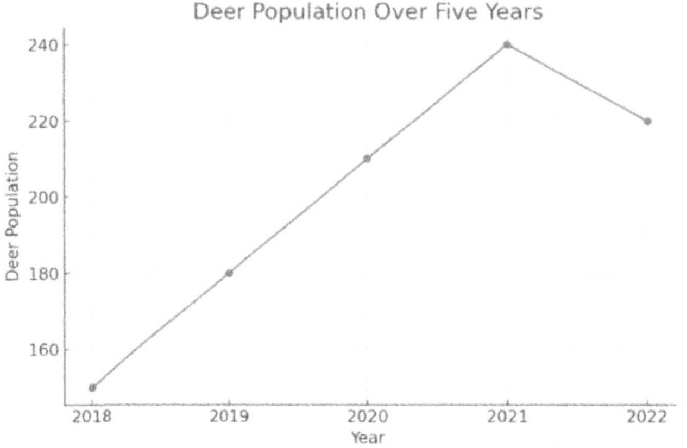

Question:
In which year did the deer population peak?
Answer: The deer population peaked in **2021** with 240 deer.

Question 2
The bar graph below displays the monthly rainfall (in mm) in a region over five months:

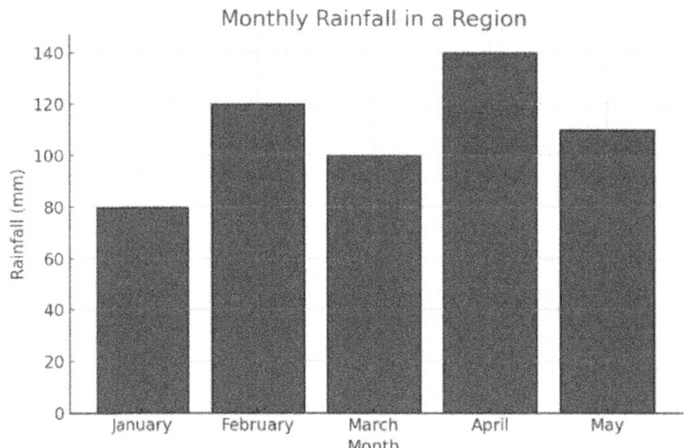

Question:
Which month received the highest rainfall?
Answer: The month with the highest rainfall is **April** with 140 mm.
Question 3
The pie chart shows energy sources used in a town:

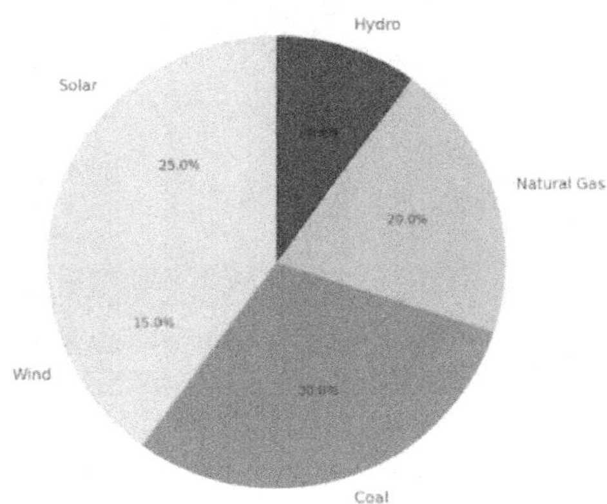

Question:

What is the most commonly used energy source in the town?
Answer: The most commonly used energy source is **coal** at 30%.

Question 4

The following scatter plot shows the relationship between hours studied and test scores:

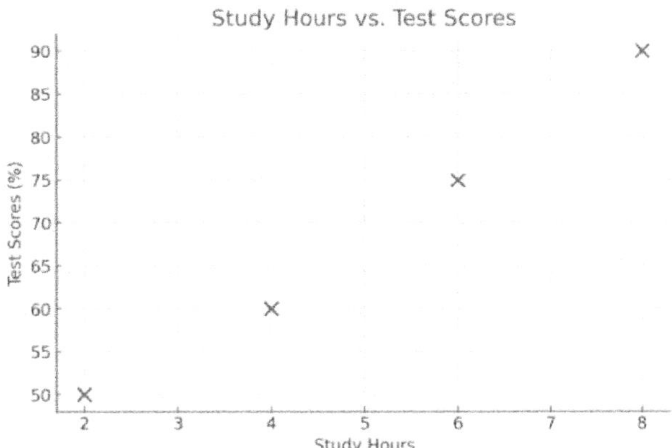

Question:

What trend does the scatter plot show about studying and test scores?
Answer: The scatter plot shows a **positive correlation**: as study hours increase, test scores improve.

Question 5

The bar graph shows the number of different tree species in three parks:

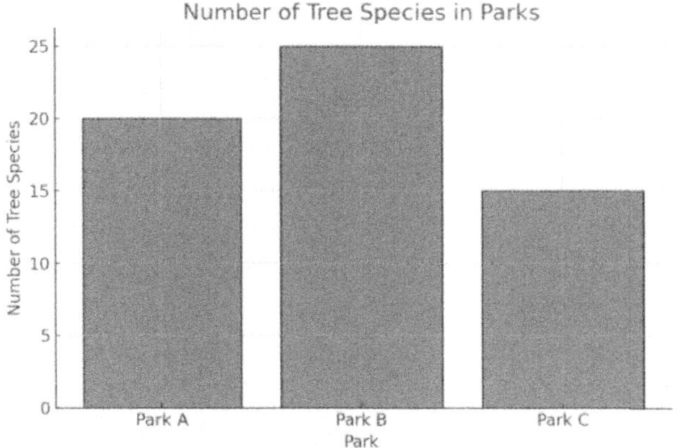

Question:

Which park has the highest biodiversity in terms of tree species?
Answer: Park B has the highest biodiversity with 25 tree species.

Question 6

A line graph shows the population growth of a city:

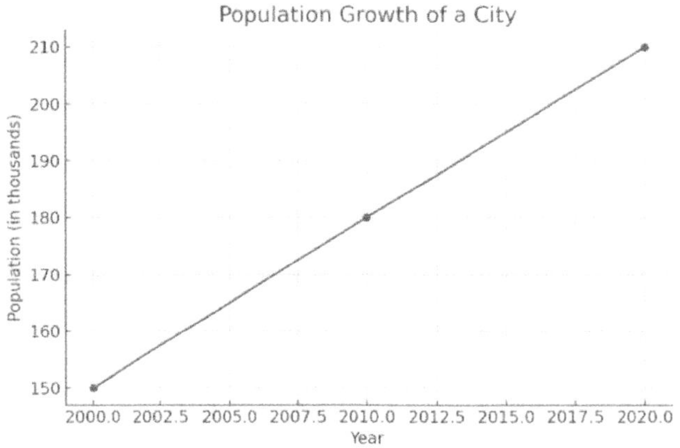

Question:

What is the population growth from 2000 to 2020?
Answer: The population grew by **60,000** from 150,000 in 2000 to 210,000 in 2020.

Question 7

The pie chart shows the percentages of nutrients in a plant fertilizer:

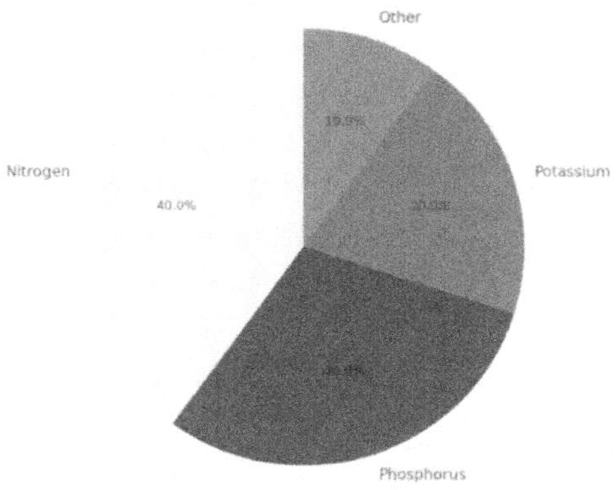

Question:

What is the largest nutrient component in the fertilizer?
Answer: The largest nutrient component is **nitrogen** at 40%.

Question 8

The graph below shows the average temperature (°C) for four cities in a week:

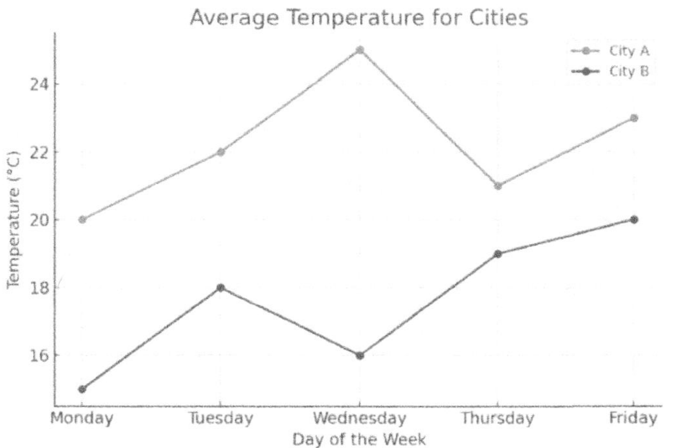

Question:

Which city had the highest average temperature on Wednesday?
Answer: **City A** had the highest temperature on Wednesday with **25°C**.

Question 9

The following graph shows the productivity (in units) of a factory over four months:

Factory Productivity Over Four Months

Units Produced: 0, 100, 200, 300, 400, 500, 600

Month: January, February, March, April

Question:

In which month was productivity the lowest?
Answer: Productivity was the lowest in **January** with 500 units.

Question 10

A bar graph shows the population of birds in a sanctuary:

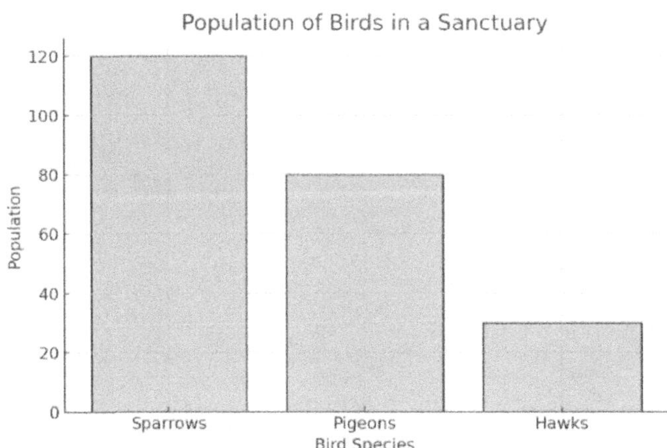

Question:

What is the combined population of sparrows and pigeons?
Answer: The combined population of sparrows and pigeons is **200** (120 + 80).

10 Scenario-Based Questions

Question 1: Environmental Science
Scenario:
A lake has experienced a sudden decrease in fish population. Scientists suspect that fertilizers from nearby farms are causing algae to grow excessively, reducing oxygen levels in the water.
Question:
What is the most likely cause of the fish population decrease?
Answer: The excessive algae growth, caused by runoff of fertilizers, leads to oxygen depletion in the lake, which negatively impacts fish survival.
Question 2: Human Health
Scenario:

A new vaccine has been developed to prevent a viral disease. In a clinical trial, 5,000 people received the vaccine, and 4,750 of them remained disease-free after a year.

Question:

What is the efficacy rate of the vaccine?

Answer: The efficacy rate is $\frac{4750}{5000} \times 100 = 95\%$.

Question 3: Physics

Scenario:

A car travels 120 kilometers in 2 hours on a highway. Later, it takes 3 hours to travel 150 kilometers on a mountain road.

Question:

What is the car's average speed during the entire trip?

Answer: The total distance is $120 + 150 = 270$ kilometers, and the total time is $2 + 3 = 5$ hours.

The average speed is $\frac{270}{5} = 54$ kilometers per hour.

Question 4: Biology

Scenario:

A scientist is studying the effects of light on plant growth. They grow three groups of plants: one in full sunlight, one in partial sunlight, and one in darkness. After two weeks, the plants in full sunlight are tallest, while those in darkness are shortest.

Question:

What can the scientist conclude about the effect of light on plant growth?

Answer: The scientist can conclude that increased light exposure promotes plant growth.

Question 5: Chemistry

Scenario:

A student adds baking soda to vinegar and observes bubbling and the release of a gas. They measure the gas and find it to be carbon dioxide (CO_2).

Question:

What type of reaction is occurring between baking soda and vinegar?

Answer: It is a chemical reaction, specifically an acid-base reaction, producing carbon dioxide gas as a result.

Question 6: Climate Change

Scenario:

The average global temperature has increased by 1.2°C over the past century. Scientists note that carbon dioxide levels in the atmosphere have risen during the same period.

Question:

What is the likely relationship between carbon dioxide levels and global temperature?

Answer: The increase in carbon dioxide levels is likely causing the global temperature rise due to the greenhouse effect.

Question 7: Genetics

Scenario:

A scientist crosses two plants, one with purple flowers (dominant trait) and one with white flowers (recessive trait). In the offspring, 75% have purple flowers, and 25% have white flowers.

Question:

What does this indicate about the genotype of the parent plants?

Answer: The parent plants are likely heterozygous for the flower color gene (Pp × Pp), resulting in the observed 3:1 phenotype ratio.

Question 8: Astronomy

Scenario:

A student observes that the Moon appears to change shape throughout the month.

Question:

What causes the Moon to appear in different phases?

Answer: The Moon's phases are caused by its position relative to the Earth and Sun, affecting how much of the illuminated portion is visible from Earth.

Question 9: Earth Science

Scenario:

A river has widened significantly over the past 50 years. Scientists attribute this to erosion caused by increased water flow and deforestation along the riverbanks.

Question:

What is the primary factor contributing to the widening of the river?

Answer: The primary factor is increased erosion due to higher water flow and reduced vegetation stabilizing the soil.

Question 10: Nutrition

Scenario:

A nutritionist observes that a patient consumes excessive amounts of saturated fats and has high cholesterol levels.

Question:

What dietary change should the nutritionist recommend?

Answer: The nutritionist should recommend reducing saturated fat intake and increasing consumption of fruits, vegetables, and unsaturated fats to improve cholesterol levels.

Question 11: Ecosystem Balance

Scenario:

A forest experiences a sudden decline in its wolf population. Over the next few years, the deer population in the area increases dramatically, leading to overgrazing and damage to vegetation.

Question:

What role did the wolves play in maintaining the ecosystem balance?

Answer: The wolves acted as predators, controlling the deer population. Their decline led to an overpopulation of deer and overgrazing, disrupting the ecosystem balance.

Question 12: Renewable Energy

Scenario:

A city plans to replace coal-fired power plants with solar panels and wind turbines. However, citizens are concerned about the reliability of these energy sources.

Question:

What could the city do to address concerns about renewable energy reliability?

Answer: The city could implement energy storage systems, such as batteries, to store excess energy during sunny or windy days for use during low production periods.

Question 13: Human Body

Scenario:

A person is experiencing fatigue, shortness of breath, and pale skin. A doctor determines they have a low red blood cell count.

Question:

What condition might this person have, and how could it be treated?

Answer: The person might have anemia. Treatment could include increasing iron intake through diet or supplements to support red blood cell production.

Question 14: Conservation Biology

Scenario:

An endangered species of bird is losing its habitat due to urban development. Conservationists are creating protected areas to help preserve the species.

Question:

What additional steps could conservationists take to support the bird population?

Answer: Conservationists could plant native vegetation, reduce human disturbances, and implement breeding programs to increase the bird population.

Question 15: Water Pollution

Scenario:

A factory releases untreated wastewater into a nearby river, causing fish to die and algae to grow excessively.

Question:

What is the primary cause of these environmental issues, and what could the factory do to mitigate the impact?

Answer: The untreated wastewater contains pollutants that harm fish and promote algae growth. The factory could install water treatment systems to remove harmful substances before discharging wastewater.

Question 16: Physics of Motion

Scenario:

A car traveling at 60 mph suddenly applies its brakes and comes to a stop. The driver notices that it takes longer to stop on a wet road than on a dry road.

Question:

What causes the increased stopping distance on wet roads?

Answer: The stopping distance increases on wet roads because reduced friction between the tires and the road surface decreases the car's ability to stop quickly.

Question 17: Climate Patterns

Scenario:

A coastal town experiences warmer winters and more frequent flooding over the past decade. Scientists attribute these changes to rising sea levels and shifts in ocean currents.

Question:

What global phenomenon is likely responsible for these changes?

Answer: The changes are likely caused by climate change, which leads to rising sea levels and altered ocean currents.

Question 18: Scientific Method

Scenario:

A student wants to test whether the amount of sunlight affects the growth of bean plants. They grow three groups of plants: one with full sunlight, one with partial sunlight, and one with no sunlight.

Question:

What is the independent variable in this experiment?

Answer: The independent variable is the amount of sunlight.

Question 19: Genetics and Heredity

Scenario:

A child has blue eyes, even though both parents have brown eyes. Blue eyes are a recessive trait, while brown eyes are dominant.

Question:

What does this indicate about the parents' genotypes?

Answer: Both parents are likely heterozygous for eye color (Bb), carrying one dominant allele for brown eyes and one recessive allele for blue eyes.

Question 20: Greenhouse Gases

Scenario:

A country implements policies to reduce its greenhouse gas emissions by increasing the use of electric vehicles and renewable energy sources.

Question:

How do these policies help mitigate climate change?

Answer: These policies reduce the burning of fossil fuels, decreasing the release of greenhouse gases like carbon dioxide, which contribute to global warming.

PART V

SOCIAL STUDIES

CHAPTER 26

OVERVIEW OF THE SOCIAL STUDIES EXAM

The GED Social Studies exam is designed to evaluate your understanding of key concepts in U.S. history, civics and government, economics, geography, and world history. It also assesses your ability to interpret social studies data, think critically about historical and current events, and draw meaningful conclusions based on evidence.

This section of the GED exam is not simply about memorizing facts but about applying your knowledge to analyze scenarios, interpret documents, and make informed decisions. The Social Studies test prepares you for real-world decision-making, encouraging you to engage with the broader historical, civic, and global context.

Format of the Social Studies Exam

The Social Studies exam consists of multiple-choice questions, drag-and-drop items, fill-in-the-blank responses, and hotspot questions, where you interact directly with maps or diagrams. Some questions will require you to interpret data from charts, graphs, or political cartoons, while others will focus on written passages or excerpts from historical documents.

- **Test Duration**: 70 minutes
- **Total Questions**: Approximately 35 questions
- **Question Types**:
    - Multiple-choice
    - Drag-and-drop
    - Hotspot
    - Fill-in-the-blank
- **Skills Focus**: Analysis, critical thinking, and reasoning

Key Topics Covered

1. **U.S. History**
   Includes founding documents like the Declaration of Independence and the Constitution, major historical events, influential figures, and movements such as the Civil Rights Movement.
2. **Civics and Government**
   Explores the principles of democracy, government structure, civic responsibilities, and understanding laws and policies.
3. **Economics**
   Discusses economic systems, supply and demand, government roles in the economy, personal finance, and global trade.
4. **Geography and World History**
   Covers major geographic features, their impacts on societies, and key global historical events and technological developments.
5. **Interpreting Social Studies Data**
   Requires analyzing maps, graphs, tables, and political cartoons, as well as understanding primary and secondary sources.

Skills Required

To succeed in this exam, you'll need to demonstrate the following abilities:

- **Critical Thinking**: Evaluate arguments, analyze cause-and-effect relationships, and identify bias or point of view.
- **Data Interpretation**: Understand and interpret charts, graphs, and maps to answer questions accurately.
- **Historical Understanding**: Use knowledge of historical events and their contexts to analyze and answer questions.
- **Civic Knowledge**: Demonstrate an understanding of civic responsibilities and governmental processes.

Why This Exam Matters

The GED Social Studies exam prepares you for situations where you'll need to analyze and apply knowledge of history, economics, and government. This skillset is crucial for informed citizenship and real-life problem-solving. Whether it's understanding your role as a voter, managing finances, or appreciating cultural and historical contexts, this test equips you with valuable tools for everyday decision-making.

26.1 Structure and Question Types

The GED Social Studies exam features a variety of question formats designed to test your ability to analyze, interpret, and apply knowledge across key social studies topics. Understanding the structure of the exam and the types of questions you will encounter is essential to your preparation and success.

Exam Structure

The Social Studies exam consists of approximately 35 questions, covering topics in U.S. history, civics and government, economics, geography, and world history. These questions are presented in different formats to assess your comprehension and reasoning skills.

- **Test Duration**: 70 minutes
- **Sections Covered**:
  - U.S. History
  - Civics and Government
  - Economics
  - Geography and World History

Types of Questions

The Social Studies exam includes a mix of question types to evaluate your ability to interpret information, analyze scenarios, and draw logical conclusions.

1. **Multiple-Choice Questions**
   You will select the best answer from four options. These questions often involve interpreting text, charts, or historical documents.
   Example:
   What year was the Declaration of Independence signed?

a) 1776
b) 1783
c) 1801
d) 1812

Answer: a) 1776

2. **Drag-and-Drop Questions**

   In these questions, you'll organize items into categories, match terms to definitions, or place events in chronological order.

   Example:

   Drag the following historical events into chronological order:

   - American Revolution
   - Civil War
   - World War I
   - Great Depression

   Answer:

5. American Revolution

   - Civil War
   - World War I
   - Great Depression

3. **Hotspot Questions**

   Hotspot questions require you to interact directly with visual elements such as maps, graphs, or political cartoons. You'll click on specific areas to answer.
   Example:
   On a map of the United States, click the state where the Boston Tea Party occurred.
   Answer: Massachusetts

4. **Fill-in-the-Blank Questions**

   These questions require you to type a word, number, or short phrase to complete a statement or answer a question.
   Example:
   The U.S. Constitution was written in the year __________.
   Answer: 1787

5. **Scenario-Based Questions**

   These questions involve reading a scenario or passage and answering multiple questions based on the information provided.
   Example:
   Scenario: A new law proposes limiting carbon emissions by 50% over the next decade.
   Question: What is the primary goal of this law?
   Answer: To reduce the impact of climate change.

Focus on Interpretation and Analysis

Unlike other exams that emphasize rote memorization, the GED Social Studies exam tests your ability to:

- **Analyze historical and current events** to understand their significance.
- **Interpret graphs, maps, and charts** for key insights.
- **Apply civic knowledge** to answer questions about government and policies.
- **Reason critically** to identify cause-and-effect relationships in social and economic contexts.

Time Management

Efficient time management is crucial for completing the test. You'll need to allocate your time wisely to ensure you can thoroughly analyze the more complex scenarios and data interpretation questions. Use these strategies:

- Spend more time on scenario-based and graph-related questions.
- Tackle straightforward multiple-choice questions first to build momentum.
- Keep an eye on the clock to ensure all questions are answered.

26.2 Skills Tested: Analysis, Interpretation, and Reasoning

The GED Social Studies exam evaluates your ability to think critically, interpret information, and apply reasoning skills across key areas such as U.S. history, civics and government, economics, and geography. Success on the exam requires more than just factual knowledge; you must analyze scenarios, draw conclusions, and assess evidence to answer questions effectively.

Key Skills Assessed

The exam focuses on three primary skill areas:

1. Analyzing Historical and Contemporary Events

This skill requires you to evaluate historical events and their implications, as well as connect them to contemporary issues. You will often encounter questions that involve comparing past and present events to identify trends or analyze their impacts.

Example Question:

- **Scenario**: During the Great Depression, unemployment rates soared due to a lack of consumer spending and economic downturns.
  Question: How did New Deal policies, like public works programs, aim to address these issues?
  Answer: New Deal policies aimed to create jobs, stimulate economic growth, and restore consumer confidence.

2. Interpreting Data in Graphs, Charts, and Maps

Interpreting visual data is a critical skill. Questions may present information in the form of bar graphs, line charts, pie charts, or maps. You'll need to extract relevant details, compare data points, and use the information to answer questions.

Example Question:

A bar graph shows voter turnout in three recent elections:

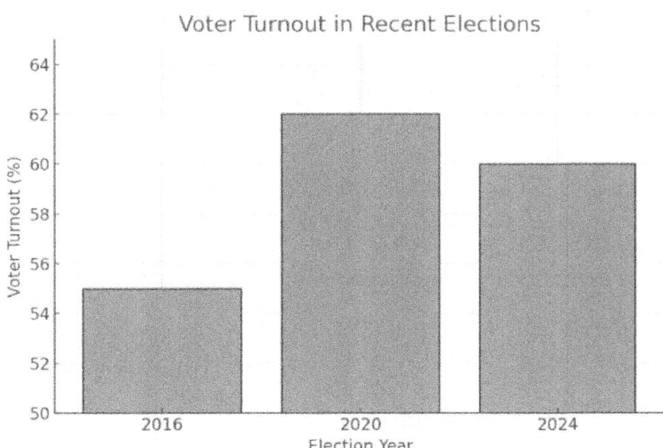

Question: What trend can be observed in voter turnout?
Answer: Voter turnout increased from 2016 to 2020 but slightly decreased in 2024.

3. Critical Reading and Reasoning

This skill focuses on analyzing written passages, identifying the author's purpose, evaluating arguments, and understanding cause-and-effect relationships. Passages may include excerpts from historical documents, speeches, or contemporary news articles.

Example Question:

- **Passage**: "We hold these truths to be self-evident, that all men are created equal…" (Declaration of Independence)
  Question: What principle is emphasized in this passage?
  Answer: The principle of equality and inherent rights for all individuals.

Analysis and Interpretation in Different Contexts

1. **U.S. History**
- Evaluate the significance of major historical events, such as the Civil War or World Wars.
- Analyze the impact of founding documents like the Declaration of Independence and the Constitution on the development of democracy.
2. **Civics and Government**
- Understand the functions and responsibilities of government branches.
- Analyze policies and laws to determine their impact on citizens and society.
3. **Economics**
- Interpret supply and demand graphs to understand economic principles.
- Evaluate the role of government in regulating the economy and supporting financial stability.
4. **Geography and World History**
- Assess the impact of geographic features on human development and historical events.
- Understand how technological advancements shaped societies globally.

Reasoning Skills in Practice

1. **Cause-and-Effect Relationships**
   You'll identify how events or actions lead to specific outcomes. This is especially relevant in questions about historical events or policy impacts.

Example Question:

What was one effect of the Emancipation Proclamation during the Civil War?

Answer: It declared enslaved people in Confederate states to be free, shifting the war's focus to abolition.

2. **Identifying Bias or Point of View**
   You must assess whether a source or argument presents information objectively or reflects a specific bias.

Example Question:

- **Scenario**: A political cartoon depicts a businessman controlling the government.
  Question: What perspective does this cartoon likely represent?
  Answer: It reflects a critique of corporate influence over politics.

3. **Synthesizing Information**
   You'll combine details from multiple sources to form a conclusion.

Example Question:

A map shows regions experiencing drought, while a graph displays decreased crop yields in those regions.

Question: What conclusion can be drawn?
Answer: Drought conditions are likely contributing to reduced agricultural productivity.

Strategies for Developing These Skills

1. **Practice Active Reading**
- Summarize passages in your own words to ensure understanding.
- Highlight key details, such as dates, statistics, or main arguments.
2. **Work with Visual Data**
- Practice reading and interpreting different types of graphs and charts.
- Focus on understanding trends and relationships between data points.
3. **Connect Concepts to Real Life**
- Relate historical events to current issues to better understand their significance.
- Use examples from personal experience or news stories to practice reasoning skills.
4. **Use Elimination Techniques**
- For multiple-choice questions, eliminate answers that don't align with the evidence or context provided.

CHAPTER 27

U.S. HISTORY

27.1 Founding Documents: Declaration of Independence, Constitution

The founding documents of the United States, the **Declaration of Independence** and the **Constitution**, serve as the bedrock of American democracy. These documents define the nation's principles, outline the framework of government, and ensure the protection of individual rights. Understanding their content, context, and significance is essential for excelling in the GED Social Studies exam and for grasping the foundational values of the United States.

The Declaration of Independence

Background and Purpose

- **Adopted**: July 4, 1776
- **Author**: Primarily written by Thomas Jefferson, with input from other members of the Continental Congress, including John Adams and Benjamin Franklin.
- **Purpose**: To formally announce the colonies' separation from Great Britain and justify the decision to seek independence.

Key Sections

1. **Preamble**:

   The introduction explains why the colonies felt compelled to declare independence. It highlights the belief in universal principles, such as equality and natural rights.

   Example Text:

   "We hold these truths to be self-evident, that all men are created equal, that they are endowed by their Creator with certain unalienable Rights, that among these are Life, Liberty and the pursuit of Happiness."

2. **List of Grievances**:

   Details the colonists' complaints against King George III, including unfair taxation, denial of representation, and the imposition of military rule.

3. **Declaration of Independence**:

   Officially states the colonies' intention to separate from Great Britain and form an independent nation.

Significance

- Articulated the ideals of democracy and self-governance.
- Inspired future democratic movements worldwide, serving as a model for other declarations of independence.
- Marked the beginning of the Revolutionary War, uniting the colonies under a common cause.

The U.S. Constitution

Background and Purpose

- **Adopted**: September 17, 1787 (Ratified in 1788).
- **Authors**: Drafted by delegates to the Constitutional Convention, including James Madison (often called the "Father of the Constitution").
- **Purpose**: To establish the framework for the federal government, ensuring a balance of power and protecting the rights of citizens.

Key Features of the Constitution

1. **Preamble**:

The opening statement outlines the goals of the Constitution: to form a more perfect union, establish justice, ensure domestic tranquility, provide for the common defense, promote the general welfare, and secure the blessings of liberty.

Example Text:

"We the People of the United States, in Order to form a more perfect Union..."

2. **Articles**:

   The Constitution is divided into seven articles, each detailing a specific aspect of government:

   - **Article I**: Establishes the legislative branch (Congress), its structure (House of Representatives and Senate), and its powers.
   - **Article II**: Defines the executive branch, led by the President, and its responsibilities.
   - **Article III**: Creates the judicial branch and outlines the powers of the Supreme Court and lower courts.
   - **Articles IV-VII**: Address issues such as state relationships, the amendment process, federal supremacy, and ratification.

3. **Amendments**:

   - The first ten amendments, known as the **Bill of Rights**, were added in 1791 to ensure the protection of individual freedoms.
   - Examples of key amendments:
     - **First Amendment**: Protects freedom of speech, religion, press, assembly, and petition.
     - **Fourth Amendment**: Protects against unreasonable searches and seizures.
     - **Fifth Amendment**: Guarantees due process and protection from self-incrimination.

Significance

- Created a system of checks and balances to prevent any one branch from becoming too powerful.
- Ensures federalism, balancing power between the federal and state governments.
- Continues to serve as a living document, adaptable through amendments to meet the evolving needs of society.

Comparison Between the Two Documents

Aspect	Declaration of Independence	U.S. Constitution
Purpose	Declared independence from Britain.	Established the framework for U.S. government.
Focus	Ideals and grievances.	Laws, structure, and functions of government.
Tone	Philosophical and revolutionary.	Legal and pragmatic.
Timeframe	Written during the Revolutionary War (1776).	Written post-Revolution to create a stable government (1787).

Impact on the GED Exam

Questions on this topic often involve analyzing excerpts from these documents. You may be asked to:

- Identify the main ideas or purposes of specific passages.
- Compare principles in the Declaration and the Constitution.
- Apply the concepts to historical or modern contexts.

Example Question:

- **Excerpt**: "That to secure these rights, Governments are instituted among Men, deriving their just powers from the consent of the governed."
  Question: What principle is expressed in this statement?
  Answer: The principle of government by consent of the people.

Example Question:

- **Question:** What does the Bill of Rights primarily protect?
  Answer: Individual freedoms and rights from government overreach.

27.2 Major Historical Events and Movements

Understanding the significant events and movements that have shaped the history of the United States is essential for the GED Social Studies exam. This comprehensive chapter covers key moments from the founding of the colonies to modern times, providing the context, causes, and consequences of these pivotal events.

Colonial America and Early Settlements (1607–1776)

- **Founding of Jamestown (1607):** The first permanent English colony in North America, established for economic ventures.
- **Mayflower Compact (1620):** An early form of self-governance by the Pilgrims in Plymouth, laying a foundation for democratic principles.
- **Bacon's Rebellion (1676):** Highlighted class tensions between wealthy landowners and frontier settlers, leading to increased reliance on enslaved labor.
- **French and Indian War (1754–1763):** A conflict between Britain and France over North American territory, leading to increased British taxation of the colonies.

The American Revolution (1775–1783)

- **Causes of the Revolution:**
  - Unfair taxation, such as the Stamp Act (1765) and Tea Act (1773).
  - Events like the Boston Massacre (1770) and Boston Tea Party (1773) escalated tensions.
- **Key Events of the Revolution:**
  - **Declaration of Independence (1776):** Proclaimed the colonies' separation from Britain.
  - **Battle of Saratoga (1777):** A turning point that secured French support for the American cause.
  - **Treaty of Paris (1783):** Officially ended the war, recognizing U.S. independence.

The Early Republic (1780s–1830s)

- **Articles of Confederation:** The first governing document, which proved too weak to manage the growing nation, leading to the drafting of the U.S. Constitution.
- **Constitutional Convention (1787):** Established the framework for the federal government, balancing powers between states and the federal government.
- **War of 1812:** A second war with Britain that solidified U.S. independence and spurred nationalism.
- **Monroe Doctrine (1823):** Declared that European interference in the Americas would be viewed as an act of aggression.

Westward Expansion and Manifest Destiny (1800s)

- **Louisiana Purchase (1803):** Doubled the size of the U.S., purchased from France.
- **Lewis and Clark Expedition (1804–1806):** Mapped the newly acquired territory and established relations with Native tribes.
- **Indian Removal Act (1830) and Trail of Tears:** Forced relocation of Native Americans, resulting in significant loss of life and culture.
- **Mexican-American War (1846–1848):** Gained territories like California and Texas through the Treaty of Guadalupe Hidalgo.

Impact:

This period of expansion led to economic growth but also fueled debates over slavery and displaced Native populations.

The Civil War and Reconstruction (1861–1877)

- **Causes:**
  - **Slavery:** The primary cause of sectional tensions.
  - **States' Rights:** Southern states argued for their right to govern independently.
  - **Economic Divides:** Industrial North versus agrarian South.
- **Key Events of the Civil War:**
  - Election of Abraham Lincoln (1860): Prompted Southern secession.
  - Emancipation Proclamation (1863): Freed enslaved people in Confederate states.

    - Battle of Gettysburg (1863): Turned the tide in favor of the Union.

- **Reconstruction Era:**
    - **13th, 14th, and 15th Amendments:** Abolished slavery, granted citizenship, and ensured voting rights.
    - **Failures of Reconstruction:** The Compromise of 1877 led to the withdrawal of federal troops from the South, allowing the rise of Jim Crow laws.

Industrialization and the Progressive Era (1870s–1920s)

- **Industrial Revolution:** Transformed the economy with factories, railroads, and urbanization.
- **Labor Movements:** Workers fought for fair wages, safe conditions, and shorter work hours through strikes like the Pullman Strike (1894).
- **Progressive Reforms:**
    - Child labor laws and workplace safety regulations.
    - Women's suffrage movement, culminating in the 19th Amendment (1920).

World Wars and the Great Depression (1914–1945)

- **World War I (1914–1918):** The U.S. joined in 1917, tipping the balance in favor of the Allies.
- **The Great Depression (1929–1939):** Triggered by the stock market crash, leading to widespread poverty.
    - **New Deal Programs:** FDR's initiatives like Social Security and public works projects helped alleviate economic hardship.
- **World War II (1939–1945):** The U.S. played a critical role in defeating Axis powers, emerging as a global superpower.

The Civil Rights Movement (1950s–1970s)

- **Key Figures:**
    - Martin Luther King Jr.: Leader of nonviolent protests.
    - Rosa Parks: Sparked the Montgomery Bus Boycott.
- **Legislation:**
    - **Civil Rights Act (1964):** Ended segregation.
    - **Voting Rights Act (1965):** Prohibited discriminatory voting practices.

Modern Era (1970s–Present)

- **Cold War (1947–1991):** A geopolitical rivalry between the U.S. and the Soviet Union, marked by events like the Cuban Missile Crisis.
- **Technological Advancements:**
    - The Moon landing (1969) symbolized American innovation.
    - The rise of the internet transformed communication and industry.
- **Social Movements:**
    - LGBTQ+ rights, including the legalization of same-sex marriage in 2015.
    - Environmental movements advocating for sustainable practices.

Key Takeaways for the GED Exam

Questions on this section may ask you to:

- Place events in chronological order.
- Identify the causes and effects of major historical movements.
- Analyze the significance of specific events, policies, or amendments.

Example Question:

Question: What was the primary goal of the Monroe Doctrine?
Answer: To prevent European interference in the Americas.

27.3 Influential Figures in U.S. History

The story of the United States is shaped by individuals whose vision, leadership, and courage made an indelible mark on the nation's history. Understanding the contributions and legacies of these influential figures is essential for the GED Social Studies exam, as questions often focus on their roles and the impact of their actions on society and governance.

George Washington: The Founding Leader

As the first President of the United States and Commander-in-Chief of the Continental Army during the Revolutionary War, George Washington played a pivotal role in the nation's founding. His leadership secured key victories, such as the Battle of Trenton, and his refusal to accept absolute power set a precedent for democratic governance. Washington's legacy includes his farewell address, where he warned against political factions and foreign alliances, principles that resonate in U.S. politics to this day.

Thomas Jefferson: Author of Liberty

Thomas Jefferson, the principal author of the Declaration of Independence, articulated the ideals of equality and unalienable rights that define American democracy. As the third President, Jefferson oversaw the Louisiana Purchase, doubling the nation's size, and supported the exploration of new territories through the Lewis and Clark expedition. His advocacy for limited government and individual freedoms influenced the nation's development for generations.

Abraham Lincoln: The Great Emancipator

Abraham Lincoln's presidency during the Civil War was a defining moment in U.S. history. His commitment to preserving the Union and ending slavery culminated in the Emancipation Proclamation and the passage of the 13th Amendment. Lincoln's Gettysburg Address, delivered in 1863, reframed the war as a struggle for equality and democracy, embodying the nation's highest ideals. His leadership during the nation's most perilous period solidified his place as one of America's most revered leaders.

Frederick Douglass: Voice of Abolition

Frederick Douglass, an escaped slave turned abolitionist, became one of the most powerful voices against slavery. His autobiographies, including *Narrative of the Life of Frederick Douglass*, exposed the brutal realities of enslavement and inspired movements for abolition and civil rights. Douglass's speeches, writings, and advocacy helped shape public opinion and contributed to the eventual abolition of slavery.

Susan B. Anthony: Champion of Women's Rights

A tireless advocate for women's suffrage, Susan B. Anthony was instrumental in the fight for equal rights. As a leader in the women's suffrage movement, she co-founded the National Woman Suffrage Association and worked to secure the passage of the 19th Amendment, granting women the right to vote. Anthony's dedication to justice and equality left an enduring legacy in the struggle for gender equality.

Franklin D. Roosevelt: Architect of the New Deal

Franklin D. Roosevelt's leadership during the Great Depression and World War II transformed the nation. Through his New Deal programs, FDR provided jobs, reformed the financial system, and established Social Security, laying the foundation for modern economic stability. His leadership during World War II helped secure Allied victory and positioned the U.S. as a global superpower. Roosevelt's unprecedented four-term presidency reshaped the role of the federal government in American life.

Martin Luther King Jr.: Leader of Civil Rights

Martin Luther King Jr. remains one of the most iconic figures in the fight for racial equality. Through his philosophy of nonviolent resistance, King led pivotal events like the Montgomery Bus Boycott and the March on Washington, where he delivered his famous "I Have a Dream" speech. His efforts were instrumental in the passage of the Civil Rights Act of 1964 and the Voting Rights Act of 1965. King's legacy of justice and nonviolence continues to inspire social movements worldwide.

John F. Kennedy: Visionary of a New Frontier

As the 35th President, John F. Kennedy championed a vision of progress and innovation. His commitment to civil rights, exemplified by his support for desegregation, and his push for space exploration through the Apollo program defined his presidency. Kennedy's famous declaration, "Ask not what your country can do for you—ask what you can do for your country," encapsulates his call for civic responsibility and public service.

Rosa Parks: The Mother of the Civil Rights Movement

Rosa Parks ignited the modern civil rights movement by refusing to give up her seat on a segregated bus in Montgomery, Alabama, in 1955. Her act of defiance sparked the Montgomery Bus Boycott, a landmark event in the fight against racial segregation. Parks became a symbol of courage and resistance, demonstrating the power of ordinary citizens to create extraordinary change.

Barack Obama: The First African American President

Barack Obama's election in 2008 marked a historic milestone as the first African American president of the United States. His presidency focused on healthcare reform, economic recovery following the 2008 financial crisis, and progressive social policies. The passage of the Affordable Care Act (Obamacare) stands as one of his signature achievements, expanding healthcare access to millions of Americans.

Key Takeaways for the GED Exam

Understanding the contributions of these figures is essential for the GED Social Studies exam. You may encounter questions that require you to:

- Identify the roles and achievements of specific individuals.
- Analyze the impact of their actions on historical events or movements.
- Connect their contributions to broader themes, such as civil rights or democratic governance.

Example Question:

- **Question:** Which President issued the Emancipation Proclamation?
  Answer: Abraham Lincoln.

Example Question:

- **Question:** What was Susan B. Anthony's primary focus as an activist?
  Answer: Securing women's right to vote.

27.4 Civil Rights and Social Justice Movements

The Civil Rights and social justice movements in the United States have played a pivotal role in addressing inequality and securing rights for marginalized groups. These movements have not only reshaped laws and policies but have also challenged societal norms and inspired global human rights initiatives. This chapter explores the key events, figures, and outcomes of these movements, providing the context needed to excel in this section of the GED Social Studies exam.

The Civil Rights Movement (1950s–1970s)
Overview

The Civil Rights Movement aimed to end racial segregation and discrimination against African Americans, primarily in the Southern United States. It sought to ensure equal rights and opportunities for all citizens, as guaranteed under the U.S. Constitution.

Key Events and Milestones

- **Brown v. Board of Education (1954):**
  This landmark Supreme Court decision declared racial segregation in public schools unconstitutional, overturning the precedent set by *Plessy v. Ferguson* (1896).
  Impact: It marked the beginning of the dismantling of institutionalized segregation.

- **Montgomery Bus Boycott (1955–1956):**
  Sparked by Rosa Parks' arrest for refusing to give up her bus seat to a white passenger, this year-long boycott led to the desegregation of public buses in Montgomery, Alabama.

- **Civil Rights Act of 1964:**
- Signed into law by President Lyndon B. Johnson, this act prohibited discrimination based on race, color, religion, sex, or national origin in employment and public accommodations.

Impact: It was a major legislative victory for the Civil Rights Movement.

- **Voting Rights Act of 1965:**
  Addressed discriminatory practices like literacy tests and poll taxes that disenfranchised African American voters, especially in the South.

Key Figures

- **Martin Luther King Jr.:**
  Advocated nonviolent resistance and led significant events like the March on Washington (1963), where he delivered his famous "I Have a Dream" speech.
- **Malcolm X:**
  Promoted Black empowerment and self-reliance, offering an alternative perspective to King's nonviolence.
- **Rosa Parks:**
  Her courage in refusing to yield her bus seat became a symbol of resistance against racial injustice.

The Women's Rights Movement

Overview

The Women's Rights Movement sought to achieve gender equality in areas such as voting, education, employment, and reproductive rights.

Key Events and Milestones

- **Seneca Falls Convention (1848):**
  The first women's rights convention in the U.S., where activists like Elizabeth Cady Stanton and Lucretia Mott called for gender equality.
- **19th Amendment (1920):**
  Granted women the right to vote after decades of advocacy by leaders like Susan B. Anthony and Alice Paul.
- **The Equal Rights Amendment (ERA):**
  Proposed in 1923, the ERA aimed to guarantee equal rights regardless of sex. Though it has not been fully ratified, it remains a cornerstone of the movement.

Modern Advocacy

In recent decades, the movement has expanded to address issues like the gender pay gap, sexual harassment, and reproductive rights.

The LGBTQ+ Rights Movement

Overview

The LGBTQ+ Rights Movement emerged to combat discrimination based on sexual orientation and gender identity, advocating for equal rights and acceptance.

Key Events and Milestones

- **Stonewall Riots (1969):**
  A series of protests in New York City after police raided the Stonewall Inn, a gay bar. These riots are often considered the birth of the modern LGBTQ+ rights movement.
- **Obergefell v. Hodges (2015):**
  The Supreme Court ruled that same-sex marriage is a constitutional right.
  Impact: This decision marked a significant victory for marriage equality.

Key Figures

- **Harvey Milk:**
  One of the first openly gay elected officials in the U.S., Milk championed LGBTQ+ rights and inspired generations of activists.

The Labor Rights Movement

Overview

The Labor Rights Movement fought for fair wages, reasonable working hours, and safe working conditions for workers across industries.

Key Events and Milestones

- **Haymarket Affair (1886):**
  A peaceful rally for workers' rights turned violent after a bomb exploded, drawing attention to the harsh conditions faced by laborers.
- **Fair Labor Standards Act (1938):**
  Established minimum wage, overtime pay, and child labor protections.

Modern Advocacy

Unions continue to advocate for worker protections, particularly in the gig economy and industries with low wages.

The Environmental Movement

Overview

The Environmental Movement aims to protect natural resources, combat pollution, and address climate change. It has shaped policies and public awareness about sustainability.

Key Events and Milestones

- **Earth Day (1970):**
  The first Earth Day mobilized millions of Americans to demand environmental protections.
- **Clean Air Act and Clean Water Act (1970s):**
  Landmark legislation that set standards for reducing pollution.

Modern Advocacy

Efforts now focus on combating climate change, promoting renewable energy, and protecting endangered species.

The Disability Rights Movement

Overview

This movement advocates for equal rights and access for people with disabilities.

Key Events and Milestones

- **Americans with Disabilities Act (ADA) (1990):**
  Prohibited discrimination based on disability and ensured access to public spaces and employment.

Impact:

The ADA has improved accessibility and raised awareness about the rights of individuals with disabilities.

Key Takeaways for the GED Exam

On the GED exam, you may encounter questions that require you to:

- Analyze the causes and outcomes of these movements.
- Identify significant legislation and its impact on society.
- Interpret quotes or data related to these movements.

Example Question:

- **Question:** What was the primary goal of the Voting Rights Act of 1965?
  Answer: To eliminate discriminatory practices that prevented African Americans from voting.

Example Question:

- **Question:** What event is considered the beginning of the modern LGBTQ+ rights movement?
  Answer: The Stonewall Riots.

CHAPTER 28

CIVICS AND GOVERNMENT

28.1 Principles of Democracy

Democracy is a form of government in which power ultimately rests with the people. In the United States, this democratic framework is implemented through a representative system, where elected officials govern on behalf of the people. The principles of democracy ensure fairness, accountability, and the protection of individual rights. These principles form the foundation of the U.S. government and guide its function.

Popular Sovereignty

At the heart of democracy is the idea of **popular sovereignty**—the belief that the authority of the government comes from the consent of the governed. Citizens express their consent through voting and other forms of civic participation. Without this principle, the government would lack legitimacy.

Example in Action:

Elections allow citizens to choose their leaders, from the president to local officials. When citizens vote, they exercise their sovereignty by determining who will represent their interests.

Rule of Law

The **rule of law** ensures that no one, not even government officials, is above the law. The U.S. Constitution serves as the highest law of the land, and all individuals and institutions must comply with it. This principle protects citizens from arbitrary use of power.

Example in Action:

If a public official abuses their authority, they can be held accountable through legal processes, such as impeachment or criminal prosecution.

Separation of Powers

The **separation of powers** divides the government into three branches—legislative, executive, and judicial—to prevent any one branch from becoming too powerful. Each branch has distinct responsibilities:

- The **legislative branch** makes laws.
- The **executive branch** enforces laws.
- The **judicial branch** interprets laws.

Why It Matters:

This division creates a system of checks and balances, ensuring that power is distributed and not concentrated in one entity.

Checks and Balances

Closely tied to the separation of powers, **checks and balances** allow each branch of government to limit the power of the others. This system prevents abuse of power and ensures cooperation among branches.

Example in Action:

- The president can veto a bill passed by Congress.
- Congress can override the president's veto with a two-thirds majority.
- The Supreme Court can declare laws unconstitutional, limiting legislative and executive power.

Individual Rights

Democracy prioritizes the protection of individual rights and freedoms. In the United States, these rights are enshrined in the Constitution, particularly in the Bill of Rights. Examples include freedom of speech, religion, and the press, as well as the right to a fair trial.

Example in Action:

Freedom of the press allows journalists to report on government actions without fear of censorship, holding leaders accountable to the public.

Majority Rule with Minority Rights

In a democracy, decisions are often made based on **majority rule**, but the rights of minority groups are protected to prevent oppression. This principle ensures that everyone, regardless of their background or beliefs, has equal protection under the law.

Example in Action:

Laws may pass with majority support, but they cannot violate constitutional rights, such as freedom of religion or equal protection under the law.

Citizen Participation

Active participation by citizens is essential to democracy. This includes voting, attending public meetings, joining advocacy groups, and engaging in community activities. Citizen involvement ensures that government decisions reflect the will of the people.

Example in Action:

Public protests and petitions often influence policymakers to address social issues, such as climate change or healthcare reform.

Why These Principles Matter

The principles of democracy create a framework for fair and effective governance. They ensure that power is distributed, rights are protected, and citizens have a voice in how they are governed. For the GED exam, understanding these principles is crucial for analyzing how the U.S. government functions and for answering questions that involve real-world scenarios or historical contexts.

Example GED Question:

Question: What principle of democracy ensures that government officials are not above the law?
Answer: Rule of law.

28.2 Structure and Functions of Government

The structure and functions of the U.S. government are designed to balance power, protect individual rights, and ensure effective governance. This system, established by the Constitution, divides authority among three branches—legislative, executive, and judicial—while also maintaining a federalist system that distributes power between national and state governments.

The Three Branches of Government

1. Legislative Branch

The legislative branch, represented by Congress, is responsible for making laws. It ensures that citizens' needs and interests are addressed through legislation.

- **Structure of Congress**:
  - **House of Representatives**:
    - Comprised of 435 members, with representation based on state population.
    - Members serve two-year terms.
  - **Senate**:
    - Comprised of 100 members, with two senators from each state.
    - Senators serve six-year terms.
- **Key Powers**:
  - Drafting and passing laws.
  - Approving federal budgets.
  - Declaring war.
  - Confirming presidential appointments (Senate only).

    - Ratifying treaties (Senate only).

Example in Action: Congress passed the Civil Rights Act of 1964 to address racial discrimination, demonstrating its legislative authority to create impactful laws.

2. Executive Branch

The executive branch is tasked with enforcing and administering laws. It is headed by the President, supported by the Vice President, Cabinet, and federal agencies.

- **President's Roles and Powers**:
    - Acts as Commander-in-Chief of the armed forces.
    - Signs bills into law or vetoes them.
    - Negotiates treaties with other nations (subject to Senate approval).
    - Appoints federal officials, including Supreme Court justices and Cabinet members.
- **Vice President's Role**:
    - Serves as President of the Senate, casting tie-breaking votes when necessary.
    - Assumes the presidency in the event of the President's incapacity.
- **Federal Agencies**: Agencies like the Environmental Protection Agency (EPA) and Federal Bureau of Investigation (FBI) enforce specific laws and policies.

Example in Action: The President enforces laws passed by Congress, such as implementing the Affordable Care Act to expand healthcare access.

3. Judicial Branch

The judicial branch interprets laws and ensures they are consistent with the Constitution. This branch resolves disputes and protects individual rights.

- **Structure**:
    - **Supreme Court**: The highest court, consisting of nine justices appointed for life.
    - **Lower Courts**: Includes district courts, appellate courts, and specialized courts (e.g., bankruptcy courts).
- **Key Powers**:
    - Judicial review: The ability to declare laws or executive actions unconstitutional (*Marbury v. Madison*, 1803).
    - Resolving disputes involving federal laws, treaties, or the Constitution.

Example in Action: The Supreme Court's decision in *Brown v. Board of Education* (1954) ended segregation in public schools, showcasing the judiciary's power to shape social policy.

Federalism: The Division of Powers

Federalism divides power between the national and state governments to address both local and national needs. The Constitution specifies which powers belong to each level of government.

Powers of the Federal Government:

- Regulating interstate and international trade.
- Printing money.
- Declaring war.
- Managing foreign relations.

Powers of State Governments:

- Regulating education.
- Issuing licenses (e.g., driver's licenses, marriage licenses).
- Conducting elections.
- Managing public health and safety.

Shared Powers (Concurrent Powers):

- Taxation.
- Building and maintaining infrastructure.
- Enforcing laws.

Example in Action: While the federal government sets national education standards, states determine specific curricula and teacher certification requirements.

Checks and Balances in Practice

The system of checks and balances ensures that no branch becomes too powerful. Each branch has specific mechanisms to limit the power of the others.

- **Legislative Branch Checks**:
  - Can override a presidential veto with a two-thirds majority.
  - Approves judicial appointments.
- **Executive Branch Checks**:
  - Can veto legislation passed by Congress.
  - Appoints federal judges.
- **Judicial Branch Checks**:
  - Can declare laws or executive actions unconstitutional.

Example in Action: If Congress passes a controversial law, the Supreme Court can review it and strike it down if it violates constitutional principles.

The Role of Citizens in Government

Citizens play a critical role in ensuring government accountability and effectiveness. Civic participation, such as voting, attending public meetings, and contacting representatives, allows citizens to influence policies and hold officials accountable.

- **Voting**: Citizens elect representatives who make decisions on their behalf.
- **Jury Duty**: Participating in the judicial system ensures fairness and justice.
- **Advocacy**: Citizens can petition the government or join advocacy groups to promote social change.

Example in Action: Grassroots movements, such as the civil rights protests of the 1960s, demonstrated how citizen involvement can lead to transformative policy changes.

Key Takeaways for the GED Exam

Understanding the structure and functions of government is essential for analyzing real-world scenarios on the GED Social Studies exam. You may encounter questions that require you to:

- Identify the responsibilities of each branch of government.
- Explain how federal and state powers are divided.
- Analyze examples of checks and balances in action.

Example Question:

Question: Which branch of government has the power to declare war?
Answer: The legislative branch (Congress).
Example Question:
Question: What is the primary role of the judicial branch?
Answer: To interpret laws and ensure they align with the Constitution.

28.3 Understanding Policies, Laws, and Civic Responsibilities

The functioning of any democratic society relies on its citizens' understanding of policies, laws, and their civic responsibilities. This chapter explores how laws are made and enforced, the role of policies in shaping society, and the responsibilities citizens have to ensure a well-functioning government. These topics are crucial for the GED Social Studies exam, as they form the basis of questions related to governance and civic participation.

Understanding Policies and Laws

What Are Policies?

Policies are guidelines created by governments, organizations, or institutions to address specific issues and direct decision-making. They often precede laws, serving as a framework for legislative or executive action.

Example: A city policy promoting the use of renewable energy may lead to laws mandating solar panels on new buildings.

What Are Laws?

Laws are formal rules established by governing bodies to regulate behavior, resolve disputes, and protect citizens' rights. In the U.S., laws must align with the Constitution to ensure they are fair and just.

Types of Laws:

Criminal Laws: Address actions considered harmful to society, such as theft or assault.
Civil Laws: Resolve disputes between individuals or organizations, such as contract disagreements.
Constitutional Laws: Interpret and apply the Constitution to legal cases.

The Lawmaking Process

The process of creating laws varies between federal, state, and local governments, but it generally follows these steps:

Proposal: A law begins as a bill introduced in either the House of Representatives or the Senate at the federal level.
Committee Review: Committees analyze the bill and may suggest changes or amendments.
Debate and Voting: Both chambers of Congress debate the bill and vote. If both approve, it moves to the President.

Presidential Action:

The President can sign the bill into law or veto it.
Congress can override a veto with a two-thirds majority vote.

Example: The Civil Rights Act of 1964 went through extensive debate and revisions before becoming law, addressing racial discrimination in public spaces and employment.

Role of Policies in Society

Policies shape how governments address social, economic, and environmental issues. They provide a roadmap for achieving specific goals and often reflect societal priorities.

Economic Policies:

Aim to regulate taxes, control inflation, and manage unemployment.
Example: The New Deal policies during the Great Depression created jobs and stabilized the economy.

Social Policies:

Address healthcare, education, and welfare.
Example: Policies like Medicaid and Medicare provide healthcare to vulnerable populations.

Environmental Policies:

Focus on preserving natural resources and reducing pollution.
Example: Clean Air and Clean Water Acts protect public health and the environment.

Civic Responsibilities

Citizens play a vital role in maintaining a functioning democracy. Civic responsibilities go beyond legal obligations; they involve active participation in shaping and improving society.

Key Civic Responsibilities

Voting

The most fundamental way citizens influence government policies and leadership.
Importance: Voting determines who represents citizens' interests at local, state, and federal levels.

Serving on Juries

Ensures fair trials by allowing citizens to participate in the judicial system.
Responsibility: Jurors must assess evidence impartially and make decisions based on the law.

Obeying Laws

Following the law maintains order and protects the rights of all citizens.
Example: Traffic laws ensure safety on roads.

Paying Taxes

Taxes fund essential services such as schools, roads, and public safety.
Importance: Without taxes, governments would lack the resources to function effectively.

Engaging in Community Service

Volunteering helps address local needs, such as supporting schools, shelters, or environmental initiatives.

Staying Informed

Citizens should educate themselves about current events, policies, and political candidates to make informed decisions.
Example: Reading about ballot measures before voting ensures that citizens understand the implications of their choices.

Balancing Rights and Responsibilities

While citizens have rights protected by the Constitution, such as freedom of speech and the right to a fair trial, they also have corresponding responsibilities to ensure these rights are upheld for everyone.

Example: The right to free speech is balanced by the responsibility not to spread harmful misinformation.

Challenges to Civic Participation

Despite its importance, civic engagement faces challenges, including:

Voter Suppression: Practices that make it difficult for certain groups to vote.
Misinformation: False information that can mislead voters or create mistrust in the system.
Apathy: Lack of interest in participating in governance or societal issues.

Addressing These Challenges:

Educating citizens about their rights and how to exercise them.
Promoting transparency and accountability in government.

Key Takeaways for the GED Exam

Understanding policies, laws, and civic responsibilities is crucial for the GED Social Studies exam. You may encounter questions that require you to:

Analyze how a law is passed or the impact of a policy.
Identify examples of civic responsibilities and their importance.
Evaluate the role of citizens in maintaining a functioning democracy.

Example Question:

Question: What is one civic responsibility required by law in the U.S.?
Answer: Paying taxes.

Example Question:

Question: Why is serving on a jury important in a democracy?
Answer: It ensures fair trials and upholds the rule of law.

CHAPTER 29

ECONOMICS

29.1 Supply and Demand

Supply and demand are fundamental principles of economics, forming the foundation of how markets operate. These principles explain how the interaction between buyers and sellers determines prices and quantities of goods and services in a market. For the GED Social Studies exam, understanding supply and demand will help you analyze real-world economic scenarios, such as pricing trends, shortages, and surpluses.

Understanding Supply and Demand

What Is Supply?

Supply refers to the quantity of a good or service that producers are willing and able to sell at various price levels during a specific period.

- **Law of Supply**: When prices rise, producers are more willing to supply goods because higher prices can lead to increased profits. Conversely, when prices fall, producers may supply less.

Example: If the price of smartphones increases, manufacturers may produce more smartphones to take advantage of higher profits.

What Is Demand?

Demand refers to the quantity of a good or service that consumers are willing and able to buy at various price levels during a specific period.

- **Law of Demand**: When prices rise, consumers tend to buy less because the product becomes more expensive. When prices fall, consumers are more likely to purchase because the product is more affordable.

Example: If the price of movie tickets drops, more people might go to the theater, increasing demand.

The Interaction Between Supply and Demand

Equilibrium

The point at which supply equals demand is called the **equilibrium price**. At this price, the amount of goods supplied matches the amount demanded, and the market is considered stable.

Example: A coffee shop sells lattes for $5 each. At this price, the number of lattes the shop produces equals the number customers are willing to buy.

Surplus

A surplus occurs when supply exceeds demand, often leading to a price reduction to encourage sales.

Example: If a clothing store overproduces winter coats, they may offer discounts to sell the extra inventory.

Shortage

A shortage happens when demand exceeds supply, often resulting in higher prices as consumers compete to buy limited goods.

Example: A popular video game console sells out during the holidays, leading to increased resale prices online.

Factors That Influence Supply and Demand

1. **Price**
    - **Supply**: Higher prices encourage producers to make more goods.
    - **Demand**: Higher prices discourage consumers from buying.
2. **Consumer Preferences**

Trends and cultural shifts can increase or decrease demand.

Example: A health trend promoting plant-based diets increases demand for vegetarian products.

3. **Income Levels**
   - When incomes rise, people have more money to spend, increasing demand.
   - When incomes fall, demand for luxury items decreases.
4. **Production Costs**

   Changes in the cost of production can affect supply.

   Example: If the cost of raw materials rises, producers may decrease output.

5. **External Factors**

   Events like natural disasters, pandemics, or wars can disrupt supply chains and alter demand.

   Example: A hurricane damages crops, reducing the supply of fresh produce and raising prices.

Supply and Demand in Real-Life Scenarios

Housing Market

When more people want to buy homes than there are houses available, demand exceeds supply, causing prices to rise. If new housing developments increase supply, prices may stabilize or decrease.

Gasoline Prices

Global events like oil shortages or increased production affect gasoline prices. A reduction in supply leads to higher prices, while increased supply lowers prices.

Technology and Trends

The release of a highly anticipated smartphone creates high demand, often leading to shortages at launch. Over time, as supply increases, prices may decrease.

Graphs of Supply and Demand

A supply and demand graph visually represents how these principles interact.

1. **Supply Curve**: Slopes upward, showing that higher prices lead to more goods being supplied.
2. **Demand Curve**: Slopes downward, showing that higher prices lead to less demand.
3. **Equilibrium Point**: The intersection of the supply and demand curves, where the market stabilizes.

Example Graph:

A graph showing supply and demand for concert tickets might indicate an equilibrium price of $50, where 1,000 tickets are sold.

(Graphs can be created if required for further understanding.)

Key Takeaways for the GED Exam

The concepts of supply and demand frequently appear in GED questions. These questions may ask you to:

- Analyze supply and demand charts.
- Predict the effects of price changes on supply and demand.
- Identify scenarios of surplus or shortage.

Example Question 1:

Question: What happens to the price of a product when supply exceeds demand?
Answer: The price usually decreases to encourage sales.

Example Question 2:

Scenario: A new gaming console is released, and demand far exceeds supply.
Question: What is the likely effect on the console's price?
Answer: The price will likely increase due to the shortage.

29.2 The Role of Government in the Economy

The government plays a crucial role in regulating, stabilizing, and influencing the economy. Its involvement ensures fair practices, provides public goods, and addresses market failures that may arise in a free market system. For the GED Social Studies exam, understanding how the government impacts the economy through policies and interventions is essential.

Government's Economic Roles

1. Regulating the Economy

The government establishes rules to ensure fairness and safety in economic transactions. These regulations protect consumers, workers, and businesses from unethical practices.

- **Examples of Regulations**:
  - **Consumer Protection Laws**: Ensure product safety and prevent false advertising.
    Example: The Food and Drug Administration (FDA) regulates food and medicine to ensure safety.
  - **Labor Laws**: Protect workers' rights, ensuring fair wages, safe working conditions, and prohibiting child labor.
    Example: The Occupational Safety and Health Administration (OSHA) enforces workplace safety standards.
  - **Environmental Regulations**: Limit pollution and encourage sustainable practices.
    Example: The Clean Air Act reduces industrial emissions to protect air quality.

2. Providing Public Goods and Services

Public goods are services and infrastructure that benefit society and are typically funded by taxes because the private sector cannot efficiently provide them.

- **Examples of Public Goods**:
  - **Infrastructure**: Roads, bridges, and public transportation systems.
  - **Education**: Public schools and state universities.
  - **Healthcare**: Programs like Medicare and Medicaid.
  - **National Defense**: Ensuring the safety of citizens through a military presence.

Why It Matters: Public goods benefit everyone, regardless of their ability to pay directly for them.

3. Stabilizing the Economy

The government takes measures to stabilize the economy during periods of recession, inflation, or economic uncertainty. These efforts ensure steady growth and prevent extreme fluctuations.

- **Fiscal Policy**:
  - The government adjusts its spending and taxation policies to influence economic activity.
  - *Example*: During a recession, the government may increase spending on public projects to create jobs.
- **Monetary Policy**:
  - Managed by the Federal Reserve, this involves controlling the money supply and interest rates to regulate inflation and stimulate growth.
  - *Example*: Lowering interest rates to encourage borrowing and investment during a slowdown.

4. Addressing Market Failures

Market failures occur when the free market cannot efficiently allocate resources. The government intervenes to correct these issues.

- **Types of Market Failures**:
  - **Monopolies**: When one company dominates a market, leading to unfair practices.
    Example: Anti-trust laws break up monopolies to promote competition.
  - **Externalities**: Unintended side effects of economic activities, such as pollution.
    Example: Imposing taxes on carbon emissions to reduce environmental damage.

Government Programs That Impact the Economy

Social Welfare Programs

The government provides support for individuals and families facing economic hardships.

- **Examples**:
  - **Unemployment Insurance**: Temporary financial assistance for people who lose their jobs.
  - **Social Security**: A retirement program funded by payroll taxes.
  - **Food Stamps (SNAP)**: Helps low-income families afford basic groceries.

Economic Stimulus Programs

During economic downturns, the government implements programs to boost spending and job creation.

- **Examples**:
  - **New Deal (1930s)**: Programs like the Works Progress Administration (WPA) created millions of jobs during the Great Depression.
  - **COVID-19 Relief Packages (2020–2021)**: Stimulus checks and loans to businesses helped stabilize the economy during the pandemic.

Balancing Government Involvement

While government intervention is crucial for stability and fairness, excessive involvement can lead to inefficiencies, such as bureaucracy or overregulation. Striking the right balance is essential for fostering innovation and growth while protecting citizens and the environment.

Key Takeaways for the GED Exam

Understanding the role of government in the economy is essential for analyzing real-world scenarios on the exam. Be prepared to identify how government policies impact individuals, businesses, and society.

Example GED Questions:

Question: Why does the government regulate monopolies?
Answer: To promote competition and prevent unfair practices.
Question: What is the purpose of fiscal policy during a recession?
Answer: To increase government spending or reduce taxes to stimulate economic growth.
Scenario: A factory emits pollution that affects nearby residents.
Question: How might the government address this market failure?
Answer: By imposing fines or regulations to limit emissions.

29.3 Personal Finance Basics

Understanding personal finance is a critical life skill that helps individuals make informed decisions about earning, saving, spending, and investing their money. For the GED Social Studies exam, personal finance basics often appear in scenarios or questions requiring analysis of financial concepts, budgets, or economic decisions. This chapter will explore the core principles of personal finance, providing the tools and knowledge needed to manage money effectively.

Key Areas of Personal Finance

1. Income and Budgeting

Managing personal finances starts with understanding income and creating a budget.

- **Income**:
  - Refers to the money earned from work, investments, or other sources.
  - Types of income include wages, salaries, bonuses, interest, and dividends.
- **Budgeting**:
  - A budget is a plan that tracks income and expenses to ensure financial stability.

- The **50/30/20 Rule** is a common budgeting method:
    - 50% for necessities (e.g., rent, utilities, groceries).
    - 30% for discretionary spending (e.g., entertainment, dining out).
    - 20% for savings and debt repayment.

Example Question:

If someone earns $3,000 per month, how much should they allocate to savings if they follow the 50/30/20 rule?

2. Saving and Emergency Funds

Saving is essential for achieving financial goals and preparing for unexpected expenses.

- **Short-Term Savings**: Funds set aside for immediate goals, like vacations or appliances.
- **Long-Term Savings**: Money saved for future goals, such as buying a home or retirement.
- **Emergency Fund**:
  - A safety net for unexpected expenses, such as medical bills or car repairs.
  - Experts recommend saving 3–6 months' worth of living expenses.

3. Managing Debt

Debt can be a useful financial tool when managed responsibly, but excessive debt can lead to financial stress.

- **Types of Debt**:
  - **Good Debt**: Borrowing for education, a home, or a business, which can provide long-term benefits.
  - **Bad Debt**: High-interest debt for non-essential items, like credit card purchases.
- **Debt Management Tips**:
  - Pay more than the minimum payment on credit cards to reduce interest costs.
  - Avoid payday loans due to their high interest rates.
  - Consolidate loans if it lowers interest rates and simplifies payments.

Example Question:

If a credit card has a balance of $1,000 with a 15% annual interest rate, how much interest will accrue in one year if no payments are made?:

$1{,}000 \times 0.15 = \$150$.

4. Credit Scores

A credit score is a numerical representation of your creditworthiness, which lenders use to assess the risk of lending money.

- **Components of a Credit Score**:
  - Payment history (35%).
  - Credit utilization (30%).
  - Length of credit history (15%).
  - New credit inquiries (10%).
  - Types of credit used (10%).
- **Improving Credit Scores**:
  - Pay bills on time.
  - Keep credit utilization below 30%.
  - Avoid opening too many new accounts at once.

Why It Matters: A high credit score can lead to lower interest rates on loans and better financial opportunities.

5. Investing

Investing helps individuals grow their wealth over time through assets like stocks, bonds, and mutual funds.

- **Types of Investments**:
  - **Stocks**: Shares of ownership in a company, offering high potential returns but with higher risk.
  - **Bonds**: Loans to companies or governments that pay regular interest with lower risk.

    - **Mutual Funds**: Pooled investments managed by professionals, diversifying risk.
- **The Power of Compound Interest**:
    - Investing early allows your money to grow exponentially over time.
    - Example: If $1,000 is invested at an annual interest rate of 5%, compounded yearly, it will grow to $1,276 in 5 years.

6. Taxes

Understanding taxes is vital for managing finances effectively.

- **Types of Taxes**:
    - **Income Tax**: Paid on earnings from work or investments.
    - **Sales Tax**: Paid on goods and services at the time of purchase.
    - **Property Tax**: Paid on owned real estate.
- **Filing Taxes**:
    - Individuals must file tax returns annually, reporting income, deductions, and credits.
    - Tools like tax software or professional tax preparers can help.

Applying Personal Finance Concepts

Scenario 1: Creating a Budget

Imagine you earn $4,000 per month. Using the 50/30/20 rule, allocate your income:

- Necessities: 4,000 × 502,000.
- Discretionary Spending: 4,000 × 301,200.
- Savings/Debt: 4,000 × 20800.

Scenario 2: Debt Management

You have a student loan of $10,000 at a 6% annual interest rate. To reduce costs, you decide to pay an extra $50 monthly toward the principal. This accelerates repayment and reduces the total interest paid.

Key Takeaways for the GED Exam

Personal finance questions on the GED exam may ask you to:

- Analyze and create budgets.
- Calculate interest on loans or savings.
- Interpret financial scenarios to recommend actions.

Example GED Questions:

- **Question:** If a person earns $3,600 per month, how much should they save using the 50/30/20 rule?
  Answer: $3,600 × 20% = $720.
- **Question:** What is one benefit of having a high credit score?
  Answer: Access to lower interest rates on loans and credit cards.

29.4 Global Trade and Economic Systems

Global trade and economic systems are the cornerstones of the interconnected world economy. Nations exchange goods and services across borders, creating interdependence and fostering international relationships. Understanding these concepts is essential for the GED Social Studies exam, as questions often address the principles of trade, the types of economic systems, and their impact on society.

What Is Global Trade?

Global trade refers to the exchange of goods, services, and resources between countries. It allows nations to access products they cannot produce efficiently themselves while exporting goods they produce in surplus.

Key Benefits of Global Trade

- **Economic Growth**: Trade stimulates economic activity, creating jobs and wealth.
    - Example: The export of high-tech products, like computers and software, boosts the U.S. economy.
- **Access to Resources**: Countries can obtain materials not available domestically, such as oil or rare minerals.
- **Lower Prices for Consumers**: Increased competition from international markets often reduces prices for goods.
    - Example: Imported electronics from countries with lower production costs are typically more affordable.
- **Cultural Exchange**: Trade promotes the exchange of ideas, technologies, and cultural practices.

Barriers to Trade

While global trade has numerous benefits, certain barriers can limit its effectiveness.

- **Tariffs**: Taxes imposed on imports to protect domestic industries or generate revenue.
    - Example: A country may impose a tariff on foreign cars to encourage consumers to buy domestic vehicles.
- **Quotas**: Limits on the quantity of a specific good that can be imported.
    - Example: A country might limit the import of sugar to protect local farmers.
- **Trade Embargoes**: Government-imposed bans on trade with specific countries, often for political reasons.
    - Example: The U.S. trade embargo on Cuba restricted economic exchanges for decades.

Types of Economic Systems

Economic systems determine how a society organizes the production, distribution, and consumption of goods and services. The main types of economic systems include:

1. Market Economy

- In a market economy, decisions are made by individuals and businesses based on supply and demand.
- **Characteristics**:
    - Minimal government intervention.
    - Prices are determined by market forces.

Example: The United States operates as a mixed-market economy, where private businesses play a significant role, but the government regulates certain industries.

2. Command Economy

- In a command economy, the government controls all aspects of production and distribution.
- **Characteristics**:
    - Centralized decision-making.
    - State ownership of resources.

Example: North Korea has a command economy, with the government directing all major economic activities.

3. Mixed Economy

- A mixed economy combines elements of both market and command economies.
- **Characteristics**:
    - Private businesses operate alongside government regulations.
    - Public services, such as healthcare or education, are often government-funded.

Example: Canada has a mixed economy, with free-market practices and strong government involvement in public services.

4. Traditional Economy

- In a traditional economy, customs, traditions, and cultural beliefs guide economic decisions.
- **Characteristics**:
    - Often found in rural or undeveloped areas.
    - Reliance on agriculture and bartering.

Example: Indigenous communities that trade goods locally based on cultural traditions.

Global Organizations Facilitating Trade

Several international organizations aim to promote global trade and economic stability:

- **World Trade Organization (WTO)**: Regulates international trade and resolves disputes between countries.
- **International Monetary Fund (IMF)**: Provides financial assistance to countries facing economic crises.
- **World Bank**: Offers loans and grants to developing countries to reduce poverty and support economic development.

Key Concepts in Global Trade

Comparative Advantage

Countries specialize in producing goods or services they can produce most efficiently relative to other countries. This principle underpins global trade.

Example:

The U.S. specializes in producing high-tech goods, while Brazil specializes in exporting coffee. Both benefit from trading with each other.

Trade Agreements

Trade agreements establish rules and reduce barriers between countries to encourage economic cooperation.

- **Examples**:
  - **NAFTA (Now USMCA)**: A trade agreement between the U.S., Canada, and Mexico that reduces tariffs and promotes cross-border trade.
  - **European Union (EU)**: A political and economic union that allows free trade among its member countries.

Challenges of Global Trade

While global trade has many advantages, it also presents challenges:

- **Economic Inequality**: Wealthier nations often benefit more from trade than poorer ones.
- **Environmental Concerns**: Increased production and transportation contribute to pollution and climate change.
- **Job Displacement**: Domestic industries may suffer when cheaper imported goods dominate the market.

Example: A local textile factory may close due to competition from cheaper overseas manufacturers.

Key Takeaways for the GED Exam

Questions on global trade and economic systems may ask you to:

- Analyze trade policies or agreements and their impact on nations.
- Evaluate the advantages and disadvantages of different economic systems.
- Interpret trade data, such as import/export statistics or production comparisons.

Example GED Question 1:

Question: What is a tariff?
Answer: A tax imposed on imported goods to protect domestic industries or raise government revenue.

Example GED Question 2:

Scenario: A country produces cars more efficiently than any other country but imports most of its oil. Why does it engage in trade?
Answer: The country benefits from comparative advantage, specializing in car production while importing oil, which it cannot produce efficiently.

CHAPTER 30

GEOGRAPHY AND WORLD HISTORY

30.1 Major Geographic Features and Their Impact on Societies

Geographic features such as mountains, rivers, plains, and deserts have significantly shaped human history, influencing where civilizations developed, how economies grew, and how cultures evolved. Understanding the relationship between geography and society is essential for the GED Social Studies exam, as questions often focus on how geographic factors affect human activities and historical events.

Key Geographic Features and Their Influence

1. Rivers and Waterways

Rivers have been vital to the growth of civilizations by providing water for drinking, agriculture, transportation, and trade.

Example: The Nile River (Egypt)

The predictable flooding of the Nile created fertile farmland, enabling ancient Egypt to thrive as one of the earliest agricultural civilizations.

The Nile also served as a transportation route, facilitating trade and communication.

Example: The Mississippi River (United States)

The Mississippi has been a critical trade route, linking agricultural regions in the Midwest to international markets.

Impact on Society: Rivers promote settlement, trade, and the exchange of ideas, but they can also present challenges, such as flooding or territorial disputes.

2. Mountains

Mountains act as natural barriers, influencing settlement patterns, trade, and defense.

Example: The Himalayas (Asia)

These towering mountains isolate the Indian subcontinent, contributing to the development of distinct cultural and religious traditions.

Example: The Rocky Mountains (United States)

These mountains served as a barrier to early westward expansion but later became a hub for mining and tourism.

Impact on Society: Mountains can protect societies from invasion and create unique cultural identities but may hinder transportation and communication.

3. Deserts

Deserts are arid regions with limited water and vegetation, presenting challenges for human settlement.

Example: The Sahara Desert (Africa)

The Sahara acted as a barrier to migration and trade but also supported the development of trans-Saharan trade routes, linking sub-Saharan Africa to North Africa and the Mediterranean.

Example: The Mojave Desert (United States)

Despite its harsh environment, technological advances in irrigation have enabled settlements and agriculture.

Impact on Society: Deserts limit population density but encourage innovation in water management and transportation, such as camel caravans or railways.

4. Plains and Grasslands

Plains and grasslands offer fertile soil and flat terrain, making them ideal for agriculture and settlement.

Example: The Great Plains (United States)

Known as the "breadbasket" of the U.S., this region produces much of the nation's wheat and corn.

Example: The Steppes (Eurasia)

These grasslands supported nomadic cultures, such as the Mongols, who relied on herding and horse-riding.

Impact on Society: Plains promote farming and settlement but may leave societies vulnerable to invasion due to the lack of natural barriers.

5. Coastlines

Coastal regions facilitate trade, exploration, and cultural exchange due to their proximity to oceans and seas.

Example: The Mediterranean Coast

Ancient civilizations like Greece and Rome flourished due to access to the Mediterranean Sea, which enabled trade and military expansion.

Example: The East Coast (United States)

Early European settlers established colonies along the Atlantic Coast, benefiting from access to trade routes and resources.

Impact on Society: Coastlines encourage trade and urbanization but may face challenges such as storms, flooding, and overpopulation.

The Role of Geographic Features in Historical Events

1. Natural Barriers and Defense

Geographic features often serve as protective barriers during conflicts.

Example: During World War II, the English Channel provided a natural defense for Britain, complicating Germany's invasion plans.

2. Trade Routes and Economic Growth

Geographic features like rivers and coastlines have historically facilitated trade, fostering economic development.

Example: The Silk Road, spanning deserts and mountains, connected Asia to Europe, enabling the exchange of goods, ideas, and technology.

3. Migration and Cultural Exchange

Geography influences migration patterns and cultural diffusion.

Example: The Appalachian Mountains shaped the migration of settlers westward in early American history, influencing regional cultures.

Human Impact on Geography

While geography shapes societies, human activities also alter geographic features.

Deforestation: Clearing forests for agriculture or urbanization disrupts ecosystems.
Urbanization: Expanding cities change natural landscapes and strain resources.
Climate Change: Human activity, such as burning fossil fuels, contributes to rising sea levels and desertification.

Example: The construction of dams, such as the Hoover Dam, transforms rivers into reservoirs, providing water and energy but altering ecosystems.

Key Takeaways for the GED Exam

On the GED exam, questions about geography may require you to:

Analyze maps and identify key geographic features.
Understand how geography influences economic activities and cultural development.
Evaluate the impact of human activity on geographic features.

Example GED Question 1:

Question: How did the Nile River contribute to the development of ancient Egyptian civilization?

Answer: The Nile provided fertile soil for agriculture, enabling sustained food production and population growth.

Example GED Question 2:

Question: What is one challenge faced by societies located in deserts?

Answer: Limited access to water resources makes agriculture and settlement difficult.

30.2 Key Global Historical Events and Their Effects

Global historical events have shaped societies, economies, and governments, leaving profound impacts that continue to influence the modern world. These pivotal moments, driven by a combination of political, economic, and social forces, reveal patterns of growth, conflict, and resolution that define human history. Below is an expanded exploration of some of the most significant global events and their lasting effects.

The Fall of the Roman Empire (476 CE)

The fall of the Western Roman Empire marked the end of ancient European civilization and the beginning of the Middle Ages. This event resulted from centuries of internal instability and external pressures.

- **Political Instability**: Corruption and weak leadership weakened the empire's administrative structure. Constant power struggles among emperors destabilized governance.
- **Economic Decline**: Reliance on slave labor hindered technological innovation, while over-taxation and inflation burdened citizens.
- **Military Issues**: Repeated invasions by Germanic tribes, including the Visigoths and Vandals, overwhelmed Roman defenses.

Effects:

The fall led to the decentralization of power, giving rise to feudalism across Europe. Infrastructure such as roads and aqueducts fell into disrepair, hindering trade and communication. The Catholic Church emerged as a unifying force, influencing politics, culture, and education throughout the Middle Ages.

The Age of Exploration (15th–17th Century)

The Age of Exploration was a period of global maritime expansion, driven by European nations seeking new trade routes, wealth, and knowledge. This era significantly altered the political and economic landscape of the world.

- **Technological Advancements**: Innovations such as the compass, astrolabe, and improved ship designs like the caravel made long sea voyages possible.
- **Exploration Highlights**:
  - Christopher Columbus's voyages opened the Americas to European colonization.
  - Vasco da Gama's discovery of a sea route to India expanded trade networks.

Effects:

European colonization reshaped entire continents, leading to cultural exchanges and the exploitation of indigenous populations. The Columbian Exchange introduced new crops, animals, and diseases, revolutionizing diets and economies but also decimating native populations due to the spread of smallpox and other illnesses. The transatlantic slave trade, initiated during this period, caused profound demographic and social changes.

The Industrial Revolution (18th–19th Century)

The Industrial Revolution transformed economies from agrarian to industrial and urban, with advancements in technology and manufacturing.

- **Key Inventions**:
  - The steam engine revolutionized transportation and industry.
  - The spinning jenny and power loom increased textile production.
  - Railroads expanded markets and connected cities.

Effects:

Urbanization led to the growth of industrial cities and increased job opportunities, but also overcrowding, pollution, and poor working conditions. Labor unions emerged to demand fair wages and safer environments. Globally, industrialization widened the gap between industrialized nations and those reliant on traditional economies.

The American Revolution (1775–1783)

The American Revolution established the United States as an independent nation and influenced other independence movements worldwide.

- **Causes**:
  - Taxation without representation fueled resentment toward British rule.
  - Enlightenment ideals promoted self-governance and individual rights.

Effects:

The Revolution resulted in the drafting of the U.S. Constitution and Bill of Rights, providing a model for democratic governance. It inspired the French Revolution and revolutions in Latin America, challenging colonial rule and monarchical systems.

World War I (1914–1918)

World War I was a global conflict triggered by militarism, alliances, imperialism, and nationalism.

- **Major Events**:
  - The assassination of Archduke Franz Ferdinand of Austria-Hungary ignited the war.
  - Trench warfare and the use of new technologies, such as tanks and chemical weapons, defined the conflict.

Effects:

The Treaty of Versailles imposed harsh penalties on Germany, contributing to economic instability and the eventual rise of Adolf Hitler. The war also led to the collapse of the Austro-Hungarian, Ottoman, and Russian Empires, reshaping borders and creating new nations in Europe and the Middle East.

World War II (1939–1945)

World War II was a global conflict fueled by the unresolved issues of World War I, the rise of totalitarian regimes, and territorial expansion.

- **Key Events**:
  - Germany's invasion of Poland in 1939 sparked the war.
  - The Holocaust resulted in the systematic genocide of six million Jews and millions of others.
  - The war ended with the Allied victory and the atomic bombings of Hiroshima and Nagasaki.

Effects:

World War II established the United Nations to promote peace and prevent future conflicts. The U.S. and Soviet Union emerged as superpowers, initiating the Cold War. Decolonization movements gained momentum, leading to the independence of many African and Asian nations.

The Cold War (1947–1991)

The Cold War was a geopolitical struggle between the capitalist United States and the communist Soviet Union, characterized by ideological conflict and proxy wars.

- **Major Events**:
  - The Cuban Missile Crisis brought the world to the brink of nuclear war.
  - The Space Race highlighted technological competition between the superpowers.

Effects:

The Cold War shaped global alliances, such as NATO and the Warsaw Pact. Its end marked the dissolution of the Soviet Union, the reunification of Germany, and the spread of democratic ideals in Eastern Europe.

The Civil Rights Movement (1950s–1970s)

In the United States, the Civil Rights Movement sought to end racial segregation and discrimination.

- **Key Events**:
    - The Montgomery Bus Boycott highlighted the power of peaceful protest.
    - The Civil Rights Act of 1964 outlawed discrimination in public places and employment.

Effects:

The movement achieved significant legal and social advancements for African Americans and inspired other social justice movements worldwide, including women's rights and LGBTQ+ rights.

The Information Age (Late 20th–21st Century)

The Information Age revolutionized communication and knowledge dissemination through digital technology.

- **Key Developments**:
    - The rise of the internet connected people globally.
    - Advances in artificial intelligence and biotechnology transformed industries.

Effects:

Access to information democratized education and innovation, while challenges like cybersecurity threats and digital inequality emerged as new societal issues.

30.3 Cultural and Technological Developments Through Time

Cultural and technological developments have shaped human societies, driving progress and transforming how people live, communicate, and interact with the world. These advancements, rooted in human ingenuity, reflect the evolving needs, aspirations, and challenges of societies across different periods. From ancient innovations to modern breakthroughs, cultural and technological progress has consistently altered the trajectory of history.

Ancient Technological Innovations

Early civilizations laid the groundwork for technological and cultural advancement by addressing basic human needs like shelter, food, and transportation.

- **Agriculture and Irrigation Systems**
  The development of agriculture allowed humans to shift from nomadic lifestyles to settled communities. Irrigation systems, such as those in Mesopotamia and Egypt, supported large-scale farming and population growth. The surplus food supply enabled the specialization of labor, fostering cultural achievements in art, architecture, and governance.

- **Writing Systems**
  Writing emerged as a revolutionary tool for record-keeping, communication, and preserving knowledge. The cuneiform script of Mesopotamia and Egyptian hieroglyphs provided the first methods for documenting laws, trade transactions, and historical events.

- **The Wheel and Transportation**
  The invention of the wheel revolutionized transportation and trade. Carts and wagons facilitated the movement of goods and people, linking distant regions and fostering cultural exchange.

Cultural Achievements in Ancient Civilizations

Art, literature, and philosophy flourished as civilizations stabilized and grew. Cultural advancements often reflected societal values and religious beliefs.

- **Greek Philosophy and Science**
  Ancient Greek thinkers like Socrates, Plato, and Aristotle explored ethics, politics, and natural sciences, laying the intellectual foundation for Western thought. Their ideas influenced subsequent scientific and cultural developments.

- **Roman Engineering**
  The Romans excelled in engineering, constructing aqueducts, roads, and monumental architecture like the Colosseum. These structures enhanced urban living and facilitated cultural exchange across the vast Roman Empire.

The Medieval Period

The medieval era saw technological progress intertwined with religious and cultural shifts.

- **Technological Advancements**

Innovations like the heavy plow, windmills, and water mills improved agricultural efficiency, supporting population growth. The development of the mechanical clock reflected advances in timekeeping and organization.

- **Cultural Contributions**
  Gothic architecture, exemplified by cathedrals like Notre-Dame, showcased advancements in engineering and artistry. Manuscript illumination preserved and disseminated knowledge, particularly within monastic communities.

The Renaissance and Scientific Revolution

The Renaissance marked a cultural rebirth that celebrated human potential and creativity, while the Scientific Revolution transformed the understanding of the natural world.

- **Art and Literature**
  Renaissance artists like Leonardo da Vinci and Michelangelo achieved new levels of realism and expression in their works. Writers such as Shakespeare explored universal themes of human nature and society.

- **Scientific Discoveries**
  Figures like Galileo, Copernicus, and Newton challenged traditional beliefs, laying the groundwork for modern science. The development of the scientific method emphasized observation, experimentation, and reasoning.

The Industrial Revolution

The Industrial Revolution ushered in an era of unprecedented technological progress, reshaping economies and societies.

- **Technological Innovations**
  The steam engine, spinning jenny, and mechanized loom revolutionized manufacturing, while the telegraph transformed communication. These inventions facilitated the rise of industrial cities and expanded global trade networks.

- **Cultural Shifts**
  The Industrial Revolution altered social structures, leading to the rise of the working class and labor unions. It also inspired artistic movements like Romanticism, which emphasized emotion and nature in reaction to industrialization.

The Modern Era

The 20th and 21st centuries have witnessed exponential advancements in technology and significant cultural transformations, driven by globalization and digital connectivity.

- **Technological Milestones**
  The invention of the automobile, airplane, and computer revolutionized transportation and communication. The internet and smartphones further connected people, enabling instant access to information and fostering global collaboration.

- **Cultural Developments**
  Movements for civil rights, gender equality, and environmental sustainability have reshaped societal norms. Popular culture, driven by advancements in media and entertainment, reflects the diversity and dynamism of modern societies.

Challenges and Ethical Considerations

Technological and cultural progress often brings challenges and ethical dilemmas. Balancing innovation with sustainability, privacy, and social equity remains a critical focus for societies.

- **Environmental Impact**
  Industrialization and technological growth have contributed to climate change and resource depletion. Addressing these issues requires sustainable practices and global cooperation.

- **Ethical Questions**
  Advances in biotechnology, artificial intelligence, and genetic engineering raise questions about privacy, human rights, and the implications of altering life itself.

CHAPTER 31

INTERPRETING SOCIAL STUDIES DATA

31.1 Analyzing Maps, Graphs, and Political Cartoons

Interpreting visual data, such as maps, graphs, and political cartoons, is a critical skill for understanding historical, economic, and political events. These tools present complex information in a concise and visual format, helping individuals analyze trends, relationships, and underlying messages. This chapter delves into how to interpret these forms of data, providing essential strategies and examples to prepare for the GED Social Studies exam.

Analyzing Maps

Maps are graphical representations of geographic areas, often used to illustrate physical features, population density, political boundaries, or historical events. To analyze a map effectively, you need to understand its components.

Key Elements of a Map

- **Title**: Explains the purpose of the map (e.g., "Population Density of the U.S. in 2020").
- **Legend/Key**: Explains the symbols and colors used on the map.
    - *Example*: A map showing migration routes may use arrows of different colors to represent various time periods.
- **Scale**: Indicates the relationship between map distances and actual distances.
    - *Example*: 1 inch = 100 miles.
- **Compass Rose**: Shows cardinal directions (North, South, East, West).
- **Labels**: Identify important places, such as cities, rivers, or landmarks.

Types of Maps

- **Physical Maps**: Show natural features like mountains, rivers, and lakes.
    - *Example*: A physical map of North America highlights the Rocky Mountains and the Mississippi River.
- **Political Maps**: Show political boundaries, such as countries, states, and cities.
    - *Example*: A political map of Europe in 1945 shows the division between East and West during the Cold War.
- **Thematic Maps**: Focus on specific topics, such as economic activity, climate, or historical events.
    - *Example*: A map showing the spread of the Black Plague across Europe in the 14th century.

Analyzing Graphs

Graphs visually represent data to show trends, relationships, or comparisons. Understanding how to read and analyze graphs is essential for interpreting historical and economic information.

Types of Graphs

- **Bar Graphs**: Used to compare quantities across categories.
    - *Example*: A bar graph comparing industrial output in the North and South during the Civil War.
- **Line Graphs**: Show trends over time.
    - *Example*: A line graph tracking unemployment rates during the Great Depression.
- **Pie Charts**: Represent proportions of a whole.
    - *Example*: A pie chart showing the percentage of U.S. government spending allocated to different sectors.
- **Histograms**: Similar to bar graphs but represent data grouped into ranges.
    - *Example*: A histogram showing age distribution in colonial America.

Key Steps for Analyzing Graphs

- **Read the Title**: Understand the topic being addressed.
- **Examine Axes or Categories**: Look for labels on the x-axis (horizontal) and y-axis (vertical) to understand the variables.
- **Identify Trends**: Observe patterns, such as increases, decreases, or steady levels.
- **Compare Data**: Evaluate differences between categories or time periods.

Practice Example:

Question: A line graph shows U.S. unemployment rates from 1929 to 1945. What conclusion can you draw about the Great Depression and World War II?

Answer: Unemployment peaked during the early 1930s, reflecting the Great Depression, and declined sharply during World War II as wartime production increased.

Analyzing Political Cartoons

Political cartoons use symbolism, exaggeration, and humor to comment on current events, policies, or historical issues. Understanding the message behind a political cartoon requires critical thinking and familiarity with historical or political contexts.

Elements of Political Cartoons

- **Symbols**: Represent larger ideas or concepts.
  - *Example*: An eagle may symbolize the United States.
- **Exaggeration**: Certain features or elements are exaggerated to emphasize a point.
  - *Example*: A political leader's oversized hat might highlight their arrogance.
- **Labels**: Key objects or people may be labeled to clarify their role in the cartoon.
  - *Example*: A labeled factory represents industrialization.
- **Captions and Speech Bubbles**: Provide context or dialogue to explain the cartoon's theme.
- **Irony or Satire**: Highlight contradictions or criticize policies in a humorous way.

Steps for Analyzing Political Cartoons

- **Identify the Context**: Consider the time period and event being depicted.
- **Interpret Symbols and Exaggeration**: Analyze how these elements convey the cartoonist's message.
- **Understand the Perspective**: Determine whether the cartoon supports or criticizes the subject.

Practice Example:

Question: A cartoon from the 1930s shows a large, bloated figure labeled "Big Business" stepping on a smaller figure labeled "Workers." What is the cartoonist's message?
Answer: The cartoon criticizes the unequal power dynamics between large corporations and workers during the Great Depression.

Key Skills for Analyzing Maps, Graphs, and Political Cartoons

- Pay close attention to details like titles, labels, and legends.
- Use historical or economic knowledge to interpret trends and messages.
- Practice comparing different types of visual data to draw conclusions.

31.2 Understanding Primary and Secondary Sources

Primary and secondary sources are critical tools for analyzing historical events and understanding social studies concepts. These sources provide insights into the past, offering evidence that allows historians and students to reconstruct and interpret historical narratives. For the GED Social Studies exam, recognizing the differences between these sources and knowing how to evaluate them is essential.

What Are Primary Sources?

Primary sources are original, firsthand accounts or evidence created during the time of an event or by someone who directly experienced it. These sources provide raw materials for understanding history and are often used to answer questions about what happened, who was involved, and why it mattered.

Examples of Primary Sources

- **Documents**: The Declaration of Independence, letters, diaries, and speeches.
  - *Example*: Abraham Lincoln's Gettysburg Address is a primary source reflecting his thoughts on national unity.
- **Artifacts**: Tools, clothing, and weapons from specific historical periods.
  - *Example*: A musket from the Revolutionary War.
- **Photographs and Videos**: Visual records of events.

- *Example*: Photographs of soldiers in World War I trenches.
- **Oral Histories**: Interviews or recorded recollections of events from individuals who experienced them.
  - *Example*: An interview with a Civil Rights Movement activist.

What Are Secondary Sources?

Secondary sources interpret, analyze, or summarize information from primary sources. These sources are created by individuals who did not experience the events firsthand but instead study, compile, and explain the evidence provided by primary sources.

Examples of Secondary Sources

- **Books and Textbooks**: Interpretations or overviews of historical events.
  - *Example*: A history textbook summarizing the American Revolution.
- **Articles and Essays**: Analysis of events by historians or scholars.
  - *Example*: A journal article examining the causes of the Great Depression.
- **Documentaries**: Films that analyze historical events.
  - *Example*: A PBS documentary about the Civil Rights Movement.

Differences Between Primary and Secondary Sources

Feature	Primary Sources	Secondary Sources
Time of Creation	Created during the event or shortly after.	Created after the event, often much later.
Perspective	Firsthand, direct account of events.	Analytical or interpretive perspective.
Examples	Letters, diaries, photographs, artifacts.	Textbooks, academic articles, documentaries.
Purpose	Provide evidence or firsthand details of events.	Analyze, explain, or provide context for events.

Evaluating Sources

How to Evaluate Primary Sources

- **Context**: Understand the time period and circumstances in which the source was created.
  - *Example*: A propaganda poster from World War II reflects the values and concerns of the time.
- **Purpose**: Determine why the source was created.
  - *Example*: Was the source meant to inform, persuade, or document an event?
- **Bias and Perspective**: Recognize the creator's viewpoint or agenda.
  - *Example*: A diary entry from a soldier might emphasize personal struggles rather than the larger conflict.

How to Evaluate Secondary Sources

- **Credibility**: Check the author's credentials and the publication's reliability.
  - *Example*: A peer-reviewed academic article is more credible than an unsourced blog post.
- **Use of Evidence**: Ensure the secondary source cites primary sources accurately.
  - *Example*: Does the textbook refer to original documents or reliable data?
- **Perspective**: Be aware of the author's interpretation or bias.
  - *Example*: A historian writing about the Civil War may emphasize economic causes over political ones.

Using Primary and Secondary Sources Together

Historians and researchers often use primary and secondary sources in tandem to gain a deeper understanding of events. Primary sources provide the evidence, while secondary sources help analyze and interpret that evidence.

Example: Understanding the Great Depression

- **Primary Source**: Letters from farmers describing the Dust Bowl and its effects on their lives.
- **Secondary Source**: A history book explaining how agricultural policies of the 1930s impacted farming communities.

Using both sources provides a comprehensive view of the event, combining personal experiences with broader historical context.

Practice Example

Scenario:

You are studying the Civil Rights Movement. You have the following sources:

- A photograph of the March on Washington (primary source).
- A textbook chapter discussing the significance of the event (secondary source).

Question: Which source would provide direct evidence of the event, and which would offer an analysis of its importance?

Answer:

- The photograph provides direct evidence of the event as a primary source.
- The textbook chapter offers an analysis and is a secondary source.

Another Example:

Question: Why is it important to use both primary and secondary sources when studying history?

Answer: Primary sources provide firsthand evidence, while secondary sources offer context and interpretation, helping to create a more complete understanding of historical events.

31.3 Drawing Conclusions from Historical and Political Data

Drawing conclusions from historical and political data is a vital skill for understanding events, trends, and their implications. On the GED Social Studies exam, this involves analyzing evidence, identifying patterns, and interpreting relationships between causes and effects. This chapter focuses on strategies for evaluating historical and political data, providing examples to develop critical thinking and analytical skills.

Key Strategies for Drawing Conclusions

1. Identify the Source and Context

Understanding the origin and purpose of the data is the first step in drawing accurate conclusions. Ask:

- Who created the data, and why?
- What historical or political context surrounds it?
- Is the source reliable and unbiased?

Example:

A government census from the 19th century provides demographic information about population growth but may omit marginalized groups due to systemic biases of the time.

2. Analyze Trends and Patterns

Look for recurring themes, upward or downward trends, or abrupt changes in the data. These patterns often reveal underlying causes or consequences.

Example:

A chart showing rising industrial production during the late 19th century reflects the growth of the Industrial Revolution. An accompanying dip during the 1930s could indicate the effects of the Great Depression.

3. Consider Cause and Effect Relationships

Historical and political events are often interconnected. Understanding these relationships helps explain why events occurred and how they influenced subsequent developments.

Example:

The Treaty of Versailles imposed harsh penalties on Germany after World War I. This economic and political pressure contributed to the rise of Adolf Hitler and World War II.

4. Evaluate Multiple Perspectives

Historical and political data may present different interpretations based on the source's perspective. Comparing multiple sources ensures a well-rounded understanding.

Example:

An American textbook might emphasize the successes of the Marshall Plan, while a Soviet perspective from the same era could critique it as an act of Western imperialism.

5. Use Evidence to Support Your Conclusions

Base your conclusions on specific details from the data. Avoid assumptions or generalizations without concrete evidence.

Example:

If a graph shows a sharp increase in voting participation after the Voting Rights Act of 1965, the conclusion should highlight the direct impact of the legislation.

Types of Historical and Political Data

1. Statistical Data

Statistics like population figures, economic output, or election results are commonly used to analyze historical trends.

Example:

A table showing unemployment rates during the Great Depression highlights the economic severity of the era.

2. Maps

Maps provide geographic and spatial information, showing territorial changes, migration patterns, or resource distribution.

Example:

A map of colonial America illustrates how geography influenced settlement patterns and economic activities.

3. Textual Sources

Documents like treaties, speeches, and laws offer direct insight into historical decisions and political motivations.

Example:

The Gettysburg Address emphasizes themes of unity and democracy during a pivotal moment in the Civil War.

4. Visual Data

Photographs, political cartoons, and propaganda posters convey cultural and political messages.

Example:

A World War II propaganda poster encouraging war bond purchases reflects the government's strategy to fund the war effort.

Practice Examples

Example 1: Statistical Data

Scenario: A chart shows the U.S. unemployment rate dropping from 25% in 1933 to 10% in 1941.
Question: What conclusion can you draw about the U.S. economy during this period?
Answer: The data suggests that New Deal policies and increased wartime production contributed to significant economic recovery.

Example 2: Textual Analysis

Scenario: The Declaration of Independence asserts the right to "life, liberty, and the pursuit of happiness."
Question: How does this phrase reflect the ideals of the American Revolution?
Answer: It emphasizes the colonists' demand for freedom from British control and the establishment of self-governance based on individual rights.

Example 3: Political Cartoon

A political cartoon from the Cold War depicts a bear (symbolizing the Soviet Union) looming over a map of Europe while an eagle (representing the United States) stands in opposition.
Question: What does this cartoon suggest about the Cold War?
Answer: The cartoon highlights the ideological and geopolitical tensions between the U.S. and the Soviet Union over control and influence in Europe.

Tips for the GED Exam

1. **Read Carefully**: Always analyze titles, labels, and legends in data presentations.
2. **Look for Relationships**: Identify connections between events, causes, and outcomes.
3. **Be Specific**: Base your answers on concrete evidence from the data.
4. **Avoid Bias**: Be aware of potential biases in sources, especially when interpreting political data.

Example GED Questions

Question 1: A bar graph shows a sharp increase in women entering the workforce during World War II. What conclusion can you draw?
Answer: The war created labor shortages, leading to increased employment opportunities for women.
Question 2: A map shows the westward expansion of the United States in the 19th century. What factors might explain this movement?
Answer: The availability of land, economic opportunities, and government policies like the Homestead Act encouraged westward migration.

PRACTICE TEST FOR THE GED SOCIAL STUDIES SECTION

Below is a complete full-length exam for the Social Studies section, covering various question types. The test includes questions on U.S. history, civics, government, economics, geography, and data analysis. Each question type aligns with the GED exam format.

Section 1: Multiple-Choice Questions

Question 1:
Which document declared the United States independent from British rule?
A) Articles of Confederation
B) U.S. Constitution
C) Declaration of Independence
D) Federalist Papers
Answer: C) Declaration of Independence
Question 2:
What was the main purpose of the Emancipation Proclamation issued by President Abraham Lincoln?
A) To grant women the right to vote
B) To end slavery in Confederate-held territories
C) To promote westward expansion
D) To create the 13th Amendment
Answer: B) To end slavery in Confederate-held territories
Question 3:
Which branch of government is responsible for interpreting laws in the United States?
A) Legislative
B) Executive
C) Judicial
D) Administrative
Answer: C) Judicial
Question 4:
Which event directly led to the start of World War I?
A) The invasion of Poland
B) The signing of the Treaty of Versailles
C) The assassination of Archduke Franz Ferdinand
D) The attack on Pearl Harbor
Answer: C) The assassination of Archduke Franz Ferdinand
Question 5:
What is one function of the Federal Reserve System?
A) Enforcing antitrust laws
B) Printing currency
C) Regulating the money supply
D) Collecting taxes
Answer: C) Regulating the money supply

Section 2: Drag-and-Drop Questions

Question 6:
Drag the following U.S. Constitutional Amendments to match their purposes:

1. 13th Amendment
2. 19th Amendment
3. 26th Amendment

- Abolished slavery
- Granted women the right to vote

- Lowered the voting age to 18

Answer:
1 → Abolished slavery
2 → Granted women the right to vote
3 → Lowered the voting age to 18

Section 3: Fill-in-the-Blank Questions

Question 7:
The Cold War was a geopolitical conflict primarily between the United States and ________.
Answer: The Soviet Union
Question 8:
The Great Depression began in the year ________.
Answer: 1929

Section 4: Drop-Down Questions

Question 9:
The Bill of Rights guarantees [select: freedom of speech, the right to vote, the abolition of slavery, the prohibition of alcohol].
Answer: Freedom of speech
Question 10:
The Louisiana Purchase doubled the size of the United States in [select: 1776, 1803, 1865, 1900].
Answer: 1803

Section 5: Hotspot Questions

Question 11:
Click on the Northwest Territory on the provided U.S. map.
Answer: The region should highlight modern-day Ohio, Indiana, Illinois, Michigan, Wisconsin, and parts of Minnesota.

Section 6: Graph and Data Interpretation Questions

Question 12:
A bar graph shows the following data about U.S. government spending in 2020:

- Defense: 30%
- Education: 15%
- Healthcare: 40%
- Infrastructure: 15%

Question: Which category received the largest share of government spending?
Answer: Healthcare

Question 13:
A line graph shows unemployment rates increasing from 4% in 1929 to 25% in 1933. What historical event does this trend illustrate?
Answer: The Great Depression

Section 7: Extended Response Questions

Question 14:
Analyze how the New Deal addressed the economic challenges of the Great Depression. Use evidence from the provided text about Social Security, public works projects, and financial reforms.
Answer:
The New Deal tackled unemployment through public works projects, such as the construction of roads and bridges, creating jobs for millions. Programs like Social Security provided financial security for the elderly and disabled, reducing poverty. Financial reforms, including bank regulations, restored public confidence in the financial system.

Section 8: Scenario-Based Questions

Scenario: The following text describes the Civil Rights Movement of the 1960s:
"Key events included the Montgomery Bus Boycott, the March on Washington, and the passage of the Civil Rights Act of 1964. Leaders like Martin Luther King Jr. advocated for nonviolent protest to combat racial segregation and discrimination."
Question 15:
What method did Martin Luther King Jr. use to achieve civil rights goals?
Answer: Nonviolent protest

Question 16:
What was the significance of the Civil Rights Act of 1964?
Answer: It outlawed discrimination based on race, color, religion, sex, or national origin.

PART VI

FULL EXAM SIMULATIONS

COMPLETE GED EXAM SIMULATION

GED RLA Section

Question 1

Read the passage below and answer the question: *"The children played joyfully in the park, their laughter echoing through the air as the sun began to set."*

What is the tone of this sentence?

A) Excited

B) Melancholy

C) Joyful

D) Suspenseful

Question 2

Which sentence contains a grammatical error?

A) Everyone is responsible for their own actions.

B) He don't know the answer to the question.

C) The book, which is on the table, belongs to Sarah.

D) After the meeting, we decided to go for coffee.

Question 3

Which of the following is the best way to combine these two sentences?

She studied for hours. She still failed the test.

A) Although she studied for hours, she still failed the test.

B) She studied for hours; she still failed the test.

C) She studied for hours, but she still failed the test.

D) All of the above.

Question 4

Which word in the sentence below is a pronoun?

"After Mark finished his homework, he went to the park with his friends."

A) After

B) Mark

C) He

D) Friends

Question 5

Identify the main idea of the paragraph:

"Recycling is one of the easiest ways to reduce waste and protect the environment. By recycling materials like paper, glass, and plastic, we can conserve natural resources and reduce the amount of trash in landfills. Many communities have programs that make recycling convenient and accessible."

A) Recycling is inconvenient for most communities.

B) Recycling helps protect the environment by reducing waste.

C) Landfills are running out of space.

D) Natural resources are unlimited.

Question 6

Choose the sentence with correct punctuation:

A) "The cat slept on the mat; while the dog barked."

B) "The cat slept on the mat while the dog barked."

C) "The cat, slept on the mat, while the dog barked."

D) "The cat slept on the mat, while the dog barked."

Question 7

In the sentence, *"Maria hesitated before making her final decision,"* what is the function of the word "hesitated"?

A) Noun

B) Verb

C) Adjective

D) Adverb

Question 8

What is the purpose of an argumentative essay?

A) To entertain the reader with a story.

B) To explain a complex process.

C) To persuade the reader to adopt a specific viewpoint.

D) To describe an event in detail.

Question 9

Choose the correct version of the sentence:

I couldn't hardly believe what I was hearing.

A) I could hardly believe what I was hearing.

B) I couldn't believe what I was hearing.

C) Both A and B are correct.

D) Neither A nor B is correct.

Question 10

Which of the following best supports the claim that education is important for personal success?

A) "Some people are naturally talented and don't need education."

B) "Those with higher levels of education tend to earn more money."

C) "Many people prefer working instead of studying."

D) "Education systems differ around the world."

Question 11

Which sentence uses the correct form of "its" or "it's"?

A) Its a beautiful day outside.

B) The cat licked it's paw after eating.

C) It's been raining all afternoon.

D) The tree lost all of it's leaves.

Question 12

What is the best replacement for the word *"big"* in the sentence below to make it more precise?

"The company faced a big problem when sales dropped unexpectedly."

A) Giant

B) Huge

C) Significant

D) Immense

Question 13

Which sentence is written in active voice?

A) The cake was eaten by the children.

B) The children ate the cake.

C) The cake was being eaten by the children.

D) The cake had been eaten by the children.

Question 14

Read the sentence:

"Despite the storm, the crew continued working on the ship, repairing the sails and securing the mast."

Which word is a conjunction?

A) Despite

B) Continued

C) Working

D) Securing

Question 15

In the sentence, *"To achieve success, one must be persistent and work diligently,"* what does the word "diligently" mean?

A) Lazily

B) With determination

C) Carelessly

D) Without enthusiasm

Question 16

Choose the sentence that is correctly capitalized:

A) "My favorite book is To kill a mockingbird."

B) "My favorite book is to Kill a Mockingbird."

C) "My favorite book is To Kill a Mockingbird."

D) "My favorite book is To kill A Mockingbird."

Question 17

What is the best way to improve the clarity of this sentence?

"There were lots of interesting animals in the zoo."

A) The zoo had interesting animals.

B) The zoo displayed a wide variety of fascinating animals.

C) Interesting animals could be seen at the zoo.

D) There were many animals in the zoo.

Question 18

Which sentence demonstrates parallel structure?

A) "She likes swimming, to jog, and biking."

B) "She likes to swim, jogging, and bike."

C) "She likes swimming, jogging, and biking."

D) "She likes to swim, to jog, and biking."

Question 19

Read the following:

"The mayor argued that increasing taxes was necessary to improve infrastructure, while the council members debated the proposal."

What is the author's purpose in this sentence?

A) To entertain readers.

B) To provide factual information.

C) To present an argument.

D) To analyze a historical event.

Question 20

Which sentence is written in correct formal style?

A) "Hey, can you gimme that report?"

B) "Could you please provide the report?"

C) "I need that report ASAP."

D) "Give me that report right now."

Question 21

Which of the following sentences uses a metaphor?

A) The wind howled through the trees.

B) Her voice was music to his ears.

C) The car screeched to a halt.

D) He ran as fast as a cheetah.

Question 22

What is the main purpose of a persuasive essay?

A) To entertain the audience with an engaging story.

B) To describe a person, place, or event in detail.

C) To inform readers about a specific topic.

D) To convince readers to adopt a specific point of view or take action.

Question 23

Choose the correctly punctuated sentence:

A) "My brother who lives in Texas, is coming to visit us."

B) "My brother, who lives in Texas, is coming to visit us."

C) "My brother who lives in Texas is coming to visit us."

D) "My brother, who lives in Texas is coming to visit us."

Question 24

Which of the following words is a synonym for "important"?

A) Trivial

B) Significant

C) Minor

D) Negligible

Question 25

Read the passage and answer the question:

"Many scientists agree that climate change poses a significant threat to ecosystems around the world. Rising temperatures, melting ice caps, and extreme weather events are among the effects being observed. Governments, organizations, and individuals are working together to address this global issue."

What is the main idea of this passage?

A) Extreme weather is the main cause of climate change.

B) Climate change affects ecosystems globally and requires collective action to address.

C) Governments alone are responsible for solving climate change.
D) Rising temperatures are the only effect of climate change.

Question 26
Which sentence is an example of passive voice?
A) The artist painted a stunning portrait.
B) The stunning portrait was painted by the artist.
C) The artist creates beautiful works of art.
D) The stunning portrait inspired many viewers.

Question 27
In the sentence, *"She walked briskly through the park, enjoying the crisp autumn air,"* which word is an adverb?
A) Walked
B) Briskly
C) Enjoying
D) Autumn

Question 28
What does the prefix "un-" in the word "unbelievable" mean?
A) Very
B) Opposite of
C) Similar to
D) About

Question 29
Which of the following sentences demonstrates correct subject-verb agreement?
A) The group of students are planning a trip.
B) The group of students is planning a trip.
C) The group of students planning a trip.
D) The group of students has planning a trip.

Question 30
Read the following passage:
"Although the industrial revolution brought many advancements, it also led to significant environmental challenges, such as pollution and deforestation."
What can you infer from this statement?
A) The industrial revolution had no positive outcomes.
B) The industrial revolution created both progress and problems.
C) Environmental challenges were ignored during the industrial revolution.
D) Pollution and deforestation were not significant issues during the industrial revolution.

Drop-Down Questions

Question 1
The U.S. Constitution was ratified in [select: 1776, 1788, 1803, 1865].

Question 2
The Civil Rights Act of 1964 primarily aimed to [select: end segregation in public places, abolish slavery, grant women the right to vote, lower the voting age to 18].

Question 3
The Declaration of Independence was adopted on [select: July 4, 1776; September 17, 1787; December 15, 1791; April 12, 1861].

Fill-in-the-Blank Questions

Question 1
The Emancipation Proclamation was issued by President ________.

Question 2
The Great Depression began in the year ________.

Question 3
The first ten amendments to the U.S. Constitution are called the ________.

Extended Response (Essay) Question

Question:
Analyze the impact of the Civil Rights Movement on American society. Discuss key events, such as the Montgomery Bus Boycott, the March on Washington, and the passage of the Civil Rights Act of 1964. Use evidence to explain how these events contributed to social and legal changes in the United States and consider how the movement's legacy continues to influence the nation today.

GED Mathematical Reasoning: Multiple-Choice Questions

Question 1
What is the value of $5x + 3$ when $x = 4$?
A) 17
B) 18
C) 19
D) 20

Question 2
Simplify: $8 + 3 \times (2^2 - 1)$.
A) 14
B) 17
C) 18
D) 23

Question 3
Solve for x: $2x - 5 = 15$.
A) $x = 5$
B) $x = 10$
C) $x = 15$
D) $x = 20$

Question 4
Which fraction is equivalent to $\frac{3}{4}$?
A) $\frac{6}{8}$
B) $\frac{9}{12}$
C) $\frac{12}{16}$

D) All of the above

Question 5

A rectangle has a length of 10 cm and a width of 4 cm. What is its area?

A) 14 cm^2

B) 28 cm^2

C) 40 cm^2

D) 44 cm^2

Question 6

If you travel 60 miles in 1.5 hours, what is your average speed?

A) 30 mph

B) 40 mph

C) 50 mph

D) 60 mph

Question 7

What is 20% of 250?

A) 40

B) 50

C) 60

D) 70

Question 8

Which of the following represents a linear equation?

A) $y = 2x + 3$

B) $y = x^2 + 4$

C) $y = 5x^3$

D) $y = \sqrt{x} + 2$

Question 9

The graph of $y = -3x + 2$ has a slope of:

A) -3

B) 2

C) 3

D) 1

Question 10

Convert 3.5 into a fraction.

A) $\frac{3}{5}$

B) $\frac{7}{2}$

C) $\frac{5}{3}$

D) $\frac{5}{7}$

Question 11

Which is greater: 25% of 80 or 30% of 60?

A) 25% of 80

B) 30% of 60

C) They are equal

D) Cannot determine

Question 12

What is the greatest common factor (GCF) of 36 and 48?

A) 6

B) 8

C) 12

D) 18

Question 13

If $f(x) = 3x + 5$, what is $f(2)$?

A) 10

B) 11

C) 12

D) 13

Question 14

Solve for x: $\frac{4x}{3} = 8$.

A) $x = 4$

B) $x = 6$

C) $x = 8$

D) $x = 12$

Question 15

A circle has a radius of 7 cm. What is its circumference? (Use $\pi = 3.14$)

A) 21.98 cm

B) 43.96 cm

C) 49.02 cm

D) 153.86 cm

Question 16

Which of the following is a prime number?

A) 15

B) 27

C) 37

D) 49

Question 17

A company spends $\frac{1}{4}$ of its budget on marketing, $\frac{1}{3}$ on operations, and $\frac{5}{12}$ on salaries. What fraction of the budget remains?

A) $\frac{1}{12}$

B) $\frac{1}{6}$

C) $\frac{5}{6}$

D) $\frac{7}{12}$

Question 18

Solve for x: $5x - 10 = 2x + 20$.

A) $x = 5$

B) $x = 10$

C) $x = 15$

D) $x = 20$

Question 19

Which of the following sets contains only even numbers?

A) {2,4,7,10}

B) {2,6,8,12}

C) {1,3,5,7}

D) {3,5,9,11}

Question 20

Simplify: $3x^2 + 5x^2$.

A) $8x$

B) $15x^2$
C) $8x^2$
D) $3x^4$
Question 21
A box contains 6 red, 4 blue, and 5 yellow balls. What is the probability of randomly selecting a red ball?
A) $\frac{2}{15}$
B) $\frac{1}{3}$
C) $\frac{2}{5}$
D) $\frac{6}{15}$
Question 22
Convert 5% to a decimal.
A) 0.05
B) 0.5
C) 0.005
D) 5.0
Question 23
What is the volume of a cube with side length 3 cm?
A) 6 cm^3
B) 9 cm^3
C) 27 cm^3
D) 81 cm^3
Question 24
Simplify: $\frac{5}{8} + \frac{3}{8}$.
A) $\frac{8}{8}$
B) $\frac{15}{8}$
C) 1
D) $\frac{1}{2}$
Question 25
The mean of five numbers is 20. If four of the numbers are 15, 25, 30, and 10, what is the fifth number?
A) 10
B) 15
C) 20
D) 30

GED Mathematical Reasoning: 25 Multiple-Choice Questions

Question 1
What is the value of $5x + 3$ when $x = 4$?
A) 17
B) 18
C) 19
D) 20
Question 2
Simplify: $8 + 3 \times (2^2 - 1)$.
A) 14
B) 17
C) 18
D) 23
Question 3
Solve for x: $2x - 5 = 15$.
A) $x = 5$
B) $x = 10$
C) $x = 15$
D) $x = 20$
Question 4
Which fraction is equivalent to $\frac{3}{4}$?
A) $\frac{6}{8}$
B) $\frac{9}{12}$
C) $\frac{12}{16}$
D) All of the above
Question 5
A rectangle has a length of 10 cm and a width of 4 cm. What is its area?
A) 14 cm^2
B) 28 cm^2
C) 40 cm^2
D) 44 cm^2
Question 6
If you travel 60 miles in 1.5 hours, what is your average speed?
A) 30 mph
B) 40 mph
C) 50 mph
D) 60 mph
Question 7
What is 20% of 250?
A) 40
B) 50
C) 60
D) 70
Question 8
Which of the following represents a linear equation?
A) $y = 2x + 3$
B) $y = x^2 + 4$
C) $y = 5x^3$
D) $y = \sqrt{x} + 2$
Question 9
The graph of $y = -3x + 2$ has a slope of:
A) -3
B) 2
C) 3
D) 1
Question 10
Convert 3.5 into a fraction.
A) $\frac{3}{5}$
B) $\frac{7}{2}$

C) $\frac{5}{3}$

D) $\frac{5}{7}$

Question 11

Which is greater: 25% of 80 or 30% of 60?

A) 25% of 80

B) 30% of 60

C) They are equal

D) Cannot determine

Question 12

What is the greatest common factor (GCF) of 36 and 48?

A) 6

B) 8

C) 12

D) 18

Question 13

If $f(x) = 3x + 5$, what is $f(2)$?

A) 10

B) 11

C) 12

D) 13

Question 14

Solve for x: $\frac{4x}{3} = 8$.

A) $x = 4$

B) $x = 6$

C) $x = 8$

D) $x = 12$

Question 15

A circle has a radius of 7 cm. What is its circumference? (Use $\pi = 3.14$)

A) 21.98 cm

B) 43.96 cm

C) 49.02 cm

D) 153.86 cm

Question 16

Which of the following is a prime number?

A) 15

B) 27

C) 37

D) 49

Question 17

A company spends $\frac{1}{4}$ of its budget on marketing, $\frac{1}{3}$ on operations, and $\frac{5}{12}$ on salaries. What fraction of the budget remains?

A) $\frac{1}{12}$

B) $\frac{1}{6}$

C) $\frac{5}{6}$

D) $\frac{7}{12}$

Question 18

Solve for x: $5x - 10 = 2x + 20$.

A) $x = 5$

B) $x = 10$

C) $x = 15$

D) $x = 20$

Question 19

Which of the following sets contains only even numbers?

A) $\{2,4,7,10\}$

B) $\{2,6,8,12\}$

C) $\{1,3,5,7\}$

D) $\{3,5,9,11\}$

Question 20

Simplify: $3x^2 + 5x^2$.

A) $8x$

B) $15x^2$

C) $8x^2$

D) $3x^4$

Question 21

A box contains 6 red, 4 blue, and 5 yellow balls. What is the probability of randomly selecting a red ball?

A) $\frac{2}{15}$

B) $\frac{1}{3}$

C) $\frac{2}{5}$

D) $\frac{6}{15}$

Question 22

Convert 5% to a decimal.

A) 0.05

B) 0.5

C) 0.005

D) 5.0

Question 23

What is the volume of a cube with side length 3 cm?

A) 6 cm^3

B) 9 cm^3

C) 27 cm^3

D) 81 cm^3

Question 24

Simplify: $\frac{5}{8} + \frac{3}{8}$.

A) $\frac{8}{8}$

B) $\frac{15}{8}$

C) 1

D) $\frac{1}{2}$

Question 25

The mean of five numbers is 20. If four of the numbers are 15, 25, 30, and 10, what is the fifth number?

A) 10

B) 15

C) 20

D) 30

Drag-and-Drop Questions

Question 1
Match the following mathematical terms to their definitions:

1. **Perimeter**
2. **Area**
3. **Volume**

Definitions:
A) The amount of space inside a 3D object.
B) The distance around a 2D shape.
C) The amount of space inside a 2D shape.

Question 2
Arrange the following numbers in ascending order:

- $\frac{3}{4}, 0.6, \frac{5}{8}, 0.85$.

Question 3
Match the algebraic expressions to their simplified forms:

1. $3x + 2x$
2. $4x - 2x$
3. $5x \cdot 2x$

Simplified forms:
A) $2x$
B) $5x^2$
C) $5x$

Fill-in-the-Blank Questions

Question 1
What is 25% of 160?
Answer: ________.

Question 2
Solve for x: $2x + 5 = 15$.
Answer: x = ________.

Question 3
A triangle has a base of 8 cm and a height of 5 cm. What is its area?
Answer: ________ cm^2.

Hotspot Questions

Question 1
On a coordinate plane, identify the quadrant where the point $(-3,4)$ is located.

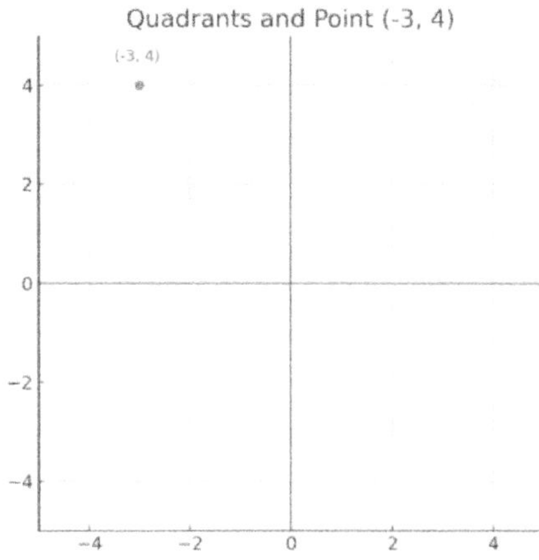

Question 2
Identify the vertex of the parabola $y = x^2 - 4x + 3$ on the graph.

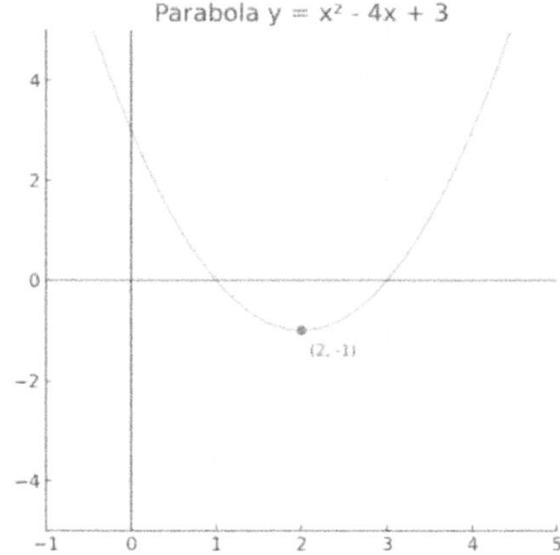

Short Answer Questions

Question 1
Explain why $2x - 3 = 7$ is a linear equation.

Question 2
A car travels 120 miles in 3 hours. Calculate the car's average speed.

GED Science Section: Multiple-Choice Questions

Question 1
Which cell structure is responsible for producing energy in animal cells?
A) Nucleus
B) Ribosome
C) Mitochondria
D) Golgi apparatus

Question 2
Which of the following best describes the process of photosynthesis?
A) Conversion of glucose into energy
B) Conversion of sunlight into chemical energy
C) Release of oxygen into the atmosphere
D) Breakdown of carbon dioxide

Question 3
Which body system is primarily responsible for transporting oxygen and nutrients throughout the body?
A) Digestive system
B) Circulatory system
C) Respiratory system
D) Nervous system

Question 4
Which of the following is an example of a chemical change?
A) Melting of ice
B) Dissolving salt in water
C) Burning of wood
D) Breaking glass

Question 5
What type of energy transformation occurs in a battery-powered flashlight?
A) Chemical to mechanical
B) Electrical to chemical
C) Chemical to electrical
D) Mechanical to electrical

Question 6
What is the primary cause of tides on Earth?
A) The gravitational pull of the Sun
B) The gravitational pull of the Moon
C) Earth's rotation
D) Ocean currents

Question 7
Which layer of the Earth is composed primarily of solid iron and nickel?
A) Crust
B) Mantle
C) Outer core
D) Inner core

Question 8
What is the formula for calculating density?
A) Mass ÷ Volume
B) Mass × Volume
C) Volume ÷ Mass
D) Mass − Volume

Question 9
Which of the following elements is most abundant in Earth's atmosphere?
A) Oxygen
B) Nitrogen
C) Carbon dioxide
D) Argon

Question 10
Which type of rock is formed from cooling magma?
A) Igneous
B) Sedimentary
C) Metamorphic
D) Fossil

Question 11
What process in the water cycle is responsible for the formation of clouds?
A) Precipitation
B) Evaporation
C) Condensation
D) Runoff

Question 12
Which of the following is an example of kinetic energy?
A) A book sitting on a shelf
B) A stretched rubber band
C) A rolling ball
D) A charged battery

Question 13
Which planet in our solar system has the most moons?
A) Mars
B) Saturn
C) Jupiter
D) Neptune

Question 14
Which of the following best describes an ecosystem?
A) A group of organisms of the same species living in an area
B) The physical and biological components of an environment interacting together
C) A collection of abiotic factors in a region
D) A single food chain within a habitat

Question 15
What does DNA stand for?
A) Deoxyribonucleic acid
B) Dinucleic acid
C) Dioxynucleic acid
D) Deoxyribosomal acid

Question 16
What is the acceleration of an object in free fall near Earth's surface?
A) 5 m/s^2
B) 9.8 m/s^2
C) 15.6 m/s^2

D) 20 m/s^2

Question 17
What is the role of decomposers in an ecosystem?
A) Convert sunlight into energy
B) Break down dead organisms and recycle nutrients
C) Control population sizes
D) Provide shelter for other organisms

Question 18
Which law explains why a balloon deflates when pricked?
A) Newton's first law of motion
B) Boyle's law
C) Charles's law
D) Law of conservation of energy

Question 19
Which of the following is an example of renewable energy?
A) Coal
B) Oil
C) Solar power
D) Natural gas

Question 20
Which part of the human brain is responsible for processing visual information?
A) Frontal lobe
B) Temporal lobe
C) Parietal lobe
D) Occipital lobe

Question 21
What is the pH of a neutral substance?
A) 0
B) 7
C) 14
D) -1

Question 22
Which of the following is a physical property of matter?
A) Flammability
B) Reactivity
C) Melting point
D) Combustion

Question 23
What is the unit of force in the metric system?
A) Joule
B) Newton
C) Pascal
D) Watt

Question 24
Which gas is released during photosynthesis?
A) Carbon dioxide
B) Oxygen
C) Nitrogen
D) Methane

Question 25
What is the main reason for seasons on Earth?
A) Earth's distance from the Sun
B) Earth's tilted axis
C) Earth's rotation
D) The Sun's activity

Question 26
Which of the following organisms is classified as a producer?
A) Lion
B) Oak tree
C) Mushroom
D) Rabbit

Question 27
What is the primary function of red blood cells in the human body?
A) Fight infections
B) Carry oxygen
C) Regulate body temperature
D) Remove waste products

Question 28
Which phenomenon is caused by the refraction of light?
A) A rainbow
B) Shadows
C) The phases of the Moon
D) Tides

Question 29
Which type of boundary occurs where two tectonic plates move away from each other?
A) Convergent boundary
B) Transform boundary
C) Divergent boundary
D) Subduction zone

Question 30
What is the term for an organism's role within its ecosystem?
A) Habitat
B) Population
C) Niche
D) Community

Question 31
Which element is represented by the symbol *Na*?
A) Neon
B) Sodium
C) Nitrogen
D) Nickel

Question 32
Which law states that energy cannot be created or destroyed?

A) Newton's second law
B) Law of conservation of energy
C) Law of thermodynamics
D) Boyle's law

Question 33
What is the boiling point of water at standard atmospheric pressure?
A) 0°C
B) 50°C
C) 100°C
D) 212°C

Question 34
Which of the following best explains why the Moon appears to change shape?
A) The Earth's shadow falls on the Moon.
B) The Moon emits less light at different times.
C) The Moon's rotation causes its phases.
D) The Moon's phases are caused by its position relative to Earth and the Sun.

Question 35
What type of bond is formed when two atoms share electrons?
A) Ionic bond
B) Covalent bond
C) Hydrogen bond
D) Metallic bond

Question 36
Which is the smallest unit of life?
A) Atom
B) Molecule
C) Cell
D) Tissue

Question 37
What type of energy does a compressed spring have?
A) Kinetic energy
B) Potential energy
C) Thermal energy
D) Electrical energy

Question 38
What is the process by which plants lose water through small pores in their leaves?
A) Photosynthesis
B) Respiration
C) Transpiration
D) Absorption

Question 39
Which part of a plant is responsible for absorbing water and nutrients from the soil?
A) Stem
B) Leaves
C) Roots
D) Flowers

Question 40
Which layer of the atmosphere contains the ozone layer?
A) Troposphere
B) Stratosphere
C) Mesosphere
D) Thermosphere

Drag-and-Drop Questions

Question 1
Match the following parts of the cell to their primary functions:

Nucleus
Mitochondria
Ribosome
Cell Membrane

Functions:
A) Regulates what enters and exits the cell
B) Produces energy for the cell
C) Synthesizes proteins
D) Stores genetic material

Question 2
Arrange the following steps of the water cycle in the correct order:

Precipitation
Evaporation
Condensation
Runoff

Question 3
Match the following types of energy to their examples:

Potential Energy
Kinetic Energy
Thermal Energy
Chemical Energy

Examples:
A) A stretched rubber band
B) A rolling ball
C) Energy stored in a battery
D) Heat from a fire

Question 4
Place the planets in order from closest to farthest from the Sun:

Mars
Earth
Venus
Mercury

Question 5

Match the layers of Earth to their descriptions:

Crust
Mantle
Outer Core
Inner Core

Descriptions:
A) Solid layer made of iron and nickel
B) Liquid layer composed of molten iron and nickel
C) The outermost solid layer of Earth
D) Semi-solid layer with convection currents

Fill-in-the-Blank Questions

Question 1
The chemical formula for water is ________.

Question 2
The Earth takes ________ days to complete one orbit around the Sun.

Question 3
The process by which green plants make their food using sunlight is called ________.

Hotspot Questions

Question 1
On a diagram of the water cycle, identify where evaporation occurs.

Question 2
Using a chart of the solar system, locate the planet known as the "Red Planet."

Short Answer Questions

Question 1
Explain why plants are considered producers in an ecosystem.

Question 2
A scientist observes that a chemical reaction releases heat and light. Explain whether this reaction is endothermic or exothermic and why.

GED Social Studies Section: Multiple-Choice Questions

Question 1
What was the primary purpose of the Declaration of Independence?
A) To establish a new Constitution for the United States
B) To declare independence from Great Britain
C) To create a framework for the U.S. government
D) To abolish slavery

Question 2

Which branch of the U.S. government is responsible for interpreting laws?
A) Executive
B) Legislative
C) Judicial
D) Electoral

Question 3
The Great Depression began in what year?
A) 1920
B) 1929
C) 1933
D) 1945

Question 4
Which of the following was a result of the Civil Rights Movement?
A) The Emancipation Proclamation
B) The passage of the Voting Rights Act of 1965
C) The end of Reconstruction
D) The adoption of the Monroe Doctrine

Question 5
Which economic term refers to the scarcity of resources compared to wants and needs?
A) Opportunity cost
B) Demand
C) Scarcity
D) Supply

Question 6
What does the term "separation of powers" mean?
A) Dividing government responsibilities into three branches
B) Separating the state and national governments
C) Allowing citizens to vote on all laws
D) Ensuring equal rights for all citizens

Question 7
Which of the following amendments guarantees freedom of speech?
A) First Amendment
B) Second Amendment
C) Fifth Amendment
D) Tenth Amendment

Question 8
Which geographic feature contributed most to the development of early civilizations?
A) Mountains
B) Rivers
C) Deserts
D) Forests

Question 9
Who is known as the "Father of the Constitution"?
A) George Washington
B) Benjamin Franklin
C) James Madison
D) Thomas Jefferson

Question 10
What economic system is characterized by private ownership and the goal of profit?
A) Socialism
B) Communism
C) Capitalism
D) Feudalism

Question 11
What is the primary role of Congress in the U.S. government?
A) To enforce laws
B) To make laws
C) To interpret laws
D) To veto laws

Question 12
What event led directly to the start of World War I?
A) The signing of the Treaty of Versailles
B) The assassination of Archduke Franz Ferdinand
C) The bombing of Pearl Harbor
D) The invasion of Poland

Question 13
Which U.S. document begins with the words "We the People"?
A) The Declaration of Independence
B) The Constitution
C) The Bill of Rights
D) The Emancipation Proclamation

Question 14
What is the main function of the Federal Reserve?
A) To print money
B) To control the money supply and interest rates
C) To collect taxes
D) To regulate trade

Question 15
What term describes the exchange of goods and services without using money?
A) Inflation
B) Bartering
C) Capitalism
D) Trade deficit

Question 16
Which movement aimed to end racial segregation in the United States?
A) The Abolitionist Movement
B) The Civil Rights Movement
C) The Suffrage Movement
D) The Labor Movement

Question 17
Which Supreme Court case established the principle of judicial review?
A) Brown v. Board of Education
B) Marbury v. Madison
C) Plessy v. Ferguson
D) Roe v. Wade

Question 18
Which of the following is an example of a renewable resource?
A) Coal
B) Oil
C) Timber
D) Natural gas

Question 19
What is the purpose of the Electoral College?
A) To directly elect members of Congress
B) To vote on state laws
C) To formally elect the President and Vice President
D) To pass constitutional amendments

Question 20
Which of the following best describes the purpose of tariffs?
A) To encourage international trade
B) To protect domestic industries
C) To eliminate trade restrictions
D) To reduce government spending

Question 21
What was the main cause of the Cold War?
A) Economic rivalry between the U.S. and China
B) The spread of communism and containment policies
C) Territorial disputes over Alaska
D) Alliances formed during World War II

Question 22
What document officially ended slavery in the United States?
A) The Emancipation Proclamation
B) The 13th Amendment
C) The Declaration of Independence
D) The Gettysburg Address

Question 23
What term refers to the total value of goods and services produced within a country in a year?
A) Gross Domestic Product (GDP)
B) National Debt
C) Trade Balance
D) Federal Reserve Index

Question 24
What river was most important to the development of ancient Egypt?

A) Amazon River
B) Nile River
C) Yangtze River
D) Mississippi River

Question 25
What is the primary goal of supply-side economics?
A) To reduce inflation by limiting consumer spending
B) To stimulate economic growth by increasing production
C) To promote social welfare through government programs
D) To regulate monopolies and protect competition

Fill-in-the-Blank Questions

Question 1

The United Nations was founded in the year ________.

Question 2

The first ten amendments to the U.S. Constitution are called the ________.

Question 3

The economic system based on private property and profit is called ________.

Question 4

The movement to end slavery in the United States was known as the ________.

Question 5

The U.S. entered World War II after the bombing of ________.

Drop-Down Questions

Question 1

The U.S. Constitution was ratified in [select: 1776, 1781, 1788, 1791].

Question 2

The Great Depression began in [select: 1914, 1929, 1941, 1950].

Question 3

The primary purpose of the Bill of Rights is to [select: establish state governments, protect individual freedoms, create the judicial system, regulate trade].

Question 4

The Treaty of Versailles officially ended [select: the American Revolution, World War I, World War II, the U.S. Civil War].

Hotspot Questions

Question 1

On a world map, identify the Atlantic Ocean.

Question 2

On a map of the U.S., locate the Mississippi River.

Question 3

On a political map of Europe, select the country of Germany.

Extended Response (Essay)

Question:

Analyze the causes and effects of the Civil Rights Movement in the United States. Include key events, figures, and outcomes, such as the Civil Rights Act of 1964, Martin Luther King Jr.'s leadership, and the March on Washington. Discuss the movement's legacy and how it shaped American society

TEST SIMULATION ANSWERS

Answer Key RLA SECTION

Multiple Choice Questions

1. C
2. B
3. D
4. C
5. B
6. B
7. B
8. C
9. A
10. B
11. C
12. C
13. B
14. A
15. B
16. C
17. B
18. C
19. C
20. B
21. B
22. D
23. B
24. B
25. B
26. B
27. B
28. B
29. B
30. B

Drop-Down Questions

1. 1788
2. End segregation in public places
3. July 4, 1776

Fill-in-the-Blank Questions

1. Abraham Lincoln
2. 1929
3. Bill of Rights

Extended Response (Essay) Answer

The Civil Rights Movement profoundly impacted American society by addressing systemic racial discrimination and advocating for social and legal equality. Key events such as the Montgomery Bus Boycott, the March on Washington, and the passage of the Civil Rights Act of 1964 illustrate the movement's transformative influence.

The Montgomery Bus Boycott of 1955–1956 marked a pivotal moment in the fight against segregation. Sparked by Rosa Parks' refusal to give up her bus seat to a white passenger, this year-long boycott showcased the power of nonviolent resistance and community organization. It led to a Supreme Court ruling declaring segregation on public buses unconstitutional, setting a precedent for further desegregation efforts.

The March on Washington in 1963 demonstrated the movement's ability to unite diverse groups around a common goal. Over 250,000 people gathered to demand civil and economic rights, and Martin Luther King Jr.'s "I Have a Dream" speech became a defining moment in American history. This event highlighted the widespread support for racial equality and pressured lawmakers to address systemic injustice.

The passage of the Civil Rights Act of 1964 was a direct result of the movement's persistent advocacy. This landmark legislation outlawed discrimination based on race, color, religion, sex, or national origin, addressing inequalities in public accommodations, employment, and education. It represented a significant step toward dismantling institutionalized racism and promoting equal rights for all Americans.

The legacy of the Civil Rights Movement continues to influence contemporary society. It paved the way for subsequent movements advocating for gender equality, LGBTQ+ rights, and other marginalized groups. The principles of nonviolent resistance and grassroots activism remain powerful tools for social change.

In conclusion, the Civil Rights Movement reshaped the United States by challenging discriminatory practices and securing critical legal protections. Its impact is enduring, serving as a reminder of the importance of collective action in the pursuit of justice and equality.

Answer Key MATH SECTION

Multiple Choice Questions

1. C
2. D
3. B
4. D
5. C
6. C
7. B
8. A
9. A
10. B
11. A
12. C
13. B
14. D
15. B
16. C
17. A
18. C
19. B
20. C
21. C
22. A
23. C
24. C
25. D

Drag-and-Drop Questions

Question 1

1 → B (The distance around a 2D shape.)
2 → C (The amount of space inside a 2D shape.)
3 → A (The amount of space inside a 3D object.)

Question 2

Arrange in ascending order:

$\frac{5}{8}$, 0.6, $\frac{3}{4}$, 0.85

Question 3

1 → C ($3x + 2x = 5x$)
2 → A ($4x - 2x = 2x$)
3 → B ($5x \cdot 2x = 10x^2$)

Fill-in-the-Blank Questions

Question 1

25% of $160 = 0.25 \times 160 = 40$

Answer: 40

Question 2

$$2x + 5 = 15$$

Subtract 5: $2x = 10$

Divide by 2: $x = 5$

Answer: $x = 5$

Question 3

Area of a triangle $= \frac{1}{2} \times$ base $\times$ height

$$= \frac{1}{2} \times 8 \times 5 = 20 \text{ cm}^2$$

Answer: 20 cm^2

Hotspot Questions

Question 1

The point $(-3,4)$ is located in **Quadrant II**.

Question 3

The vertex of the parabola $y = x^2 - 4x + 3$:
Rewrite as $y = (x - 2)^2 - 1$ (vertex form).
The vertex is at $(2, -1)$.

Short Answer Questions

Question 1

The equation $2x - 3 = 7$ is linear because it has the variable x raised to the power of 1. Linear equations form straight lines when graphed and follow the general format $ax + b = c$.

Question 2

Average speed $= \frac{\text{Total Distance}}{\text{Total Time}}$

$$= \frac{120}{3} = 40 \text{ mph}$$

Answer: 40 mph

Answer Key SCIENCE SECTION:

Multiple Choice Questions

Answer Key (Letters Only)

1. C
2. B
3. B
4. C
5. C
6. B
7. D
8. A
9. B
10. A
11. C
12. C
13. C
14. B
15. A
16. B
17. B
18. B
19. C
20. D
21. B
22. C
23. B
24. B
25. B
26. B
27. B
28. A
29. C
30. C
31. B
32. B
33. C
34. D
35. B
36. C
37. B
38. C
39. C
40. B

Drag-and-Drop Questions

Question 1

1 → D (Stores genetic material)

2 → B (Produces energy for the cell)
3 → C (Synthesizes proteins)
4 → A (Regulates what enters and exits the cell)

Question 2

Correct order:
Evaporation → Condensation → Precipitation → Runoff

Question 3

1 → A (A stretched rubber band)
2 → B (A rolling ball)
3 → D (Heat from a fire)
4 → C (Energy stored in a battery)

Question 4

Correct order:
Mercury → Venus → Earth → Mars

Question 5

1 → C (The outermost solid layer of Earth)
2 → D (Semi-solid layer with convection currents)
3 → B (Liquid layer composed of molten iron and nickel)
4 → A (Solid layer made of iron and nickel)

Fill-in-the-Blank Questions

Question 1
The chemical formula for water is **H_2O**.
Question 2
The Earth takes **365** days to complete one orbit around the Sun.
Question 3
The process by which green plants make their food using sunlight is called **photosynthesis**.

Hotspot Questions

Question 1
Evaporation occurs at the **surface of water bodies (e.g., oceans, lakes, or rivers)** where heat causes water to convert into vapor.
Question 2
The "Red Planet" is **Mars**.

Short Answer Questions

Question 1
Plants are considered producers in an ecosystem because they produce their own food through photosynthesis. Using sunlight, water, and carbon dioxide, plants create glucose, which serves as an energy source. They also release oxygen as a byproduct, which is essential for other organisms.

Question 2
The reaction is **exothermic** because it releases heat and light. Exothermic reactions transfer energy to the surroundings, often observed as an increase in temperature or light emission.

Answer Keys SOCIAL STUDIES SECTION:

Multiple Choice Questions

1. B
2. C
3. B
4. B

5. C
6. A
7. A
8. B
9. C
10. C
11. B
12. B
13. B
14. B
15. B
16. B
17. B
18. C
19. C
20. B
21. B
22. B
23. A
24. B
25. B

Drag-and-Drop Questions

Question 1

1 → C (U.S. Civil War begins → 1861)
2 → A (Signing of the Declaration of Independence → 1776)
3 → B (U.S. Constitution ratified → 1788)
4 → D (End of World War II → 1945)

Question 2

Correct order:

- American Revolutionary War
- U.S. Civil War
- World War I
- World War II

Question 3

1 → B (Inflation → General increase in prices and fall in purchasing value)
2 → D (GDP → Total value of goods and services produced in a year)
3 → A (Scarcity → Limited resources to meet unlimited wants)
4 → C (Opportunity cost → The cost of the next best alternative)

Question 4

Correct order:

- Legislative
- Executive
- Judicial

Question 5

1 → D (Abraham Lincoln → Signed the Emancipation Proclamation)
2 → B (Susan B. Anthony → Advocated for women's suffrage)
3 → C (Martin Luther King Jr. → Delivered the "I Have a Dream" speech)
4 → A (Franklin D. Roosevelt → Led the U.S. during the Great Depression and World War II)

Fill-in-the-Blank Questions

Question 1

The United Nations was founded in the year **1945**.

Question 2

The first ten amendments to the U.S. Constitution are called the **Bill of Rights**.

Question 3

The economic system based on private property and profit is called **capitalism**.

Question 4

The movement to end slavery in the United States was known as the **Abolitionist Movement**.

Question 5

The U.S. entered World War II after the bombing of **Pearl Harbor**.

Drop-Down Questions

Question 1
The U.S. Constitution was ratified in **1788**.

Question 2
The Great Depression began in **1929**.

Question 3
The primary purpose of the Bill of Rights is to **protect individual freedoms**.

Question 4
The Treaty of Versailles officially ended **World War I**.

Extended Response (Essay)

Question:
Analyze the causes and effects of the Civil Rights Movement in the United States.

Answer:
The Civil Rights Movement in the United States was driven by a combination of systemic racial discrimination, segregation, and the denial of basic rights to African Americans. Key causes included the Jim Crow laws in the South, widespread inequality in education, employment, and housing, and the lack of voting rights for Black Americans. The post-World War II period, which saw African American soldiers returning to a segregated society, further highlighted the need for change.

The movement's major events were critical in shaping its outcomes. The Montgomery Bus Boycott (1955–1956) marked a significant start, with Rosa Parks' arrest sparking a year-long protest that ended in desegregation of public buses. Martin Luther King Jr. emerged as a prominent leader, advocating for nonviolent resistance. The March on Washington in 1963, where King delivered his iconic "I Have a Dream" speech, galvanized national support. Legislative victories followed, including the Civil Rights Act of 1964, which outlawed discrimination based on race, color, religion, sex, or national origin, and the Voting Rights Act of 1965, which aimed to eliminate barriers to voting for African Americans.

The effects of the Civil Rights Movement were profound. It dismantled legal segregation and created a foundation for future social justice movements. While significant progress was made, challenges remain in addressing racial inequality. The movement's legacy continues to inspire activism and reminds us of the importance of collective action in achieving justice and equality.

Made in the USA
Las Vegas, NV
08 June 2025

23338963R10164